The World of Perception

THE DORSEY SERIES IN PSYCHOLOGY

FLEISHMAN   *Studies in Personnel and Industrial Psychology*

FISKE & MADDI   *Functions of Varied Experience*

BARNETTE   *Readings in Psychological Tests and Measurements*

BENNIS, SCHEIN, BERLEW, & STEELE   *Interpersonal Dynamics: Essays and Readings on Human Interaction*

RATNER & DENNY   *Comparative Psychology: Research in Animal Behavior*

COURTS   *Psychological Statistics: An Introduction*

DEUTSCH & DEUTSCH   *Physiological Psychology*

VON FIEANDT   *The World of Perception*

The World of Perception

Kai von Fieandt
INSTITUTE OF PSYCHOLOGY
UNIVERSITY OF HELSINKI

An English adaptation,
by the author, of his
HAVAITSEMISEN MAAILMA
with the consultation of
Michael Wertheimer,
University of Colorado

1966 · THE DORSEY PRESS · HOMEWOOD, ILLINOIS

Library of Congress Catalog Card No. 66–11820

Printed in the United States of America

Preface

Three versions of this volume on the psychology of perception preceded the present edition; the first of these was published in Finnish in 1951. It was followed by a Swedish edition in 1956 and another Finnish one in 1962. The successive drafts profited from the author's experience in using the text in classes in Finland, Sweden, and Norway. Results from continuing experimental work in the psychology of perception, conducted at the University of Helsinki's Institute of Psychology, were incorporated into the manuscript, and the presentation was rewritten in accord with the results of classroom tryouts of the various drafts; hence each book was essentially a new and separate work.

The idea of preparing an American edition was that of my Scandinavian friend, Dr. Per Saugstad of Oslo. His 1958 review of the book in *Contemporary Psychology* closed with the suggestion that in order for it to reach an appropriate audience it should be reworked into a new textbook on the psychology of perception in English.

The time-consuming job of undertaking new experiments, searching recent bibliographic material, translation, and rewriting would not have been economically possible without a grant in 1964 from the Esko Aaltonen Foundation in Tampere, Finland. During the same year I had the good fortune to receive a Senior Foreign Scientist Fellowship from the National Science Foundation in Washington, D.C. This enabled me to spend the academic year 1964–65 at the University of Colorado, which decisively facilitated my efforts in carrying the plan through.

The present text aims to serve the same purpose, at the advanced undergraduate and graduate levels, as that filled by comparable chapters in, say, Woodworth and Schlosberg's *Experimental Psychology*. It tries to combine significant European material with recent American contributions to the field. The teacher may want to use it together with some kind of complementary source book, or else as his main textbook in psychology classes. In the latter case, the order of presentation indicated by chapter numbers need not be strictly followed. Some chapters, for instance, Chapter 1, might preferably be taken up for discussion at the very end of a course in perception. The author is aware of how incomplete the book is in many respects, but decided to hazard this first version nevertheless, and to rely on experience with it and comments about it in preparing a more adequate later edition.

When possible, American measures and units (cps, jnd, etc.) have been introduced instead of current continental ones. So, also, have all symbols for tones been converted to fit the international standard system (see Chapter 5).

The book is the product of the close cooperation of my friend Professor Michael Wertheimer, who during my stay in Colorado went over the text with me in great detail and made many helpful suggestions.

Miss Teresa Pressman of Palo Alto, California, helped with proof reading and with many of the chores associated with seeing the manuscript through the press.

Ristiina, Finland   KAI VON FIEANDT
June 10, 1966

Table of Contents

CHAPTER | PAGE
INTRODUCTION 1

Why Perceptual Psychology? Related Sciences. Basic Considerations. The Phenomenal and the Physical Approach. The Constancy Hypothesis and Its Limitations.

1. CURRENT TRENDS IN PERCEPTUAL PSYCHOLOGY 11

Historical Background. The Evidence from Ambiguity. Percepts as End-Products of Development. The Sensory-Tonic Theory. New-Look Theory, Set, and the Role of Cognition.

2. ASPECTS OF SENSORY EVOLUTION 23

Primary Irritability and the Origins of Sensation. Sense Classification. The Evolutional Differentiation.

3. THE DIFFERENT SENSES AND THEIR RECEPTORS 30

VISION. HEARING. SMELL AND TASTE. THE SKIN SENSES: The Sense Organs. Opinions about Touch and Pressure. Temperature Sensitivity. Pain Sensitivity. KINESTHETIC AND LABYRINTHINE SENSITIVITY.

4. PERCEPTION OF COLOR 76

LIGHT AND COLORS: Ostwald's Color System. Appearances of Color. Effects of Different Illuminations. Memory Colors or Invariances? Laws of Color Mixture. Color Contrast and the Purkinje Shift. ON COLOR THEORIES: The Young-Helmholtz Theory. The Hering Theory. The Ladd-Franklin Theory. The G. E. Müller Theory. The Edridge-Green Theory. Recent Contributions. Color Deficiencies.

5. PERCEPTION OF SOUND 112

SOUND STIMULI. PSYCHOPHYSICS OF SOUNDS: Attributes and Dimensions. Pitch. Loudness. Timbre. Volume and Density. Beats. Combination Tones. Modulation and Vibrato. Masking. Musical Scales. The Human Voice. Brightness and Tonality.

6. PERCEPTION OF TOUCH, VIBRATION, AND TEMPERATURE . . 141

Stimulus-Systems of Touch. Vibratory Stimuli. Interpretation of the Vibratory Experience. Perceptual Qualities of Warmth and Cold.

7. ON SMELL AND TASTE EXPERIENCES 150

Significance of Odors in Our Everyday Life. Sensorial Models and Terminology of Odor. Theories of Smell. Thresholds and Classification of Odors.

8. PRINCIPLES OF SENSORY FUNCTIONING AND INTERACTION . 160

STIMULUS BASIS OF SENSATIONS: Neural Transmission. General Considerations about Threshold Phenomena. Weber's and Fechner's Laws.

CHAPTER   PAGE

Hecht's Work. ADAPTATION: Recent Studies in Sensitivity and Adaptation. INTERACTION OF MODALITIES: Hartshorne's Dimensional Explanation. Pfaffmann's Studies. Evaluation of Hartshorne. Polymodal Impressions. Criticism.

9. PERCEPTUAL CONSTANCY AND THE FRAME OF REFERENCE . 203
Shapes at Different Angles of Inclination. The Problem of Shape Constancy. Relational Invariances in Size Perception. Dimensions of Perceptual Space. Orthogonality and Anisotropy of Space. Inadequacy of the Learning Assumption. Size and Distance. MEASUREMENT OF THE DEGREE OF CONSTANCY: Size Constancy. Color Constancy. Degree of Color Constancy. Theoretical Explanations. Wallach's Contribution. Hue and Brightness Constancy. The Factors of Field Size and Complexity.

10. THE DIFFERENTIATION OF VISUAL-TACTUAL SPACE . . . 227
Biological Origins of Perceptual Space. COMPONENTS OF VISUAL SPACE: Gradual Differentiation of a Homogeneous Space. Ambiguous Patterns—Figure and Ground. Learning Effects Closely Investigated. Organization of Three-dimensional Space. Depth Cues for Perceptual Space. THE INDEPENDENCY OF TACTUAL SPACE: Structuration Principles of Tactual Forms. Analogies between Tactual and Other Modal Space Determinants.

11. MOVEMENT AND TIME PERCEPTION 258
THE ANALYTIC CHARACTER OF MOVEMENT PERCEPTION: Conditions for Apparent Motion. Stroboscopic and Pure Motion as Compared. Investigating the Wertheimer Phenomenon. Johansson's Contributions. Stereokinetic Motion. Perceived Motion Directions. Perception of Velocity. Perception of Time and the Phenomenal Present. TIME AND MOTION RELATIONSHIPS: Michotte's Experiments.

12. DIFFERENTIATION OF AUDITORY PERCEPTION 282
ANALOGIES BETWEEN VISUAL AND AUDITORY SPACE: Temporal Units. Direction and Distance Localization. 1. Binaural Intensity Differences. 2. Binaural Time Differences. 3. Binaural Phase Differences. Other Cues for Scanning and Localization. THE ROLE OF DIFFERENTIATION: Interaction of Visual and Auditory Cues. The Problem of Auditory Space.

13. COMPLEX ARTICULATIONS IN TACTUAL PERCEPTION . . . 298
Dimensions of Touch and Modes of Appearance. Intermodal Correspondence. Preferred Forms. Expressive Value of Works Made by Congenitally Blind. The Gestalt Completion in Tactual Experiments.

14. THE PERCEPTION OF OBJECTS BY THE PRIMITIVE SENSES . 313
PSYCHOPHYSICS OF ODORS: Modes of Appearance. Analogies in Perceiving Smells and Colors. SCALING OF TASTE EXPERIENCES: Various Systems of Reference for Taste.

15. PERCEPTION OF THE SELF DIRECTLY AND AS A MIRROR
IMAGE 322
The Shaving Paradox. Role of Objectified Sense Material. Origins of the Body Image. PHANTOM-LIMB PHENOMENA: Vividness and Mobility of Phantom Limbs. Body Image Explained as a Thing Constancy Phenomenon. Our Body as an Object of Our Perception. Additional Findings.

CHAPTER   PAGE

16. PERCEPTION OF PICTORIAL ART 336

SOME PRINCIPLES OF ARTISTIC CONSTRUCTION AND COMPOSITION.
THREE-DIMENSIONAL PICTORIAL SPACE: Jaensch's Studies in Picto-
rial Space. COLORS AND ILLUMINATION IN PICTORIAL SPACE. SOME
SPECIAL FEATURES OF THE USE OF COLORS IN THE MIDDLE AGES.
THE PROBLEM OF DIRECTED ILLUMINATION IN RENAISSANCE AND
MODERN ART. ART AND PERSONALITY DYNAMICS.

17. THE RELATIONAL INVARIANCES OF PERCEPTION 378

BIBLIOGRAPHY 385

ACKNOWLEDGMENTS 405

INDEX 409

INTRODUCTION

THE STUDY of perception is generally considered to be the basic, traditional part of the young science of psychology. It was in the field of perceptual psychology that experimental investigation of mental phenomena was begun; Fechner, Wundt, von Helmholtz, Hering, Külpe, J. Müller, Titchener, G. E. Müller, and von Kries, the great early sensory physiologists, could also be regarded as pioneers in perceptual psychology. It seems that the development of particular research methods in a special field of a science may strongly influence the kinds of problems studied by the whole science. That is what happened in psychology. Even the analysis of social phenomena began with the aid of concepts taken over from the perceptual psychologists. Introductory courses in psychology have, therefore, often started with perception. It seems appropriate to introduce general laws of mental processes by way of the rather concrete, easily grasped perceptual events which occur in living organisms.

Why Perceptual Psychology?

One may ask why perception should be investigated as a field of its own. Doesn't or shouldn't traditional sensory physiology already cover the study of perceptual phenomena? It is true that physiology and psychology are related when dealing with these problem areas. Sometimes it is even hard to decide what should be regarded as a physiological and what a psychological approach. The question of how analysis of our perceptions fits in with the most central problems of psychology could be answered most appropriately by discussing some frequent misunderstandings connected with the interpretation of our visual functions.

Quite recently the analogy between the human eye and a camera

1

was taken almost literally. It was believed that our nervous system, like "a little man inside," gets a kind of mental image which consists of a faithful duplication of the inverted retinal image. No wonder that one of the most persistent and hardest-fought controversies in the nineteenth century was concerned with the problem of how we nevertheless see things right side up. One could hardly imagine a more misleading conception than this point-to-point projective model of our visual functions. As Boring has pointed out, the *camera obscura* analogy has led investigators to mechanistic, stimulus-oriented interpretations of perceptual events. Sensory physiology is inclined to restrict itself to that kind of explanation, avoiding more central relationships. (Let us not forget, however, that this does not always happen, and particularly not with the most outstanding sensory physiologists.)

Physical and physiological models of our visual processes ought, therefore, to be supplemented and completed by psychological ones. When we receive *visual impressions*, they are never limited to events in the peripheral sense organs in the retina. Differentiated vision consists of processes in which cortical brain centers are involved. Even in human beings the role played by the retina sometimes is predominant (e.g., in the phenomenon of physiological after-images), and sometimes the influence of the cortex is decisive (e.g., in connection with surface color constancy). In any case peripheral receptors, afferent neural events, and central mechanisms act together, forming a wonderful system of organized interaction.

An observation made by ophthalmologists shows us that if the two eyes are simultaneously presented with slightly different stimulations (e.g., circular patterns with a segment cut out from the whole circle), the visual impressions combine, resulting in a single image of a complete round figure. The formation of a uniform, consistent gestalt succeeds up to certain limit, up to a certain threshold value of binocular disparity. As long as the disparity of the two patterns is not beyond this threshold, the visual organization is determined by the relations among the various parts of the figural patterns.

Related Sciences

The investigation of visual experiences therefore requires cooperation among a number of sciences. *Physics* and *chemistry* are concerned with *stimuli*, with the light sources and with the radiation emerging from them. *Physiology* deals with how neural activity is initiated by the incoming stimulation and with the *functional interrelations* between the receptor tissues and the higher-order neural processes in the central nervous system. *Psychology*, on the other hand, is interested in perceptual wholes, i.e., in the *phenomenal experiences* which accompany the above-mentioned events. It certainly is important to try to discover the role of the peripheral factors which the retina is able to discriminate, e.g., of retinal gradients, to borrow a term from Gibson.[1] It seems that early European perceptual psychology neglected the part played by these factors. However, as the experiments of Gelb and Goldstein[2] with brain-injured people have shown, the role played by cortical visual centers is crucial for the genesis of "gestalten" or patterned configurations in visual perception. Some of the patients, even though their retinas were intact, nevertheless were unable to articulate visual stimulation patterns, because their cortical centers were damaged.

David Katz[3] often pointed out—e.g., in his "gestalt psychology" —that textbooks in perception are mainly limited to a consideration of visual problems. This criticism is well-founded, and he has presented excellent discussions of phenomena and experimental results in other modalities, which he has successfully explained by using concepts and points of view derived from the study of visual phenomena. It is the aim of this textbook to proceed further in the same direction. The conceptions introduced by Katz will be applied to findings from all sense modalities. The point of view stressed above generally holds true for all kinds of modalities. The sense of vision was chosen as an example, since it is less difficult to give a concrete description of functional and phenomenal sequences in that modality.

Basic Considerations

The task of perceptual psychology, then, is to discover and refine the regularities and lawful connections governing the central coding and experiencing of sensory messages. A perception is an experienced sensation, i.e., a phenomenal impression resulting function-

---

[1] J. J. Gibson, *The Perception of the Visual World* (New York: Houghton Mifflin Co., 1950).

[2] A. Gelb, and K. Goldstein, "Optische Analysen gehirnpathologischer Fälle." *Zeitschrift für Psychologie*, 83 (1920).

[3] D. Katz, *Gestaltpsychologie* (Basel: Benno Schwabe & Co., 1944).

ally from certain inputs. Sensations are initiated by changes in the environmental conditions of our *receptors*. These changes have been called *stimuli*. The receptors have generally been grouped into *exteroceptors* (eye, ear, mouth cavity and tongue, nose, skin), *interoceptors* (nerve endings connected with inner organs) and *proprioceptors* (sensors of muscle tensions, posture, and equilibrium of head and body). Helmholtz was thinking of *distance receptors* (sight, hearing, smell) when he distinguished between *distal* and *proximal* stimuli. As distal he regarded the remote sources of environmental alterations and influences upon receptor cells (objects and events which give rise to visual and auditory impressions). He called the processes directly affecting the receptor tissues proximal stimuli. These energy changes are therefore sequences of events described by physics and chemistry (radiations, chemical stimuli, sound waves, etc.). A remote chair, when seen from a distance, is, according to Helmholtz, a distal stimulus for the sensation of a chair; on the other hand, the incoming radiation from the surface of the chair (or better: the chemical processes evoked by it in the visual cells) must be called a proximal stimulus for that same sensation.

Actually perception cannot be regarded as a matter of merely recording and coding stimuli; it is in part an autonomous creative process within the organism. Everybody creates a perceptual world of his own, a kind of behavioral environment built upon percepts. There has been much controversy about the term sensation during recent years. Can it really be considered indispensable? If one wants to preserve the word sensation, it should preferably be used for denoting the *functional interaction processes* between peripheral end organs and the corresponding loci in the brain. Perception would then be reserved for the reactive creative counterpart, the content of the message as built up and coded by the organism.

The Phenomenal and the Physical Approach

How far is perceptual psychology able to describe these phenomena? Apparently either a completely functional or a completely phenomenal language could be applied. The famous Danish psychologist E. Rubin[4] definitely chose a phenomenal approach. He points out that a dichotomy of this kind cannot even arise when an

---

[4] E. Rubin, "Om det psykiske og det fysiske," *Tidskrift för psykologi och pedagogik*, Nos. 1–2 (1947).

unsophisticated human being starts describing his experience of his behavorial environment. It is not until a *physical picture of the world* has been invented that one can speak about alternative descriptions. Members of primitive tribes, or preschool children in our culture, would not understand the difference between the two ways of looking at our behavioral world—the functional and the phenomenal, as indicated respectively by the inner circle and the enclosing ring in Figure I–1.

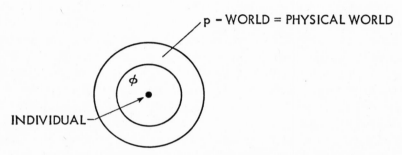

FIG. I–1. Developmental stages in the perceived environment (Rubin).

An unsophisticated person experiences the whole surrounding world in a phenomenal way. Even a sophisticated adult retains this world of immediate experiences. Around it he constructs a conventional conceptual world based upon discoveries made primarily in the field of inorganic nature. The physical picture of the world has arisen as a result of educational tradition and forces itself on our conventions for describing even mental experiences. The strict natural sciences such as physics and even physiology, according to Rubin, restrict themselves to investigations of this second-order construction of environmental phenomena. They cannot be of any help whatsoever to a scientist who is interested in the way we immediately perceive our stimulus world. Thus psychology is forced to deal with systematic phenomenal descriptions, since the other sciences neglect them.

It is impossible, however, to work out a perceptual psychology based merely on phenomenal descriptions. Even the research performed by Rubin himself provides many instances in which physical and physiological factors (p-correlates) corresponding to the analyzed phenomenal events (ϕ-events) can be found. That perceptual psychology can employ either of these two descriptive modes has been convincingly shown in investigations of amputees. The comments made by patients regarding experiences of their phantom limbs can mostly be supplemented in a valuable way by observing their overt behavior when moving around in their everyday geographical environment.

It is the aim of this textbook to give parallel descriptions of physical, physiological events on the one hand and of phenomenal experience on the other. Functional descriptions will be supplemented by an analysis of experience.

This mode of approach, however, does not imply that ϕ-sentences could completely and without remainder be translated into p-sentences. A recent philosophical form of behaviorism, represented e.g. by Ryle,[5] has proposed a perfect degree of correspondence. As an experimental science, psychology could, of course, construct a conceptual framework based entirely on physical measurements. To the extent that it aims at using a language which is common to all experimental sciences, it most conveniently could take the form of *psychophysics*. That would mean a psychology restricted to metric statements, equally expressible in phenomenal and in physical sentences. Perceptual events, as treated by psychophysics, are phenomena to be described quantitatively in terms of measurable stimulus conditions. It should not be forgotten, however, that by tracing back ϕ-experiences in that manner to p-events, rich amounts of ϕ-contents will inevitably be lost, because they cannot be directly translated into these kinds of measurements. This point was made, among others, by the late Finnish philosopher Eino Kaila, in his posthumous work.[6]

Although attempts to find constant, systematic psychophysical relations in the sense of broad, general invariances will be repeatedly encountered throughout the following chapters, it would be impossible for a textbook to limit its scope to the extent implied by a complete acceptance of a principle of correspondence. Many of the phenomenal descriptions used by continental psychologists may sound rather strange to Anglo-American students for the simple reason that English, as somewhat of a matter-of-fact language, lacks corresponding expressions. When Ryle argues that we are compelled to use everyday language and therefore have to give up

---

[5] G. Ryle, *The Concept of Mind* (New York: Barnes & Noble, Inc., 1949).

[6] E. Kaila, "Arkikokemuksen perseptuaalinen ja konseptuaalinen aines, *Ajatus*, 23 (1960).

phenomenal descriptions, his point of view may reflect just this particular linguistic state of affairs. It is probable that Koffka, for instance, never succeeded fully in making the gestalt point of view intelligible to Americans.[7] His big textbook seems to have been partially misunderstood in the United States. In order fully to understand ϕ-analyses as carried out by gestaltists, one should ideally study them in their original language.

The Constancy Hypothesis and Its Limitations

Perception has not always been regarded as an active, creative function. When carrying out psychological research, however, we should be interested precisely in this *active creation* of a phenomenal environment. Former psychologists generally held the opinion that our *perceptions* are built up from *sensation-elements*, which in turn exhibit a point-to-point correspondence with *stimulus-elements* in the proximal stimulation. This is the often mentioned *constancy hypothesis* in its classical form. If it were literally true, we could scarcely call perceptual processes *psychological* in the strict sense of the word.

Contrary to the assumptions made by the constancy hypothesis, it has been repeatedly confirmed that the same receptor cells and the same sensory nerve endings can yield many different phenomenal qualities. One and the same receptor surface can, depending on the circumstances, give rise to numerous different experiences—especially if one takes the prevailing total situation into account. We need only think about some of the qualities—colors, shapes, dimensions, directions, and movements—given us by our visual sense under the same invariant physico-physiological stimulus conditions. Moreover, these factors even combine to yield occasional experiences of cosmic significance. Another instance: The receptors on the surface of the skin can do remarkably different things. One and the same part of the skin is able under different conditions to transmit differences among touched surfaces with a precision seldom found in engineering devices. As these examples show, nature takes advantage of various possibilities in a most efficient manner, a fact which is undeniably important in the physiological economy of the organism. It is rather tempting to consider this utilization of prevailing conditions as an expression of the principle of economy or

---

[7] K. Koffka, *Principles of Gestalt Psychology* (London: Kegan Paul, 1935).

the law of least effort, as it was formulated in the systematic view of Mach. He maintained that this law is generally valid and holds especially with regard to perceptual events.

The organism does not need to develop ever more and more specialized organs for all its different purposes—though it must be admitted that the division of labor has gone far in everything that concerns our receptive functions. Within wide limits the same receptor surfaces or the various cell tissues are able to transmit messages with widely differing perceptual contents.

The far-reaching abilities of the retina have already been mentioned in several connections. This cellular tissue enables us to discriminate among different brightness levels with an astonishing accuracy. The retina adjusts its sensitivity according to changes in illumination. It opens to us the world of colors; it gives us the opportunity to distinguish among the *brightness*, the *hue*, and the *saturation* of perceived colors. The retina also manages to record directly the general level of illumination when picking up radiations from surrounding surfaces—an achievement so far unmatched by any camera. In addition to all these performances, however, the eyes can transmit patterns which are articulated as gestalten, i.e., contours, things, surfaces, and figure-background organizations. With the aid of this sensory tissue we experience the familiar things surrounding us as relatively constant, even when they are viewed from different angles, from different distances, and at varying illuminations. We experience the table surface as an uninterrupted plane regardless of the inhomogeneity of its detailed structure.

As a consequence of the fact that we have two eyes, we are able to perceive differences in depth; we immediately are aware of distance in the third dimension. Moreover, the retina mediates the organization of discrete successive stimulations into perceived movement, producing a fusion of distinct, brief, disparate local stimulations with a smoothness which is only roughly imitated in motion pictures or television. The visual receptors furnish us with material for the entire complex processes of reading and thus get involved with higher-order symbolic functions. And last but not least: through our eyes we also keep in social contact with our fellow human beings; we decode the expressions on the faces of our neighbors and develop corresponding attitudes toward them.

Surprisingly rich in variety and economically well organized also is the receptor-system which consists of the hand surface and fingertips with their sensitive end organs. Katz and Révész have clarified the functions of these sensory tissues with many ingenious experiments. If a blindfolded person is asked to touch a number of objects which he has not seen, he can, with remarkable accuracy, report what he is touching and how the surface appears to him. These achievements include recognition of familiar tactual shapes or gestalten, such as cups, books, inkstands, etc. Yet the statements made by subjects are sometimes more general in nature; they can give detailed analyses of the structure of surfaces.

Through the codes transmitted by the tactual receptors we are astonishingly well informed about the roughness or smoothness of objects, about their hardness or softness, about their stiffness or flexibility. With the aid of these receptors we obtain numerous impressions which enable us to distinguish among surfaces ranging from sandpaper to polished metal bodies. With an accuracy far exceeding the level achieved by vision, we can discriminate degrees of hardness and softness ranging from pillows to stone pillars. Our everyday experiences convincingly show that when selecting sheets of paper or some other thin material we do better to trust our fingertips than our visual organs. According to Katz, we are able to discriminate differences in thickness even down to a threshold of a 0.001 mm. difference in the thickness of membranes. And besides all that, the skin surface can mediate a wide range of vibratory stimuli. Katz has shown that the skin receptors can sense vibrations down to a minimum of 0.00008 mm. in amplitude. A psychological fact so far almost overlooked is our ability to perceive degrees of roughness on the paper sheet through our pen when writing. There are differences which are scarcely audible in the scratch of the pen but which are clearly distinguishable with the receptors of our fingertips.[8]

When we knock on objects we give rise to vibrations which tell something about their qualities. An observation time of 0.03 sec. is often enough to yield a correct impression. Medical doctors since long ago have used ausculation, tapping on their fingertips which are placed upon the tissue to be investigated. Our hands also mediate remarkable information concerning the temperature conductance of surrounding things. And furthermore, the pain receptors in the skin of the hands are numerous. The principle of shape constancy holds true in the touch sense as well as in vision. Let us only hint at the

---

[8] D. Katz, "Der Aufbau der Tastwelt," *Zeitschrift für Psychologie, Ergänzungsband*, 11 (1925).

everyday familiar psychological event of placing our hands *outside* the pocket in order to check through the cloth material whether we brought the keys along. The sensitive skin surface does not directly get in touch with the keys at all. Yet on the touch receptors the variations in pressure give rise to a remarkable differentiation: we are able to feel on the very same spot something *hard behind the softness*.

The above-mentioned few instances have been rather casual and restricted to just a few modalities. But the general principle which we illustrated is valid for all fields of perception: A manifold and qualitatively rich variety of experiences is based on the remarkable capacities of only a few types of receptors. These capacities most efficiently fulfill the requirements of the total situation.

CHAPTER 1

Current Trends in Perceptual Psychology

PERCEPTUAL RESEARCH during the early 1960's has been dominated by two basic tendencies. Both of them are modern in that they
are based upon experimental, functionally observable, and measurable events. We shall call these ways of thinking

 a. Stimulus-response oriented or *mechanistic*.
 b. Organism-centered or *organismic*.

Historical Background

These trends are represented in both European and American
theoretical psychology. Each has an historical background; the first
is consistent with the approach of radical behaviorism, while the
second has been more influenced by European traditions.

The study of perception has never managed fully to bridge a gulf
which separated early European and American psychology. European perceptual psychology originated in philosophy. The Europeans have always been interested in how things look, how they
appear to the perceiving organism. The stimulus-experience relationship was for most European psychologists the fundamental
problem to be investigated. The Americans, on the other hand,
started at the output end of the organism, at the recorded responses.

Following the 1890 functionalism of Angell, and later Watson at
Chicago, the early behaviorists were inclined to deny the existence
of mental processes except in the form of measurable behavior.
Even the concept of consciousness (as in Wundt and James) was
abandoned. The sensory processes were regarded as an interesting
research area only to the extent that changes in stimulus conditions
really did change responses. This inevitably meant a focusing on
learning processes, since modification of responses by varying the

stimulus is related to learning. It is not purely a matter of chance that behavioristic interest in perception began with an interest in perceptual learning. In the kind of perceptual theory which grew out of this early mode of approach only direct connections between *stimulus* (S) and *response* (R) were considered. S–R relationships were held to be crucial for drawing conclusions about what is happening in the perceiving organism. Central mediating processes were regarded as intervening variables. Whatever could have been presumed to mediate between S and R was declared a part of the

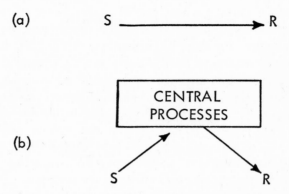

FIG. 1–1.   Two models of stimulus-response interrelationships.

inaccessible black box, impossible to investigate with the exact methods of psychology.

The influence of this trend is clearly reflected in *modern psychophysics*. This method, as represented, e.g., by J. J. Gibson, G. Ekman,[1] and G. Johansson,[2] involves a metric, quantified mapping of the process of perception and of the resulting percepts in terms of stimulation. Whatever you say about perception can and should always be reduced to measurable relationships within the stimulus pattern. A point-to-point correspondence between stimulus and perception is assumed to exist.

The traditions of the organismic approach can be traced back to the phenomenological school in Austria in the late 1800's (Husserl, Mach, Meinong, and von Ehrenfels). What these research workers pointed to with their ideas concerning the interrelated influences of

---

[1] See G. Ekman, *Psykologi*, 1953, and *Journal of Psychology*, 38 (1954).

[2] G. Johansson, *Configurations in Event Perception* (Uppsala: Almquist and Wiksell, 1950).

the whole organic system on the perceptual apparatus reminds us of the teachings of the later gestaltists. Actually their main emphasis does not lie so strongly in the direction of orthodox gestaltism. Probably the too frequently forgotten *structural psychology* founded by F. Krueger[3] in Leipzig would reflect the clearest form of organismic psychology, as it does not make use, as do the gestaltists, of hypothetically formulated explanations in terms of cortical fields.

An organismic explanation of perceptual events does not restrict itself to S–R connections but also includes consideration of any organic changes and processes in the perceiving subject which might influence perceptual events. It is, for instance, regarded as quite probable that conflicting alternative organizing tendencies are typically involved in human perception. Modes of organization could eventually be traced back to early genetic stages. If we call the S–R approach mechanistic, we can regard the other approach as pseudomechanistic in that it also relies on experimental, functional evidence but still considers an ontogenetically definable set of factors to be chiefly responsible for the nature of perception.

No one working with perception would be inclined to question the outstanding contribution of modern psychophysics to the development of a scientific explanation of receptive processes. On the other hand, this branch of perceptual psychology still is burdened with some mechanistic tendencies. The most precarious manifestation of this is probably the omission of the contributions of the perceiving organism. Yet the experimenter should remember that an organism, even in a cross-sectional type of experiment, always represents a continuously changing system, which is altered even by a single act of measurement.

The Evidence from Ambiguity

Representatives of the organismic approach ask for opportunities to check the possible influences of longitudinal changes within the organism. Would it be possible to test the effects of early developmental stages on the structure of an actually observed later perception?

Since the early 1950's G. S. Klein[4] and some of his collaborators

---

[3] Krueger's contributions were published in *Neue Psychologische Studien* in the 1920's and early 1930's.

[4] G. S. Klein, "The Personal World Through Perception" in R. R. Blake and G. V. Ramsey (eds.), *Perception* (New York: Ronald Press Co., 1951).

at the Menninger Foundation and at New York University have been engaged in research centered around these problems. Organismic psychologists point to these investigations as potential answers to the demands for verification. Klein and his co-workers regard our consciously experienced perceptions as developmental end products of organizing processes extended in time. It has long been known that various unconscious tendencies influencing apparently definite and clear-cut perceptions can be revealed through appropriate experimental procedures.

One of the differences between mechanistic and organismic ways of thinking is easy to see in their different attitudes toward so-called ambiguous patterns. If we look, for instance, at the well-known

FIG. 1–2. Duck or rabbit? An ambiguous picture which can be perceived in either of two different ways depending on which of the halves, the left or the right, is more emphasized during observation. One and the same pattern can be perceived in several ways.

pictures shown in Figures 1–2 and 1–3, we generally see either of the two animals, the duck or the rabbit, in Figure 1–2 or either of the two female heads in Figure 1–3. While structuralists and early gestaltists found stimulus patterns like these extremely interesting, behaviorists have regarded them merely as rather atypical special cases, in which there happens to be too much ambiguity in the sensory input.

For psychophysicists, ambiguous patterns cannot be anything other than bothersome exceptional cases. Because of the point-to-point correspondence assumed to exist between stimulus and perception, perceptual wholes should be entirely determined by the stimulus. An organism experiencing a single stimulus pattern in two or more different ways must be regarded as behaving exceptionally. Illusions was thus considered to be the right word to use for these exceptional cases.

According to the organismic psychologists, on the other hand, our perceptions generally are end results of simultaneously competing alternative tendencies. Certainly in ordinary perceptions we are not aware of all of them. Who knows, however, how much ambiguity there is in our naively perceived stimulus world?

The other error made in this connection by extreme S–R behaviorists is that of assuming that the language of phenomenal description (ϕ-description) can be perfectly translated into the language of behavioristic p-description. As has been shown by Eino Kaila in his posthumous work, this assumption depends on a series of misunderstandings.[5]

FIG. 1–3. Ambiguous picture after Hill. Here the alternatives are "the mother-in-law" or "the wife," the latter with her head turned slightly away from the observer. Are our apparently stable percepts, too, just an outcome of a superior alternative chosen from among several competing possibilities?

Charles Osgood[6] enumerates three procedures that might affect which one of several alternative percepts arise and that can reveal hidden unconscious tendencies which might influence even our definite and unambiguous ordinary percepts.

These methods are:

1. Reduction of the clarity of the stimulus pattern.
2. Production and analysis of after-images.
3. Tachistoscopic exposure.

The Klein group has mainly used the tachistoscopic method.

Percepts as End-Products of Development

The Swedish psychologist, G. Smith, together with Klein and Spence, in 1959, reported a convincing experiment in the paper,

---

[5] A reference to Kaila's contribution is made above on p. 6.

[6] Charles Osgood, *Method and Theory in Experimental Psychology* (New York: Oxford University Press, 1953).

"Subliminal Effects of Verbal Stimuli."[7] If an ambiguous pattern (Figure 1–4) of a human face (stimulus pattern B) is preceded by the word HAPPY (stimulus pattern A), giving a definitely subliminal exposure to A (say 5 thousandths of a second) as against a supraliminal one to B (say 130 thousandths of a second), subjects report having seen a smiling, pleasant-looking face. If, on the other hand, another stimulus word, ANGRY, is substituted for HAPPY and is followed by the same B-pattern, subjects tend to report angry or unhappy expressions. Two years earlier a similar kind of experiment had already been done by Klein, Spence, Holt, and Gurevitch.

The unconsciously activated determining tendencies of the per-

FIG 1–4. The supraliminal stimulus employed in the tachistoscopic experiment of Smith, et al. It was preceded either by the stimulus word HAPPY or by ANGRY.

ceptual process could in these cases be regarded as dynamically motivated, e.g., in terms of Freudian psychology.

However, recent experiments using quite simple line patterns have shown that competing perceptual tendencies can be evoked by successive, emotionally neutral subliminal stimulations. This effect was demonstrated by Smith and Henriksson[8] working with the familiar Ehrenstein illusion. This illusion, as shown in Figure 1–5, involves a square embedded in a pattern of fanning lines. On the other hand, Ulf Kragh, a colleague of Smith, using thematic pictures, threw new light upon our percepts as compromise solutions among fast successive supraliminal stimulations.[9]

[7] G. Smith, D. P. Spence, and G. S. Klein, "Subliminal Effects of Verbal Stimuli," *Journal of Abnormal and Social Psychology*, 59 (1959).

[8] G. Smith, and M. Henriksson, "The Effect of an Established Percept of a Perceptual Process Beyond Awareness," *Nordisk Psykologi*, 7 (1955).

[9] U. Kragh, "The Actual Genetic Model of Perception Personality," *Studia psychologica et paedagogica*, Ser. 2, VII (1955).

According to Smith, experiments like these can suggest how perceptions arise and develop as a reflection of the total personality. Apparently the perceptual process contains unconscious or half-conscious early stages which are more ambiguous and unstable than is the clearly unambiguous end product. Stabilization of a perceptual whole actually means increasing the role played by better-articulated and consciously operating systems of reference. In experimental situations these roles can temporarily be weakened with the aid of various kinds of technical restrictions (procedures of reduction). Organismic psychologists look upon the final, stabilized, definite percepts as the result not only of consciously conceived stimulations but also of the inner influences contributed by the living organism.

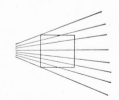

FIG. 1–5.   Ehrenstein illusion.

Both lines of research, the mechanistic as well as the organismic, force us to reformulate the old question of the correspondence between stimulus and perception.

The Sensory-Tonic Theory

Wapner, Werner, and Chandler[10] investigated the effect of changes in tonic muscle tensions on the perception of various stimulus objects in reduced experimental situations. In the main experiment the subject was seated in a dark room viewing a tilted, straight, luminous line. The line was adjusted according to the subject's instructions until it appeared vertical to him. The position of the line, when considered vertical by the average subject, actually was inclined a few degrees counterclockwise in the absence of any other stimuli. If the subject was stimulated acoustically or electrically on his right side, the light line had to be inclined in the opposite direction in order to appear vertical. Tilting of the observer in his chair also required compensatory inclinations in the apparent vertical line. Optical as well as other stimuli evoked *tonic* effects apart from their specific responses. These tonic movement reactions combined in a total interactive field. Thus a kind of functional

---

[10] S. Wapner, "Experiments on Sensory-Tonic Field Theory of Perception: IV. Effect of Initial Position of a Rod on Apparent Verticality," *Journal of Experimental Psychology*, 1952.

equality was demonstrated between "sensory" and "tonic" effects, that is to say, they are equivalent to each other in that both can produce the same end result. Thing perception is furthermore greatly influenced by impressions of the use value, the tool potential of the objects. In this sense, our perceptions not only reflect discriminations but also, and for the most part, manipulations as well.

Werner and Wapner applied their findings and conjectures in an attempt to interpret some of the very interesting experimental results obtained by I. Kohler.[11] He used spectacles, mirrors, and other kinds of optical devices to produce gross distortions in the space and color aspects of the habitual visual world. After wearing these distorting glasses for weeks, subjects gradually became able to compensate for these distorted stimulations. As Kohler himself has pointed out, the old constancy hypothesis failed from one point of view only. If stimuli could be defined not as punctiform elements but as higher-order complexes (including relationships between elements), the constancy hypothesis would be consistent with the findings of gestalt psychology.

Kohler's results can be interpreted by taking either renewed movement coordinations or perceptual changes as points of departure. When resorting to explanations in terms of motion coordinations, one encounters scarcely any difficulties at all. The events investigated could be looked upon as cases of *relearning*. This interpretation, of course, immediately forces us to consider the significance of postural stimuli and their relation to visual cues.

On the other hand, if one prefers to lean on transformations of perceptions, an appropriate *perceptual theory* is needed. At any rate, it does not seem impossible that the same particular retinal stimulation could give rise to two or more different perceptions as a function of the state of movement-innervation prevailing within the organism.

Werner and Wapner[12] therefore point out that our perceptual processes are also based on organismic factors rather than due

---

[11] I. Kohler, *Über Aufbau und Wandlungen der Wahrnehmungswelt* (Vienna, 1951).

[12] S. Wapner, and H. Werner, "Experiments on Sensory-Tonic Field Theory of Perception: Effect of Body Rotation on the Visual Perception of Verticality," *Journal of Experimental Psychology*, 1952.

Also referred to in F. Allport, *Theories of Perception and the Concept of Structure* (New York: John Wiley & Sons, Inc., 1955), pp. 183–207.

merely to the immediately relevant receptor stimulations. On the other hand, anyone who feels inclined to admit the role played by "organic states" upon perception, runs into the so-called interaction paradox, a consequence rather surprising to strict behaviorists. We shall return to this question in Chapter 8.

Werner and Wapner's sensory-tonic theory has four postulates: (1) Stimulation is a tonic process, regardless of the kind of receptor input, that is, whether it be either extero-, proprio- or intero-ceptive in its origins. Sensory (visual, auditory, etc.) as well as motor (postural, kinesthetic, etc.) functions contribute to a simultaneous sensory tonic state of tension. (2) The sense modalities possess some degree of functional equality in that they can give rise to identical perceptual consequences. A sound and an electric shock can substitute for one other in bringing about the same apparent deviation of a visual line. (3) A sensory quality is an experience which corresponds to a stable organism-stimulus relationship. If, for instance, the tonic state is symmetrically distributed relative to the longitudinal axis of the body, the sensory quality of vertical emerges. (4) Whenever a persistent stimulus has an unstable relationship to the prevalent state of the organism, there arises a tendency to bring about a change in the tonic state of the organism in order to return the relationship between organic state and stimulation to equilibrium.

The return to equilibrium which occurs with the distorted perceptual world in Kohler's experiments can, for example, be regarded as a stabilizing tendency within the organism. The degree of efficiency of such a stabilization process can be seen in the fact that one of Kohler's subjects finally was able to ski in the Alps with his distorting lenses on after having had sufficient opportunity to become accustomed to them.

Werner and Wapner argue that their theory, as a genuine field explanation, can handle the interactions between the organism and its surroundings, so that the theory goes beyond what could have been achieved by classical gestalt theory or by psychophysics.

This does not imply that we should avoid functional descriptions of the physical correlates of experienced perceptual events. On the contrary, it is appropriate to use a level of description similar to that of the natural sciences, which rely on measurements and calculation. This would permit us to describe essential relationships between stimuli. Among others, *information theory* has made it possible to be more precise about such formerly vague expressions as good, organized, well-articulated gestalten, etc. These previously rather tentative and vague expressions can be given strict mathematical definitions. It may suffice here to point out that descriptions can be improved, can be quantified, if one makes use of terms like information, noise, and redundancy. What formerly was referred to by speaking of stronger or better articulations, which make some gestalten more "efficient" than others, can be expressed succinctly and elegantly as a greater redundancy inherent in certain perceptual alternatives. *Measurements of the degree of organization, quantifications of gestalt qualities, and specifications of visual identification*, such as the measurement of shape constancy, are among the tasks which can be accomplished with the aid of modern computers programmed according to the concepts of information theory.

The old problem of the correspondence between stimulus and perception thus has been reformulated into new tasks, which are to be analyzed in terms of modern conceptual formulations. As stated above, Kohler's investigations already showed the significance of systems of relations among single stimuli. Comparably, one of the most important points in Gibson's perceptual theory is the emphasis laid upon the effectiveness of geometrically definable systems of relations within the stimulation pattern itself. So far this method has not been able to account for all of the determinants of perception, and yet many of the older phenomenal concepts have already been reformulated into quantitative scale values. Gibson is convinced that perceptual psychology should avoid any central mediating explanations until the explanatory potential of all the possible measurable relationships in the peripheral proximal stimulation have been exhausted. This, he feels, is the only way we can continue to keep pace with the language used by the other empirical sciences.

New-Look Theory, Set, and the Role of Cognition

A point of view more far-reaching than the one referred to as organismic is represented by the so-called new-look psychologists, e.g., Bruner and Postman.[13] Directive states of the organism are stressed by them as having an influence on perception. These directive states are mechanistically explained as products of learning strongly influenced by motivational factors in the organism.

---

[13] J. S. Bruner, and L. Postman, "Emotional Selectivity in Perception and Reaction," *Journal of Personality*, 16 (1947).

According to Allport there are six kinds of evidence in favor of the so-called influence of motivation upon perceptual events.[14]

1. The needs of the organism seem to affect its perception. The learning of discriminations by dogs has been shown to be most effective when the animals are hungry and expect food. Human subjects who have been deprived of food produce more food associations when presented with ambiguous visual patterns than do control subjects who have not undergone deprivation.

2. Perception is affected by rewards and punishments. For example, there is a change in recognition thresholds for stimuli which are associated with reward or with punishment.

3. The recognition of objects depends on their subjective value. Included in one of Goldstein's sorting tests among a variety of tools and other materials was a ripe, red apple. When required to recall the items in this collection, hungry subjects usually recalled the apple first. In tachistoscopic experiments the recognition threshold is different for words loaded with emotional meanings.

4. Brunswik and some of his students, as well as Bruner, have shown that the apparent or phenomenal size of objects depends on the impression of their value. A silver coin exposed for a few seconds together with equal size paper and wooden disks was reported by most subjects to be the biggest of them all.

5. The *directedness*, the *omissions*, and the *completions* of our perceptions depend on our personality. If we take a walk with a little boy, we may ignore a number of stimuli quite significant to him. On the other hand, he may not perceive the sex appeal of a woman passing by.

6. Freud has shown the effects of our unconscious dynamisms on what we perceive or fail to perceive.

When discussing these newest applications of the concept of "perception," it might be advisable to consider, among others, the admonitions of Hochberg and Johansson. As they pointed out, the relation of perception to the states which are supposed to be directive in some way or another has not been clearly specified. According to Johansson, it is not only a matter of different language when Gibson and his colleagues use the term perception.[15] They apparently mean something else by this term than do Bruner and

---

[14] Allport, *op. cit.*, pp. 337–39.

[15] Oral communication made by G. Johansson at a symposium in Copenhagen, September, 1960.

the new-look psychologists. Experimenters with motivated perception are not sufficiently careful in distinguishing between *perception* proper on the one hand and *cognition* or *recognition* on the other. Admittedly, organismic factors become decisive whenever cognition is involved, over and above perception. We must not forget, however, that motivational factors can become more influential when configurational conditions are weakened or ambiguous. When a fisherman boasts about the big trout which escaped from his hook, we assume that his description reflects his strong motivation. Yet the influence of these motivational tendencies may well have been strengthened a great deal by the vague and diffuse stimulus conditions. Elongated objects, like fish, viewed through a murky medium may look even longer, and after all, its longitudinal movements could also provide some extra apparent length to the big fugitive.

In this particular field of research, it must be admitted, precise measurements are harder to carry out than has been true with Gibson's method of investigation.

CHAPTER 2

Aspects of Sensory Evolution

BEFORE TAKING UP the question of the detailed function of the senses and the corresponding perceptual events, we shall consider some regularities which generally hold for all the sense modalities. Although perceptual scientists often warn against ill-founded generalizations and against premature syntheses concerning such matters, there is, on the other hand, much evidence in favor of some far-reaching analogies about the way the various senses function. If we could carry out more thorough investigations than we can today with our restricted methodology, we would probably discover even further analogies. Based on numerous investigations in the field of comparative physiology, Hecht already in 1934 claimed that, regardless of the specific sensory tissue examined, the *basic function* of a receptor cell is always the same from modality to modality. It produces firing in the receptor's neural fibers. He refers to the fact that every receptor cell, from whatever sensory tissue, consists of three clearly different parts. The outer, peripheral part picks up the changes in the environment for which the receptor organ is specifically sensitive. The middle part plays a mediating role, "transforming" the sensed energy (e.g., radiations, sound waves, chemical processes) into neural processes. This middle part is roughly similar in the receptor cells of all kinds of sense organs. The third basic part, as mentioned above, gives rise to similar and functionally equivalent physiological processes in the neural fibers. When traditional sensory physiologists grouped and divided our sense organs according to their specificity, they apparently forgot about the fundamentally analogous performance of the so-called different, specific receptors. We certainly would have reason to be surprised, Hecht remarks, if this conformity did not exist.

Primary Irritability and the Origins of Sensation

Even today, in some psychological texts, the false assumption is made that phylogenetically the earliest perceptions occur at that stage of development in which the sensing organism can be shown to be aware of the contents of its receptors' messages. However, it seems inadvisable to limit the term perception only to conscious experiences. If considered functionally, perception starts with an organism's *irritability*, which is already encountered at the level of unicellular animals. Irritability can be demonstrated by observing the behavior of living organisms; it is reflected in adjustments to varying environmental changes which are characteristic for any stimulated animal or human being. The environmental influences picked up by the receptors thus get transformed into appropriate patterns of behavior at phyletic levels much lower than those in which conscious coding of messages can be presumed to occur. A perceptual content, which for a highly developed human adult is an essential condition for the enjoyment of life (e.g., some artistic experience), probably takes the place of what in the life of primitive organisms are simple signals for biologically relevant and critical events in the behavioral environment. Receptive functions on that level are required in order to trigger adjustive responses to given situations. These responses must be understood as, in a primitive sense, answering the demands of the stimulus patterns. We should never forget that the functional basis for what we call human perception is also that broad and that we humans perform a wide range of reactions which do not necessarily presuppose awareness of the receptive sensory messages. Metabolic and homeostatic functions provide clear examples of this fact.

We can take for granted that different individuals' perceptions are basically similar. To be sure, there are differences. One person likes a particular taste which might be disgusting to somebody else. A smell which some people would consider pleasant might, in the opinion of others, be just awful. However, even if we think of the different motivational sets, which can tune our perceptual world, these are all differences based upon highly subtle advanced differentiations among individuals.

If one wants to decide whether perceptual contents do exist at lower phylogenetic stages, one clearly runs into greater difficulties. The behavior of our familiar domestic animals shows us that cats, dogs, horses, sheep, and rabbits have visual, auditory, olfactory, gustatory and tactual impressions. Since their receptors show a far-reaching resemblance to human sense organs, one feels tempted to assume that they might also perform analogous coding of messages. But the perceptions of even the most advanced animals differ from ours in remarkable ways: A dog can discriminate a high-frequency whistle which is inaudible to any human being. Dogs sense smells which we cannot discern; on the other hand, they might be insensitive to some kinds of smells which are quite familiar to us. Dogs also have difficulty in seeing remote objects which are clearly visible to us. The more we descend from the human level, the more difficult is it to find precise comparability of function. Should we permit ourselves to describe the performance of the ommatidia of the insect eye with the terms our *retinal vision* deserves? Can we extend the word smell to cover the messages sent by female butterflies to call males from distances of several miles? Some animals have receptors which are completely lacking in human beings. If we should presuppose corresponding sensory qualities, these would clearly appear extremely strange to human beings; presumably we could not even imagine what the experience would be like. Certain fishes have receptors along their sides which transmit not only touch stimuli but also vibrations in the surrounding water. There is reason to believe that the human ear differentiated out of such telereceptors, in the same way as the sense organs in our mouth cavity can be regarded as relics of earlier diffuse chemical receptors which can still be found on the body surfaces of certain kinds of animals. Some primitive species have light-sensitive spots all over their body surfaces. This occurs even at developmental stages in which no organized nervous system exists. It would hardly sound sensible to call the function of these spots vision in the human sense of the word. Nevertheless, these light-sensitive spots clearly affect the behavior of their owners. Sea polyps, which lack a central nervous system, still have receptors: the tentacles and the trunk respond differently to various stimulations. Even the unicellular amoeba has its receptive system: it is equipped with the remarkable sensitivity characteristic of all living cells, and with the aid of this ability, manages to adapt to and answer the demands of its environment.

Receptors for all modalities have, then, developed slowly and gradually. A diffuse general sensitivity grows more precise and turns into specific sensory functions. Yet, even within the frame of a human organism, there are modalities capable only of rather gross differentiations. This is to some extent the case in the senses of taste and smell.

Sense Classification

In everyday language, we talk of five modalities: sight, hearing, smell, taste, and touch, a way of grouping suggested by Aristotle. This traditional classification is consistent with the concept of exteroceptors (if we follow Sherrington's terminology). Sight and hearing show such a great degree of differentiation in human beings that they have been called the higher senses. It is thus perhaps natural that we tend superficially to regard all the other modalities as distinct and clearly separable from each other to the same extent as vision and hearing. Yet most other sense modalities in human beings are capable only of rather poor differentiations and are not as clearly specialized. We still depend a great deal on diffuse, common sensory contents of messages, and the boundaries separating the various different modalities are by no means sharp. Even a phenomenally homogeneous experience may result from an interaction of several different types of receptors. Yet, when speaking of physiologically determined fields of sensory activity, we generally prefer to rely on the term *sensory modality*.

Let us consider some examples. The boundary between smell and taste is generally very confused in human perception. There are foods and flowers whose aroma does not stimulate the diffuse chemical receptors in the nose and mouth cavities at all. On the other hand, these receptors are strongly influenced by other substances, e.g., onions or ammonia. According to older opinions this would require classification into several different senses. The stimulation of these diffuse chemical receptors not only reflects itself as nasal sensations, but they can also be felt all over the body surface wherever there are mucous membranes. Furthermore, man has a quite rudimentary structure, the *organ of Jacobson*, a sense organ located along the *vomer*, a bony area separating the two nostrils. In many species this organ swells up in response to stimulation by particular corpuscles in the air, and its function is apparently connected with the physiology of smell. The role played by it in human perception has not been fully investigated.

Traditional opinion regarding our sense of taste holds that what appears as a *taste* should always depend on stimulation of receptors on the tongue and in the walls of the mouth cavity. A systematic analysis of *taste experiences* shows, however, that discriminations of finer nuances of flavors in our foods or drinks would be impossible without the cooperation of both gustatory and olfactory receptors. Even experiences of touch and temperature, mediated by mucous membranes in the oral and nasal cavities, have been shown to contribute to the discrimination of complex qualities of flavor.

Similar circumstances hold within the range of all those modalities which, as a consequence of an unfounded procedure of generalization, are all too often combined under the single broad term of touch. On the one hand, our skin receptors record and transmit a number of sensory experiences (e.g., touch and pain) which differ in quality as well as along quantitative continua. On the other hand, we are able to discern differentiated perceptual wholes on the basis of messages coming simultaneously from many skin receptors. A reevaluation of the traditional concept of vision could also be performed along this very same line. We know about sensation of brightness on the one hand and about sensations of hues on the other. At least in part these two dimensions are mediated by different kinds of receptors. In fact, if one tries to determine how many senses we have by looking for different specific receptors, one runs into difficulties. As Moncrieff put it, one inevitably needs a greater number than five, but one would scarcely be apt to agree upon any higher alternative. Should we regard perception of red, green, and violet as due to different senses, in keeping with the three-color theory? People are more likely to accept salt, bitter, sour, and sweet as expressions of separate, specific modality functions than they are ready to admit separate specific color senses within the field of vision. Yet, in both cases, after all, they would actually be making equally artificial classifications. Psychologically speaking, we can avoid this tricky problem of physiological correspondence by resorting to the concept sense modality and considering these modalities as they are experienced. There are doubtless phenomenally discernible qualities, but it seems irrelevant whether these qualities depend upon one, two, or a manifold of activated receptor-systems.

Thus, there is no real reason to classify our senses at all; nor is there any ground for arguing about their number. Strictly speaking, judgments like these are always *matters of definition*. It has proved virtually impossible to differentiate clearly among the many sensory functions which we know are simultaneously active when we perceive a particular smell. To a certain extent this issue has been clarified by the phenomena of fatigue and satiation within the olfactory modality. If one and the same olfactory substance is continuously presented, smell sensitivity to this stimulus is eventually decreased. There is a process of adaptation: when our smell receptors are stimulated by a certain oil, 10 minutes may be enough to make the whole experience disappear. If, at this moment, a sufficiently different chemical substance, say camphor, is introduced, we promptly perceive it. Sensitivity to most kinds of oils, however, remains reduced.

The Evolutional Differentiation

When we look at the sense modalities and how they differ from each other, it is hard to avoid considering them *products* of *evolution*. Out of a group of diffuse, unspecified prototypes the various receptor systems became organized in diverging directions. Events in two or more modalities can only rarely be directly compared when perceptual phenomena are described. What can be considered comparable depends on the level of evolution assumed when comparisons are made. Two modalities may approach each other on one phyletic level; they may differ strongly on another. Conversely, there are modalities which in human organisms operate on such different levels that they can hardly be compared at all.

All receptor functions gradually developed out of the primitive irritability of the protozoa; one would hardly wish to assume sudden entirely new types of behavior at certain levels of evolution. Amoebas and ciliates show no sensory specialization of any kind. At most one can observe in them a diffuse receptive chain which immediately connects with corresponding patterns of action, resulting in continuous receptor-effector units. Even at the level of the medusa there is a diffuse unspecified general sensitivity to chemical substances, temperature, and touch. Out of this undifferentiated primordial receptor function the so-called higher senses have probably developed. The *diffuse chemical sense* is differentiated out from this function at an early stage of evolution. Already, at the level of earthworms and medusas there are light-sensitive spots; in a manner typical of such primordial functions, these spots are also highly sensitive to *temperature differences*. *Smell* and *taste*, important for the process of nourishment, also branch out at this relatively primitive level. *The sense of smell may reasonably be regarded as the first primitive long-distance receiver* (exteroceptive sense), and in spite of its poor neural equipment it, in its own way, exhibits a remarkable degree of efficiency. It is an excellent aid for a number of animal species when they scan their food from afar. Some deep sea fishes (Siluridae) have their surface completely covered with taste buds. If you take a piece of cotton and touch the side of one of these fishes, it will move, turn around, without any snapping response. But if the cotton has been impregnated with, say, broth, touching the fish's side will cause snapping movements, aimed at the stimulus. Careful experiments, cutting the seventh cranial nerve, have shown that this sensory pathway is responsible for these reactions.

Together with the functional differentiation of the receptors has gone their increased spatial specialization. The taste buds in the mouth cavity of higher animals originated in receptors which entirely cover the surface of some fishes. These prototypes of the mouth receptors in turn serve as evolutionary bases for the human gustatory receptors. In adults they mediate a few rather specific classes of qualities, and they occur on strictly circumscribed regions of the surface of the tongue.

There is much evidence in favor of the proposition that the senses of smell and taste, even during the descent of man, have played a more dominant role than we are generally inclined to think nowadays. It is well known that preschool children have a tighter network of olfactory and gustatory receptors than do teen-agers and adults. Some children are more accurate than older people in discriminating taste stimuli. They are often better able to discriminate differences in smells also. Parents and teachers have observed the remarkable skill with which some preschool children identify persons by their specific professional odor or the odor of their clothing. It has also been claimed that smell discriminations are more precise, and smell thresholds lower, in women than in men.

CHAPTER 3

The Different Senses and Their Receptors

VISION

THE RECEPTOR ORGAN for vision consists of the light-sensitive cell tissue, the *retina* inside the eye. If one starts from the outermost surface of the eyeball, this would be the third of the successive layers. The outer cover is the *sclera*, a tough tissue formed of tightly connected fibers. The second of the layers is the *choroid*, which supports metabolic processes inside the eye and consists largely of freely interlaced blood vessels. Thus the outer layer of the eyeball is protective, the middle one nutritive, and the inner one sensory. In the front of the eyeball the outer and middle layers are transformed into transmitting and refracting agents for the reception of light. The transparent front part of the sclerotic coat is called the *cornea*. Behind the cornea lies the modified part of the choroid, known here as the *iris*. Acting like the iris of a camera, it regulates the amount of incoming light. The opening in its center is the *pupil*. The tissue of the iris surrounding the pupil is largely muscular, one set of muscle cells being arranged circularly to make a sphincter, the other set forming radial muscles which, when they contract, enlarge the pupil. Eye color is determined by the color of the pigment contained in the iris. There are great individual differences in the amount of this pigment; the iris looks dark in the eyes of some people, light in the eyes of others. When bright light strikes the retina, the pupil may constrict to an opening less than 2 mm. in diameter; in the absence of light the pupil may dilate to more than 8 mm. in diameter. When it is dilated, it admits about 40 times as much light as when it is constricted. At the junction of iris and choroid is the *ciliary body*, a muscular tissue.

The *crystalline lens*, a remarkable part of the eye, lies immediately behind the pupil. It is attached to the ciliary body by ligaments. The lens is completely encased in a transparent encapsulating membrane, and tension exerted on the capsule by the ciliary muscle produces a change in curvature, especially of the front surface, which is always less rounded than the back surface.

The lens divides the eyeball into two cavities. The front cavity in turn is divided by the iris into two chambers, both filled with a dilute salty solution, the *aqueous humor* (watery substance). The

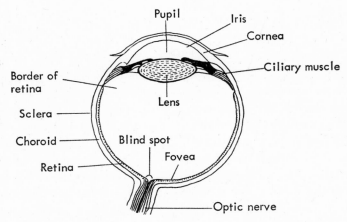

FIG. 3–1. The structure of the human eye as seen from above.

great bulk of the eyeball, the space between the back of the lens and the retina, is filled with the transparent *vitreous humor* (gelatinous substance).

The inner receptive coat, the retina, has two areas of particular interest in terms of the retina's sensory function. Close to the focus of the optical system formed by the lens and its supporting tissues, and almost directly behind the pupillary opening, the retina has a shallow pit. It is called the *fovea centralis*. The other notable area is the colliculus or *optic disc*, known generally as the "blind spot." It is located about 3.5 mm. to the nasal side of the fovea. It is here that the neurons from the retina come together and leave the eye, forming the *optic nerve*.

Figure 3–2 shows a schematic cross section of the retina. There are three main facts to note when considering its structure. The first is that at least two types of nerve endings are present, *cones* and *rods*, so named from the shape of their conical or cylindrical tips. Second, they are oriented *away* from the source of light, the front of the eye, their tips pointing toward the choroid. It is for this reason that the human eye, like other vertebrate eyes, is said to have an inverted retina. Finally, there are three consecutive neurons from the receptor cells to the fibers of the optic nerve (see Figure 3–3).

The outermost nerve cells are the rods and cones. They are synaptically connected with the *bipolar cells* in the next layer. These

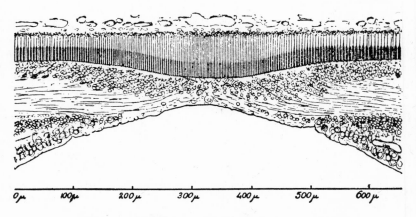

FIG. 3–2.   Cross section of the foveal part of the retina.

in turn deliver their messages to the *ganglion cells*, whose processes form the optic nerve. These three successive neural layers are separated by corresponding regions of *synapses*.

The classical tradition of strictly separating two kinds of retinal receptors (the rods and cones) was started by M. Schultze in 1866 with his famous *duplicity theory*. Functional investigations of the retina had shown that a central and a peripheral part were clearly distinguishable. The foveal region and its immediate surround proved to be best equipped to receive and transmit light impulses during periods of normal daylight illumination. This part also provided the most sensitive receptors for hue discrimination. By contrast, the periphery of the retina improved in sensitivity in twilight conditions but was also found incapable of recording color stimuli other than differences in brightness. What could have looked more natural and logical to investigators dominated by Wundt-Titchenerian modes of thought than to presuppose two distinctly separate sets of receptors?

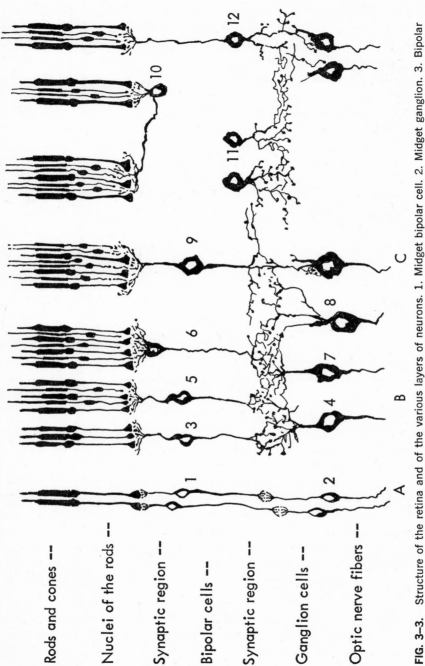

Rods and cones — —

Nuclei of the rods — —

Synaptic region — —

Bipolar cells — —

Synaptic region — —

Ganglion cells — —

Optic nerve fibers — —

FIG. 3–3. Structure of the retina and of the various layers of neurons. 1. Midget bipolar cell. 2. Midget ganglion. 3. Bipolar cell connected only with cones. 4, 7, 8. Various types of ganglion cells. 5, 6. Bipolar cells fed by both cones and rods. 9. Giant bipolar cell. The rest of the numbers refer to transverse cells.

Measurements performed by Österberg in 1935 yielded the distribution of rods and cones shown in Figure 3–4. Plotted is the number of end organs per unit area from the fovea to the extreme periphery of the retina. Although according to these measurements there is a rod-free area in the foveal region, it is apparently very small, subtending an angle of only 1.5°. It should also be observed that the tips of foveal cones are extremely thin, so that superficially

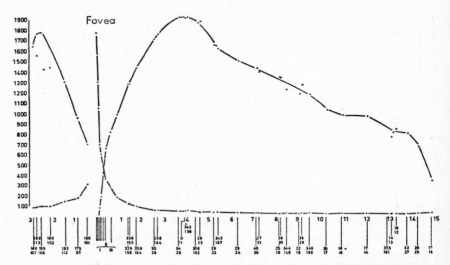

FIG. 3–4. Distribution of rods and cones throughout the retina. The zero value on the horizontal axis represents the fovea. The small numbers refer to the frequencies of visual cells per unit area at various distances in mm., large numbers, from the fovea.

they cannot be distinguished from rods at all. Because of the lack of clear structural differences between the two kinds of visual cells some research workers (e.g., Willmer, 1946) have expressed doubt about the infallibility of the duplicity theory in the extreme form in which it was formulated by Schultze. In Schultze's formulation:

1. Two completely separate functions were assumed.
2. The rods were considered insensitive to chromatic differences.
3. There was no allowance for the possibility of more than two types of receptor cells.

Saugstad and Saugstad carefully evaluated the entire experimental literature favoring or opposing the duplicity theory. They arrived at the conclusion that the theory does have considerable explanatory value, although it nevertheless needs to be revised.

Experiments on peripheral regions of the fovea in particular point in the direction of some anatomical as well as functional overlap among the receptor cells. The role played by the various kinds of retinal sense organs is *relative*, in that they all contribute to a certain extent to all kinds of color perception. Even the basic question concerning the homogeneity of foveal tissue, that is, whether it consists of more than one type of receptor, still remains unsettled.

Until recent years investigators have customarily pointed to at least one clear structural difference which they claimed had been demonstrated to exist between rods and cones. As can be seen in schematic drawings of the retina (e.g., Geldard's Figure 5),[1] cones were believed to be connected individually to bipolar cells. Although this might be the case with *foveal cells*, one cannot say with certainty that they are always and only cones. The thinner visual cells, mainly regarded as rods, have multiple connections. Each bipolar cell synapses with at least two, and usually more, of them. Thus, in extremely peripheral parts of the retina, as many as 400 cells can jointly be connected to one bipolar. As Saugstad and Saugstad have pointed out, the careful investigations of Polyak weaken the evidence for even this structural argument. On the other hand, in fairness they admit that whatever other characteristics these cells may have, only such a kind of anatomical arrangement (increasing multiplicity of connections toward the periphery) can explain the marked differences in sensitivity between the fovea and the periphery.

In early sensory physiology it was customary to assume that the whole *macula lutea*, an area surrounding the fovea and including it, was free of rods. It subtends an angle of 4°. It is called the yellow spot because of its appearance when viewed through an ophthalmo-scope.

According to Österberg the human retina contains about 6½ million cones, and 120 million rods. Krause has estimated the number of fibers in the optic nerve at about 1 million in all.

The blind spot was first discovered by Mariotte in 1666. Everybody with normal sight can convince himself of its existence by doing the following experiment: Close the left eye and arrange Figure 3–5 so that the small cross is straight ahead of your right eye. While fixating on the cross move the whole page closer to and

---

[1] F. A. Geldard, *The Human Senses* (New York: John Wiley & Sons, Inc., 1953), p. 24.

further from your eye. At a distance of about 30 cm. the black circle disappears.

An estimate made by Trendelenburg gives an idea of the size of this spot: 14 retinal projections of the full moon placed side by side would just about cover its area.

The axons of the retinal ganglion cells form the optic bundle or *optic nerve*. It was formerly considered the second cranial nerve; nowadays anatomical textbooks regard it as a protrusion of cortical tissue. The bundles of fibers from the two eyes converge to join and appear to cross at the *optic chiasma* (from the Greek chi: Χ). But the complete crossing is only apparent. Animals below the level of mammals do exhibit a complete crossing, but in humans and other mammals only half the fibers cross (see Figure 3–6). Half the

FIG. 3–5. To demonstrate the blind spot.

fibers continue on their own side, and the other half cross to the opposite side of the brain. The fibers which cross over in each optic nerve are those originating from the inner or nasal half of the retina. The effect of this arrangement is to include in the right optic tract, behind the chiasma, all fibers coming from the right halves of the two retinas, while fibers from the left halves go to the left side of the brain.

Beyond the chiasma the fibers proceed to the thalamus and terminate chiefly in the *lateral geniculate body* of that center. Both of the geniculate bodies act as important way stations for messages traveling to the corresponding cortical lobe. It is in these bodies that the axons of the ganglion cells in the retina terminate. They make synaptic connections with brain-stem neurons, whose axons in turn reach up to the visual centers in the cortex. Studies done on brain-injured patients, especially on disabled war veterans, have provided a crude localization of the cortical visual fields (retinae corticales).

Figure 3–7, after Wright, shows the prevailing opinion concerning the relative representation of different retinal regions in the

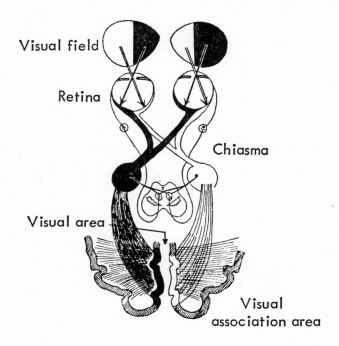

Visual field

Retina

Chiasma

Visual area

Visual
association area

FIG. 3–6. Crossing-arrangement of the visual pathways.

corresponding occipital lobe of the brain. Note the strong representation of the macula lutea on a wide area farthest back in the cortex. In spite of the anatomical correspondence shown in the picture, we should never forget that a functional interaction prevails in the whole system. It is doubtless not just coincidental that some of the thalamic optic fibers branch up to other parts of the cortex. The cortical coding of "retinal messages" thus is not just a matter of specified brain centers but is an instance of dynamic interaction.

HEARING

The sense organs for hearing are divisible into three parts: the *outer* ear, the *middle* ear, and the *inner* ear (see Figure 3–8). We all know the *earlobe* or *pinna*, the most visible part of our auditory organ. It serves to funnel sounds into the inner parts of the ear and is less well developed in man than in most other mammals, in which it is bigger and can be turned to receive the sound waves rather efficiently. The external *auditory canal*, a tube 0.7 cm. in diameter

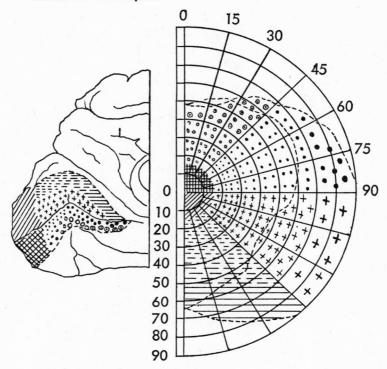

FIG. 3–7. The cortical representation in the left occipital lobe of the right half of a monocular visual field.

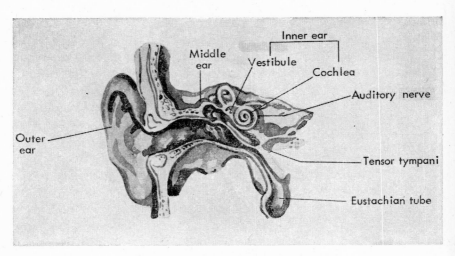

FIG. 3–8. Gross structure of the ear.

and about 2.5 cm. long, leads from the pinna to the *eardrum* (the *tympanic membrane*). This thin membrane is shaped like a flat cone, with its tip toward the middle ear. In fact, the eardrum separates the external from the middle ear. Functionally, it acts like the diaphragm of a microphone; it is made to vibrate by the sound frequencies which impinge upon it. On the inner side of the eardrum there is a relatively wide ventricle, the *middle ear cavity*, 1–2 cc. in volume. In the temporal bone near the middle of this cavity there are two openings, the *oval window* and the *round window*.

The oval opening is located above the round one. Vibrations of

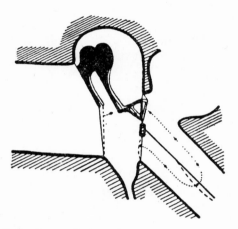

FIG. 3–9. Transmission of vibration to the inner ear.

the eardrum can be transmitted immediately by air conduction through the middle ear cavity, but the oscillations are intensified by the lever system of the three *ossicles* which form a chain from the eardrum to the oval window. These tiny bones are the *hammer* (malleus), *anvil* (incus), and *stirrup* (stapes). The hammer is attached to the center of the eardrum and vibrates with it. The vibrations are transferred to the anvil, which is connected to the hammer by an elastic ligament. The anvil in turn activates the stirrup through the lever system of another ligament. As a consequence of these transmitted movements the stirrup is driven back and forth in the oval window. The drum is about 20 times as big as the footplate of the stapes, and the ossicles provide a small mechanical advantage. Thus a considerable pressure, about 25 to 30 times as great per unit area as at the drum, but with a reduced amplitude of oscillation, is concentrated on the oval window.

The *Eustachian tube*, which runs from the middle ear cavity to the throat, plays an important role in equalizing the pressure between the external and the middle ear. Normally closed, it opens during swallowing. Soldiers serving in heavy artillery usually have learned to swallow and then to keep their mouths open during the firing of a series of shots. When the drum is subjected to extreme atmospheric pressure variations, it is advantageous for the pressure to be the same inside as outside.

Attached to the ossicles are two muscles, the *stapedius* and the *tensor tympani*. The former is attached to the stapes. When it contracts it changes the articulation between the foot of the stirrup and the oval window. Contraction of the tensor tympani, attached to the malleus, places the drum under greater tension. The two muscles thus act as antagonists, the action of each being opposite to that of the other. When both muscles contract at the same time, as they normally do, motion of the ossicles is dampened, and there is a more favorable response to high tones. When the stimulus intensity exceeds a certain threshold, both muscles contract reflexively. This reflex contraction of the ear muscles may have an essentially protective function. For that matter, the muscles can be compared with the ciliary body of the eye.

A third way in which vibrations can be conducted to the cochlea, in addition to the two ways already mentioned (air conduction and transmission through the ossicles), is via bone conduction through the walls of the middle ear cavity. This alternative is important only in cases in which some temporary damage or permanent defect has rendered normal function of the middle ear impossible.

The actual auditory cells are located in the inner ear. Structurally, the inner ear corresponds to its name, the *labyrinth*. It is entirely embedded in the *bony labyrinth*, a system of cavities in the temporal bone (Figure 3–10). It contains a transparent, watery fluid, the *perilymph*. The inner labyrinth is composed of a series of sacs; it is usually known as the *membranous labyrinth*. This labyrinth has three major divisions, the *vestibule*, the *cochlea* and the *semicircular canals*. In the vestibule are two sac formations, the *utricle* and the *saccule*. Together with the semicircular canals they form a sense organ for body position and equilibrium. They will be described in more detail in the section devoted to the proprioceptors.

The vestibule, about 5 mm. long and 5 mm. wide, constitutes an immediate continuation of the middle ear cavity. The membranous labyrinth is filled with a clear fluid, the *endolymph*.

The bony cochlea is composed of a central axis, the *modiolus*, and a tube, which during an early embryonic stage coiled on itself, forming a spiral cavity around the modiolus. The modiolus supports and forms the inner wall of the *cochlear duct*. In a fully developed human being the spiral makes about 2¾ turns.

Two elastic membranes divide the cochlea longitudinally into

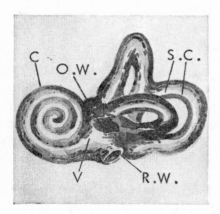

FIG. 3–10.   The bony labyrinth.
C = cochlea.
O.W. = oval window.
R.W. = round window.
S.C. = semicircular canals.
V = vestibule.

three chambers, the *scala vestibuli* on top, the *scala tympani* underneath, and the *ductus cochlearis* in the middle. In the longitudinal section shown in Figure 3–11, the scala vestibuli is separated from the cochlear duct by *Reissner's membrane*, and this duct, in turn, is separated from the scala tympani by the *basilar membrane*. This membrane does not, however, divide the indicated cavities completely. At the extreme tip of the modiolus it leaves an opening between the two scalae, the *helicotrema*, which has a diameter of only 0.25 mm. Thanks to this organization, the scala vestibuli and the scala tympani are connected with each other around the cochlear duct, which ends in a blind alley. The whole system is schematically represented in Figure 3–12.

Extending from the modiolus part of the way to the outer wall of the cochlea is a bony shelf; the basilar membrane completes the division of the cochlea, attached on one side to this bony shelf and to the outer wall of the cochlea on the other. Upon the basilar membrane are situated the endings of the auditory nerve. Together

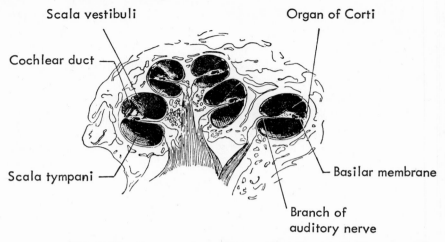

FIG. 3–11.   Cross section of the cochlea of a guinea pig.

with epithelial hair cells they form a structure called the *organ of Corti*. Its structure and organization are schematically shown in Figure 3–13. Two rows of column cells (the *rods of Corti*) form a triangular tunnel, which divides the organ into an inner and an outer part. In the outer part there are several rows of receptive hair cells (3 or 4), in the inner part there is only one. The afferent pathways extending to the outer receptors run through the tunnel. The auditory nerve bundle is embedded in the modiolus. A large system of ganglions is wound around the modiolus, following the bony part of the intersection between the cochlear duct and the scala tympani. From this *spiral ganglion of Corti* the single afferent fibers branch out into the organ of Corti.

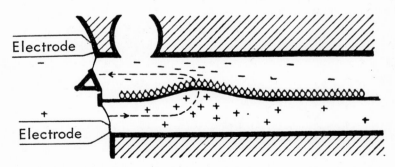

FIG. 3–12.   Role of the basilar membrane in the field of electric potentials.

The tiny hair cells or ciliary cells must be regarded as the real receptors for sound stimuli. A number of theories have been proposed to explain what happens in these hair cells at the very moment the mechanical vibrations in the inner ear are transformed into neural events. The best founded nowadays is the description given by Békésy.[2] Pressure waves in the endolymph produce a pattern of standing waves on the basilar membrane. This pattern is specific for vibrations of different frequency and for their combinations. When the basilar membrane bends upwards it results in a

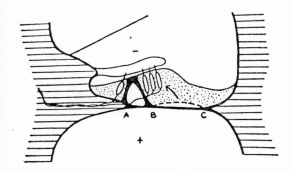

FIG. 3–13.   Structure and function of the basilar membrane.

contact between the free endings of the hair cells and the *tectorial membrane*, the membrana tectoria. This membrane is rather rudimentary and is attached only on one side—to the bony shelf.

Békésy did not expressly stress the importance of a locally specific contact between the receptor endings and the tectorial membrane. Should this prove to be the essential event in the whole procedure of stimulation, we are faced with the question of whether the mechanism for firing the sensory neurons is basically chemical, tactual, or electrical. The fact that the tectorial membrane strikes the hair cells could provide the basis for an explanation in terms of the *piezo-electric effect*. It has, on the other hand, been pointed out that the contact could presumably unbind proteins in the receptor cells. In that case the resulting processes would not look entirely different from the events started by the breakdown of rhodopsin or iodopsin in visual cells.

As is shown in the longitudinal section, the cochlea gets narrower

[2] G. v. Békésy, *Experiments in Hearing* (New York: McGraw-Hill Book Co., 1960).

from its base towards its apex. The basilar membrane, on the other hand, gets wider farther from the oval window. At the base of the cochlea, the membrane is 0.16 mm. wide, while it reaches a width of 0.52 mm. at the helicotrema. In Figure 3–14 the human basilar

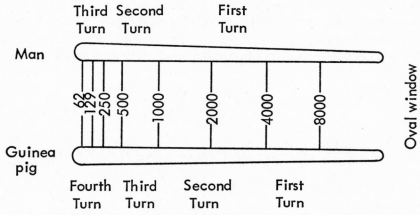

FIG. 3–14.   Frequency sensitivity along the basilar membrane.

membrane is schematically compared with the same organ in the guinea pig. The location of the regions most sensitive to certain frequencies are indicated in parallel fashion for both organisms. Note that the lowest frequencies, about 60 to 70 cycles, stimulate the portions nearest to the helicotrema, while the highest frequencies are picked up nearer the oval window.

It is clear that a *place theory* like the one proposed by Békésy accounts pretty well for the facts of pitch discrimination. As to the question of loudness perception, place theories during recent years have been complemented by frequency mechanisms. The intensity of the stimulus, that is, the amplitude of the vibration, is mediated in neural transmission by the rate at which each neuron fires and by the number of neurons activated at a given time. The investigations of these rather intricate mechanisms has proceeded with unforeseen efficiency; recent improvements in electrophysiology have permitted the use of new recording techniques and electronic aids. Above all the cathode-ray oscilloscope and modern amplifiers have made auditory physiology a promising field for further research.

In 1930 Wever and Bray tried to study action potentials in the auditory nerve of a cat by hooking a pair of electrodes to the nerve, and amplifying and reproducing the electrical changes in a loudspeaker. The electrical waves proved to be faithful reproductions of the stimuli, indeed so faithful that the listener at the loudspeaker could identify the person speaking into the cat's ear. After a period of intensive research, criticism, and reexamination, it turned out that the Wever-Bray effect could not be considered due merely to genuine neural transmission, since it would have required action potentials at rates up to 5,000 per second and beyond, clearly much faster than any neuron can fire. Actually the effect is a compound of two different phenomena: *auditory nerve potentials* and *cochlear microphonics*. The high frequencies in the Wever-Bray experiment were due only to the latter.

Because the auditory nerve cannot transmit *action potentials* at the rate presupposed by early frequency theories (which argued that pitch is mediated by the frequency of neural firing), Wever and Bray proposed their volley theory. According to it, not all nerve fibers are identical in their response characteristics. Some have short refractory periods, others long. With a low frequency tone it may be possible for all fibers to keep up with the stimulus and thus respond to every wave, but they cannot do this with high frequency tones. As frequency increases, various fibers, with different refractory periods, respond to waves skipped by others. The net result is a high frequency of response in the entire bundle of neurons but only relatively infrequent discharges in any individual neuron.

The fact of aural or cochlear microphonics nevertheless shows that the cochlea can transform mechanical oscillations into electric currents. The explanation given by Stevens and Davis is based on the piezo-electric effect. The hair cells, under the pressure of the tectorial membrane, become charged at their bases and at their tips, the degree of pressure determining the phase and direction of alternating discharge-charge patterns. Figure 3–12 provides a very schematic illustration of the presumed distribution of positive and negative charges. The assumption of such antagonistic loadings has already been strengthened by some evidence from animal experiments.

It is easy, when looking at Figure 3–13, to think that the basilar membrane must be more flexible transversely than longitudinally. The portion AB beneath the tunnel is stiff, while the outer part is elastic. A weak oscillation causes a bending movement restricted to the distance B–C only. On such an occasion only the outer hair cells are stimulated. At higher frequencies the oscillation spreads out over the entire organ of Corti, including the AB section. To activate the inner hair cells, the pressure must be increased 50 times relative to what is required for stimulation of the portion B–C.

The *psychophysics of hearing* has for practical reasons concentrated mainly upon measurements of thresholds. The absolute threshold can be determined either by measuring the minimum pressure on the eardrum or the minimum intensity in the stimulus field which evokes a sensation. Figure 3–15 shows *audiograms*

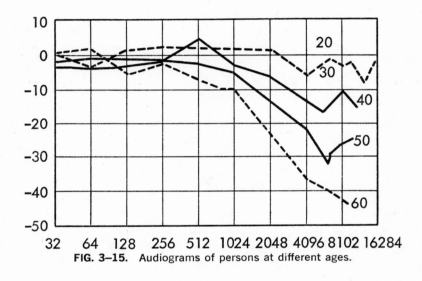

FIG. 3–15. Audiograms of persons at different ages.

obtained with both methods of measurements. *Binaural* test situations regularly yield lower thresholds for stimulus intensities than do *monaural* situations. The normal *auditory area* (Figure 3–16) is computed on the basis of these auditory thresholds. The limits of the auditory area are determined by the absolute threshold curve at the bottom and the threshold for feeling (pressure) at high intensities at the top. Standard equipment for carrying out threshold measurements is the *audiometer*. Most commercial audiometers are electronic; they consist of audiofrequency oscillators arranged to generate eight or more frequencies, usually the octaves from 64 to 8,192 cycles. The audiogram is a graph connecting the recorded threshold values.

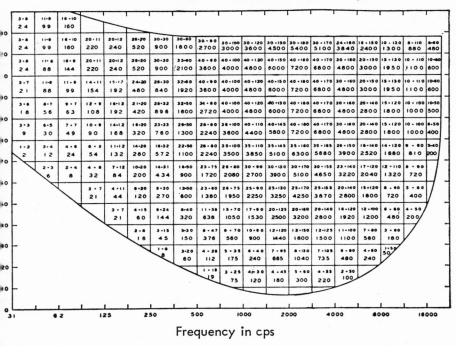

Frequency in cps

FIG. 3–16. Number of tones which can be distinguished within the auditory area.

According to Geldard, "Large-scale audiometric surveys have been made in an effort to establish the picture of normal hearing characteristics in the general population and to ascertain the nature of age and sex differences."[3] In the course of making the National Health Survey, conducted in 1935–36, 4,662 people, all of whom had had a clinical history of normal hearing, were measured. The age range was from 10 to over 60 years. The following trends could be clearly observed: (1) In males, advancing age has no deteriorating effect on perception of frequencies below 1,000 cycles. (2) With increasing age there do occur large and significant losses for high tones. This is particularly true for the highest frequencies measured (4,096–8,192 cycles). (3) At all age levels females show somewhat more loss for low-frequency tones, but less for tones of high frequency. This sex difference is such that women of advanced age do not normally suffer partial high-tone deafness to as great a degree as do aged men.

---

[3] Geldard, *op. cit.*, pp. 116–17.

SMELL AND TASTE

Both in vision and in hearing there is the possibility that the proximal stimuli are chemical processes. More undifferentiated than these senses, and more primary in their level of phylogenetic development, are the modalities which respond directly to chemical irritations in the environment of human beings: *the chemical senses.* Three of them are customarily distinguished: *smell, taste,* and the *diffuse chemical sense.* The mucous membranes in the nose and mouth cavities are differentiated from the regions sensitive to general chemical influences, which are encountered everywhere around the openings of the body surface (eyes, mouth, intestinal region, and sex organs). Animals at lower evolutionary levels, such as some types of fishes, have chemical receptors all over their surfaces, especially along their sides.

The receptors for smell and taste are called *olfactory* and *gustatory* respectively. To stimulate these cells, as well as the receptor cells of the diffuse chemical sense, the substance must be dissolved in some liquid. The most differentiated among these receptors are the olfactory ones; the most primitive are the diffuse chemical receptors.

The location and function of the olfactory receptors is based upon the aerodynamics of the nose cavities. The average volume of the human nasal chamber is 34.2 cc. for the two nostrils combined. Their position and relative size is shown in Figure 3–17.

Starting at the tip of the nose, we first encounter the *nostrils* (*nares anteriores*) as the outermost part of the system. Correspondingly, there is a pair of outlets into the nasal chambers at the rear, the throat openings (*nares posteriores*). The inner surface of the nostrils is covered with a sensitive epithelial layer, an immediate continuation of the skin of the nose. This epithelium is called *regio respiratoria.* The nostrils are separated by a partly bony and partly cartilaginous wall, the *septum nasale.* The bone forming the top and rear framework for the nasal structure is the *vomer,* which was mentioned in connection with the organ of Jacobson.

Most of the inspired air passes through to the pharynx and lungs without affecting the olfactory region at all. Air masses generally do not circulate around the *turbinate bones* (Figure 3–18), but instead follow the less complicated route of a high arc in the nasal cavity. By both convection and diffusion odorous particles escape from the

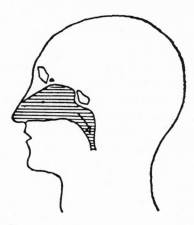

FIG. 3–17. Location of the nasal cavities.

mainstream and find their way to the uppermost reaches of the nasal chamber, where the sensitive *olfactory epithelium* (*regio olfactoria*) is located.

In the septum are some additional organs sensitive to smell. They

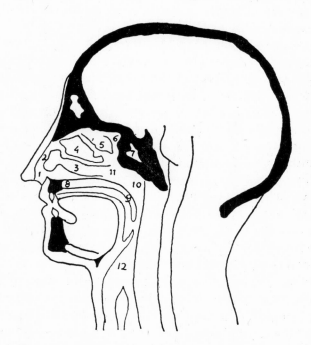

FIG. 3–18. The nasal passages. The olfactory epithelium is at 6.

are clearly rudimentary in the human adult. In the human embryo and during early infancy they are visible as openings in the inner walls of the two nostrils, one in each. They belong to the *Jacobsonian organ (organon nasovomerale Jacobsoni)*. In mammals other than humans this organ is mainly composed of spongy tissue which can swell in order to affect the influx of air. When the organism is engaged in the process of olfactory sensation, the swelling slackens, producing an air-sucking effect in the passages. It is not impossible that some of the peculiarities we ascribe to the perceptual world of dogs, and the differences in their sensory behavior relative to that of man, might be due to their more developed vomeral organ. While sight and hearing are better in human beings, their olfactory organs seem to have degenerated.

The main task of the nasal cavity is not the conduction of incoming air to the olfactory epithelium. It serves primarily as a kind of heater and filter mechanism. The horizontal turbinate bones provide an extended surface which produces this preparatory treatment of the air. This is why the nasal cavity is folded and complicated in structure.

The olfactory epithelium is about 5 cm. square in size, and yellowish-brown in color. The diffusion which results in odorous particles escaping from the mainstream of air passing through occurs during expiration as well as during inspiration. Many of the experiences we call taste are based upon particles escaping from swallowed foodstuffs in the throat, which reach the olfactory region when we breathe out air while chewing or swallowing. The olfactory sensory qualities mix with messages sent by the *gustatory* receptors proper in the mouth cavity. In the cross section of the nasal chamber shown in Figure 3–19 the olfactory epithelium is indicated by arrows at the top of the diagram. The cell tissue of that epithelium consists of the ordinary olfactory rods (O) and many columnar or sustentacular cells (S) intermixed with them (Figure 3–20).

The column cells form a kind of supporting tissue through which the thinner receptor cells send their endings to the surface. The column cells are also pigmented; they are responsible for the yellowish color of the area. There are 160 olfactory rods for every 100 columnar cells. The third type of nasal epithelium cells, the mucus-secreting *goblet cells* (G), are rare in the olfactory region, although they are common in other parts of the respiratory epithe-

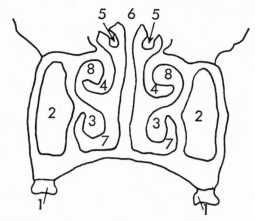

FIG. 3–19. Cross section of the nasal passages.

lium. The several million olfactory cells are tiny endings of the first cranial (olfactory) nerve.

The olfactory rods are in a sense archaic since they represent a combination of receptor and ganglion function in the same unit of tissue. There is no synapse at the level of the epithelial tissue, each rod serving the role of both generator and conductor of nerve impulses. This structural organization indicates the relatively primitive nature of this modality because a similar duality of function is typical in nervous systems of the lower vertebrates. From their distal ends, the receptor cells send out a dozen or so hairs to the surface of the nasal cavity. The dissolved particles of olfactory substances are presumed to stimulate these hair endings directly.

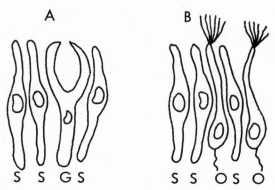

FIG. 3–20. Examples of cells from the nasal mucous epithelium.

The density of receptors in the rabbit's mucosa, which has been more thoroughly studied than the same tissue in human subjects, is estimated to be 120,000 per square millimeter. The basic layer of the mucous respiratory region is formed by the *basal cells*, which have a pyramidal form and a spherical nucleus.

The olfactory region also contains free nerve endings. They mediate sensations of *touch* and are sensitive to *diffuse chemical influences*. When carrying out olfactory experiments we must not forget the role of these receptors. The hairs of the olfactory rods are kept damp by the mucous fluid secreted by the goblet cells. It is supposed that the dry particles carried by the air must be dissolved in this secretion before they can produce any olfactory stimulation. If the fluid thickens because, for example, of an infection of the mucous epithelium, the hairs of the olfactory rods can no longer function. It is remarkable that in addition to our lack of smell experiences when suffering from a cold we, as a rule, cannot discriminate tastes as before. This very fact proves that most of our experienced taste qualities depend on interactions between gustatory *and* olfactory receptors. The stimulation of the olfactory rods might occur just on the membranes of the tiny hairs or as a chemical reaction inside the more bulbous portion of the cells.

Careful examination of the rabbit's olfactory region shows a lack of lateral connections joining one part of the sensitive area with another. As the nerve fibers leave the epithelium they converge into larger and larger bundles. After passing through perforations in the plate of the ethmoid bone, at the roof of the nasal cavity, they immediately enter the *olfactory bulb*. In the glomeruli near the surface of the bulb are the first synapses of the system. It is not until the level of the *mitral cells* that lateral connections can be found. From the olfactory bulb the first cranial nerve leads to the cortical olfactory area, located in the cingulate gyrus (Figure 3–21).

It is curious to note that despite a rudimentary sense of smell, the human species after all ended up with the most complicated system of olfactory nervous conduction. Moreover, the olfactory tract differs from all other sensory systems in that it bypasses the thalamus on its way to the cortex.

The gustatory receptors of man are located on the tip, the sides, and the back of the dorsal tongue surface. There are also regions responsive to taste stimuli on the palate, in the pharynx and larynx, and on the tonsils and epiglottis. Adults are devoid of sensory

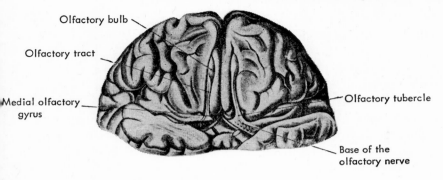

Olfactory bulb

Olfactory tract

Medial olfactory gyrus

Olfactory tubercle

Base of the olfactory nerve

FIG. 3–21. Human frontal lobes as seen from below, with some olfactory centers and pathways.

organs for taste on the underside of the tongue, on the middle of the tongue's upper surface, and on the inner side of the lips and cheeks. By contrast, children, at least during their first decade, have taste receptors widely scattered around on the whole surface of the tongue and even on the side walls of the mouth cavity. These particular receptors are especially sensitive to sweet, so it is hardly accidental that children, with their numerous taste recorders in the mouth, are particularly fond of sweets. The delicacies of the adult are spiced foods which, as we know, contain components that stimulate the olfactory receptors in the nose. In 3-month-old human embryos the gustatory cells are already clearly visible, scattered on a wider area than in newborn infants. This pattern of organization is not unexpected, because these receptors have also been shown to be indiscriminately abundant at earlier phyletic levels. Higher levels of evolution involve a gradual increase in distinctiveness and restriction in their spatial distribution.

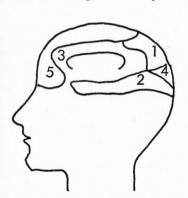

FIG. 3–22. Location of the olfactory cortex (3).

The receptor cells proper are located in *taste buds*, onion-shaped clusters, each of which contains 2 to 12 sensory cells together with *supporting* (sustentacular) cells. The supporting cells are arranged around the taste cells somewhat in the manner of barrel staves, and

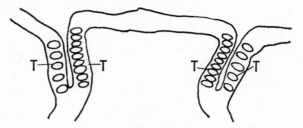

FIG. 3–23. Cross section of a papilla (schematic); T = taste buds.

are columnar in form, while the gustatory cells themselves tend to be spindle-shaped. The taste buds are collected in papillae; each papilla is filled with taste buds, horizontally oriented along its edges, as can be seen in Figure 3–23.

The papilla is surrounded by a moat, into which the pores of the taste buds open. Inside each taste bud there is a narrow passage, the *porus gustatorius*. The stimulus material diffuses from the moat to the nuclear part of the taste bud through this passage. The tips of the sense cells protrude beyond the surrounding epithelium and are presumably stimulated by direct contact with taste solutions. Unlike the olfactory receptor cells the taste cell appears to be constructed to serve only as a generator of nerve impulses. Nerve fibers supplying taste cells terminate in arborizations at the cell surfaces; they do not enter the cell bodies proper. Furthermore, the strength of taste experience depends in part on the surface area stimulated; a process of summation is typically involved in the mediation of increased stimulus intensity.

Three different forms of papillae are traditionally distinguished: (1) *fungiform papillae*, mushroom-like in appearance, are scattered irregularly over the upper tongue surface; (2) *foliate papillae* are continuations of a series of folds in the midlateral border of the tongue; (3) *circumvallate papillae* are the largest of all, consisting of rather massive but low protrusions, which form a kind of ridge near the back of the tongue, usually 7 to 10 in number. Figure 3–24 schematically shows the location of these different types on the tongue of an adult man. The *filiform* papillae are without importance for the receptor functions as they are devoid of taste buds. They are scattered over the whole upper surface of the tongue, as well as on its tip and sides and give the tongue surface its roughness, useful for softening food.

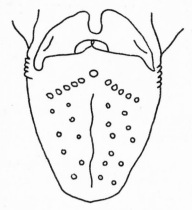

FIG. 3–24. Different types of papillae on the tongue surface.

Contrary to what was hitherto rather mechanistically assumed concerning the functional basis of taste experiences, recent investigations have pointed to the interactive complexity of taste phenomena. All naturally occurring tastes are a result of parallel stimulation of olfactory, temperature, and touch receptors, as well as of the taste buds proper. The doctrine according to which taste perception is a mere additive result of some combined primaries or taste fundamentals is now out of date. Admittedly, *if we close our nostrils* and taste only solutions which are approximately at body temperature (about +37° C.), we do experience a reduced world of tastes. In that sense of the word we are justified in distinguishing the traditional four taste primaries: *sweet, salt, sour, and bitter.* It is obvious, however, that a bare series of qualities like this does not do justice to the richness of nuances encountered in free natural tasting situations. All attempts to find and classify specific taste organs must be viewed against this background. Figure 3–25 shows the parts of the tongue which, when experimentally isolated, have been shown to respond specifically to different gustatory stimuli. This functional localization can, of course, be directly compared with the differences found in the location and structure of the papillae (Figure 3–23). The same stimulus material can apparently give rise to different taste experiences, depending on which part of the tongue it stimulates.

On the other hand, the structure of taste receptor cells does not exhibit a high degree of differentiation. Öhrwall examined 125 papillae, stimulating them with solutions of sugar, salt, vinegar, and quinine. On the regions devoid of papillae no sensations could be provoked. All papillae responded readily to changes in pressure and temperature, but only 98 proved sensitive to changes in the chemical composition of the stimulus. Some papillae responded specifically to only one type of stimuli, while other papillae proved sensitive to certain combinations of the primaries. *Öhrwall apparently inclines toward the assumption of four specific types of nerve fibers.* Their relative distribution in different types of papillae could be quite different.

The determination of specific thresholds for the four types of receptors began a new epoch by introducing Pfaffmann's superb experimental techniques. By means of a series of electronic devices he was able to record the flow of discharges directly from the nerve fibers mediating gustatory stimulations. Thresholds for both sodium chloride and acid were readily obtained by noting the minimum concen-

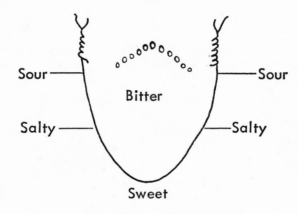

FIG. 3–25.   Sensitivity areas for the four taste primaries.

tration which elicited a discharge of neural impulses. A modified method of constant stimuli was employed in which series of stimuli were dropped in random order on the tongue surface. "The presence or absence of a response in the nerve was judged by the appearance of the oscilloscope and the sound of the discharge in the loudspeaker of the recording system. The frequency of occurrence of a response was an increasing ogival function of the stimulus concentration. A threshold was then computed from the midpoint of this curve."[4]

Pfaffmann was able to present average specific thresholds for five categories of chemical stimuli: viz., sugar, sodium chloride, hydrochloric acid, saccharine, and quinine sulfate. The differences in the order of magnitude of the thresholds were considerable, varying from a 0.2–0.7 percent concentration for sodium chloride and sugar to 0.00003–0.0005 percent for quinine sulfate and saccharine.

[4] Carl Pfaffmann, "Somesthesis and the Chemical Senses," *Annual Review of Psychology* (1951). Also in Carl Pfaffmann, "Taste and Smell," Stevens (ed.), *Handbook for Experimental Psychology* (New York: John Wiley & Sons, 1951), pp. 1145–58.

Sugar produced almost no effect. Some activity following quinine stimulation could be detected in the more optimal preparations. Pfaffmann assumes that the nerve fiber system conveying impulses for sweet may be of relatively smaller diameter. It could, according to him, even be unmyelinated so that action potentials in these fibers would prove quite difficult to record.

As Pfaffmann points out, taste impulses are mainly carried by the 7th, 9th, and 10th cranial nerves. The facial afferent nerves for touch and pain do, on the thalamic level, interfere with the gustatory pathways. So, also, are the cortical centers for taste located close to the loci for facial sensitivity.

Among the investigations of the absolute thresholds, those concerned with the influence of the temperature of the stimuli have proved especially successful. The threshold curves for dulcine, sodium chloride, hydrochloric acid, and quinine show quite specific trends if the temperature of the stimulus is varied from 17 to 42 degrees centigrade. The acid solution maintained its threshold at an almost invariable level of concentration; the sodium chloride threshold rose steadily as a linear function of the temperature; the trend for the quinine rose progressively; but the threshold for dulcine appeared lowest at 32–37 degrees centigrade, rising again at higher temperatures.

All attempts to point out correlations between variations in the chemical structure of the stimulating solutions on the one hand and the gradients of qualitative taste impressions on the other have proved unavailing so far.

Instead, Pfaffmann has decisively contributed to our knowledge of the physiological determinants for affective values of our taste impressions. They will be discussed in connection with a later topic.

From a phyletic point of view, Morgan's hypothesis concerning the determinants of differentiation of gustatory receptors deserves some attention. According to him the differential capacity of the nerve endings serving corresponding receptor cells would account for the development of the receptor cells themselves. As an explanation for the important but controversial "law of specific nerve energies" his opinion could have far-reaching consequences. These questions will be dealt with further in Chapter 8.

Lasareff's assumption concerning the physiological chemistry of gustatory stimulation is analogous to what we know about comparable processes in visual cells. According to him the chemical substance contained in the stimulating solution penetrates the receptor cell and produces chemical reactions. The proximal stimuli proper would then be the chemical by-products of the absorption process. Consequently phenomena of thresholds and of adaptation in taste could be explained in the same way they are in visual perception.

THE SKIN SENSES

The traditional sense of touch, as mentioned above, is actually a rather complicated modality which now is regarded as composed of a number of separate recording systems. Generally, psychologists have been more interested in the functions of tele-exterceptors, primarily in sight and hearing. Among the three ways to group sensory processes mentioned by Geldard (*qualitative*, according to the *stimulus*, and *anatomical*), the last one seems to have been most favored. When we proceed from the telereceptors to systems sensitive to stimulation of the skin and of the internal organs, however, the anatomical basis turns out to be rather indefinite. The question of which nerve endings in the skin and in deeper tissues respond to common touch and pressure is far from settled. This lack of knowledge is noticeably reflected in the wide variation in terminology and in the classification of these modalities among textbooks. Following Geldard once more, the skin might best be considered as housing three sensory systems, one for *pressure* reception, one for *pain* sensitivity, and one responsive to *temperature* changes. Those belonging to the deeper tissues, muscles, and visceral organs, as well as the receptor system located in the nonauditory labyrinth of the inner ear, constitute the *internal senses*, sometimes also called either the *intero-* or the *proprioceptors*.

Among the interoceptors we find, e.g., the taste system and the sensors for internal pain (as distinguished from the pain mediated by the skin tissues); further, there are sensory systems for hunger, thirst, and the sensations of sexual excitement. The kinesthetic and postural receptors in muscles, joints, and in the labyrinth of the ear are also regarded as proprioceptors.[5]

This section is confined to a survey of the skin receptors.

---

[5] C. T. Morgan and E. Stellar, *Physiological Psychology* (New York: McGraw-Hill Book Co., 1950).

The Sense Organs

A kind of mapping procedure has been applied in order systematically to explore the organs located in the skin tissues. The common laboratory technique is to utilize a rubber stamp prepared in the form of a square grid, 20 mm. on each side, with a total of 400 squares each one 1 mm. square in size. This then specifies a standardized sample area of the skin for exposure to experimental stimulation.

For investigations extended over longer periods of time, a technique devised by Dallenbach has proved feasible: a small dot of india ink is hypodermically injected at the corners of the grid. The grid can thus be easily reproduced if it has faded away in the interim.

At the turn of the century Blix and Goldscheider observed that experiences of warmth or cold could not be obtained at all places on the skin surface. On the contrary, the specific temperature receptors are restricted to rather definite, circumscribed regions. Blix, after having investigated temperature-sensitive loci of the skin, was the first to define the different spots for warmth and cold. A little later Frey was able to extend the observation of punctate differential sensitivity to pain and pressure. That was why he classified the skin receptors *qualitatively*. As tools Frey used hairs, both human and animal, attached at right angles to the end of a matchstick or other wooden holder. These hairs, varying from 0.05 mm. to 0.2 mm. in diameter, made it possible to carry out accurate point-by-point serial explorations of the skin samples.

In order to explore warm- and cold-sensitive spots, investigators apply temperature stimulators, in which water, at a controlled temperature, circulates and keeps the tip of the stimulator at a constant temperature. The best known of those temperature cylinders was designed by Dallenbach. For prick, pain, and allied sensations any sharp-pointed device, typically a needle, has proved sufficient.

With these methods Frey also tried to determine the specific end organs corresponding to the various categories of spots. At first such studies explicitly followed the principle of specific sense energies. Nowadays the interest in distinctions among different end organs has lessened. As Lewis puts it, nerve fibers are of interest at their endings rather than in their length.[6] The traveling of impulses is quite analogous from fiber to fiber, no matter what kind of energy has elicited them. A survey of the different types of end organs requires first a brief presentation of the structure of the skin. The main features are shown schematically in Figure 3–26.

Three major skin layers are conventionally distinguished: the *epidermis* or cuticle, the *corium* or true dermis, and the *subcutaneous* tissue.

The last-mentioned layer is not actually part of the skin. Yet it acts as it were as a chief mediator for the biological functions of the two outer layers. Most of the larger blood vessels, nerve trunks, sweat glands, and hair follicles of the skin are located in it. The

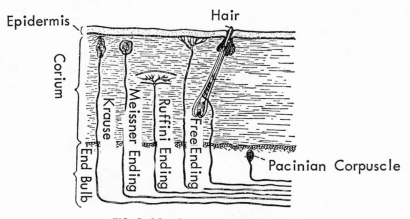

FIG. 3–26.   Cross section of the skin.

epidermis in turn consists of two chief layers: the *corneum* and a deeper *germinative* (or Malpighian) layer. The cells of the corneum arise from the last. The separation between epidermis and corium is irregular, the uppermost layer of the corium consisting of conical mounds which project into the floor of the epidermis. The papillae, some of which house the specialized nerve endings, are confined mostly to the corium, although some of them may stretch out into the germinative layer. The uppermost layer of epidermis is devoid of nerves and receptors. Blood vessels are richly distributed throughout the corium.

Most numerous among the skin receptors are the "free nerve endings." In some parts of the skin they end at all kinds of levels so

---

[6] Thomas Lewis, *Pain* (New York: Macmillan Co., 1946), p. 34.

that they branch out to make contact with any of the cells included in that region. In their structure the free endings show considerable variation. There are *bundles* (plexuses), which do not occur in the epidermis but which are quite numerous in the corium and in the subcutaneous layers. Apart from the corium the free nerve endings thus extend and cross over into virtually any layer of the skin. Phyletically they are sometimes regarded as the prototype of all other categories of skin receptors. An unbroken continuum runs from these free nerve endings to the large, complicated *Pacinian corpuscles* at the other extreme. While the free nerve endings terminate—mostly without any myelin sheath—in the layers of the epidermis, in recent decades even more types of encapsulated receptors have been identified. In addition to free nerve endings some of the main types of encapsulated terminations are shown in Figure 3–26. Among them are *Meissner's corpuscles*, found in the papillae of hairless skin regions. *Krause end bulbs* are distributed throughout the corium; they have been found near the edge of the cornea in the eye, in the tissues of the external genitalia, and on the tongue. *Ruffini cylinders*, also known as arboriform terminations, occur in the dermis near its border with deeper layers; sometimes they have also been found in subcutaneous tissue proper. Not to be forgotten also are the *bases of the skin hairs, the hair follicles, with basket-like free endings* coiled around them.

Related to the encapsulated endings just mentioned are the *Golgi-Mazzoni corpuscles* and the Pacinian corpuscles (the figure shows only the latter). Both are rather large egg-shaped formations which can be seen with the naked eye; they are quite widely distributed, extending through and penetrating several tissues. Golgi-Mazzoni endings are found especially in the junctions of tendons and muscles. Pacinian corpuscles also occur in the joints, the ligaments of the leg and forearm, in the external genitalia, in the coverings of bones, in the connective tissue of the abdominal cavity, and near the walls of large blood vessels.

Opinions about Touch and Pressure

At different stages of research on these structures several attempts were made to group the various receptors so as to correspond with the phenomenal qualities presumed to be mediated by them. Best known of these was Frey's effort; he tried to list specific separate receptors for touch, pain, and temperature. Such assumptions must, however, be regarded as premature. Especially the theory that the Ruffini and Krause structures serve respectively as specific organs for the warm and cold spots must be viewed with suspicion, because we know that the latter are especially responsive to slow changes of temperature within deeper and larger portions of tissue rather than to punctate stimuli on the skin surface.

Best founded are Frey's opinions concerning *touch and pressure* receptors. Touch spots differ in number from one part of the skin to another, and there is some degree of correlation between their density and the density of Meissner's corpuscles and of hair base endings. In most cases the nerve endings at the bases of hairs do appear to act as touch receptors, but there is still insufficient experimental evidence concerning Meissner's corpuscles. It is most likely that they mediate sensations of light pressure from the hairless parts of the skin surface. In addition, there is evidence to suggest that some free endings in the epidermis participate in the mediation of touch.

Temperature Sensitivity

Temperature sensitivity has proved troublesome for investigators. It has turned out to be difficult to specify particular terminations corresponding to the loci for warmth or cold sensitivity. Considering the physical stimulus conditions, one certainly could ask about the need to distinguish between two separate senses: it is a commonplace fact that conduction operates to make a surface either lose temperature or gain it from surrounding bodies. Why should we postulate two senses? But as Katz noted, the leveling of temperature differences during conduction occurs in several stages. He also observed that the adaptation to these stages proceeds gradually after having started at the skin surface and before reaching the deeper layers of tissue. To use Gibson's terminology, one could put it as follows: *gradients of increasing* or of *decreasing temperature* occur between the successive adjacent layers of the body surface.

The chief argument for distinguishing two senses rests on the facts known about the location and the distribution of warm and cold spots. If a sample area of the arm is explored point by point with a metal contactor cooled well below skin temperature in a 1 cm. square area perhaps a half dozen such spots will be found. Stimulated later with a warmer contactor the same area yields perhaps one or two reports of warmth. Cold spots always seem to be far more numerous than warm. Table 3–1 gives comparisons for several body regions.

The conclusion that the temperature spots mapped by this procedure should correspond with the location of individual temperature receptors would, of course, be mistaken. The spots are products of certain specific experimental operations. The number of them found in a given investigation is dependent on at least the following factors: (1) the stimulus temperature, (2) the size of the stimulator tip, (3) concomitant mechanical pressure, (4) the state of thermal adaptation, (5) the duration of the stimulus at each

TABLE 3–1

COMPARISON OF WARM- AND COLD-SPOT CONCENTRATIONS
(After Geldard)

	Spots per cm².	
	Cold	Warm
Forehead......................	8.0	0.6
Nose....................8.0(side)–13.0(tip)		1.0
Upper lip......................	19.0	...
Chin..........................	9.0	...
Chest.........................	9.0	0.3
Upper arm, volar side.............	5.7	0.3
Upper arm, dorsal side............	5.0	0.2
Bend of elbow....................	6.5	0.7
Forearm, volar side..............	6.0	0.4
Forearm, dorsal side..............	7.5	0.3
Back of hand....................	7.0	0.5
Palm..........................	4.0	0.5
Fingers.......................2.0–9.0		1.6–2.0
Thigh..........................	5.0	0.4
Lower leg.....................4.0–6.0		...
Sole of foot.....................	3.0	...

exposure, (6) the interval between stimulation, and (7) the attitudinal set of the subject.

Because of the influence of these factors the correspondence between two successive maps is likely to run no higher than 80 percent.

In the years 1930–32 Bazett and his co-workers accurately measured the conduction through the tissue of heat from a thermal stimulator applied to the skin surface. They used tiny thermocouples embedded in the skin of the forearm. At a depth of about 1.0 mm. below the surface there proved to be remarkably little heat gained or lost when warmth or cold sensations were aroused. The

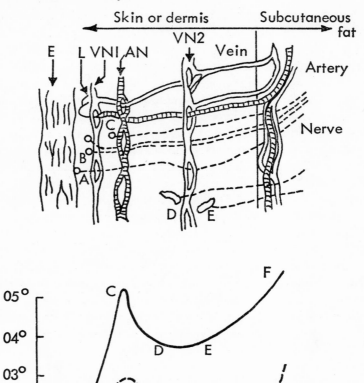

FIG. 3–27. Thermal gradient theory of temperature sensitivity.

rate of heat penetration through the layers of the skin was found to be between 0.5 and 1.0 mm./sec. Apparently the dermal blood circulation serves as a kind of cooling system, retarding direct heat penetration into the tissues. Putting together all the results of his experiments, Bazett developed his theory of thermal gradients, which is illustrated in Figure 3–27. The abscissa gives distance below the skin surface in millimeters, the ordinate temperature above that of the skin surface in degrees centigrade.

The various structures of the dermis and subcutaneous region are represented at the top in Figure 3–27. Below are pictured two different thermal gradients, one for rapid blood flow (solid line), one for more sluggish circulation (dotted line). The abscissae give distances below the skin surface in millimeters. The ordinates show temperature above that of the skin surface, in degrees Centigrade. Possible positions of cold receptors under this theory are A, B, and C; warm receptors could be at D, E, or F. The solid line depicts a situation in which blood flow is increased above normal; the more usual case is represented by the dotted line. A, B, and C denote possible locations of cold receptors, D, E, and F are loci of possible end organs for warmth. In the normal resting skin, maintaining as it does a thermal equilibrium with the external environment, the gradients for warmth and cold are apparently of opposite sign. To be effective, a warm stimulus would have to exaggerate the normal gradient. A cold stimulus, to excite cold sensations, would similarly have to steepen the normal gradient. The cold receptors occupy a region in which the gradient is already quite steep to start with. The withdrawal of heat from the system brings about a rapid increase in the temperature difference between the skin surface and the receptors. The situation for warmth is somewhat different, though similar in principle. If the skin surface is warmed, the rather gradual gradient in the region of the warmth receptors is exaggerated, which should result in stimulation of these receptors. The changes produced by high temperature on the skin should require more time than those for cold, which is in fact the case.

Some research by Katz has shown the decisive role played by specific heat in the thermal perception of different objects. The phenomenal significance of the *thermal capacity* of different objects will be examined more closely in a later chapter.

Pain Sensitivity

Pain and *ache* could in part be called skin senses, although there is a still wider variety of disagreeable sensations included in the category of visceral or organic pain.

In a number of textbooks pain is considered to be solely a result of stimulation at high intensities, i.e., intensities which exceed the upper threshold or the stimulus maximum. Whatever modality is involved, a maximal stimulus intensity would always produce sensations of pain. This opinion is supported by everyday experiences. If one applies pressure on the body surface at an intensity exceeding the mean of customary intensities, or if one persistently increases skin temperature, even an initially pleasant sensation before long changes into its opposite. But the statements made by Blix and Goldscheider, on the basis of compelling experimental findings, have brought about a change in these traditional opinions. Working independently, these investigators observed that pain is relatively specific in the sense that only one cutaneous system can be held responsible for it. Pain results from a light, quick touch with a heated wire, application of a brief pulse of electric current, a quick tug on a hair, or a jab with a fine needle. They all feel exactly alike to a subject if care is taken to keep him ignorant of supplementary information concerning the stimuli employed. Using appropriate stimuli, pain points or spots were found in most areas of the skin, yet it proved even harder to identify specific pain receptors than was the case for temperature and pressure organs. It should be noted that the intensitive and differential thresholds for pain vary in a way which does not correlate to an appreciable degree with the distribution of the density of pain spots on the body surface. One of Frey's favorite ideas was to regard pain as a system of sensitivity distinct from pressure, warmth, and cold, and furnished with receptor organs of its own, the free nerve endings. This idea is not now generally accepted.

As we know from measurements of pain spot distributions made in Frey's laboratory, in some areas of the skin 1 square cm. contains as many as 200 spots. The tip of the nose, the sole of the foot, and the radial surface of the hand are less sensitive, with 40 to 75 pain spots in the same area. Besides these regions, which were emphasized by Frey, the cornea and the eardrum also deserve considerable attention, because according to Geldard "the most exquisite pains in the body can originate from these sources." The mucous linings of the cheeks and the back parts of the mouth, including the rear portion of the tongue, are relatively analgesic. The lower part of the uvula is completely insensitive to pain. Most of the organs of the abdominal cavity are also insensitive, assuming they are not inflamed. Visceral pains can generally be felt only as a consequence of the pain mediating capacity of the muscles and bones surrounding the "hollow" viscera.

It was the widespread distribution of free nerve endings throughout the body which—according to Geldard—led Frey to believe that these organs were the specific receptors for pain. For a long time the cornea of the eye remained a center of controversy regarding the role of free endings. It is found to be devoid of all other kinds of receptor organs, and it was until recently taken for granted that no sensations except for pain could ever be elicited by corneal stimulation. As Geldard points out, experiments during the late 1930's have shown that the cornea is also sensitive to pressure. Any tissue containing free nerve endings is capable of transmitting sensations of pressure as well as those of pain. The question of whether there are specific separate receptors remains unsettled.

TABLE 3–2

DISTRIBUTION OF PAIN SENSITIVITY
(After Geldard)

Skin Region	Pain "Points"/cm².
Back of knee (popliteal fossa)	232
Neck region (jugular fossa)	228
Bend of elbow (cubital fossa)	224
Shoulder blade (interscapular region)	212
Volar side of forearm	203
Back of hand	188
Forehead	184
Buttocks	180
Eyelid	172
Scalp	144
Radial surface, middle finger	95
Ball of thumb	60
Sole of foot	48
Tip of nose	44

All phenomenal mappings of pain impressions are the result of rather subjective procedures. It has proved especially difficult to find qualities or modes of appearance of pain. Dallenbach ended up with a list of 44 qualities. We expect to be reasonably well understood when we use words like biting, burning, gnawing, pressing, tearing, and twitching pain. Yet we can probably never achieve a degree of unanimity between different individuals comparable to that of naming colors. For example, Lewis calls attention to the fact that pains of very short durations are often referred to as *pricking*. The same pain when it lasts longer is called *burning*, and so are all other pricking pains. On the other hand, the phenomena known as double pain, and the referred pain sensed in deeper layers of the body tissues in connection with slowly traveling burning messages, indicate that there might be other factors behind the experienced differences than merely duration.

Jenkins also brings up the fact that pain has for a long time often been considered as the opposite of pleasure. "But pain is not necessarily unpleasant. Some people derive pleasure from the consumption of hot spices, horseradish, etc., which appear to obtain their distinctive effects by the stimulation of pain receptors."[7]

Still to be considered is the problem of the neurobiological correlates of perceived pain. According to Lewis, superficial pain sensations are mediated by structures whose embryonic origin is the *ectoderm*, while deep pain is mediated by structures which originate in the embryonic *mesoderm*. Organs developing from the *endoderm* are generally insensitive to pain.

Animal experiments have convincingly demonstrated that pain impulses ascend ventral tracts in the spinal cord. Lehmann's observations led him to suggest that these ventral pain pathways probably mediate only the deeper pains, while dorsal tracts transmit impulses from the skin, but Lewis cautions that there is little empirical evidence to support this conjecture.

A single, brief needle prick to the fingertip produces an experience consisting of *two successive pain sensations*. First there is a sudden stroke of pain which disappears almost immediately. Soon after there follows a more persistent and generally stronger unpleasant sensation. According to Lewis, the average lag of the second response is 1.9 sec. at the toe, 1.3 sec. at the knee, and 0.9 sec. at the top of the thigh. Hence, research workers have postulated a double system of pain transmission. Certain kinds of neural fibers, called the α and β fibers, are known to have a rapid transmission rate, while others, the γ fibers, are known to transmit more slowly. Thus it does not seem unreasonable to assume that the skin may be equipped with two parallel pain mediation systems. The first-experienced, immediate pricking pain is probably due to impulses in the α and β fibers, which are thicker than the slower γ fibers, and which are myelinated, while the γ fibers are not; the later "burning" pain is probably mediated by the γ fibers. Impulse propagation speed in the γ fibers is only about 0.5 to 1.0 meter per second, while the rate in the β fibers is about 20 times this fast.

Some supporting evidence comes from observations on pathological cases. Fast reflexes, such as the withdrawal of the hand from a hot surface, are known to be mediated by the β fibers. Identical pain

---

[7] W. L. Jenkins, "Somesthesis," in Stevens (ed.), *op. cit.*, p. 1178.

experiences can, however, be mediated by all of these neural transmission systems; furthermore, the localization of surface pain and deep pain are equally accurate, irrespective of which system is innervated.

Pain experiences originating in the deeper tissues are generally more difficult to study than surface pain; there have been controversies concerning what has been called "visceral pain." Lewis holds that no differences in connecting pathways or the resulting experiences can be shown to exist between pains in muscle tissue or in visceral organs; he feels that to avoid difficulties in the operational definitions, it is wiser to confine our studies to muscle pains.

Part of the controversy is due to the insufficiency of our knowledge about afferent pathways from the visceral organs. Much of what we know about proprioceptive sensory systems is really information concerning the transmission of visceral pain; the best assumption seems to be that free nerve endings typically act as the chief receptors, whether in the deeper layers of the skin or in the inner organs. They probably receive larger and more global masses of stimulation than the rather punctate and locally specific pain spots on the skin surface. There are several different conjectures about the afferent visceral pathways. Ross (1887), supported by his follower Wernøe, assumed that impulses are transmitted along two different paths. Direct visceral pain is presumably mediated by the vagus nerve; coordinate with this system is another, presumably consisting of more peripheral subcutaneous neural tissues. Pain transduction is assumed to be a function of "vegetative reflexes" that contract the capillaries and that produce other changes which affect the pain receptors in the skin. Referred pains are readily explained with this view, as are local hyperalgesia of the skin surface accompanying visceral pain, skin pallor, and disorders in secretory functions. Thus Ross and Wernøe postulated two parallel spinal pathways: one for *splanchnic* (= visceral) *pain*, and the other for *somatic* (= referred) *pain*.

Lewis maintains that discussion of "sensory autonomic pathways" in connection with direct visceral pain is apt to be confusing. The only thing we know is that some afferent pathways associated with the spinal column, such as the vagus nerve, connect anatomically with some structures of the autonomic nervous system; but these structures generally remain outside the spinal cord. Part of the confusion comes from the attempt to identify sympathetic ganglia as pain centers despite the fact that these ganglia lack afferent fibers.

The connections of the vagus and the somatic nerves with the spinal cord are all in the dorsal roots. Although some visceral tissues may lack pain-transmitting nerve endings, Lewis does not deny the possibility that there may be some direct neural pain mechanisms; he says that pain cannot be referred to the visceral organs. Phenomenally, all we can do is point to the general region from which the pain appears to be radiating, and to say that the pain is somewhere deep under the skin. We can often report whether the pain is located on the ventral or dorsal side of the body.

When muscle and connecting tissue are involved in referred pain, the picture is different. Nerves located in the same parts of the body, whether visceral or muscle paths, produce identical pain sensations, which are always projected to some indeterminate part of the skin surface. Schematic diagrams of the body surface have been developed to show how skin segments are innervated by known pain-transmission systems; they also identify the segments on the surface of the skin to which experimental subjects refer deeper pains originating in muscle tissues. Some controversy has surrounded the issue of the origin of deeper referred pain. Does it originate in the visceral organs themselves, or in surrounding tissue, affected by the changes in the damaged organ? Lewis feels that conjectures like this are apt to be fruitless; if we want to look for the regions in which the deepest pains originate, we could also list the visceral structures or the inner walls of the abdominal cavity as areas sensitive to pain. One primary fact does stand forth, Lewis says. "Some internal pains must arise from receptors that are more specific than those of the skin. Not only are they specific in yielding only pain, but they can be stimulated only in certain specific ways."[8]

Finally, we should consider one of Lewis' remarks concerning the mode of action of the pain terminals in the skin. Sometimes the triggering stimulus is a chemical process, a small chemical change in the cellular tissue.

If blood circulation in a limb is artificially reduced and then, after a time, the muscles of the limb are forced to move, the person investigated suffers a diffuse, hardly definable pain which has a quality different from any experience of pain sensations at the skin. Some investigators have considered it profitable to make a distinction between *superficial* or *epicritic* and *deep* or *protopathic* pain. Experiences of dull burning deep in muscle tissues are so peculiar

---

[8] Lewis, *op. cit.*, p. 34.

that even the common expression pain sounds inappropriate to them. Probably we should consider ache as synonymous with protopathic pain.

KINESTHETIC AND LABYRINTHINE SENSITIVITY

In terms of the above classification, pain, as we have seen, involves more than exteroceptors. We have encountered sense organs for pain which, with good reason, should be grouped as proprio- or interoceptors. Morgan lists five ways in which these receptors differ from the exteroceptors we have considered so far:

1. They are stimulated by the action of the body itself.
2. In contrast to the intermittent action of exteroceptive stimuli, stimulation is always with the organism, guiding its every movement.
3. Generally there is an awareness of the activity of the exteroceptors, while one seldom is aware of proprioceptive events.
4. The qualities of proprio- and interoceptive experiences are indistinct.
5. Proprioceptive sensations tend to form a background as it were, against which exteroceptive sensations stand out as figures.[9]

It has often been pointed out that the proprioceptors must be regarded almost entirely as mechanoceptors, which means that they are primarily fired by mechanical stimuli. Yet pain receptors, even if they are not interoceptors, may be activated by chemical stimuli.

Most important among the proprioceptors are deep subcutaneous end organs sensitive to pressure and kinesthetic stimulation; they can be found in muscles, tendons and joints. Also in this class are the peculiar labyrinthine organs, which have been known since the days of Bastian (1880).

Kinesthetic and postural receptor organs, according to Geldard, are present in different sets, some of them embedded in muscle proper, some in tendons, and some in the fascia associated with muscles. Their extensive and painstaking examination was undertaken by the British physiologist Matthews. He designated the kinesthetic organs A_1, A_2, B_2, and C endings; their anatomical arrangement is illustrated in Figure 3–28. The A_1 type is found at the end of the small diameter fiber, d. The terminations of A_2 (b in the diagram) are called "annulospiral" endings. Receptors of the B type are presumably the tendon organs of Golgi (designated as g in

---

[9] Morgan and Stellar, *op. cit.*

the diagram). They have been considered *general tension recorders*, while both the A_1 and A_2 fibers continue to fire when the muscle is slightly stretched.

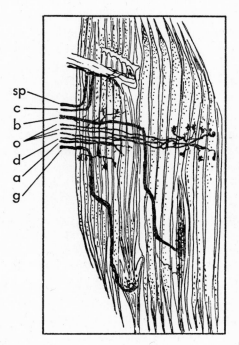

FIG. 3–28. Nerve endings in muscle: (*a*) flower-spray endings, Matthews type A_1; (*b*) annulospiral endings, type A_2.

The receptors designated "C" by Matthews are presumably Pacinian corpuscles. They are widely distributed throughout the inner organs, and are especially numerous in muscles and tendons. Apparently their contribution is to report mechanical deformations, whether *deep pressure* or changes caused by muscle movements. The blood vessels of muscle tissue are well supplied with free nerve endings. Probably they can arouse sensations of pain. The details are as yet obscure, but free nerve endings in all these organs, as in the skin, have generally been regarded as pain receptors.

Of the labyrinthine sense one could say that under normal conditions it yields no sensations. The neural systems connected with it make no direct report to the cortex. Nevertheless, it controls processes through which experiences of movement and of equilibrium are indirectly aroused.

The structure of the labyrinth was described in the section on the sense of hearing. It was pointed out that the utricle and saccule contribute to the control of equilibrium, while the semicircular canals are sensitive to changes in direction and rate of motion. The old opinion assuming a clear-cut division of labor between the canals and the other labyrinthine organs has been abandoned in this modality too. Although destruction of the saccule in animal experiments does not result in obvious defects of equilibrium, it ought to be remembered that branches of the eighth cranial nerve, the auditory-vestibular, originate at the surface of both utricle and saccule. The saccular *macula* is oriented in a plane approximately at right angles to that of the utricular macula. The nerve terminations are hair cells embedded in a gelatinous substance. These cells have tiny crystals of calcium carbonate, the so-called *otoliths*, suspended above them. The inertia of the otoliths presumably brings about a bending of the hair cells whenever the motion of the body is changed. Tilting of the head in any direction would be expected to produce the same results.

In congenital deaf-mutes, whose inner ears have been completely destroyed by infection, postural adjustments are still possible in most everyday situations. Only when the patient is asked to stand on one leg with his eyes closed does the abnormal state of his utricle and saccule become apparent in his behavior. Perhaps the labyrinthine modality should be named *the sense of spatial orientation*. Some evidence in favor of this opinion is gained from the orthogonal arrangement of the receptor surfaces, which holds not only of the vestibular sacs but also of the semicircular canals. The six canals of both ears together form a three-coordinate system to which gross bodily motions may be referred. In human depth perception, the system of orthogonal coordinates represented by the direction of the force of gravity and the horizontal dimension have played a predominant role.

At both of their ends the canals enter the vestibule. One of the ends has an enlargement known as the *ampulla*. The ampulla contains the receptors for sensation of *change in the direction and rate of movement*. The entire system is filled with endolymph. The nerve endings have a familiar form: they are hair cells, as are the cochlear receptors for hearing. These terminations are housed in elastic structures called the *cristae*, 10 to 20 hair cells stretching out from each crista. The hair cells project into a gelatinous mass, the *cupula*, which extends from one wall of the crista to the opposite one (see Figure 3–29).

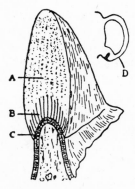

The principle of the function of labyrinthine stimulation is simple: every new movement or every change of speed in a previously continuous movement brings about a change in the direction of flow of the endolymph. Presumably, motion of the cupula stretches the hair cells on the windward side of the bending cupula and slackens those on the lee side (Figure 3–30). Impulses set up in some such fashion in the endings of vestibular fibers are transmitted to the medulla, where synaptic endings occur in the vestibular nuclei. In addition to stimulation by motion, there are several other ways of exciting the semicircular canals. Heat or cold, pressure, and electric shocks have proved capable of eliciting the symptoms familar from experiments with rotation: dizziness, nystagmic movements, and nausea.

FIG. 3–29. Structure of a crista and its location within an ampulla.

The activity of the labyrinthine proprioceptors in human beings is more complicated than it is lower on the phyletic scale. The human vestibular apparatus is more intimately associated with postural re-

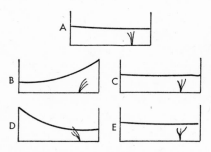

FIG. 3–30. Schematic representation of stimulation in the semicircular canals. A. Stationary state. B. Left acceleration. C. Constant speed. D. Stopping of motion. E. Stationary state.

sponses controlled by other sense modalities. Contrary to what has been observed in reptiles and birds, man, even when his labyrinths are degenerate, is able to compensate for this loss by his senses of sight, touch, and kinesthesis. The labyrinthine receptors are richly connected with the thalamus and the cerebellum. For that reason even *tonic changes* in muscle tissues are determined to a high degree by labyrinthine stimulation. Because the labyrinthine receptors can be stimulated in a variety of ways they make it possible to investigate cross-modal interaction in terms of observable and measurable *tonic reflexes*, especially nystagmus which can be elicited by a variety of different parallel sense stimuli.

CHAPTER 4

Perception of Color

WE ALL have seen a ribbon of moonlight glittering on a water surface. Described in terms of physics this surface is, as we know, reflecting the light radiation emanating from the moon. This process of reflecting goes on as long as the moon is visible. Yet, would we claim that the glittering ribbon is there unless viewed by a spectator either directly or as a result of the mediating procedure of a camera? Again, should events like these be described *physically* rather than *phenomenally*?

The history of color psychology is the story of two kinds of explanations applied to the world of color phenomena. It thus is a bit of history of scientific reasoning. In this connection two different theoretical trends or approaches could be distinguished. One of them is physicalistic; it is based upon stimulus description, beginning with Newton's optics and ending with the modern sensory physiologists supported by the authority of Helmholtz. The other one, which is phenomenalistic and consequently primarily interested in experiences, originates in Geothe's philosophy and reaches over Hering to the most recent gestalt psychologists. It is somewhat amusing to note the extent to which preference for one or the other of these theoretical points of view has influenced the methods chosen and the progress made in empirical research. When, for example, the retinal zones for specific color sensitivity were mapped, the procedure was prescribed by Hering's theory of paired *color substances*, assuming paired opposite primaries. The same thing happened in the study of after-images and adaptation. In a corresponding way the two approaches are mirrored in diagrams of color systems, i.e., by the "solids" and "scales" which have been proposed from different quarters. Those using a physical approach feel satisfied with the spectrum to represent the system of stimuli. The phenomenalists believe in the possibility of depicting their system of color experiences as some kind of solid, such as the color solid of Ostwald, which will presently be given as an example.

LIGHT AND COLORS

The basis of our visual stimulation consists of radiant energy, emanating from bodies around us or reflected by their surfaces. Within the wide frequency limits of electromagnetic radiation, the portion affecting our visual recep-
tors is very small. No agreement has been reached concerning the nature of this small visible portion of electromagnetic radiation. For practical purposes it is described in terms of wave motion. That part of the electromagnetic spectrum which falls between wavelengths of 380 and 760 nanometers (nm)

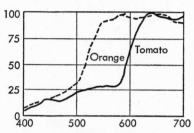

FIG. 4–1. Spectrum energy distributions of two reflecting surfaces.

has been regarded as light. In textbooks, sometimes the angstrom unit (A) is used, one A being equal to a ten-millionth of a millimeter. In physical optics a convenient way to specify the composition of a light beam is to depict the relative amount of energy present at the various wavelengths in the visible spectrum. The wavelengths of the spectrum are plotted on the X-axis (the spectral axis), and the measured intensity at each of the different wavelengths is plotted along the y-axis. The resulting graph is called the *spectrum energy distribution curve*. Two energy spectra, one representing the radiation reflected from the skin of a tomato, the other from an orange, are shown in Figure 4–1.

Not infrequently we encounter the opinion that our visual apparatus should be considered primarily an *analytical system*. On the contrary, our organs of sight are fundamentally *integrative*. Regardless of the complex wavelength composition of the radiation, ordinarily just a single color is perceived. When looking at the skin of an orange we do not have parallel perceptions of the blue, blue-green, orange, and red colors whose wavelengths are included in the radiation. We simply see a kind of unitary orange. Our ability to experience color mixtures depends on this integrative ability.

The process of vision involves the three successive stages already mentioned in the Introduction (page 2 ff.): (1) stimulation, (2) sensation and (3) perception. Physics, physiology, and psychology have all been concerned with the facts of color vision. Their fields of research cannot be strictly distinguished. After briefly noting some physical fundamentals of vision, we shall in the following discussion concentrate more on the role of physiology and especially that of psychology. In addition to investigating organic processes, the

FIG. 4–2. The pattern of reflected radiation constitutes phenomenal forms. Depending on whether there are sharp or gradual discontinuities in the reflected light, either edges or bending surfaces are perceived.

psychologist is interested in the *appearances of colors.* The presentation will therefore gradually change from a physicalistic to a phenomenal orientation.

Probably the progress of scientific research would have been smoother if the comparison between the human eye and a camera had never been made, because such a comparison locks theoretical assumptions to a quite mechanistic explanatory model. As we know, different parts of the retina are rather precisely presented in a kind of "point-to-point" arrangement in the visual cortex. Apparently it would nevertheless be mistaken to assume that the correspondence is similar to that between a photographic plate and the pattern of light radiation focused upon it. Within an organism we encounter a play of *dynamic interaction,* more specific than a sheer point-to-point elementistic correspondence. The entire stimulus pattern is significant for the fate of all its constituent elements. The status and the previous condition of the visual organs influence the appearance of a given actual sensation.

In our everyday experience, objects are perceived as located in a certain place. There is articulation and organization within the visual field, and we are able to discriminate among the relative size, distance, color, and shape of given objects. Along the edges of every area seen as an "object" there is a gradient of light reflectance, a rather pronounced step which we recognize as a *contour*. Colors can exhibit a gradual variation or they can appear as continuous surfaces forming the extended areas of figures. In the *optical array impinging upon our retinas, there is no primordial form, no inherent contour enclosing some figure areas.* The colors are immediately sensed; were there no discontinuities in the chromatic reflected radiation, we would not perceive any shapes at all.

Ostwald's Color System

In order to present the perceived colors systematically, various diagrams of phenomenal colors, in the form of "spindles" and "solids" which differ from the physically developed spectrum, have been worked out. Usually you can tell the theoretical viewpoint held by the designer of a color solid by looking at its structure. It has been held that all the colors in our natural environment could, without remainder, be represented by a three-dimensional body. The Ostwald color system will be described here as representative of this kind of approach.

The phenomenal colors are traditionally classified as:

1. *Chromatic* or *spectral* colors.
2. *Achromatic* or *neutral* colors.

Achromatic are the shades of grey ranging from deep black to brightest white. Since they can only be ordered on a single scale, they can be said to possess one dimension only, the dimension of *brightness*.

All the other colors are called chromatic. Aside from variations in brightness, they exhibit different *hues*. Even if we throw achromatic light on the object surfaces, they are selective in what they reflect. Depending on the nature of the incident radiation, object surfaces absorb a portion of it and reflect other parts, and surfaces of different qualities absorb and reflect different parts of the spectrum.

The greater the reflective selectivity of a surface, the more saturated is the perceived chromatic hue; and conversely, the more a reflected array contains radiation of wavelengths other than one dominating the chromatic impression, the more *unsaturated* does the hue appear. In other words, the greater the difference between the intensity of the absorbed and the reflected light, the higher the saturation, and vice versa.

FIG. 4–3. Some standard grey values and their symbols in Ostwald's color system. The sizes of the sectors show the relative amount of black and white needed to create the corresponding grey mixture.

The relations between different hues and saturations can be well represented by Ostwald's color circle. As his starting point he chose the yellow primary (5,750 A) and gave it the number 1. Of all spectral colors, pure yellow shows the highest degree of brightness in normal daylight. It is also the spectral color most easily recognized in that we are very sensitive to whether other radiations are mixed with it. In a clockwise direction from this primary yellow are arranged the successively redder hues from orange to primary red. The circle continues over purple and violet to primary blue (4,400 A) and from there to deep blue, which is located at the bottom of the circle, opposite primary yellow. Then follow green-blue, blue-green, leaf green and primary green. Over olive hues we return to yellow, number 1. Ostwald distinguished among 24 hues along his color circle, proposing his system of numbers as norms for referring to chromatic colors. Complementaries are always diametrically opposite each other on the circle. The four primaries are given the numbers 1, 7, 13, and 19. For practical purposes a hue gradation with 24 steps has turned out to be sufficient. Every hue on the circle could be produced by mixing an equal amount of both neighboring hues (i.e., their spectral radiations) in a single stimulus. Furthermore, if the existence of a process of complementarity is assumed, and if only the colors of one half were known, we could produce all of the rest, because the unknowns would then be complementaries of the knowns (see Plate I).

Note that the brightness of the colors varies along the circle. As said before, yellow is the brightest one in daylight, and from there on in either a clockwise or a counterclockwise direction we find ever darker hues until we reach the darkest, 13, at the bottom of the circle. As to the size of the brightness steps from hue to hue, they cannot all be considered equal. There are smaller differences

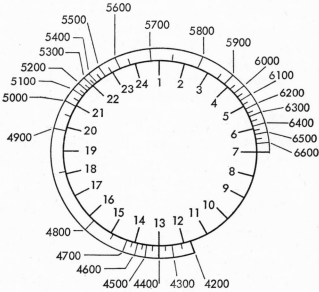

FIG. 4–4. Ostwald's circle corresponds to a "bent" spectrum. Note the gap in the region of the phenomenal purples (values 8–11).

between successively adjacent hues in the red and green zones than in those of yellow and blue.

Chromatic colors are rarely very saturated, and even spectral colors vary in brightness. The third of Ostwald's dimensions represents *saturation*. The purity of a hue can be defined as the distance between it and the main axis, which is imagined as running through the center of the color circle at a right angle to it. Because in our natural environment we have mostly rather unsaturated chromatic colors, our eyes are able to discriminate between degrees of brightness combined with degrees of saturation. These shades are called the *valences* of a hue. In the primary red, 100 valences have been observed. Ostwald uses isotonic triangles to represent this system. The vertical white-black axis serves as a common base for all these triangles; their apices are located along the Ostwald circle. The resulting three-dimensional solid is called Ostwald's double cone.

The purpose of this double cone, like that of other diagrammatic descriptions and other psychological color systems, was to symbolize phenomenal reality. As shown by Katz, this purpose has not been fully achieved. As a consequence of Newtonian physicalism, laboratory work used to confine itself exclusively to investigations of *spectral colors.* Thus one of the most remarkable dimensions of the phenomenal mode of appearance of colors, or the form of *illumination,* was completely left out. Because of this omission a three-dimensional model of the color system must remain incomplete.[1]

Appearances of Color

Let us look at an ordinary piece of red paper. The red color seems to belong to the surface of the seen object, can be strictly localized, and even shows structural features typical of the colored object. The color of the paper looks firmer and thicker than a spectral color, and one feels unable to penetrate it with the eyes. The experience of color seems to be of something "covering" or "coating" the thing surface, which "lies behind a sheet of color." For that reason the color of the paper, when perceived under such conditions, is called a *surface color.* A surface color is in many respects different from the spectral colors known from early laboratory experiments. The colors we perceive on the objects of our natural world are just what is meant by surface colors. There is an impression of "thingness," of a solid three-dimensional object, connected with these percepts. The surface color "spreads out" along the sides of the object and can thus appear at any angle of orientation toward the line of sight. Experience of the quality of the seen surface, i.e., of its microstructure, is included in this impression. On the other hand, the colors of the spectrum are flat and lack "solid" three-dimensionality. Katz called them *film colors.* They used to be regarded as a kind of basic form of color percept, which they certainly are not. The most primordial color experience is of the surface color which belongs to objects. The distance of a film color from the observer is more

---

[1] D. Katz, *The World of Colour* (London: Kegan Paul, 1935), pp. 1–57.

difficult to determine—another difference to remember. This is because our gaze seems to penetrate the ethereal, translucent film color. If we look at a cloudless sky, we get an idea of this experience. An almost unlocalized diffuse transparency is characteristic of a film color. It does not seem to belong to a particular object, looks "immaterial," and mostly appears vaguely oriented at right angles to our line of sight. When twilight falls in our room, the surface colors around us gradually disappear. Finally we see just contours and dark shades of "thingless" film colors surrounding us at vague distances.

A third appearance of color mentioned by Katz is *space color.* Phenomenally, it fills up the space between the observer and the rigid objects he perceives. It forms a sort of "medium" through which the objects are seen, or else it is simply referred to as the prevailing illumination. These experiences can be elicited by means of colored spectacles or of a strongly chromatic illumination. Special cases are a dim twilight, a dense fog, and a drizzle. Our *immediate experience of the colored illumination* of a room or of a landscape demonstrates the existence of space colors. This phenomenon has proved hard to explain in terms of traditional sensory physiology. In the early literature on perceptual psychology perception of the illumination was not mentioned as a kind of space color, although illumination must be considered just as much of a perceptual reality as are the surface colors of objects.

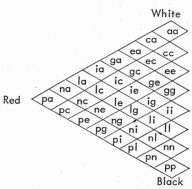

FIG. 4–5. One isotonic triangle from Ostwald's system.

"Close your eyes," Katz asks us, in order to give a demonstration; "open them again for just a brief moment, and after closing them once more try to report what you perceived during the moment they were open. I expect you will grant me that what you saw was the prevailing illumination. In an experiment like this you more easily get an impression of the illumination than of the object colors in the visual field. In this experiment you probably would not be able to report anything about the colors in the periphery, although even there your impression of the illumination is reasonably good. The experience of an illumination is quite immediate, as immediate as that of local surface colors."[2]

Other instances of space colors are *transparent film and surface colors*, *reflections*, *luster*, *shine*, and *glow*. Katz also points out that any surface color can be transformed into a film color by reducing the visual field of the color surface. Viewed through a 2 cm. diameter opening cut out of a large piece of cardboard, the opposite wall of the room, for example, looks closer (hold the cardboard sheet about an arm's length in front of your eyes). Not only is the opening completely "filled up" with the color of the wall, but the appearance of the color is also changed. It has lost its character of a surface color and looks like a film color which *conforms to the plane of the cardboard surface*. The piece of cardboard with the hole in it is called a *reduction screen*. With the aid of a device like this, surface colors can be reduced to film colors. Some evidence from experiments with brain-injured people shows that the perception of surface colors presupposes articulation processes at the level of the visual cortex.[3]

Effects of Different Illuminations

In some respects Katz's excellent perceptual experiments and descriptions have undergone a considerable reevaluation, as has classical color psychology generally. Specifically, this refers to the conclusion regarding our capacity to distinguish between *illumination* and *illuminated objects* as separate appearances of colors. The following statement would be more appropriate: *within certain limits* our organism is capable of that kind of discrimination, and it has reached a developmental level which corresponds to biologically relevant natural life conditions.

The revolution was brought about by the introduction of *fluorescent lamps* in connection with several kinds of indoor and outdoor illumination. The rich findings and experimental results of famous color psychologists like G. E. Müller, Bühler, and Katz were obtained under daylight conditions or in illumination from *incandescent lamps*, which was not very different from sunlight in its spectral composition.

Physically speaking, light sources can be classified as *glowing* or

---

[2] D. Katz, "Några fakta ur modern färgpsykologi," *Tidning för Sveriges teckningslärare* (Stockholm, 1938).

[3] D. Katz, *Der Aufbau der Farbwelt* (Leipzig: Barth, 1930), pp. 67–71.

fluorescent bodies. The former are often called "hot," the latter "cold," sources. With a candle or a carbon arc lamp the radiation originates from a burning material. The "cold" light sources give radiations from a fluorescent substance which is made to flash by the impact of an electric current.

In two respects the introduction of fluorescent lights proved revolutionary:

1. Higher intensities became possible, bringing about an increase in the sheer amount of light reflected by all colors. For that reason alone the hues measured in the laboratory are changed in their modes of appearances in comparison with traditional colors.

2. Depending on the material composition of the flashing substance, fluorescent light shows a wide variation of intensity across the conventional band of the spectrum. Most fluorescent lamps contain more energy at the short end of the visible spectrum than in the illumination provided by incandescent lamps. Sharp maxima, spikes and peaks, caused by strong reactions within rather narrow bands of the spectral continuum, occur on the spectral energy distribution curves of fluorescent lights. If the high points of the light-source distribution and the high points of the specific reflection curves of surface colors do not coincide, even slight discrepancies can bring about great changes in the colors seen.

Suppose that the human eye developed especially for the purpose of facilitating man's locomotion and orientation in a variety of natural daylight conditions. As we know, the brightness of our surrounding objects and of our "behavioral space" varies considerably during the hours of the day. The specific modality responsible for recording the *general proportions* of reflected radiations must be remarkably sensitive. Generally speaking, it must be admitted that a rather high degree of *constancy* is typical of our *brightness perception*.

In natural daylight conditions differences between successive hues throughout the chromatic continuum are generally minimal and gradual. There is indeed a shift in the appearance of some portions of the spectrum caused by the rods taking over when the cones fail during dark adaptation. Yet variations in the intensity level, which are the greatest variations during biologically natural sight conditions, scarcely affect the chromaticity of the hues. Even when incandescent light in laboratories was substituted for daylight, the flat or gently curving slope of the light energy distribution remained essentially intact. The curve of relative spectral intensity was moved as a whole, as it were, toward the red end of the spectrum, where relatively more energy was gained. It is only when the distribution curves of the illuminating light and of the specific reflecting illuminated surfaces are irregular that great changes occur in perceived hue. In such cases chromatic color constancy can disappear almost completely.

As will be shown later, the experience of *hue constancy* (or invariance) is probably brought about as much by certain *stimulus-proportions of reflected surface intensities* (i.e., degrees of brightness) as by their spectral chromaticity proper.

Memory Colors or Invariances?

Color "invariance" or color "constancy" is a concept which can be traced back to the terminology of Hering, in his main work on the "light sense," more than 40 years ago. He coined the expression *"memory color"* (*Gedächtnisfarbe*), which he considered peculiar to each object we experience. To us the familiar objects appear to have relatively constant colors; we assign them their memory color even in very different illuminations. According to Hering we always call grass green, coal black, chalk white, etc., regardless of the conditions under which we look at them.

Helmholtz was the first perceptual theorist to pay attention to the difference between the reflecting characteristics of the surface of an object and the prevailing conditions of illumination.

As a consequence of our experience we learn to distinguish between the illumination and the surface illuminated, "because we continuously have a tendency to distinguish between that aspect of the color or the appearance of an object which is caused by the illumination and that which originates from the particular surface of the object itself" ("weil wir fortdauernd die Neigung haben zu trennen, was in der Farbe oder dem Aussehen eines Körpers von der Beleuchtung und was von der Eigentümlichkeit der Körperoberfläche selbst herrührt").[4]

In terms of a strictly physicalistic stimulus language such a visual achievement would be hard to explain. The stimulus array impinging upon our photoreceptors does not contain an independ-

---

[4] H. v. Helmholtz, *Physiologische Optik*, Vol. 2 (Hamburg, 1910/11), p. 110; as quoted in *A. Gelb*, "Die Farbenkonstanz der Sehdinge," *Handbuch der normalen und pathologischen Physiologie* (ed. Bethe), 12, No. 1 (1929), p. 598.

PLATE I

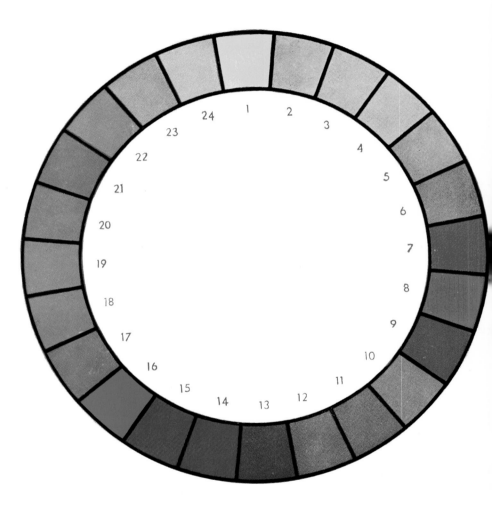

Ostwald's Color Circle

PLATE II

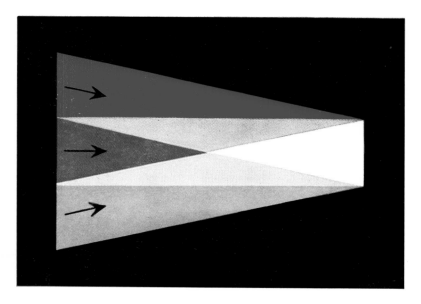

Additive Color Mixture

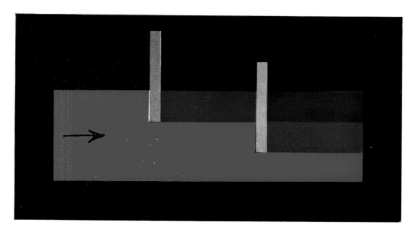

Subtractive Color Mixture

ently stimulating "illumination" and a separate color surface "behind" it. The direct radiation from the light sources and the reflected radiation are fused in the stimulus pattern. What should be seen is a "mixed color" resulting from these components. Since the perception does not actually conform to these traditionally expected conditions, Helmholtz had to postulate a higher-order perceptual regulating mechanism. The psychological nature of this "regulatory" system remains unclear throughout Helmholtz' presentation. He presumed it to be like a kind of "unconscious inference" (see Chapter 9, p. 217).

Saugstad has rightly pointed out that the precise and careful experimental contributions of Katz, even if they explain color appearances as phenomenal experiences, nevertheless reveal him as a theorist paradoxically influenced by the Helmholtzian way of thought. The dualism inherent in that influence is evident in all his efforts at explanation.[5]

The expressions he coined, like "normal illumination" and "specific object colors," are thoroughly phenomenalistic, yet they are applicable to certain laboratory conditions only. We end up with the peculiar situation that the empirical descriptions provided by Katz have left us with the appearances of colors clearly enumerated without our having any point of departure for trying to understand the correspondence between stimuli and perception.

Gelb was the first to provide us with a surprisingly modern key to the world of color constancy.

Let us start with the problem of *brightness constancy*, because it is less complex.

According to Gelb, the problem is posed incorrectly if we assume we perceive the illumination independently of the brightness of the illuminated surfaces. On the contrary, whenever some kind of brightness invariance occurs, it depends upon simultaneously perceived *relations among the intensities of reflected radiations*. Reflections from visible surfaces are organized as *gradients of intensities* ranging from the brightest surface to the least reflective. *As long as the spectral composition of the illumination remains the same, as long as there are no displacements along the wavelengths contained in the light array, the brightness gradient of the visible surfaces stays invariant.* It is our ability to receive information about

---

[5] P. Saugstad, "Värin konstanssista," *Yearbook of the Philosophical Society in Finland, Ajatus*, 24 (Helsinki, 1962).

intensity relations among reflected luminosities (albedos) which, according to Gelb, is responsible for the brightness constancy of perceived objects. This ability, incidentally, enables the organism to adapt to its familiar environment even during those hours of the day in which there are great changes in the intensity of the general illumination.

Of all object constancies, Gibson has found *visual shape* and *visual size constancy* readily explainable, but he sometimes complains about the theoretical difficulty of accounting for *color constancy*. His point relates to the ease with which we can find systems of stimulus relationships as long as we confine ourselves to the study of visual shape and size phenomena. If we do not feel satisfied with phenomenal descriptions but look for systems of stimulus relationships as a basis for impressions of constancy, *we might find a decisive invariant in shape constancy, if we take into account the form of the retinal image as related to the angle of inclination of the surface of the object.* Size constancy could be accounted for by perception of *the relationship between the retinal size and the distance of the object.* Contrary to Gibson's assumptions, Gelb's presentation contains some hints that *stimulus gradients can be used to explain color constancy as well.* It is worth noting that Gelb proposed a modern gradient theory of perceptual constancy some 20 years before Gibson did.[6]

What Gelb observed concerning the relativity of color constancy (see Chapter 9, pp. 221–22) implies that the rank order of reflected energy from surfaces adjacent to each other, in other words the gradient of intensity, will be displaced if the illumination impinging on the surfaces shows considerable spectral variation. The same thing happens, of course, to *gradients of hue* (that is, gradients of reflected intensities originating with different wavelength compositions from chromatic surfaces) if the general illumination should change noticeably in its intensity or in its spectral composition.

Actually, these displacements in familiar systems of gradients occur if after having illuminated a familiar room with incandescent light one shifts over to fluorescent. Experiments on fluorescent and incandescent light carried out at the Psychological Institute of the University of Helsinki lead us to question the universality and

---

[6] See P. Saugstad, *Ajatus*, 24 (Helsinki, 1962), pp. 119–20.

appropriateness of a concept like "color constancy," so carefully developed by Katz on the basis of his traditional experiments.

Laws of Color Mixture

Two kinds of color mixture can be distinguished in the traditional Newtonian system: *additive* and *subtractive* mixture. *Additive* mixture is produced by combining different wavelength components originating from several light sources into a single radiation. The intensities in the various chromatic components are added together, producing a mixed radiation which regularly looks *brighter* than any of its constituent components. If they have spectral values far enough apart from each other on Ostwald's circle, the resulting mixture looks almost white. The complementaries in particular, if additively mixed in appropriate proportions, will yield white as the resulting color. Correspondingly, an additive mixture is produced *if indirect radiations mediated by object surfaces* which give fairly monochromatic light are combined. An additive mixture of reflected light seldom is completely white. The object surfaces always ab-

FIG. 4–6. Color discs leave overlapping adjustable sectors when mounted concentrically on a color mixer.

sorb part of the light, and for that reason the mixture looks *grey*. In other words, reflected light components are rarely sufficiently saturated.

The laboratory device for making additive color mixtures is the color wheel, which carries rotating discs of different colors interlocked with each other in the way shown in Fig. 4–6. Varying the size of the visible sectors, which can be measured in angular degrees, the experimenter can regulate the proportions of the components in the mixture. When the discs are rotated together at a sufficient speed, the radiations reflected from them fuse, producing a mixture whose brightness is related to the sum of the various intensities reflected by the sectors. This fact is known as *Talbot's law*. It implies, in other words, that additive mixtures have an albedo equal to that which would be produced if the sectors of the wheel were spread out, so that their radiations came from the entire area of the wheel, but with an intensity reduced in proportion to the increase in surface area.

Subtractive color mixture results when reflecting surfaces are covered by material with a different selective absorption capacity from that of the surface covered. This procedure is used by painters when they mix their paints. The new pigments always absorb some of the previously reflected radiation. For that reason subtractively mixed colors look darker than their components. (See Plate II.)

Additive color mixture has been studied considerably more than subtractive. In our everyday life the latter is far more usual, although it is harder to investigate because it is dependent to a higher degree on the physical and chemical properties of the mixing pigments. Experimenters have had better control over the stimulus when mixing colors additively because then they actually mix chromatic radiations, not substances with different absorption properties. Most of our discussion will therefore be confined to additive mixtures.

Paper discs of complementary colors will, when mixed together on a color wheel, produce grey; the comparisons can be carried out simultaneously with discs of different size. If the color wheel has two small discs of complementary colors in its center and two other complementaries behind the first ones on larger discs, both pairs of complementaries giving a middle grey when mixed together, the grey produced by the middle discs can be matched against the grey of the ring formed by the larger discs. After having found settings in which the two additive grey mixtures look equal to the subject, the experimenter reads the degrees of the sectors and writes down the equation, e.g.,

> 195° red + 165° green = 70° white + 290° black.
> 205° blue + 155° yellow = 135° white + 225° black.

Empirical work has demonstrated the following laws for additive color mixture:

1. Every hue has its complementary which, when mixed with it in proper proportions, produces achromatic grey. If the proportions are not appropriate, the mixed color resembles the more strongly represented component but has a reduced saturation.

2. If hues other than complementaries are mixed together, no proportion of the components will yield an achromatic grey. The mixed color looks like the component quantitatively more strongly represented in the mixture. The weaker the saturation of the mixed color, the greater the difference between the hues of the components.

If three hues are chosen in such a way that each of them has its complementary located between the other two on the color circle, all other hues can be produced by mixing these three together in appropriate proportions.

3. If the mixtures produced by pair *a* and pair *b* look identical and two other pairs *c* and *d* also yield the identical mixed color the same color could also be obtained by mixing *a* and *c* or *b* and *d*.

Rayleigh, when asking some subjects to mix red and green so as to match a certain yellow, was astonished to find that there are people who discriminate hues correctly but are unable to mix them in the usual proportions or who would not consider the usually approved mixture to match the yellow. In accordance with the prevailing Young-Helmholtz three-color theory, Rayleigh supposed that these individuals represented an intermediate anomaly between color blindness and normal sight. Pickford later beautifully demonstrated that Rayleigh's equations can be used as diagnostic aids in order to achieve a more precise classification of deviant forms of color sensation. Red-green vision shows a normal frequency distribution except for certain color anomalies and certain forms of blindness. Measurements on certain exceptional individuals, those with red-green blindness or anomaly, fall far beyond either end of the normal distribution.

Color Contrast and the Purkinje Shift

When photoreceptor tissue is stimulated continuously by a radiation of constant intensity, adaptation occurs. The equilibrium, at first disturbed by the stimulation, is gradually reestablished. If one keeps staring at a red circular disc on a grey background, the disc may disappear after some 10–20 seconds, being "swallowed up," as it were, by the background. Removal of the disc during the period of staring produces a *complementary after-image*, a greenish spot of the same shape and size as the original disc. Increasing the distance between the spectator's eyes and the background results in an increase in the size of the after-image, in direct proportion to the square of the distance (this is *Emmert's law*). The persistent stimulation by the "red" wavelength first produces an equilibrium in the red-green metabolism of the receptor pigment, phenomenally noticeable as the fading of the red surface. The insensitivity to red causes a new shift in equilibrium. The compensatory metabolic process predominates, and a vivid sensory after-image, complementary in color, appears on the background. Because this after-image is a projection of an affected retinal area, it increases in size with increase of the distance of the background in conformity with the laws of optical projection.

These events could be labeled *successive contrast* phenomena. Induced complementary colors which appear in the visual field simultaneously with the original stimulating color are considered *simultaneous contrast* phenomena. If we notice carefully what happens in the above-mentioned experiment, we observe that the disappearing red disc at first seems covered by a dim sheet, which extends to the edge of the grey background around the red disc. This surrounding dim border of the disc looks green. In this case the expression "marginal contrast" is applied. Furthermore, a distinction is made between *brightness* and *chromatic contrast* effects. Both of them can occur *successively* as well as *simultaneously*.

Even these phenomena were previously regarded as illusions. Yet peripheral physiological stimulus factors as well as central organizing ones contribute to their occurrence. In order to produce a strong simultaneous contrast effect, the two contiguous parts of a field should be well articulated, e.g., as a figure on a ground; on the other hand, their phenomenal "object" character should be weak, the surrounding and surrounded field should be located at equal distances, the colors should be saturated, and they should be *film colors*. When surface colors are employed for contrast experiments, better results are obtained if they are covered by transparent sheets of tracing paper or are rotated on a color wheel.

Two adjoining complementaries increase each other's saturation, by reciprocal simultaneous contrast. The resulting saturations can exceed those normally found in the spectrum. On the other hand, if two contiguous colors differ in saturation only, the equality in hue brings about a decrease in contrast, that is, an assimilation effect of saturation.

If the distance between the contrast-inducing fields is increased, the effect is weakened—even with only a rather small displacement of the fields. A black contour or border has a similar effect.

When we move our eyes about in the ordinary process of obtaining visual impressions, simultaneous and even also successive contrast effects occur. In experiments on contrast in the region of the contour between two fields, the inevitable successive contrast effects have been a source of error. Successive effects can, however, be reduced by covering both reciprocally inducing chromatic fields with transparent tracing paper. In this case the surfaces produce less vivid after-images, and after removing the covering sheets one obtains maximally pure simultaneous contrast. Contrast effects make man able to improve his orientation in his natural environment. Broadly speaking, objects differ in their light-reflecting capacities, so that contrast makes them look better articulated and more clearly separated from each other.

According to the duplicity theory as mentioned above (p. 32), the rods are regarded as receptors for degrees of luminosity (brightness differences) and the cones as receptors for chromaticity (differences in hues). When the illumination decreases, all colored surfaces generally turn dimmer, as can easily be observed during twilight on a summer evening. Because the role played by the cones is weakened and only differences in brightness are clearly observed, the point of maximal brightness within the limits of the range of spectral hues undergoes a displacement. In the dark-adapted eye the luminosity maximum of the spectrum lies within the region of the "bluish-green" radiations. It is displaced from the region of "yellowish-orange" radiation, which is more effectively mediated by the cones in the foveal area of the light-adapted eye. During daylight (photopic) vision the luminosity maximum falls in the neighborhood of light yellow (5,720 A), during night (scotopic) vision around bluish green (5,110 A). This displacement, caused by the differing function of the two kinds of photoreceptors, is called the *Purkinje shift*. In our natural environment we can easily find examples of this phenomenon as convincing as the results of experiments. A blue canoe on the shore of a lake on a sunny day may look darker than the red boathouse next to it. But viewed in twilight, the blue canoe may look so bright as to seem to shine against the dark wall of the boathouse. It has been possible experimentally to produce precisely equal intensities in surface reflectances, yet the phenomenon still occurs with an undiminished clarity and distinctness.

The shift in luminosity is accompanied by a decrease in visual acuity. We may use both dark-adapted eyes to improve visual acuity because both rod retinae together undergo a physiological process of summation which is not encountered in the foveal parts of the eyes. But if it is confined to monocular vision, the dark-adapted eye is much poorer in acuity than the light adapted. A binocular telescope, because of the just mentioned summation, is a better optical device than is a monocular one during twilight.

In studies of the functions of the periphery of the retina, Katz was able to show that peripherally mediated color experiences are, at best, only film colors. The structural articulation so characteristic of surface colors seems to be a product of cooperation between the fovea and the visual cortex. Peripheral vision must be considered primordial, and if we reduce foveal surface colors, the resulting appearances correspond to what is normally seen in peripheral color vision. On the other hand, the retinal periphery is sensitive to *movement stimuli* within the visual field. If one felt inclined to do so, one could find a remarkably useful biological function in the fact that primitive visual tissue is highly sensitive to movements which, as we know, may at early levels of sensory evolution be the most important cues for prey or danger in the visual field.[7]

ON COLOR THEORIES

As mentioned above, color theories have in general conformed to Newtonian physical optics. On the other hand, Goethe is the best known and the first of those investigators who, being more concerned with the *psychology of colors* (described phenomenally), anticipated a solution diverging from those based on Newtonian optics. Yet Goethe's were mostly loosely founded speculations which could not meet strict scientific criteria. Clearly, anyone opposing Newton in those days would have failed. Methods and terminology had not yet reached a stage at which they could possibly have been applied to a phenomenal analysis from a psychophysical point of view.

Newton's discovery that a prism can split white light into its components, revolutionary as it was, influenced *all later* color research, even that done by psychologists. Yet Newton's theory, especially with regard to its view of the nature of color stimuli, was a product of its time. In many respects it reflected the early age of technological inventions, a pioneer time for the analytically oriented sciences, and an age which gave birth to the atomic theory in chemistry and inspired biologists to try descriptions even of organic nature in terms of extremely minute elements. After the spectrum had been produced and described by Newton, scientists generally

---

[7] D. Katz, *Der Aufbau der Farbwelt* (Leipzig: Barth, 1930), pp. 316–39.

tended to assume that our natural environment too should contain
"pure hues" as counterparts of precisely restricted wavelength band
widths within the spectral continuum. Admittedly, physically relatively monochromatic bands can be found in the spectrum, but these
belts are artificially obtained in spectroscopic analysis of chemical
elements. There is no reason to believe that even the complete
spectrum of sunlight, which is a compound of spectroscopically
recorded radiations from glowing elements in the sun, should
exhaustively represent the chromatic stimuli in our real natural
environment. In their role as visual stimuli the primaries have also
been thought of as special, narrow sections in the range of spectral
radiation, quite in accord with the spirit of the Newtonian era. The
law of specific sense energies, and some phenomena of color
mixture, led to the conclusion that the photoreceptors must be
considered quite specific in their functions. Even when several types
of visual receptors were allowed for, any given type was essentially
considered to be a recording device for a narrow, precisely limited
band of "pure" radiation. Put in terms borrowed from Newton's
famous experiment with the prisms, this view could briefly be stated
as follows: "A given rate of refraction always corresponds to the
same experienced hue, and a given hue always corresponds to the
same rate of refraction."

When surveying the color theories presented since the beginning
of the nineteenth century, we therefore ought to remember:

1. That either the "pure radiations" represented in the spectrum as
   primaries of certain wavelengths, or the *mixed colors* which are
   summations of such pure radiations, were regarded as the specific
   stimuli for experienced hues.
2. That the specific rate of reflectance or the range of albedos contained in a set of hues was never considered a basis for stimulation. These assumptions were produced by a too restricted understanding of Newtonian optics.

Specific retinal cells were assumed to be the receptors for certain
"pure" (monochromatic) radiations, that is, for the so-called *primaries*. This kind of reasoning completely ignored the role played by
the brightness gradient, determined by the portion of the spectral
continuum which was allowed for as a stimulus for hue. As a matter
of fact, consideration of the narrow wavelength band widths, as was
customary in classical investigations, ignored the significance of the
variations in albedo.

The Young-Helmholtz Theory

The laws for color mixture formulated by Newton implied that any perceived color could be produced by combining three "pure colors" or primaries in appropriate proportions. (Originally Newton proposed seven "pure radiations": violet, indigo, blue, green, yellow, orange, and red.) Thomas Young, at an early age, in 1801, was allowed to present to the British Royal Society his conviction that all the hues we see could be explained on the basis of three specific functions of the retina. Each of these retinal processes should correspond to a certain band of radiation (within the spectral continuum, a conception once more taken from Newton). The experienced color thus would depend upon the intensity relations of different wavelengths among radiations.

This "three-color theory," after having first been forgotten, was recreated by Helmholtz in 1860. His version was based primarily on the color mixture experiments of J. C. Maxwell, then the first-ranking physicist in England. In 1855 this superb research worker had already devised a method for producing the world's first color photograph. Maxwell took pictures of a given still life or a landscape in an ordinary way, using achromatic negatives. But each time, he took three snapshots from exactly the same spot and with the same camera focus, masking the lens alternately with red, green, and blue filters. The exposed negatives were developed into positive black and white transparencies. Using three projectors, the three diapositives were superimposed on a screen, resulting, if the same filters as those through which the pictures had been taken were placed before their respective diapositives, in a *projected color photograph. It had not only the three filter colors but contained all the colors of the originally photographed scene.* It should be expressly pointed out in this connection that *three identical black and white transparencies projected through these filters in primary colors* are not alone enough to produce the illusion. The three achromatic negatives must differ in the brightness distribution of the photographed surfaces. They must have been taken through three different filters. One would expect a fact like this to have provided food for thought for later color theorists.

Based on Maxwell's experiments, Helmholtz developed Young's theory in the direction that *all types of receptors are thought to respond to radiation of all wavelengths but are especially sensitive to narrower, more limited bands of radiation, which in turn are specific for the different types of receptors.* Figure 4–7 shows the essentials of this theory schematically.

Maxwell was able empirically to derive three curves which fit these criteria. With the aid of a color-blind dichromat, he was also able to confirm the occurrence of separate color response systems. These sensitivity distribution curves for different sets of receptors were later mathematically specified by König and Dieterici.

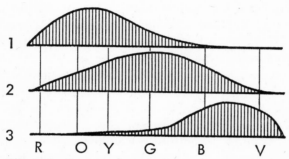

FIG. 4–7. Energy distribution and spectral composition of the three-color response systems according to the Young-Helmholtz theory.

Approximately at the same time, Schultze presented and Kries further developed the duplicity theory of the division of labor between two types of receptors in the retina. This required revision of the Young-Helmholtz theory. It proved necessary to assume three categories of cones to allow for specific sensitivity to certain wavelength bands. The following types were assumed:

I. First Type of Receptor
Most sensitive to red but responsive to radiations of other wavelengths too.
II. Second Type of Receptor
Most sensitive to green but responsive to all kinds of radiation.
III. Third Type of Receptor
Most sensitive to blue and violet but responsive to all kinds of radiation.

The emphasis of the Young-Helmholtz theory is on physiology. It explains color mixture phenomena in a satisfactory way, without omitting the relationships represented by the color triangle.[8] It has not managed as well in handling many phenomenological regularities of colors found in the experimental psychology.

Still missing is dependable information concerning which precise spectral bands are specific to each of the different types. What wavelength bands correspond to each of these sensory processes? Young's original requisites were a certain red, a certain yellow, and a certain blue as stimuli for the maxima of the three respective curves. Later he considered red, yellow, and violet as primary stimuli. Actually, if we want to be able easily to produce the complementary color of any *one* of the three primaries out of a mixture of both of the others, the ones to choose would be *orange-red*, *yellowish-green*, and *violet-blue*. We know that these components would secure us the best grey mixtures and the best complementaries. It is true that Maxwell's photographic color filters had about these spectral compositions. We must not forget, however, that all commercial filters are more or less polychromatic. Thus this kind of color photography does not provide a sufficient verifying basis for the Helmholtzian three-color theory. Because color blindness can be regarded as a "breaking down" of one total system of color receptivity, these deficiencies have often been considered in evaluating the validity of color theories. From this point of view, color blindness was thoroughly investigated by Donders, who, in his work of 1881, pointed out that his cases partly supported Helmholtz's theory and partly called for a revision of it into closer agreement with Hering's theory.

Any criticism of the Young-Helmholtz theory must consider its weakness in allowing for the phenomenal facts of color. We know that white, black, and yellow appear as independent primaries in our immediate experience. Psychologically speaking, they cannot be considered color mixtures, although physically the theory considers them such. From the point of view of our main problem, i.e., from

---

[8] *The color triangle* is a graphic representation of the laws for color mixture. It is not to be confused with the three-dimensional color diagram, because it is conceptually a description of its own. The apices of the triangle stand for the three hypothesized primaries, red, green, and blue. Maximally saturated mixtures of two primaries are located along the edge connecting the respective apices. Any other mixture of two colors, A and B, located on different edges, is represented by a point on the connecting line from A to B, if A and B are given different "weights" according to their amount in the mixture. The intermediate grey (Müller) is inside the triangle at the crossing of connecting lines between opposite complementaries.

the standpoint of an eventual correspondence between stimuli and sensations, it is important to note that according to this theory experienced hues depend on cooperation among three types of receptors.

The Hering Theory

Hering's explanatory schema had its predecessors too. In several connections Mach expressed thoughts which apparently influenced Hering's conclusions. When writing on the parallel laws of function and experience, he pointed out that yellow never can be *perceived* as a mixed color, although according to three-color theory it should be considered a mixture. White, black, and yellow are as fundamental experiences as the primaries chosen by Young. Therefore, one should expect some basic psychophysical processes to underlie all immediate fundamental color experiences.

In the same year in which Mach made his criticism (1865), another European continental investigator, Aubert, sharply opposed the Young-Helmholtz theory. He too stressed the lack of correspondence which can be shown to exist between the physiological fundamentals, i.e., the primaries, and the categories of radiation which are distinguished psychologically, e.g., by color names. Actually, it was Aubert who first introduced the term *Hauptfarbe* (main color, fundamental color), having in mind the phenomenally immediate and primary "pure" or uncombined colors. Hering's theory assumes that one of three possible processes occurs in the cellular tissue of the receptor, depending on the cell's structure. Each of these processes is a metabolic assimilation or dissimilation. (The presumed physicochemical basis for these processes is the absorption and reconcentration of the light-sensitive substance in the cells.) The change occurs in three parallel, mutually independent systems:

	Substances		
	White-Black	*Yellow-Blue*	*Red-Green*
Dissimilation	White	Yellow	Red
Assimilation	Black	Blue	Green

The table reads as follows: Dissimilation of the white-black substance causes white vision; an assimilation of the same substance causes black vision. Dissimilation of the yellow-blue substance gives rise to an experience of yellow, etc. The shifts occur in opposite directions, yet they are not considered to compensate for each other in maintaining equilibrium, except for the white-black substance, within which such an equilibrium is almost a rule. The phenomenal content corresponding to that kind of equilibrium is the perception of an intermediate grey. When the stimulus radiation does not fall within the limits of any of these six fundamental stimuli, simultaneous processes of change occur in all three different substances. There are types of radiation which call for dissimilation of one of the substances simultaneously with the assimilation of another. When white is produced by mixing complementaries, the resulting color would not be explainable as an additive compound of chromatic sensations. According to Hering, visual white is a result of equilibration between opposing processes, of a neutralization which occurs between the chromatic complementary components of a complex radiation. The chromatic valences nullify each other so that only white valences remain, resulting in a perception of white.

Difficulties arise for the Hering theory in the fact that although the primaries yellow and blue turn out to be complementary colors, this is not true for the red and the green, which we usually consider fundamental. To produce an optimal intermediate neutral achromatic grey by mixing reds and greens, it is preferable to select a purple red and an olive green or an orange-tinted red and a bluish green.

The Ladd-Franklin Theory

One approach to the foundations of color vision is to investigate the evolution of visual cells through successive phyletic levels up to their present specialization. According to a theory of this kind, too, the photosensitive substance in the receptor pigment is generally considered responsible for stimulating the sensory cells by a process of dissimilation. The theory considered here is specific in that it assumes the original "color molecules" to have been dissociable only into a kind of initiators responding to white-black stimulation. The next stage assumed by the theory appears at a later developmental period of the cones. Now the originally white-sensitive atoms of the color molecules become able to react discriminatively to radiations representing either the yellowish "long-wave half" or the bluish "short-wave half" of the spectrum. The specific capacity to sense red and green later differentiated analogously out of the earlier responsiveness to yellow. This theory is vulnerable to most of the objections, which have been directed against three-color theories. We should, e.g., expect deficiencies in the red-green color vision of a person who is abnormal in his sense of yellow. But this is not generally true.

The G. E. Müller Theory

Müller, too, makes use of a molecular model of the processes of assimilation and dissimilation. Let us suppose that a "red stimulation" results in dissociation of a molecule ab into its components $a + b$. Then a "green stimulation" should produce an assimilation of the atoms a and b to form the molecule ab. If neither of these chromatic excitations exists, equilibrium is maintained in the photochemical system. That means that at a given time as many atoms assimilate as dissociate. Any proximal stimulus thus always means activation in either of these two directions. Either of the processes is accelerated at the expense of the antagonistic one. If one and the same spot on the retina undergoes stimulation from a variety of radiations, the elicited process would be determined by the difference in intensity between the opposing transformation tendencies. If both antagonistic processes are in equilibrium, neither of them predominating, no chromatic color is perceived. The "white values" of both competing stimulations should simply combine, giving rise to an impression of white. Actually, the color mixture of complementaries equals a grey (known as endogenic grey or cortical grey), with an albedo corresponding to the sum of the albedos (white values) of the complementaries. Müller considered this constant grey a result of the molecular action of the cortex.

Müller introduced a further concept not previously used in Hering's presentations: the "inner stimulus value." In addition to excitations specific to its own type, each of the above-mentioned three main transformation processes in the retina also initiates further activations which are otherwise characteristic of the other two. Specifically, a "red" radiation fires the "red process" but also contributes to firing the "yellow" and the "white" processes as well. A red stimulus thus has additional "inner yellow and white stimulus values."

On the other hand, the optic nerve is assumed to respond to six different activation processes, grouped into three pairs. Thus the number of fundamental nerve transmission characteristics can also be set at three. *Any of the basic retinal processes* will fire *all three nerve conduction processes simultaneously.*

Later Müller expanded his theory further. He called the phase of retinal processes the *mediating substance stage.* The expression refers to the white-black, the yellow-blue, and the red-green substances respectively. Each of these can suffer two opposite transformations. Light influences these substances by means of *primary processes* in the following way:

The P_I process is initiated by red radiation.
The P_{II} process is mainly initiated by yellow radiation.
The P_{III} process is mainly initiated by blue radiation.

All of the primary processes, P_I–P_{III}, affect the white-black substance, causing white activation.

P_I produces *red* activation in the red-green substance and *yellow* activation in the yellow-blue substance.

P_{II} produces *green* activation in the red-green substance and *yellow* activation in the yellow-blue substance.

P_{III} produces *blue* activation in all of the chromatic mediating substances.

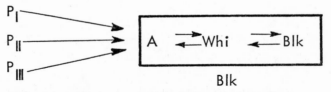

FIG. 4–8. Activation processes within the White-Black substance (Müller).

The arrangement of the white-black substance is peculiar in that here, according to Müller, all events are based on three components: the *original substance*, the *mediating substance*, and the *final substance* (the latter, in brief, are the A-, Whi- and Blk-substances). All P-processes activate these substances as shown in Figure 4–8. The A-substance is first transformed into Whi-substance, which in turn changes into Blk-substance. During both transformations an endogenic antagonistic process occurs.

The P-process hypothesis has considerable value for explaining the chromatic phases in a white light that is suddenly turned off. The time and intensity relations among the various P-processes as hypothesized by Müller conform to the model shown in Figure 4–9.

The metaphotic activation originated by the P_I-process declines much more steeply than the corresponding activation elicited by the P_{II}-process. The latter in turn descends more steeply than P_{III} activation. As to the initial rise, the P_I develops faster than the P_{II}, which in turn ascends more steeply than the P_{III}. Finally, an experience of "white" assumes simultaneous cooperation of all three processes.

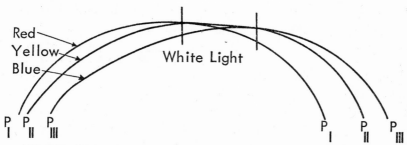

FIG. 4—9. Time and intensity relations among the various P-processes.

The Edridge-Green Theory

According to this theory, sensation of color is functionally analogous to sensation of distance or of size relationships. All depend upon the psychophysical coding of various stimulus patterns. Our sense of color is better, the more efficient our psychophysical functions are when our visual organs code wavelengths. Talking about "hues" is entirely a matter of phenomenal description. This theory also is genetically oriented. The hypothesized phyletic "phases" of differentiation resulting in four-color vision are almost the same as the stages in Ladd-Franklin's model of the development of color vision. Sensitivity to a fifth chromatic color occurs when the eye becomes able to distinguish between blue and violet, and the emergence of a sixth color involves a differentiation of orange out of yellow and red. Only after the next phase, which adds discrimination of indigo, are all spectral colors finally represented as sensational units. According to the terminology coined by this theory, "monochromats" are completely color-blind, "dichromats" are partially red-green blind, and "tetrachromats" and "pentachromats" are burdened with certain color anomalies. "Hexachromats" have normal color vision apart from their difficulty in discriminating indigo. "Heptachromats" are faultless color perceivers. The "hexachromatic" category is assumed to be the largest.

Pickford objects to this theory in that he cannot fit these seven categories, in respect to their frequency distribution, together with the well-known proportional distribution of the familiar color vision anomalies. The numerous individual differences demonstrated to date would require a much more detailed system than that proposed by the Edridge-Green theory.

Recent Contributions

Let us return to the basic point in the development of all color theories, Newton's view of "pure" chromatic stimuli, which were supposed to represent restricted wavelength bands of radiation and to yield all other colors by an additive summation of the single stimuli. Essential in Maxwell's technique of color photography (see p. 96) had been his insight of taking the three negatives through red, green, and blue filters. Thus, by a simple procedure, he managed to achieve the minimally sufficient stimulus cues for activating the retinal cells able to receive numerous and richly combined "chromaticity messages." Yet Maxwell's explanation was still burdened with the assumption of *wavelength specific color receptors, which could be stimulated by filtered, almost monochromatic radiations which, when a kind of additive stimulus pattern was fused, rendered hues appropriately.*

In 1955 Land, the inventor and producer of the American Polaroid Land camera, undertook to repeat Maxwell's experiment with the purpose of developing a camera capable of reproducing polychromatic pictures using only black and white negatives taken through appropriate filters. Working with three parallel projectors, he happened to turn off the blue-filtered projector and to remove the green filter from one of the two projectors that were still on. He was astonished to find that even now, when the screen received only a mixture of red radiation and white radiation (i.e., a radiation containing a maximum of fused single different wavelengths) both projected through two different black and white negatives, *the result was a colored picture beautifully rendering all the "real" original hues.*

The only fundamental chromatic wavelength stimulus required seemed to be red, which, when combined in this way with white, was apparently sufficient to reproduce all natural environmental colors (Plate III and IV). Land first considered his observation an artifact due to the fatigue of his eyes. Yet repetitions of the experiment consistently yielded the same result. After these initial findings he continued his experiments, varying them in several ways. He has presented rather convincing evidence for his observations and explanations in a number of articles.

It can apparently be taken for granted that as few as two negatives can suffice to create polychromatic reproductions if they have been exposed through two colored filters so chosen that they represent spectral bands far enough apart to be beyond a certain minimal wavelength separation threshold. The filters need not have the colors of the "Young-Helmholtz primaries"; even wavelengths as close together as 5,790 A and 5,990 A might be employed. *When projecting the corresponding positive black and white transparencies, either of the color filters can be removed.* Almost invariably Land himself removed the short-wave filter, e.g., the greenish one. These experiments suggest that the explanation based on Newtonian physics, which works so well, need not be restricted to *specific receptors capable of responding only to narrow wavelength bands.* A wavelength as such is not the specific stimulus for a perceived hue. A decisive role is played by the brightness distribution of the reflecting surfaces; the cues for which one of the wavelength regions would be seen predominantly consist of the reflection intensity gradients of the photographed surface. The so-called primaries of Maxwell or of Helmholtz just happened to represent sufficiently separated zones of the spectrum to produce the division of reflecting objects into the two systems mentioned by Land. Instead of assuming each color in the spectrum to be either an isolated stimulus or a stimulus composed of an additive fusion of radiations, we must consider the cues included in the intensity distribution on seen surfaces. These cues split up the reflected radiation into either "short-" or "long-wave" reflections.

If we ask on what physical conditions these two coding systems depend, we immediately encounter the brightness gradients associated with the various hues. Gelb's pioneer work has already been mentioned (pp. 87–88). He was able to demonstrate the significance of intensity gradients in brightness constancy phenomena. According to Land's findings, the visual apparatus requires a minimum of chromatic wavelength stimulation to construct a "colored world." Only so much chromatic stimulation is needed as to make the maxima of the intensity distribution characteristic of the surfaces stand out in relation to other surfaces, and thus *provide a system of reference.* The rich variety of colors we normally perceive depends wholly on the relationships of similarity and dissimilarity of the maximal regions in the energy distributions of reflected intensities.

Actually, it is astonishing that the stimulus pattern provided by the intensity gradients has not previously been taken into account in attempts to explain sensations of the hue of the reflecting surfaces of objects. This is all the more remarkable because it appears reasonable to assume that our receptors are fundamentally more sensitive to intensity variations than to shifts in the spectral composition of lights (see pp. 92–93).

It is clear that Land's point of view is important for all kinds of color psychology. If brightness gradients were not considered important, why should Maxwell have needed *three differently exposed black and white transparencies?* Would not three quite *identical* transparencies, *without* specific differences in their brightness distribution, have done even better according to traditional wavelength theory when projected through three primary-colored filters?

Land's arguments have already given rise to criticism in the psychological literature. In one of his articles, G. J. Walls points out that there is insufficient information concerning the monochromaticity of the *filters*, and we are also no better off with regard to the composition of the *projected* light. The unfiltered bundle of projected light, although called "white," probably could, if an incandescent bulb is used in the projector, well contain a sufficient amount of yellow to produce dichromatic effects when combined with the red from the other projector. Land has further been accused of never having reproduced the bluish tints very well. The reviewer does not deny Land's perceptual color phenomena altogether, but attempts an explanation in terms of the *induced or contrast colors* produced by a strongly illuminated area on all adjacent areas. It is conceivable that the Land phenomenon can be brought together with the far too little investigated *chromatic shadow* events so enthusiastically described by Goethe.

Even if sound criticism should prove that Land has been exaggerating the peculiarity of his observations, it remains a fact that he has, with the aid of achromatic transparencies using specific dominant brightness gradients from almost any restricted zone of the spectrum, produced a phenomenon of chromaticity which formerly was exclusively regarded as due to a mixture of "three primaries"—confining himself furthermore to one single filter in his technique of color reproduction. Thus the significance of the contribution of brightness gradients to our perception of surface hues and to their "belongingness" to the visual objects has been clearly demonstrated. But according to experiments performed so far, the wavelength of 5,880 A has turned out to be a limit, approached from either end of the spectrum, for the selection of filters, if the phenomenon is to be successfully demonstrated.

According to Pickford, a three-color theory cannot explain all the above-mentioned events.[9] The Young-Helmholtz version in particular encounters grave difficulties. But some of the results just presented do not fit Hering's traditional model either. As we know, the last-mentioned model would imply a decrease in green sensitivity simultaneously with an increase in red sensitivity (and we must also not forget the analogous polarity between yellow and blue). Research on color deficiency and color weakness has not come out with negative correlations between degrees of sensitivity for two complementaries. Pickford himself is, therefore, inclined to accept some later modifications of Hering's theory. Most of all he leans toward the opinions of Houstoun (cf. p. 109). As a matter of fact, Pickford's reasoning is also closely related to that of Granit, although the latter investigator is primarily interested in determining threshold values for his *modulator* and *dominator* cells (the specific receptors either for hues or for brightness discrimination assumed by his theory). Instead of postulating photosensitive substances acting in cycles of reciprocal polarity, it would be better to speak of specific types of cones arranged in pairs. As soon as one member of such a pair starts reacting to "greenish" light, the other member stops reacting to "reddish" light, etc. Svaetichin, Mac-Nichol, and some others conclude on the basis of some recently published (1964) new electrophysiological research that color vision is apt to be at least a two-stage process, consistent with the Young-Helmholtz theory at the receptor level and with the Hering theory at the level of the optic nerve.

---

[9] R. W. Pickford, *Individual Differences in Colour Vision* (London: Macmillan & Co., Ltd., 1951).

Color Deficiencies

When human performance in intelligence is investigated from the point of view of differential psychology, an almost normal distribution is taken for granted, and so are a relatively wide dispersion around the mean and positive correlations among the various tasks. But capacity for color vision, which is largely physiologically determined, scarcely shows any variability at all within a majority of about 90 percent of mankind. On the other hand, 8 percent of all males deviate markedly from the average in their color vision performance. This minority can be divided into six subgroups, the performances of which are almost completely unrelated. If we know a man is capable of successful performance in discriminating a certain color, we cannot make any inferences at all about his performance with other colors. There are no "common elements" or no "g-factor" as there are in tests of mental abilities.

Routine devices for determining color blindness have been developed for distinguishing this minority group from unselected average people. For certain practical purposes it has been most important to identify such cases, because they are unsuited for tasks requiring good color vision (e.g., driving in traffic). For this purpose Holmgren's wool yarn test and the pseudo-isochromatic plates of Ishihara or Stilling, etc., have proved sufficient. Color blindness can be detected by these crude methods, but the Ishihara and Stilling techniques cannot reveal red-green and blue-yellow anomalies. They fail to discriminate people with color weakness or color anomaly; such people are classified by these tests as no different from normal.

Carefully investigating these methods, Pickford was able to show that which of these groups a subject is classified in often depends more on the testing technique than on the individual himself. One source of difficulty consisted in the impossibility of testing all cases by a uniform procedure with at least some degree of reliability. Such a constant method was sought by Pickford when he started to work with Rayleigh's equations. The task consisted of matching two parallel colored surfaces produced by color wheels. Adjusting the color wheel sectors, the subject was to match the rotating discs in hue and brightness. One of the two color wheels had a pair of red and green sectors, and a smaller second set, concentric with the first, consisted of three sectors, one of which was orange and constantly kept at 90°, while the other two (white and black) were adjustable. The other color wheel had a large disc with yellow and blue sectors and a smaller concentric disc with a constant green (30°) and variable white and black sectors.

As mentioned above, it was shown by Pickford that red-green vision in an unselected sample yields a normal distribution. If the color sense was clearly abnormal, the extreme values were distributed along a wide range outside the distribution proper, a fact already observed by Houstoun. As a point of departure for defining his categories, Pickford used the mode of the distribution, that is, the score with the highest frequency. As for red-green blindness, cases scattered within the limits of one standard deviation from the modal score Pickford called normal, those ranging within the limits of one to two standard deviations he called deviant, and those within the limits of two to three standard deviations he regarded as color weak. The last two categories overlap considerably in the case of blue-yellow deficiency because of the greater number of deviants within this aspect of capacity for color vision. Cases of actual color vision anomalies and of color blindness fall clearly beyond the limits of these six standard deviations. These two groups are rather easily distinguished. The anomalous are generally unaware of their defect even though they are willing to accept quite exceptional color mixtures. Paradoxically, being unaware of their deficiency, they are often even more handicapped by their defect than the definitely color-blind.

It has become customary to classify color vision deficiencies as follows:

I. *Total color blindness* occurs very rarely and is clearly inherited but not sex-linked. According to the old duplicity theory it is due to defective functioning of the cones.

II. *Acquired total color blindness* may be caused by a variety of factors such as poisoning, accident, and even hysteric conditions.

III. *Night blindness* or *twilight blindness* (hemeralopia) is a deficiency in dark adaptation but does not involve impaired daylight vision.

IV. *Red-green deficiency* is inherited; it is sex-linked and recessive in females but dominant in males, occurring in about 8 percent of them. There are three kinds of red-green deficiency:

1. *Red blindness*, or *protanopia*, involves a darkening of red hues.

2. *Green blindness*, or *deuteranopia*, reveals itself as difficulty in distinguishing orange and green, although red may be seen normally.

3. *Green anomaly* involves a minor peculiarity in perceiving red and green. They are discriminated correctly but look different to the green anomalous than they look to the normal eye.

V. *Non-inherited red-green deficiencies* occur in two groups:

1. *Red-green deviation*, with a color spectrum in which either the red or the green region or both have a restricted range.

2. *Red-green weakness*, in which the differential threshold for red and green radiation is double that of the normal eye.

VI. *Blue-yellow deficiency*, which is neither sex-linked nor inherited.

The terms *protanopia* and *deuteranopia* were already introduced by Helmholtz. There are definitely more deuteranopes than protanopes, the proportion being around 10 to 3. Strictly speaking, the essential difference is that for a protanope there is an achromatic belt approximately in the spectral region from 4,900 to 4,990 A, while deuteranopes have an achromatic belt around 6,000 A. The spectrum of protanopes is shorter, but on the other hand they see as yellow certain wavelength zones which look grey to deuteranopes.

There has been a prevailing tendency to divide blue-yellow deficiencies into corresponding subgroups called *tritanopia* and *tetartanopia*. As Pickford rightly pointed out,[10] this is nothing but an artificial and unfounded parallel to protanopia and deuteranopia. Especially the term "tritanopia" looks inappropriate, because it causes the whole classification to be linked up with an implicit conviction about a three-color theory. It favors the following line of reasoning: because red-green blindness is due to faulty discrimination between two of the primaries, red and green, the other fundamental type of color blindness must be due to defective functioning of the specific receptors for the third primary, i.e., due to disturbed discrimination of yellow. As a matter of fact, all cases of blue-yellow deficiencies are "minor defects." No sex-linked hereditary influences have, for example, ever been demonstrated in connection with them.

The frequency distributions published by Pickford on the basis of his experiments with more than 1,000 individuals, normal and deficient, clearly show that protanopes, when measured with Rayleigh's equations, are distributed as an extremely small group far beyond the limits of the normal distribution. Closest to them fall the deuteranopes, who are located far out in the tails of the normal distribution. The green anomalous are close to the deuteranopes but are scattered widely throughout the tails of the continuous distribu-

---

[10] *Ibid.*

tion. The color weaks and deviants fall clearly within the range of the normal distribution.

While Pickford's contribution may be criticized, there is no question about the usefulness of his treating individual color differences dimensionally, of showing the continuity of their variation in consistently applied differential tests, and of pointing out the typical characteristics of those extreme cases which fall outside the scope of biologically normal variation.

CHAPTER 5

Perception of Sound

THE COOPERATION between three sciences, acoustics, auditory physiology, and psychology, is important for penetrating the difficult but rewarding area of the modality of hearing. The structure and function of the auditory receptors were described in Chapter 3. What we need here is an elementary survey of the acoustics of auditory stimuli and how they affect the organism.

SOUND STIMULI

An *adequate stimulus* for hearing is an oscillation, within certain wavelength limits, of the air, of water, or of other mediating bodies. The propagated oscillation is usually called a series of "sound waves." A sound wave in the air is caused by an oscillating body, e.g., a tuning fork, bringing about a condensation of the molecules of the air immediately surrounding it. Because of the elasticity of the oscillating medium, this condensation is followed by a stage of rarefaction, with alternating condensations and rarefactions being transferred to the adjacent portions of the medium. The wave of pressure changes proceeds through the immediately surrounding air waves, following the rhythm of successive rarefactions. A *pure tone* can be roughly described by specifying the *frequency* and *amplitude* of the oscillation. With certain important reservations, these two physical dimensions of the auditory stimulus can be considered the basis for our perception of sound.

The basic properties of these oscillations can be illustrated by observing a vibrating string (a so-called monocord). When the cord is oscillating, each of its elementary parts makes a complete swing and, after the excursion, returns to its original position. The oscillatory movement thus is periodic, the motion of each point

112

being repeated a given number of times within a given temporal period. Such an oscillation, which produces a pure single tone, is called *simple harmonic motion* and can be demonstrated with carefully manufactured special tuning forks. This oscillation, recorded on the surface of a rotating smoked drum (a kymograph), produces a regular sinusoidal curve (see Figure 5–1), often called a *sine wave* for short.

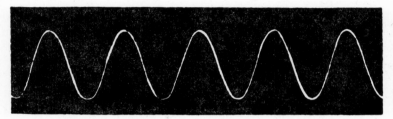

FIG. 5–1. Sinusoid graph produced by a pure tone.

We rarely encounter sine waves in our natural environment. As a rule, *several pure tones* are combined in any one sound. The sounds used in music are mainly *periodic*, although even *aperiodic* sounds or *noises* are sometimes utilized (especially in percussion instruments). Sounds containing periodic as well as aperiodic oscillations are represented especially by the human voice, the research project of *phonetics*.[1] Combinations of certain sounds are called *chords*. Despite their complexity, sound waves can be divided up or analyzed into their pure tone, sine wave components, each of which has its specific frequency and amplitude (this division is accomplished by *Fourier analysis*). The basic components of all sounds are the *fundamentals*, the lowest frequency specific to the sound, and the *harmonics*, frequencies which are multiples of the fundamental. The picture is somewhat obscured by the fact that the term "partial" is applied to the fundamental as well as to all its harmonics. In this terminology the fundamental is called the first partial, the first harmonic is called the second partial, and so on.

The terminology can be summarized as follows:

First partial   = the fundamental
Second partial = first harmonic
Third partial = second harmonic
Fourth partial = third harmonic

[1] See the works of Sovijärvi and Nadoleczny, mentioned in the bibliography at the back of this book.

The sounds made by musical instruments, e.g., by the vibrating string of a piano, have simple integral ratios between the frequencies of the partials, such as 1: 2: 3: 4, etc. A sound is named after its lowest partial, the fundamental, which is the best discerned of all the partials.

A sine wave can be considered the path followed by a point on the circumference of a wheel which is rotating counterclockwise and is simultaneously moving to the right along a straight line. Accordingly, a model like that in Figure 5–2 is usually referred to when describing the characteristics of sound waves.

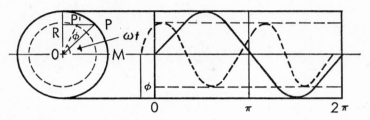

FIG. 5–2.   The oscillation pattern as produced by a rotating point moving horizontally.

The harmonic motion performed by the point P in the figure can be expressed by the equation $y = A \sin \omega t$, where y represents the displacement of the point P upwards (in the dimension OR) within a time unit t, A represents the radius of the circle ($=$ the vector OP), and ω represents the angular speed. A is equivalent to the *amplitude*, and the number of full cycles performed by P in a given unit of time indicates the *frequency* of the oscillation. The time required for one complete cycle is the *period* (T). Thus the period is the inverse of the frequency. *The amplitude of an oscillation corresponds to the intensity of the stimulation*, the density of the cycles to the frequency.

As a unit for measuring frequency, it has been customary to employ the number of complete rotations or cycles within the time of a second, *cycle/sec.* or *cps.;* German and Continental investigators generally use the abbreviation *hz* (Hertz's unit).

A concept central in acoustics is *phase*. A *phase difference* can be defined on the basis of Figure 5–2 as the angular separation between two successive positions of the vector OP as the point P moves around the circumference. Two sinusoidal curves can be formed by two points moving along different concentric circles. If the additional point on the smaller circle is called P', the angle Φ between the vectors OP and OP' indicates the phase difference of the two sine waves in Figure 5–2. When the curves were drawn, it was assumed that the two vibrations differed in frequency as well as in amptitude. The point P' moves twice as fast as P. Thus P' goes through a double cycle during one period of motion of point P. The difference between the lengths of the radii is quite clear; it represents a difference in amplitude.

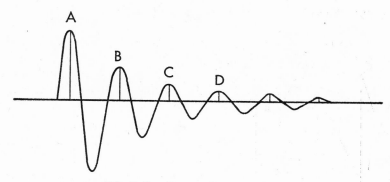

FIG. 5–3.   Decay of an oscillation.

Summation, decay, and *resonance* also are relevant aspects of physical acoustics. An oscillation can be intensified by several bodies oscillating simultaneously with comparable frequency; this is summation. Decay, which will be mentioned in a moment, is illustrated in Figure 5–3. As for resonance, when a mighty jet or propeller plane is taking off, all houses located nearby are also set in vibration, as can easily be noticed in the rattling windowpanes. Listening to a concert, we sometimes become aware that the podium, the floor, and even the farthest seats join in the vibration. If the specific frequency of oscillation of a given material or body corresponds to the frequency of the original oscillator, the induced sympathetic oscillation is called *resonance*. If one, for instance, sings a short melody near a piano, the strings of which are undamped by depressing the pedal, one is able to hear a weak reproduction of some of the sounds from the instrument. The strings are resonating to the specific frequencies contained in the inducing sound. Gradually an oscillating system returns to equilibrium because of resistance. The oscillation amplitude decays rapidly and logarithmically (Figure 5–3). The decrease in amplitude during one period can be calculated from the equation

$$k = \frac{rT}{2m},$$

in which $r =$ resistance, $m =$ mass and $T =$ the frequency of the oscillating system.

As mentioned above, every periodic oscillation can be broken down into its component harmonic partials by Fourier analysis (Figure 5–4). It is one of the achievements of the inner ear to be able to perform this analysis. Thus the auditory system is able to distinguish the components of a complex periodic vibration and even the frequency of each of them (Ohm's acoustic law).

Acoustical units of measurement are quite numerous. In addition to the already mentioned *cycles per second*, there are a few more which deserve our attention.

The intensity of the stimulus can be expressed by choosing measures either of pressure or of energy. The weakest sound recognized by a human ear has an energy of a billionth of an erg/sec. (One erg is the energy needed to lift a 1 milligram weight a vertical distance of 1 cm.). According to Morgan, the energy needed to transmit vibration through a medium varies directly with the square of the pressure. Most units of pressure are in fact calculated as square roots of the corresponding energy units.[2]

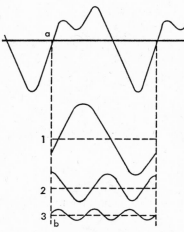

FIG. 5–4. An oscillogram of a compound sound and its components isolated by means of Fourier analysis.

A more practical unit, based on the relationship between two sound intensities, is the *decibel*, which is a measure of the ratio of the energies of two sounds.

The basic unit is the *bel*, which expresses the ratio of energies in logarithms to the base 10. A decibel on the other hand is 1/10 of a bel, usually abbreviated *db*, and corresponds roughly to the differen-

[2] C. T. Morgan, *Physiological Psychology* (1st ed.; New York: McGraw-Hill Book Co., 1943), p. 222.

tial threshold for intensity. The number of decibels or db's is given by the equation:

$$N = 10 \log \frac{E_1}{E_2} = 20 \log \frac{P_1}{P_2}$$

in which the E's are the energies being compared and the P's are the corresponding pressures.

Bels and decibels thus always denote a ratio between two intensities. If just one db value is mentioned, some "reference level" is always assumed, because db's always imply a comparison. The usual reference is the *absolute threshold intensity at a given frequency*. Expressed in units of energy, the threshold for hearing is around .0002 dyne/cm.² at 1,000 cps.; this value has been taken as a standard reference intensity. As mentioned above, the db unit has turned out to be very useful. Figure 5–5 shows the intensity of a variety of familiar sounds in db relative to the standard reference intensity.

Although the practical value of db measures has been clearly

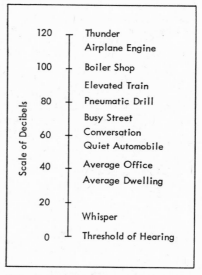

FIG. 5–5. Relative intensities of some sounds (in db).

demonstrated within the domains of acoustics and sound physiology, from the standpoint of perceptual psychology it must be pointed out that db's not only represent at best a rough approximation to what they are intended to measure but that their use is also burdened with a fallacious principle. If we want to use standard metric measurement units, we cannot simply base them on the differential threshold. Measuring units are supposed to be constant, but the differential threshold, as we know, is constant only within rather narrow limits. These questions will be dealt with more precisely in Chapter 8.

The differential threshold is not equivalent to a db unit, because the differential threshold varies. It has been shown that the differential threshold practically can be treated as constant in the zone of sounds around 1,000 cps. Within the limits of 500 to 1,000 cps., one would in 50 percent of the cases be wrong in presupposing constancy of the threshold. For a 1,000-cps. stimulus the differential threshold or just noticeable difference (jnd) is a change in energy of the order of 1/5,000 microbar ($1\ \mu b = 1\ dyne/1\ cm.^2$), but an increase of this order of magnitude would not be noticed at all if the sound is at a frequency of 100 cps. Let us not forget, furthermore, that more than half of all sounds perceived by man fall outside the limits of 500 to 6,000 cps.

Units for the measurement of *loudness* are the *phon* and the *sone*, the latter being the proper measure for *sonority* or *phenomenal loudness*, the former for loudness relative to the absolute threshold. A 1,000-cps. tone is employed as a reference tone for phons. The procedure consists of varying the intensity of the 1,000-cps. tone until it sounds equal in loudness to the unknown tone. This matching performed, the db value of the 1,000-cps. tone is determined, the zero point being the absolute threshold intensity required to hear it at all. The obtained db value is the phon value of the unknown sound. How sones are measured and what they signify will be discussed later.

PSYCHOPHYSICS OF SOUNDS

Attributes and Dimensions

In the youth of sound psychology, investigators were inclined to make errors similar to those we encountered in the field of visual perception. Here, too, there was an inclination to believe that some "point-to-point correspondence" between experienced qualities and physical stimuli would be the rule. For a time it was taken for granted that every qualitative ϕ variable would almost perfectly reflect a corresponding one-dimensional quantitative p variable. Remnants of mechanistic, elementaristic reasoning are embedded in this view. For example, formerly the phenomenal tonal qualitative dimensions of *pitch* and *loudness* were inevitably considered the counterparts of the acoustical dimensions of *frequency* and *amplitude*. Following this line of argument, it looked reasonable that pitch should always and exclusively depend on frequency, and loudness on amplitude or sound intensity. Not infrequently one encounters careless talk about frequency and intensity even in connection with what is phenomenally perceived. The phenomenal dimensions of sound are thought to be, as it were, determined exclusively and directly by these respective physical variables. Even the *timbre*, the "sound color" of tones, was believed to be determined solely by the harmonics contained in the stimulus.

Representatives of the modern psychology of sound and music (Hornbostel, Wellek, Révész, Stevens, and Davis) have vehemently opposed this mechanistic opinion. As Stevens and Davis frequently point out, one should keep phenomenal concepts and expressions separate from physical ones. Loudness as well as pitch are complex qualities which depend upon an *interaction of the components* of stimuli. It is incorrect to consider either intensity and loudness or frequency and pitch as synonyms.[3]

Following Stevens and Davis, the term *physical dimension* will in our text refer to traits and characteristics of the vibrations as acoustic phenomena, including such measures as amplitude, intensity, wavelength, period, phase, and rate of propagation. The phenomenal qualities, i.e., the ϕ experiences, will be called *attributes;* analogous to the hues of colors, they are the object of special interest in the domain of perceptual psychology.

The application of the concept of attributes seems to have freed the description of experienced sounds from the detrimental restrictions burdening earlier investigation. Contrary to the deeply rooted earlier view that at best we could distinguish between only two phenomenal dimensions, a large number of them have been identified. Wellek[4] lists seven:

1. Location
2. Duration
3. Loudness
4. Timbre
5. Pitch, including:
   a) Brightness
   b) Tonal quality
6. Vocality

Wellek defends his classification by pointing out that any sound is experienced as (1) coming from *somewhere*, (2) extended in *time*, (3) having a certain *strength*, (4) colored with a certain *timbre*, (5) being of a specific *height* or *brightness*, (6) possessing a musical quality of a certain *tonal relationship* or *tonality*, and (7)

---

[3] S. S. Stevens and Hallowell Davis, *Hearing: Its Psychology and Physiology* (New York: John Wiley & Sons, Inc., 1947), pp. 69–77, 110 ff.

[4] *Zeitschrift für Musikwissenschaft*, Vol. 16 (1934).

having a specific *vowel quality* or *vocality* (sounding like *a*, like *e*, like *i* and so on).

The list has been supplemented by later investigators with at least two further attributes: (8) space-filling quality or *volume* and (9) compactness or *density*.

Pitch

The traditional inclination to identify pitch with frequency rested upon the fact that *phenomenal* pitch does depend greatly on frequency. Thus even Révész gives the following definition in his textbook: "Pitch depends upon frequency or wave length: a higher frequency means a higher pitch."[5] Stevens and Davis, on the other hand, point out that phenomenal pitch is a function of *two* physical variables—it is determined by intensity as well as by frequency. A pure tone can, for example, be changed in pitch without affecting its frequency. These relationships deserve a closer examination.

First of all, the lower and upper limits for frequency discrimination might be pointed out. Although in principle frequencies vary far beyond these limits, only those ranging from 20 to 20,000 cps. play a role in sound perception. The lowest tone which can be discriminated by the human ear, according to Révész, has a frequency of 16 to 24 cps. (corresponding to C_1). With tuning forks an upper limit of about 22,500 cps. (F_{13}) has been found, but this number is subject to wide variations depending upon the source of the vibrations (the instrument). With stimuli at frequencies below the lower threshold Békésy was able to show surprising effects: oscillations below the threshold of hearing can initiate perceptual activities in other related modalities. These events will be examined more closely in connection with the performance of the skin receptors.

One reason for connecting pitch with frequency apparently lies in the fact that the tonal scale of our musical system is basically a frequency scale. A musically perceived tone *quality* is produced only by those oscillations whose frequency falls within the limits of 60 to 4,000 cps., or in musical terms lies between C_2 (64 cps.) and C_8 (4,138 cps.). This presentation generally follows the international standard symbols for tones agreed upon in 1962. They are given at the bottom of Figure 5–6 which shows a piano keyboard together

---

[5] G. Révész, *Einführung in die Musikpsychologie* (Bern: A. Francke Ag., 1946), p. 10.

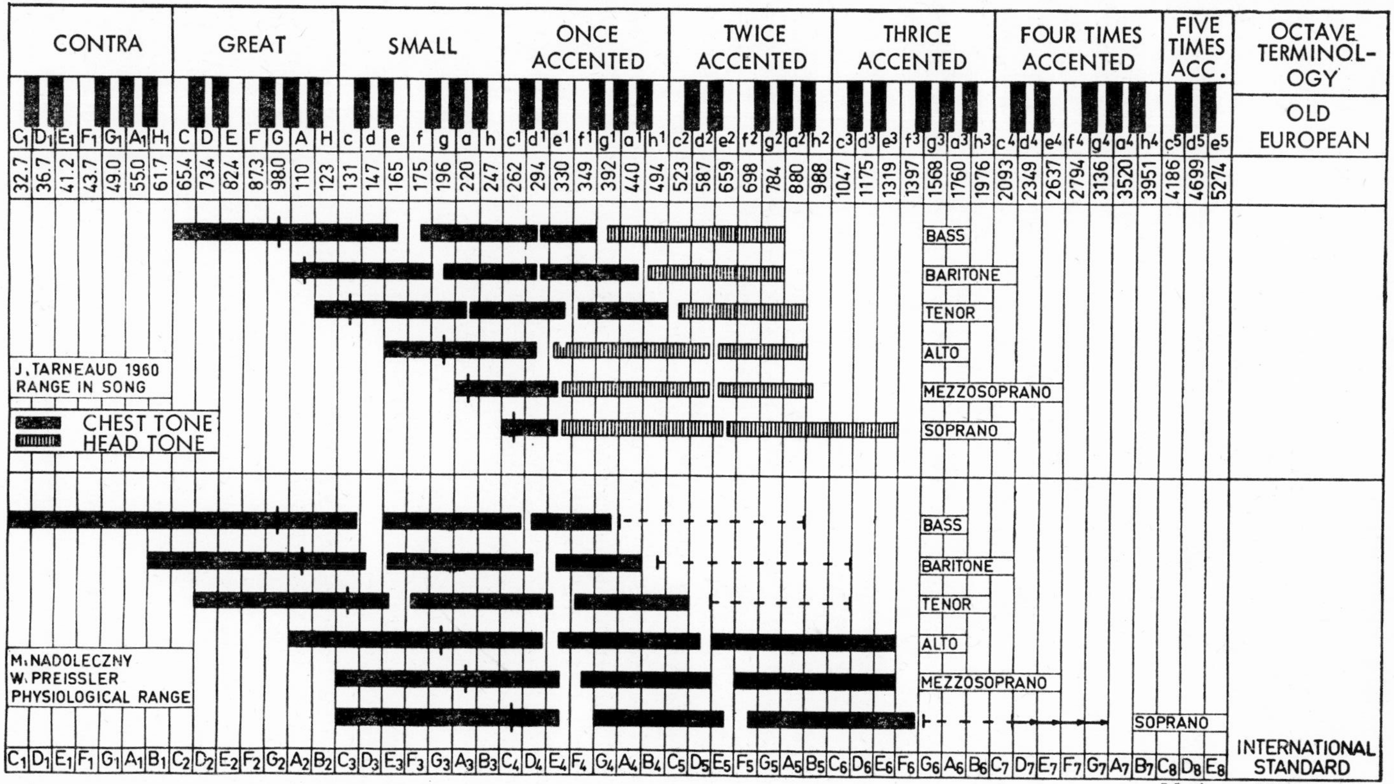

Marianne Mörner, 1962

FIG. 5–6. The various registers (ranges) of the singing voice according to Tarneaud, above, and the physiological ranges of the voice according to Nadoleczny and Preissler, below. The average fundamental frequency level of the speaking voice according to Luchsinger and Arnold is indicated in both diagrams.

with frequencies and some older notations occasionally applied in references. Human voice pitch levels are indicated in the middle.

The impetus for investigating the relationship between pitch and intensity came from an everyday experience. If a tuning fork producing ordinary C₄, is brought closer to the ear of a listener, for whom the tone accordingly becomes more intense, he cannot maintain a constant pitch if he is trying accurately to reproduce the tone by singing it. Rather, the pitch of his voice gets lower the closer the tuning fork is brought. Thus, at least for low frequency tones, more intense tones are experienced as lower in pitch. A systematic investigation of the phenomenon produces the results shown in Figure 5–7. The curves are *equal-pitch contours;* they indicate the effect of changing the intensity on the perceived pitch of tones of certain frequencies. When the intensity is increased beyond a certain level, *the pitch of a low tone* (150–500 cps.) *drops, while that of a high tone* (4,000–12,000) *rises.* The best pitch constancy across wide ranges of intensity is obtained for tones within the frequency limits of 1,000 to 4,000 cps., which, interestingly enough, corresponds to the range of maximal sensitivity of the human sound receptors.

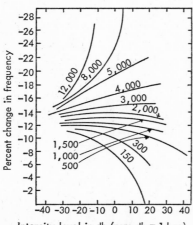

FIG. 5–7. Equal-pitch contours. All points on a given curve sound equal in pitch. The abscissa shows change in intensity in db, the ordinate percent change in frequency and the parameters frequency in cps.

One somewhat controversial phenomenon must be mentioned in connection with pitch. If a sound stimulus consists of two tones differing in frequency by at least 100 cps., the experienced pitch does not correspond to their averaged frequency. On the contrary, what is heard contains, in addition to pitches corresponding to the fundamental two-frequency components, *p* and *q*, a variety of further tones, corresponding in pitch to simple mathematical derivatives of the basic frequencies, *p* and *q*. The additional pitches might correspond to frequencies like *p + q* or *p − q* or *2p − q* or *2q − p*, etc. Further: suppose we play a sound composed of three tones with the frequencies 400 cps., 600 cps., and 800 cps., and after a while we add three more tones, at 500 cps., 700 cps., and 900 cps., then the *phenomenal pitch of the entire complex goes down by one octave.* (Because previously the lowest difference tone had a frequency of 600 — 400 or 200, but now it is 100.) A consequence of this phenomenon is that an experienced pitch can be perceived even if the fundamental to which it corresponds is not physically present in the stimulus. If the difference between the frequencies of the harmonics equals the frequency of the fundamental, the pitch is not changed by eliminating the fundamental. Between pitch and duration there prevails the relation that accuracy of determining pitch varies directly with the duration. Stimuli within a range of high thresholds for pitch discrimination must be presented for longer times in order to compensate for the decreased pitch sensitivity.

Stevens, Volkmann, and Newman have established a new quantitative scale for pitch. The unit of this scale is the *mel.* By definition 1,000 mels is the pitch of a 1,000 cps. tone at 40 db above threshold. A tone of 2,000 mels sounds half as high in pitch as a tone of 4,000 mels and twice as high as a tone of 1,000 mels. Thus this scale was constructed according to a method of fractionation. With an arbitrary loudness level of 60 db for all tones, subjects were given the task of setting the frequency of a variable so as to appear half as "high" in pitch as a standard frequency, 10 different standards distributed along the frequency dimension being used. The "half as high in pitch" judgments proved sufficiently easy to perform.[6]

Loudness

With certain reservations, the traditional view was largely correct concerning loudness too. Loudness does depend *greatly on the intensity* of the stimulus, although it is also determined by a variety of other stimulus factors. Révész simply said: "The loudness of sounds increases with the amplitude."[7] But Stevens and Davis remark in this connection, too, that *loudness is not identical with intensity* and that *db's are not measures of phenomenal loudness.*[8]

Systematic investigations have shown how much loudness varies with frequency. As in pitch perception the *mel* unit was developed, so researchers have tried to find units for measuring phenomenal

---

[6] Charles Osgood, *Method and Theory in Experimental Psychology* (New York: Oxford University Press, 1953), pp. 111–12.

[7] G. Révész, *Einführung in die Musikpsychologie* (Bern: A. Francke Ag., 1946), p. 7.

[8] S. S. Stevens and H. Davis, *Hearing* (New York: John Wiley & Sons, Inc., 1947), p. 110.

loudness. The basic unit is the *sone*. A sound has the loudness of 1 sone if it is as loud as a binaurally presented 1,000 cps. tone at an intensity of 40 db above the absolute threshold. This unit has made it possible to construct graphs showing how the loudness of tones of various frequencies changes with intensity (Figure 5–8). The curves show the loudness (in sones, on the ordinate) of tones at the

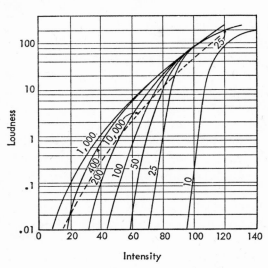

frequencies indicated on the curves, as a function of the intensity (in db above absolute threshold, on the abscissa). Low frequency tones must be presented at a much higher intensity in order to sound as loud as middle frequency tones at moderate intensities (e.g., an 80-db 25-cps. tone sounds as loud as a 40-db 1,000-cps. tone). If we consider the shape of the auditory area (see Figure 3–16, page 47), this relation is quite reasonable. Equal-loudness contours further show

FIG. 5–8. The loudness of tones (ordinate) of various intensities (abscissa) and various frequencies (parameters). The abscissa is in db, the ordinate in sones, and the parameters in cps.

that loudness rises more steeply with increasing intensity for low than for middle frequency tones. Within the most favorable limits of 1,000 cps. to 4,000 cps. a considerable loudness is already attained with relatively low intensities (0–15 db's).

The human ear can distinguish among about 1,500 levels of *pitch*. The differential threshold for *loudness* allows for about 325 separately perceived levels within the region of greatest sensitivity (about 1,000 to 4,000 cps.). Thus the number of discriminable pure tones goes up into the hundred thousands. If we multiply the number of discriminable pitches by the corresponding number of discriminable loudnesses in different regions of the auditory area, we obtain an approximation of the total number of discriminably different tones; this number is about 340,000.[9] Within the visual realm, if we add up all the discriminable shades (e.g., in Ostwald's

[9] *Ibid.*, p. 152.

system), we obtain a number of the same order of magnitude. In Figure 3–16, page 47, the auditory area was divided up into rectangles to assist in performing this multiplication operation. The first number in each square gives the number of just noticeable differences (jnd's) in intensity and the second gives the number of jnd's in frequency in that region: the former involves discriminations of various levels of db's, the latter of cps. The third number in each rectangle is the product of the other two.

In accord with the objections raised on page 117 against the usual application of the db concept, the just presented interpretation of the auditory area should preferably be entirely revised. The vertical axis of the diagram in Figure 3–16 indicates intensity in db relative to an arbitrary standard zero level. Thus a phenomenal variable is referred to a different, nonetheless phenomenal, but a mathematically unanchored, scale. A precise description in physical terms would imply an application of physical variables as coordinates. The vertical axis representing intensities should preferably be calculated purely *as a scale of varying pressure*, that is, an entirely physical, and not at all phenomenal, scale. Any such revision has been omitted in this presentation because of the firmly established practical value of the diagram.

Timbre

Sound timbres have been carefully explored by Révész. He begins with the fact that different instruments produce the fundamental as well as the harmonics in different ways. It is well known that hardly any instrument can produce all the possible harmonics. The sound made by each instrument has its own specific shape, depending on the number and intensity of the harmonics it produces. It is because of this that we hear different instruments as having characteristically different tones or timbres. Helmholtz summarized his account of the physical correlates of various timbres as follows:

Composition of Stimulus	*Timbre*
Fundamental alone	Soft
Fundamental plus first harmonic	Mellow
Fundamental plus several harmonics	Broad
Fundamental plus high harmonics	Sharp
Fundamental dominating	Full
Harmonics dominating	Hollow
Odd partials dominating	Nasal
Discordant partials dominating	Rough
High discordant partials dominating	Screeching

However, timbre does not vary only according to which partials are present in the sound. It is also affected by noises and by periodic variations in the intensity of stimulation.

In the domain of acoustics and in music theory one sometimes encounters the concept of *harmonic undertones*, parallel with the *harmonic overtones* considered here. These undertones have frequencies ½, ⅓, ¼, etc., those of the fundamental. They are, however, mainly of theoretical interest only and have not found application in the actual production of music.

Volume and Density

Most controversial of the attributes are the volume and the density of a sound.[10] Some psychologists tend especially to deny that volume can be given the status of a separate attribute. Phenomenally, what is meant by volume or "space-filling quality" becomes clear if one compares the tone of an organ with that of a flute, musically equivalent in other characteristics, i.e., equal in pitch, loudness, etc. The sounds made by the organ appear "larger," "broader," and "richer" than those of the flute. Research has concentrated on the differential threshold for volume. Some investigators claim to have shown that specific thresholds for volume cannot be obtained apart from what appear to be pitch or loudness thresholds. But the results remain controversial. Stevens was able to determine "equal-volume contours" by using a method analogous to that employed for the determination of equal pitch and equal-loudness contours. The subjects were presented alternately with two different sounds which they were to match in volume. *Even some sounds which differed in both pitch and loudness were considered equal in volume.* Equal-volume contours have the general form shown in Figure 5–9. It is clear that *volume grows with increasing intensity and with decreasing frequency* of the stimulus.

Although volume apparently must therefore be considered an attribute in its own right, Stevens and Davis accept it only with reservations. They point out that the contours just mentioned unfortunately seem to hold only within rather restricted ranges of frequency and intensity variation. Nor has it proved possible to establish unequivocal measuring units for phenomenal volume. Finally, the measurement errors in these experiments are of a high order of magnitude.

---

[10] For what is referred to here and below, cf. A. Wellek, *Zeitschrift für Musikwissenschaft*, Vol. 16 (1934), pp. 490–92.

Density is a concept which to some extent has given rise to similar comments. It has been customary to call some sounds "harder" or "tighter" than others. Stevens tried his method on this phenomenal dimension too. The subjects were confronted alternately with 200-cps. and 4,000-cps. tones. When asked about

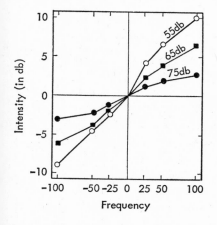

FIG. 5–9.   Equal-volume contours as functions of intensity and frequency. The ordinate shows change in intensity (in db), the abscissa change in frequency (in cps.), and the parameters the intensity of the comparison tone.

impressions of "density" they regarded the higher tones as more dense. Similarly, higher intensity tones are more dense than low intensity ones. According to such experiments, it would be appropriate to consider even density an attribute in its own right. *If two tones of different frequency are to be matched in density, the intensity of the lower one must be increased.* Thus this attribute can be distinguished from pitch, volume, and loudness.

Much guesswork surrounds the question of the acoustical and physiological correlates of volume and density. To date this guesswork is nothing more than that; there is no evidence in favor of the speculations presented so far. Yet it cannot be denied that a subject instructed to attend to density becomes more sensitive to variations in that attribute. He will react in a different way than when set to observe pitch, loudness, or volume.

The localization of sounds and the problem of brightness and tonality will be taken up later.

Beats

If two tones differing slightly in frequency are produced simultaneously, the waves summate so that sometimes they enhance and sometimes they interfere with each other according to their differences in phase. When they reinforce each other, they bring about an increase, when interfering, a decrease, in the heard intensity (Figure 5–10). These intensity oscillations are called *beats*. When one presses down two adjacent piano keys and listens to the compound sound gradually fading off, one usually can hear a periodically alternating intensification and weakening of the sound. Beats would not occur—according to Stevens and Davis—if Ohm's law were

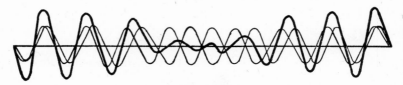

FIG. 5–10.   The production of beats.

entirely correct, i.e., if our acoustical apparatus really were able to dissect complex sounds into their components. The analysis referred to by Ohm's law clearly does not occur when stimuli produce closely overlapping vibrations of the basilar membrane.[11]

Beats have been investigated with stimuli which are initially identical in frequency but gradually differ more and more from each other. The following stages have been observed:

1. Loudness waxes and wanes periodically.
2. Beats are heard intermittently.
3. A harsh continuous sound appears.

In the first stage, the differential threshold for hearing two tones instead of one depends essentially on the patience of the subjects. During this stage the beats occur once every two minutes or a little more often. The threshold for the second stage is six to seven changes per second. A continuously heard *vibrato* has almost the same alternation frequency threshold, and as a matter of fact vibratos are not always phenomenally distinguishable from rapid beats. The third stage, the harsh sound, occurs for a 1,000-cps. tone when the beating is about 166 times per second.

Thus the beating rate clearly affects the phenomenal experiences that are produced. Minor slow beats do not bother the listener very much, but faster beats are apt to cause an irritating unpleasant wavering comparable to the disturbing flickering of a movie when the projector speed is slowed down. Even faster beats are not

---

[11] Stevens and Davis, *op. cit.*, pp. 161 ff.

discriminated as successive alternations of loudness, but instead a continuous harsh, coarse sound is perceived.

Combination Tones

One explanation offered for the phenomenon of beats is that the receptors of the cochlea are unable to act as entirely separate and independently tuned "sound analyzers." Further, *displacements of amplitudes and frequencies of heard sounds* may be produced by the asymmetry of the entire outer ear, including the external auditory canal. Fusions of two such simultaneously displaced tones are called *combination tones*. They can be either *difference* or *summation tones*. Consequently, the combination tones are outcomes of asymmetric *amplitude or frequency displacements*, whereas beats depend on periodic alterations of intensity.

The large number of combination tones created in the inner ear is astonishing. When the cochlea of a cat was stimulated by tones of 700 and 1,200 cps. at an intensity of 90 db above the absolute threshold, no less than 66 combination tones could be discriminated if electrical changes in the cochlea were again amplified. This manifold of combination tones provides a clue to the rich articulation of the spectrum of any tonal stimulus on its way to the receptors of the inner ear. If we consider the sound patterns emitted by a symphony orchestra, already in themselves composed of a rich variety of frequencies, we can hardly imagine how many tonal spectra must be produced by them when they pass through our auditory sensory apparatus.

Modulation and Vibrato

We have already mentioned *vibrato* in our discussion of beats. It is an *intentional variation of the frequency* and/or *phase* of a sound wave. Figure 5–11 shows how three superimposed components can produce either amplitude or frequency modulation depending on the phase relationships among the components. The method has considerable practical value for the procedure of analyzing *tonal spectra*. Although we cannot here present the details of this specific research area, we may note that the perception of stimulus patterns with such a degree of complexity is a kind of gestalt phenomenon. With oscillators we can vary frequencies along the entire spectrum. During such frequency variation, the listener is unable to discriminate among the separate successive spectral components. What is heard is a kind of beating of the components, *in the form of a continuous pitch variation*. Correspondingly, when amplitudes are modulated, we hear *a sound of a constant pitch continuously changing in loudness*. Beats can be considered a special case of *frequency modulation*, in which a two-component spectrum undergoes modulation.

Vibrato is the fundamental kind of frequency modulation. An

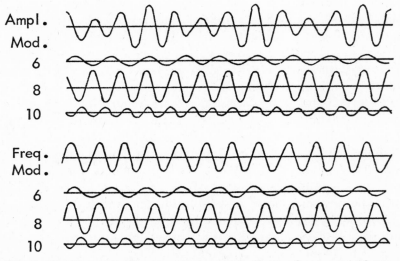

FIG. 5–11. The role of the same components (6-cps., 8-cps., and 10-cps. tones) in amplitude and in frequency modulation.

excellent example is the demonstration often given by virtuoso violinists. A fast rhythmic finger movement slightly changing the length of the oscillating string periodically produces a pleasant vibrato. Musical vibrato is usually at a speed of about seven alternations per second.

Masking

Sometimes the absolute threshold of a tone is raised by another immediately preceding or simultaneous tone. The disturbing tone is said to mask the test tone. The *masking value* is the difference in db between the absolute threshold in silence and in the presence of the masking tone. *The masking effect on simultaneously presented test tones is stronger for test tones higher in frequency than the masking tone than for test tones lower in frequency than the masking tone.* The masking effect is stronger the more similar the frequencies of test and masking tones. If two sounds are presented simultaneously, the phenomenal experience depends greatly on the relationships of frequencies and intensities of the two sounds, with the above-mentioned rules governing the impressions. The lack of linearity in our auditory system, which gives rise to the aural harmonics (a kind of high partials) that are characteristic of auditory conduction, also creates audible components if intense combination tones are used as stimuli. It is hard to mask a continuous unchanging sound with a sudden brief sound. Rather, there *occurs an articulation into figure and ground: the longer lasting sound is heard as a constant event persisting behind the shorter one.*

Musical Scales

Three principles have directed the structure of tonal systems used in European music: the *principle of consonance*, the *principle of fifths*, and the *pragmatic principle*. The comparative study of music has shown that the *octave* has played a special role in the music of many people—be they modern or ancient, civilized or primitive. The series of tones constituting a scale generally fills the interval of an octave. The octave is the fundamental interval. If tones falling inside this limit are played together, pair by pair, some of these pairs sound agreeable, others unpleasant. The former are called *consonances*, the latter *dissonances*. It was already known to the ancients that consonant intervals are based on the clearest and simplest relations between frequencies. The octave is defined as a pair of tones whose frequencies are related as 1:2 (see Figure 5–6). The other interval relations are derived from this basic one as shown below:

16:15	Diatonic semitone	3:2	Pure fifth
10:9	Minor whole step	8:5	Minor sixth
9:8	Major whole step	5:3	Major sixth
6:5	Minor third	9:5	Minor seventh
5:4	Major third	15:8	Major seventh
4:3	Pure fourth	2:1	Pure octave

If the interval relations within the limits of an octave follow this scheme, the tuning is called *pure* or *mathematical*. The most important *seven-note diatonic scale*, the so-called *major scale*, is constructed according to this principle. The tones of such a scale, and their interval relations, are the following:

$$c \; \%_8 \; d \; {}^{1}\%_9 \; e \; {}^{16}\!/_{15} \; f \; \%_8 \; g \; {}^{1}\%_9 \; a \; \%_8 \; b \; {}^{16}\!/_{15} \; c$$

The scale of the tones within the octave is articulated further if this system is replaced by the 12-note chromatic scale. It is derived from the mathematical scale by interpolating intermediate tones into all whole tone intervals. The goal can be achieved either by multiplying the frequencies of **c, d, f, g,** and **a** by $^{25}\!/_{24}$, producing tones called **c** sharp, **d** sharp, **f** sharp, **g** sharp, and **a** sharp, or by multiplying the frequencies of **d, e, g, a,** and **b** by $^{24}\!/_{25}$, which produces tones known as **d** flat, **e** flat, **g** flat, **a** flat, and **b** flat. Thus half tone steps are created which are smaller than the ones usually used in music $\left(\dfrac{20}{21}, \dfrac{256}{243}, \dfrac{16}{15} \right)$. The enharmonic scale contains all the indicated old and new tones, as follows:

c	c♯	d♭	d	d♯	e♭	e	e♯	f♭	f	f♯	g♭	g	g♯	a♭
1	$^{25}\!/_{24}$	$^{27}\!/_{25}$	$\%_8$	$^{75}\!/_{64}$	$\%_5$	$\%_4$	$^{32}\!/_{25}$	$^{125}\!/_{96}$	$\%_3$	$^{25}\!/_{18}$	$^{36}\!/_{25}$	$\%_2$	$^{25}\!/_{16}$	$\%_5$

a	a♯	b♭	b	c♭	c
$\%_3$	$^{125}\!/_{72}$	$\%_5$	$^{15}\!/_8$	$^{48}\!/_{25}$	2

Pure tuning has proved impossible for permanently tuned instruments, and it is especially poor if human singers are accompanied by these instruments. Whenever the key is changed, precise mathematical tuning of the intervals cannot be maintained. If 12 pure fifths would equal 7 pure octaves, such a discrepancy between permanently tuned instruments and singers could not occur. But we know that this condition does not hold true. Pianos and organs permanently tuned to pure constant intervals do not fit with string instruments or the human voice, because the latter can easily transform the enharmonic intervals. The solution has been to compromise the purity of sound with more constant tone step relations by constructing the equidistant or tempered scale.

The *principle of fifths* means that the scale is constructed of basic intervals. After the octave the most harmonious interval is the fifth. The outcome is the seven-tone or *Pythagorean scale*. But this solution, too, has its drawbacks. The major third, e.g., becomes too wide with this tuning, and sounds somewhat impure. The note **e**[1] in the scale corresponds to 324 cps., while in the diatonic it is 320 cps. It is precisely this deviation from the natural major third which interferes with the use of Pythagoras' scale in multiple-voice singing.

The final most widely accepted solution is based on what Révész called the *pragmatic principle*. It led first to the construction of the *partially tempered scale*. The tonal steps were created within the limits of an octave in a way which left fifths and fourths entirely pure as in the diatonic scale, while in the tuning of thirds and sixths, not to mention seconds and sevenths, a slight impurity was permitted. Alternatively, the thirds were tuned pure, which made the fifths appear too narrow and therefore impure. As even this scale produced difficulties, especially with regard to the question of *which keys* should be chosen, the octave finally was divided into *12 equidistant intervals*, which required a compromise in the purity of every interval. This construction is called the *well-tempered scale*. When the half tone steps are treated as equal in width, the difference, e.g., between **c** sharp and **d** flat, disappears. For practical reasons **d** flat and **c** sharp are considered equal, although a trained ear can distinguish them.

Because of the considerable adaptive ability of our sense of hearing, people have since the days of Johann Sebastian Bach been acquainted with impure intervals without detriment to their artistic enjoyment. On the other hand, pure intervals still have their place in any performances which permit the free play of string instruments or of the human voice if they are not tied to the hindrance of accompanying percussive instruments. When enjoying the beauty of genuine chamber music, we may be able to understand the loss that has resulted from the introduction of tempered scales.

In the new scale, pure tuning was replaced by *relative tuning*. The pragmatic scale has had to be anchored to some given frequency. If a standard reference frequency is used, the corresponding pitch is called the *normal tone*, and tuning according to it is called *absolute tuning*. During the 1500's and 1600's a^1 was decided on as the normal tone, but it had a higher pitch than the normal **a** nowadays, corresponding to a frequency of about 432–466 cps. The frequency of 435 cps. was agreed upon in Vienna in 1885. Later, in the era of radio broadcasts of music, British and American musicians made the proposal of moving the a^1 to a frequency of 440 cps., a proposal which has generally been accepted.

The Human Voice

With a few exceptions the human voice extends from C_2 to C_6, or in other words over a range from about 65 to 1,044 cps. The register of any individual, however, rarely covers more than two or three octaves. It is important to distinguish between the register of speech and the register of the singing voice. The speech register of a baritone, whose *voice range* can be symbolized by F_3, might extend from C_2 to B_3, whereas the limits of his singing range are likely to be near G_2 sharp and F_4 sharp. The schematic figure below (adapted from Sovijärvi) shows the structure of these relationships (Figure 5–12).

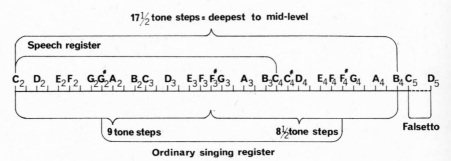

FIG. 5–12. Example of the total voice register of a man whose middle tone is f ($=F_3$ International standard tone).

The entire speaking and singing register of an individual can be characterized by the *middle tone* of his chest voice range. The median frequency of his chest voice gives his middle tone. The middle tone of a choir baritone is generally F_3. If we assume that his range extends over almost three octaves, it can be represented by the schematic picture presented in Figure 5–12, which also contains, for illustration, the successive categories of his various musical registers. *The wider the speech register, the wider too the range of the singing voice.*

The ranges of singing registers cannot be defined absolutely, because there are marked individual differences among singers within even the same voice category. Sovijärvi presents the following typical symbol tones for male and female registers. The range of the singing voice might be considered to have a width of two octaves, one on either side of the middle tone.

Soprano, mezzo-soprano, alto, and contralto are female voices, and tenor, baritone, and bass are male.[12] In addition to their registers,

---

[12] See A. Sovijärvi, *Annales Academiae Scientiarum Fennicae* B 44, No. 2 (1938), and M. Nadolecny, *Kurzes Lehrbuch der Sprach-und Stimmheilkunde* (Leipzig: Vogel, 1926).

human voices differ in timbre too. An uneducated human voice might include only 13 tonal steps. The *registers* (shown in Figure 5–12) are the following, beginning with the lowest one: *deepest range* (3 tonal steps), *deep level* (3½ steps), *mid-level* (3 steps) *high level* (2 steps) and *highest range* (1½ steps). The *chest voice* ranges through all these registers except the high **B₂** level and is followed

		International Standards
Soprano	**a¹**	**A₄**
Mezzo-soprano	**f¹**	**F₄**
Alto	**d¹**	**D₄**
Contralto	**c¹**	**C₄**
Tenor	**a**	**A₃**
Bartione	**f**	**F₃**
Bass	**d**	**D₃**

at higher pitch levels by the *head voice*, which consists, according to Sovijärvi, of high level in addition to the highest range. The chest voice is characterized by its *richer timbre*, the head voice by its *sharpness* and *shrillness*.

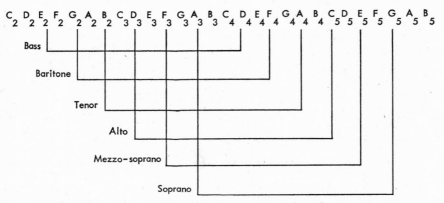

FIG. 5–13. Voice ranges.

In the 1700's the investigation of the speaking voice and speech sounds reached a systematic level. Gradually the interest of research workers centered on the physical analysis of vowels, or more precisely on discriminating their partials. This work has been continued by modern phoneticians.

The oldest experimental approach was based on the *resonance* phenomenon. A series of tuning forks, or of other kinds of *resonators* tuned to specific frequencies, will react differently to different vowels sung or spoken at them at a sufficient intensity. Resonance occurs in those resonators which are tuned to frequencies equivalent to those of the partials in the various vowels. Thus it has been shown that the vowel *o* causes a tuning fork at b^1 to resonate.[13] Nowadays analysis has been carried further with the aid of improved electronic devices, especially sound spectrographs. Their detailed description would go beyond the aims of this text.

Let us instead concentrate on Hermann's and Helmholtz' views concerning the *nature of formants*. When vowels are pronounced, one of the partials is believed to exert a dominant influence upon the phenomenal timbre of the sound. The dominant partial, determining the phenomenal quality of any vowel, has been assumed to have an *absolute, constant frequency*. What is called a formant actually is such a dominant partial, a constant partial considered to be characteristic for a given vowel. Irrespective of what note is chosen for singing the vowel into the resonators, the frequency of the formant is supposed to remain constant.

Helmholtz assumed that the formant could always be found among the harmonics of the fundamental used in singing the vowel. If he were right, each formant would be a tone the frequency of which is a simple multiple of the fundamental. Hermann, on the other hand, supposed that a formant need not necessarily be a harmonic of the tone in which the vowel is said or sung but could probably even be some nonharmonic partial. The basic problem of formants centered around this controversy.

Stumpf, on the basis of painstaking work, supported Helmholtz' opinion but complemented and extended it. A formant is not a separate tone, according to Stumpf, but is a *subregion of the frequency scale*. All vowel spectra have characteristic *maxima of intensity*. A given tone can function as a formant *only if an octave of the fundamental happens to fall within the formant region*, in which case *that particular partial will suffice to give the sound its typical vowel quality*.[14] The pitch of a formant can be called constant in the phenomenal sense of the word if a perceptual constancy is meant. Thus, according to Stumpf, if the pitch of the fundamental is raised, the pitch of the formant region will be transposed accordingly. It is only the relational, not the absolute, aspects of the tonal steps which

[13] G. Révész, *Einführung in die Musikpsychologie* (Bern: A. Francke Ag., 1946), p. 52.

[14] *Ibid.*, p. 56.

are invariant. *The lower frequency limit of the formant region is produced by the harmonic closest to this region.* Such an organization is presented in Table 5–1.

The controversy in the theory of formants ended with a compromise, with some concessions to both parties, although Helmholtz' view was given somewhat greater weight. Table 5–1 shows Révész' presentation of the formants of the common vowels in the tonal range from C_2 to C_8.

TABLE 5–1

FORMANTS OF THE VOWELS WITHIN THE TONAL RANGE
FROM C TO c^5 (STANDARD C_2 TO C_8)

Note	Frequency	Formant	
$F_{10}\#$	23410		Upper limit of audibility
C_9	8277		Upper limit of consonants and whispered vowels
C_8	4138	I	Upper limit of music
$F_7\#$	2926		
C_7	2069	E	
$F_6\#$	1463	Ä, Ö, Ü	Upper limit of the human voice
F_6	1035		
$F_5\#$	732	A	
C_5	517		
$F_4\#$	366	O	
C_4	259		
$F_3\#$	183	U	
C_3	129		Lower limit of consonants
C_2	65		Lower limit of human voice
C_1	32		Lower limit of music
$F_6\#_3$	11		Lower limit of audibility

Révész is convinced that Stumpf's results definitely invalidate the hypothesis presented by Koenig and Köhler according to which the formants of the basic vowels *u, o, a, e, i* should occur at *one octave* intervals from each other. This hypothesis was burdened with an attempt at an exaggerated analogy between phenomenal sound and color systems. The basic vowels were thought of as corresponding to the four primaries on the color circle, because they presumably represented the simple tones C_2 to C_8 on the "vowel spectrum."

Brightness and Tonality

Two attributes in our previously presented list still remain unexamined, viz., *brightness* and *tonality*. Let us first consider why pitch was represented by two separate attributes.

A pitch cannot be described acoustically by a frequency, but rather is a phenomenal auditory experience which requires description of *two* different aspects, e.g., A and $_1$ or C and $_2$. To say that a given musical tone is an A or a C is not sufficient. As a musical event a tone must be classified both at (1) being A or C, and also as (2) being high or low, etc. The latter specification symbolizes the octave level to which the tone belongs. The octave admittedly occupies a special position as a musical interval. If, for instance, we successively move up the piano keyboard, pressing down each key in turn, after passing each 12th note we always *hear a recapitulation of the just-heard qualities as a new 12-tone sequence*. Something is changed from key to key, and this change is greatest at the 12th key. At the 13th the quality "turns back" and reminds us of the first tone, the prime, more than does any of the other tones in the interval. In other words, the 13th half tone step is *in some respects different* from all the preceding tones, but *in another respect* it is maximally similar to the prime. The same rule holds true for the second half tone step when compared with the 14th, etc.[15]

If we wish to picture these phenomenal relationships in a diagram analogous to that for the description of colors, we might conceive of changes in height or *brightness* occurring along a vertically oriented *linear dimension* and changes in tonality following a *cyclic pattern*. When both dimensions are combined in a single figure, the tonal scale assumes a *spiral shape*. For any of the turns, any spot located on it, representing a single tone, will fall directly above the same tone in the lower turn, representing the next lower octave, and precisely below the same tone in the next higher turn, representing the next higher octave. Thus corresponding points on the turns are always separated by a height or brightness (vertical) interval of an octave. The linear variable was called *brightness*, the cyclic one *tonality* by Hornbostel. The schema we have described, as drawn by Révész, is shown in Figure 5–14.

This *two-component* theory was clearly and convincingly formulated by Révész in 1912. His presentation was so compelling that it made even Stumpf abandon his earlier conviction that the tonal similarity of notes separated by an octave could be described only in terms of their equivalent partials, as Helmholtz had assumed. After Stumpf had adopted Révész' view, the former's students, Köhler, Abraham, and Hornbostel, proposed their own systems of tonal

---

[15] See, e.g., A. Wellek, *Zeitschrift für Musikwissenschaft*, Vol. 16 (1934), p. 485.

dimensions. They are based on the same facts as the Révész theory, although some of them (e.g., Köhler's) have been objected to as conceptually more confusing.[16]

In his *Introduction to the Theory of Music* Révész laid out his theory in the following manner. All earlier so-called *one-component theories* agreed that variations in pitch had been satisfactorily explained by reference to one main dimension, the frequency variable. Thus a point-to-point correspondence between the tones in a musical scale and certain levels of frequency had to be assumed. The appropriate frequency was thought to be "the stimulus" for a given tone (the atomistic-mechanistic assumption). But if we pay attention to the phenomenal impression of the tonal scale, we must cope with the ambiguity of the relationship between C_3 and C_4. On the one hand, the octave of C_3, C_4, is the tone *farthest away* from C_3 within the limits of the octave interval, and in this respect it is the tone *least similar* to C_3. On the other hand, it is the *qualitatively closest* tone to C_3 and in this respect the tone most similar to C_3. This ambiguity becomes especially clear if a series of major thirds, minor thirds, or even whole tone steps are played in turn over the range of several octaves.

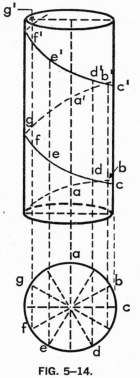

FIG. 5–14.

Musical practice has rested on these facts since ancient times, although this knowledge did not until recent decades get put in the form of a theory. Even the oldest Greek musical manuscripts that we know about used *the same symbols for tones separated by an octave*, and the same conformity for designating tonal similarity has been widespread among other peoples, e.g., medieval Europeans in various countries.

Tones separated from each other by one or several octaves are called *equivalent* by Révész. He named the two components *tonal pitch* and *tonal quality*. Tones are related either by their equivalency, that is, their *qualitative similarity*, or by their *quantitative similarity in pitch*.

---

[16] *Ibid.*

As Wellek has pointed out, a danger of serious confusions in the terminology of auditory psychology was produced by Révész' replacing Hornbostel's "tonality" with "tonal quality" and Hornbostel's successors substituting "brightness" for Révész' "tonal pitch." Following the terminology of Roiha in his psychology of music, the present text uses "tonality" for the cyclic, and "brightness" for the linear, variable. This avoids the confusion inherent in using Révész' concept of "tonal pitch" in connection with these subcategories.

Tonality is strongest and richest within the limits of the middle octave (from C_3 to C_4). The "saturation" of the tones (to borrow another expression from color psychology) is most pronounced within this tonal area. Révész tends to regard tonality as completely constant, even identical, from one octave to another. Hornbostel speaks of "similarity," while Wellek says: "Tonality may be the 'same' throughout the tonal scale, but it shows variations in its salience."[17]

In the highest and lowest frequencies of the auditory area, only pitch or brightness differences, and no variations in tonality, are experienced. Pitch discrimination is prior in evolution to the perception of tonality, and consequently, disorders of the organism do not affect the former as much as the latter. Here too, as Hornbostel ingeniously and rightly pointed out, we find another analogy between the "brightness dimensions" of colors and of tones.

---

[17] *Ibid.*, pp. 486–87.

CHAPTER 6

Perception of Touch, Vibration, and Temperature

Stimulus-Systems of Touch

A DESCRIPTION of the touch receptors was given in Chapter 3. Before we deal with *touch impressions*, let us, following our practice in discussing vision and hearing, briefly consider tactual or haptic *stimuli*.

The *adequate stimulus* for touch is a deformation of the skin surface, usually caused by some mechanical impact and appearing as a minute *compression* or *displacement* of the tissue. Displacements can be mediated by skin hairs without the skin surface as such being involved in this transmission. The displacement in such a case affects the receptors in the hair follicles directly. Although the sense of touch is sometimes referred to as specifically a pressure sense, the skin receptors apparently do not react to variations in air pressure unless some distortions or depressions of the skin are involved.

A *steady continuous pressure* cannot be experienced despite the fact that this modality is characteristically sensitive to pressure. Pressure experiences can be evoked by sudden changes in object shapes, or by compression and distention of the sensitive tissues. Clearly, here too *gradients* of touch and pressure are critical for a successful outcome of the perceptual act.

Among the *inadequate stimuli* for touch von Skramlik mentioned *vibrations*, especially electrical currents. He reminds us of a figure first presented by Adrian, whose extensive experiments showed how some direct-current stimulations are perceived as series of vibrations on the skin. Accordingly, Skramlik holds that the stimuli for vibration can be found among inadequate touch stimuli. This view will later be considered in detail.

If we continue to consider only physiologically determined classifications, the modal qualities mediated by receptors for touch and pressure could be called *experienced touch*, *pressure*, and *tickle* when there is a persistent stimulus. The term *experienced vibration* would again apply to cases of persistent intermittent pressure stimulation. In addition to *superficial* touch, physiologists speak of *deep* pressure or touch. The often claimed phenomenal differences between these two classes have produced controversies to some degree analogous to the disputes concerning the concept of deep pain. Whatever the solution of these disagreements turns out to be, it does not have much bearing on a psychological approach to this modality.

According to Head, we should distinguish among three achievements of the touch sense, depending on which layers of tissue are mainly involved:

1. *Deep sensitivity*, which enables us to experience touch qualities even without our skin receptors being activated.
2. *Protopathic sensitivity*, which gives us our impressions of *smoothness* and *roughness*, of *pain*, of *cold*, and of *warmth*.
3. *Epicritic sensitivity*, which enables us to feel light strokes on the skin, slight temperature variations, and minor peripheral deformations or displacements.[1]

Goldscheider and Hoefer have claimed the existence of:

1. *The sense of touch* proper, which depends on stimulation of the receptors in the touch spots and serves the purposes of feeling variations in the grain of surfaces and of providing body orientation.
2. *Other types of skin sensitivity*, completely independent of the location and the functions of the presumed touch spots, and probably activated by receptors interspersed among the known touch spots of the skin.
3. *Deep sensitivity*.

This classification mirrors some of the drawbacks introduced by the attempt to refer touch impressions to a system of punctiform receptors.[2]

Other investigators, especially Frey, deny the possibility of

---

[1] E. v. Skramlik, "Psychophysiologie der Tastsinne," *Archiv für die gesamte Psychologie*, Ergänzungsband 4 (Leipzig, 1937), p. 67.

[2] *Ibid.*, pp. 69–70.

distinguishing among different layers of touch sensitivity. When so-called "deep touch sensations" occur during states of local anesthesia of minute parts of the skin surface, these could in Frey's view be due to stimulus-irradiation from the local deformed area to *surrounding*, still responsive, parts of the skin. The same point of view is shared by Skramlik in his huge handbook on the sense of touch and pressure. He explicitly points out that his exposition is based upon the presumption of a single sense of touch. The peripheral touch organs in the skin must be regarded as the receptors for this unitary sense. This view, as well as the others just mentioned, can be taken as a starting point for a psychological presentation, especially if supplemented by some of Katz's important comments on these sensory functions.

The experience of *tickle* is different in many respects from perceptions of touch, pressure, and vibration. Frey was prepared to consider *skin tickle* as mediated by skin spots and *deep tickle* as due to the function of some muscle-receptors. *Itch* is a peculiar quality, apparently related to deep tickle and simultaneously containing pain components.

The absolute thresholds for touch proper and for tickle are almost the same, but only stimuli barely above the threshold can evoke tickle experiences. A further necessary condition is a movement of the stimulus along the skin surface at an appropriate speed. Thus, on the surface of the palm the pressure sufficient for evoking tickle is 0.2g, but the stimulus must move at a speed of at least 1.2 cm.p.s. As Skramlik rightly points out, the subject's attitude is quite decisive. A different set may cause one and the same stimulus to produce a touch experience at one time and tickle at another.

Vibratory Stimuli

In the chapter on sensory evolution, attention was called to the fact that some fishes have vibration receptors along their sides. They sense water vibrations in general as well as those specific waves (20 cps.–20,000 cps.) which we would call tones.

Békésy, in collaboration with some American scientists, carried out interesting experiments with sound stimuli at frequencies which exceed the limits of human auditory capacity. Their observations have certain implications for the explanation of our sensations of vibration as well. The *low sounds* in their experiments were produced at frequencies below 50 cps. For a sound of 4 cps. the absolute threshold intensity was 60 db above 1 dyne/cm². An increase in frequency brought about a stepwise successive decrease in the threshold intensity. The largest step occurred at a frequency of 18 cps. This frequency has been called the *fusion frequency* for pitch. If low frequency vibrations are gradually raised, when they reach this threshold value a fusion occurs yielding an experience of a sound. Below the fusion frequency monaural observation just produces an experience of *alternating pressure*. A binaurally presented 10-cps. frequency may be enough to produce an experience of a "space-sound" located somewhere inside the head of the observer. When stimulus frequencies sink below 50 cps., they can, when presented at sufficiently high intensities, give rise to tactual experiences of pressure, even if lower intensities of these same frequencies produce auditory impressions. According to Stevens and Davis, we can locate these nonauditory touch and pressure experiences above the upper bound of the auditory area. No matter what frequency is chosen, such experiences occur if the intensity is sufficiently great. These upper-limit values are often called "thresholds of feeling." If we use low frequencies, a stimulus originally perceived as a sound gives rise to vibration experiences when the intensity is increased. If we employ high frequencies, the outcome of the same manipulation is a strident pain sensation.[3]

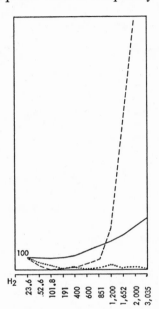

FIG. 6–1. Threshold values for stinging tickle when perceived as auditory or vibratory.
—— Electrically produced vibration.
— — — Mechanically produced vibration.
. . . . Auditory thresholds for different frequency stimulations.

Békésy reports remarkably slow adaptation for tactual sensations aroused by stimuli with a frequency of 1 cps. and a pressure of, e.g., 6,000 dynes per cm.²: the tactual sensation lasts for several minutes, showing phenomenally some similarity to touch experiences in the fingers.

---

[3] S. S. Stevens and H. Davis, *Hearing* (New York: John Wiley & Sons, Inc., 1947), pp. 44–46 and 58–59.

These brief considerations convincingly demonstrate the close relationship between the senses of vibration and hearing. The attempt of some physiologists in previous generations to explain perception of vibration as a special kind of touch experience must be considered untenable. Even resonance phenomena of our body cavities are often experienced as a kind of vibration, rather similar to the vibrations we feel when stimulated by sounds beyond the limits of the auditory area. Man has two senses for picking up mechanical vibrations in his environment: (1) the sense of vibration and (2) the sense of hearing, with the latter probably developing later for the special task of minutely recording waves within the limits of a narrower frequency band.

The sense of vibration, like the sense of hearing, has its fusion frequency. Below the threshold of 10 pulses per second the impression of continuous vibration is replaced by feeling the separate pulses. The limit is less rigid than it is in hearing. The upper frequency threshold of vibration has not been agreed upon. Katz and his successors place the upper limit for feeling vibrations between 500 and 520 cps. Becker reported a 1,500-cps. threshold, and some investigators claim to have been able to produce sensory impressions of vibration even with stimuli at 3,000 cps. if presented at a sufficiently high amplitude. There is good reason to accept Skramlik's view that the values obtained for the upper threshold reflect the inaccuracy of measuring instruments rather than an inherent deficiency of the sense organs.[4]

Theoretically speaking, we should place the upper frequency threshold for vibratory sensations at least as high as the frequencies which can still produce auditory experiences. Some interesting experiments performed by Rubin have shown that the senses of vibration and hearing operate reciprocally in strong interaction. As long as the physiological conditions allow the vibrating stimulus to be perceived as a sound, the threshold for vibratory sensations is raised. On the other hand, if the stimulus gets inaudible, it is sensed as vibration as soon and as long as possible, implying a decrease of the absolute threshold. A struck tuning fork, if made inaudible, e.g., by means of earplugs, might still be perceivable as a vibrating body. Bringing the fork closer to the ear generally causes a hearing

---

[4] Skramlik, *op cit.*, p. 95.

experience such that the vibratory impression disappears at the same moment as the stimulus is perceived acoustically.[5]

Differential sensitivity to vibrations is apparently independent of frequency. Within the limits of 16 to 1,600 cps. our receptors can discriminate 25 to 30 levels of vibration density, while our sense of hearing discriminates 1,000 shades of pitch within the same frequency range.

Interpretation of the Vibratory Experience

In his biological interpretation of vibratory perception, Katz employs a kind of duplicity principle. The receptors for touch and pressure can *record contact*, and the same receptors when mediating vibration function to *record distant events*. Thus one and the same set of sense organs has a double function. In terms of evolution, the sense of vibration is an auditory sense intermediate between touch and hearing proper. Probably this intermediate sense represents the first step of the differentiation of some touch organs into true auditory receptors. When capable of genuine hearing, these sense organs are still better equipped for the task of detecting remote invisible dangers or available prey.

Even man, at his phyletic level, lives in a *vibratory* as well as an *auditory* world. Through his sense of vibration a driver or a sailor can perceive the roughness of the surface under the wheels or the changes in air and water pressure. The vibratory sense also serves us in other daily tasks, such as shaving or writing a letter.

The organization and articulation of our touch percepts proper will be discussed in later chapters.

Perceptual Qualities of Warmth and Cold

The physiological basis of our temperature sense was discussed in Chapter 3. There we gave a description of Bazett's thermal gradient theory, which applies a principle later developed by Gibson in his investigations of the role of gradients in sensory stimulation. These recent findings controverted much of the evidence for certain anatomically well-delineated classes of skin receptors as mediators of warmth (Ruffini's cylinders) and cold (Krause end-bulbs). The main unfortunate consequence of Blix and Goldscheider's classifica-

---

[5] Edgar Rubin, "Quelques Expériences sur les rapports entre les domaines auditif et pathologique," *Journal de Psychologie*, January-March (1938), Paris.

tion was the restraints it imposed upon attempts to explore the joint interaction functions of larger groups of receptors.

The hands of human beings can become very sensitive to temperature variations in everyday working conditions. Experienced cooks and bakers, without using thermometers, are said to be able to achieve a margin of error as small as 2° in estimating temperatures up to +250° C. A drawback of such "natural thermometers" is the narrow range within which they work. Presumably, discrimination of temperatures far below the accustomed ones would not be as good and might even be seriously impaired. "Pure sensations of warmth" can, according to Skramlik, be produced only within the range of +20° C to +45° C. When stimuli at lower temperatures are applied, the experience of warmth is accompanied by *cold*-perception, and when the upper threshold is exceeded, the stimulus produces impressions of *heat* as well as of *warmth*.

Adequate stimuli for temperature sensations are the *relative temperatures* of the objects and media contacting the skin—relative in the sense of the ratio between the temperature of the contacting object and the temperature of the skin. Temperature conduction, which reduces the differences between the temperature of surfaces in contact with each other, occurs in two phases. If we consider the human body surface, the first phase involves the transmission of warmth from the skin to the surrounding bodies or to the air, or an absorption of a higher temperature from this environment by the skin. The second phase consists of corresponding equilibration of temperature differences between the skin and the deeper layers of the body.

Katz observed that the physical structure of the object or the medium brought into contact with the skin decisively influences its phenomenal temperature. A ball of cotton feels warmer than a piece of wood at the same temperature. Wood in turn feels warmer than glass and warmer yet than a metal surface. Besides the specific heat (conduction capacity) of different objects, their thermal capacity, too, plays a dominant role in the amazing relativity of our temperature perceptions. In Katz's experiments the metal plate and the glass felt hot when presented in air heated to a temperature greatly exceeding our body temperature, but wood and cotton were experienced as rather cool under the same experimental conditions. As Skramlik points out, not only the steepness of the conduction gradient, but also the time consumed by the conduction procedure, is relevant. The flatter the slope of the conduction gradient, the slower the rate of sensation, and the larger the surface area contacted, the faster the rate of sensation.

The theory of temperature perception has gradually proceeded toward the presently prevalent view that the *rate* of changes in temperature is the key stimulus. Weber was already aware of this when he claimed that our impressions of warmth and cold depend upon temperature variations in our receptors. He was also able to refer temperature adaptation phenomena to the same principle to the extent that adaptations occur within this modality. If a temperature gradient changes very gradually, the change does not affect the receptors, and we have no experience of increasing or decreasing warmth. Furthermore, if we stay continuously out in cold weather or in a strongly heated room, the gradient maintains its steepness, and there is no adaptation at all.

The most recent explanations have leaned more and more on thermal radiation. Bazett refers to the following experiment the results of which, he feels, can hardly be explained by his gradient theory. Even if we hold our hand in warm (42° C) water for as long as one hour, the water still feels warm. Clearly, a heat conduction gradient would not take so long to flatten out. The perception of an unchanged water temperature could perhaps be considered a constancy phenomenon, due to the blood circulating through the hand. In a crucial experiment the circulation in the arm was stopped while the arm was kept at body temperature. When the warm blood was again permitted to flow into the tissues whose temperature had been artificially controlled, no steep temperature gradients should have occurred. Yet the true temperature of the water was perceived, even in this case with astonishing accuracy.[6] Possibly we must consider chemical and somatic gradients occurring during intervals between temperature conduction phases and receptor stimulation. At present, however, there is no convincing evidence in favor of all these assumptions.

Within the modality of temperature perception, *tendencies to objectify*[7] can also be found. When temperature stimuli act upon

----

[6] F. Geldard, *The Human Senses* (New York: John Wiley & Sons, Inc., 1953), pp. 217–18.

[7] The term "objectify" is used here and in later pages in the sense of interpreting a sensory impression in terms of the stimulus which produces it.

our organism without being combined with simultaneous touch or pressure, we are likely to "*somatize*" our sensations. We speak of "shivers running down our backs." "Thing-gestalten" hardly ever result from pure sensations of warmth or cold unless they are objectified by reference to sensory material available from other modalities.

CHAPTER 7

On Smell and Taste Experiences

Significance of Odors in Our Everyday Life

No OTHER modalities have as strong and vivid an influence upon our prevailing mood as do smell and taste. This close connection between such sensations and the general emotional state of the organism is sometimes considered biologically significant for survival. When dealing with the role of smell in our experience of *Joie de vivre*, Skramlik eloquently described the contribution of odors to our perceptions in a good kitchen or when seated at table.

Different varieties of *wines* can be distinguished on the basis of their specific aroma, which is a combination of smell and taste ("bouquet") easily discerned by the connoisseur. Such rich flavor impressions contain olfactory as well as gustatory components. Even the complex flavor of *milk* varies considerably with local differences in the cattle fodder. It is not rare for an adult to feel disturbed by some peculiar nuances in the flavor of the milk. A five- to six-year-old child on a picnic, when offered milk by a farmer, might refuse it altogether because "it smells of strange cows." And *goat milk* is generally not appreciated even by adults.

Odors in particular are thus intimately associated with motivational aspects of our personality. Their affiliation with *sexuality* has often been pointed out. To understand the erotogenic subconscious smell sensations we must remember that an "absolute" sensory threshold usually has two different levels, the *threshold of stimulation* (Reizschwelle) and the *threshold of recognition* (Erkennungsschwelle). If we gradually increase the intensity of an initially subthreshold stimulus, the sensation develops through these *successive* stages. As soon as the stimulus intensity exceeds some absolute minimum, physiological changes, or some kind of "reaction" to the stimulus, can be observed. In the second stage a clear awareness of the stimulus becomes unequivocally evident. The threshold of recognition is even harder to determine strictly than are other thresholds. It varies widely from moment to moment. Sometimes there is hardly any difference between these thresholds, but sometimes they are surprisingly different. Henning's concept of the "threshold of perception" (*Wahrnehmungsschwelle*) is almost equivalent to our "threshold of recognition." Henning assumes that the perception threshold cannot possibly be exceeded before the organism has formed an organized, articulated impression of the odor, which generally implies a recollection of the *name* of the object producing the odor.

Clearly, the organism records a sizable portion of the components of a total stimulus situation whose intensity remains below the threshold for recognition. These unconscious nuances influence our behavior and our moods in ways of which we generally are not aware. It is well known that the *timbre* of the human voice plays an important role in arousing erotic interest in the interplay of the sexes. Some unconscious olfactory stimulus factors may strikingly influence the ineffable total impression we have of a beloved person. The characteristic odor of any person, his *personal aroma*, as it were, depends to a large extent upon the secretory products of the pores in his skin surface. *"Oft ist der Geruch der Vorläufer der Liebe"* ("Often smell is the harbinger of love").[1] Without doubt the odor of a woman's skin can in some situations act as a kind of "releasing stimulus" for a male, in Lorenz's sense of the term. Usually this personal aroma is complemented and refined by means of artificial odors. Cosmetics involve a skill as old as culture itself. Whenever the season and the climate render it possible, women have worn—and still wear—flowers in their clothing or hair. All known cultures developed methods for preserving flowers and aromatic herbs in order to make it possible to use them irrespective of the season. That was the origin of the perfume and scent industry, which uses the skill of many experts to produce cosmetic soaps, aromatic oils, pomades, etc., and which is more highly developed wherever there is a higher standard of living.

On the other hand, we know that smell impressions can be extremely disgusting, even if they are evoked only in imagination by

---

[1] E. v. Skramlik, *Handbuch der Physiologie der Niederen Sinne I* (Leipzig, 1926), p. 7.

some sensory analogy or association. Let us not forget the animals who protect themselves by means of their unbearable stench. Even the most charming odor involves—if we enjoy it to excess—the danger of becoming stunned or even intoxicated. Cherry or lily of the valley blossoms brought into the bedroom may produce strong impressions of satiation and disgust, because their odor may permeate the room's entire atmosphere during the night.

Skramlik relates the story of a lady who could not stand the smell of roses. She was visited by another lady who wore a rose in her hat. Immediately on catching sight of the hat she felt terribly ill—this time without reason, because it was an artificial flower.[2]

Unconscious smell experiences, interwound as they are with our complex perceptions, thus seem to be essential components of our sensory world, contributing to the enjoyment of life. Only if they are really missing in our environment would we have some idea of their value. It is entirely possible that appealing odors play major roles as sources of refreshment and life energy of the organism. In northern countries and in the mountains, spring and early summer are the time for nature's odors. There is something about the increased alertness of the organism that improves sensitivity to articulated details in awakening nature. The long winter is, by contrast, a rather drab period, mostly devoid of pungent smells. Phenomenally, this is even more the case because of the widespread nasal congestions of perceivers during wintertime. We don't feel as fresh and lively when deprived of our world of odors.

Sensorial Models and Terminology of Odor

Some investigators (Henning above all) have pointed out how crude and rudimentary our verbal expressions for odors and aromas are. Probably this is due to the poor differentiation of these very experiences. We have no trenchant words for "tones" or "tints" of olfactory qualities comparable to the distinct expressions for phenomenal colors. Direct *scent names* are virtually nonexistent. Olfactory qualities have to be expressed by referring to the objects connected in one way or another with the smells. One speaks of the scents of roses or lilacs or one possibly claims that a smell is that of a rotten egg.

The *verbal objectification* of smell experiences, their anchoring to the names of objects, is due to the following reasons:

---

[2] *Ibid.*, p. 9.

1. From a physical point of view, a smell is a more "substantial" event than is, e.g., light radiation.
2. Physiologically, a smell is closely tied up with a particular source of stimulation.
3. A smell impression is psychologically more concrete than an experience of color.
4. A "transposition" of expressions for smell like the transposition of tonal or color appearances would not make sense, would be perplexing.
5. Two "similar" smells would not be related in the way that colors with similar names are.
6. One can have color concepts or color ideas. Mental images of smells are amazingly weak, although we might be justified in speaking of after-sensations of odors.
7. Compared with vision, which represents some kind of luxurious complexity, smell is a biological, life-determined simple reality. It follows a kind of primitive *logic of striving* (in Brentano's sense), not a higher-level rational *logic of representation* (symbolic language).
8. The world of odors, unlike the world of colors, has not undergone a process of articulation which allows for separate names for objects and for the attributes ascribed to them.[3]

Henning presents the following list of smell "primaries":

Flowery, originating from flowers and plants.
Resinous, determined by balsam or odorous resins.
Fruity, which refers to gentle scents from fruits and wines.
Spicy, reminiscent of spices and roots.
Burnt, the smell of burning organic matter.
Foul, the smell of rotten and decayed tissue.

Aronsohn was bothered by the drawbacks of an "objectifying terminology," and developed a symbol system different from all other schemas. However, his code is so artificial and difficult to handle that it has not been generally accepted.

Smell experiences can be aroused by substances dissolved either in water or in the secretion of the nasal membranes. Exactly the same particles are said to have a *taste*, if in their dissolved state they encounter the receptor tissues in the mouth, in the throat, or around the nares posteriores. If they are to arouse olfactory experiences, substances must have some further chemical properties. It has been shown that most of them absorb ultraviolet spectral radiation. Extensive discussions have been carried out around the question of whether there exist some "odoriphora" or "aromatophora," i.e., some

---

[3] Hans Henning, *Der Geruch* (Leipzig: Barth, 1924), p. 63 ff.

common components in the chemical structure of substances that can produce olfactory stimulation. The psychophysics of odors might be described as an attempt to determine the stimulus correlates for different types of odors. Using what they call a similarity analysis of phenomenal smells, G. Ekman and his collaborators at the University of Stockholm have carried out investigations aiming at such a psychophysical system. Their work will be considered later in this presentation.

The older view was that particles of a substance responsible for stimulating the nasal membranes could be carried along only by *streams of air*. However, painstaking experiments have shown that water, too, can act as a mediating element. Yet probably a more favorable relation between the soluble substance and the solvent can be achieved if the former is inhaled as *dry particles*. In some cases a previously dissolved substance could even damage the olfactory region. According to Skramlik, a continuous constant smell experience cannot be maintained. The stimulus is sensed first during the stage of inhalation, then later during the exhalation of the same volume of air. The latter phase is especially significant for *taste* experiences. The perceptual qualities brought about by food or drink immediately as it enters the mouth are poor and monotonous. Flavor gains in richness and complexity from the olfactory stimuli present during the act of chewing or savoring. When the stream of air from the lungs transports particles of the substance from the throat into the nasal cavities during swallowing, these olfactory stimuli are added to the prevalent gustatory ones. The outcome is a complex total experience of flavor. That the expired air follows exactly the same route as the air when it is breathed in has been shown in careful experiments.

The localization of perceived smells is peculiar. Even if we abstain from objectifying odors, i.e., from referring them to objects which could act as smell sources, we never feel smells as actually located inside the nasal cavity. Even a very subjectively oriented person who does not refer the smell to anything outside himself nevertheless feels at least that it is *coming from outside the nostrils*. A patient suffering from a cold cannot sense the secretions of his infected nasal cavities *until they emerge outside his nose*. Conditions for smell experiences are optimal when the stimulus substance can fuse with the air in certain proportions. The "smell fields" of the nostrils are measurable as are the visual fields of the eyes. These receptor location fields for stimuli outside the nostrils are astonishingly narrow. This concept, presented by Zwaardemaker, should not be confused with the concept of "respiratory fields" (Atemfleck). If a small mirror is held close under the nostrils of a subject, the "respiratory fields" will appear as dim, moist spots on the mirror surface. By means of this method structural and functional differences between the two nostrils can easily be determined.

Theories of Smell

What goes on in the receptor tissue during the process of stimulation still remains an unsolved question. The situation is analogous to touch in at least one essential aspect. *Motion* of the stimulus field in relation to the receptor tissue is a *decisive* condition. *The layers of air must move across the olfactory area.* Simple diffusion and absorption of particles of a substance by the mucous tissues is insufficient as a stimulus condition. There are three prevalent theories concerning how stimuli affect the receptor field.

According to the first, the stimulus is analogous to light radiation, that is, it consists of particles emanating from the smell source. The second assumes that stimulation actually consists of direct chemical changes at the ends of the receptors. The third proposes a mechanism involving nonvisual electromagnetic radiation (ultraviolet or infrared) interacting with the inspired air after it has entered the nasal cavities.

The first assumption turns out to be too limited and one-sided. Olfactory stimuli differ in many respects from light energy. Odors travel with the wind, do not penetrate translucent membranes, and are not reflected from surrounding surfaces. They are greatly affected by temperature variations. The second assumption has been formulated more precisely by Kistiakowsky. According to him there are enzymes in the olfactory tissue in the presence of which the sensory fibers maintain their state of neutral equilibrium. Each stimulating smell substance has its specific inhibitory influence on one kind of enzyme. Presumably there are as many enzymes as there are discriminable fundamental smells. Put in this way the theory conforms well with the sensory physiology of olfaction. Its most serious difficulty lies in accounting for the amazing rapidity of initiation of smell impressions and their flexible adaptation to temporal conditions. The sensation does not appreciably outlast the stimulus, so far as can be judged. Geldard feels tempted to postulate a "gradient of absorption," not unlike the thermal gradient encountered in temperature sensation. The steepness of this gradient would depend on the velocity with which the odor-laden air strikes the olfactory area. Should this interpretation turn out to be correct, it would give us a further indication that gradients of stimulation are fundamental correlates of our phenomenal experiences, as postulated by modern psychophysics.

The third theory concerning olfactory stimulation presupposes an oscillatory interaction between the odorous vapors and the receptor tissue. That the molecules of the odorous substance are likely to undergo specific oscillations or vibrations has been assumed by several investigators. Each substance has a specific rate for absorbing light and temperature, and this rate is supposed to regulate the oscillations. A warm organism continuously emits infrared radiation, which would be absorbed at different rates by the oscillating molecules in accordance with their own specific absorption spectra. Such a mechanism would produce local cooling gradients of specific zones of the receptor tissue. The actual stimuli, according to this theory, would consist of temperature changes within relatively circumscribed parts of the receptor area. But this theory, too, runs into difficulties: there are substances with precisely equivalent absorption properties which nevertheless have easily distinguishable smells.[4]

The smell-producing capacity of a substance depends on the *vapor tension* it requires. To maintain its power as an olfactory stimulus, the substance must be suspended in vapor on an object surface. The more the vapor tension rises, the faster is the evaporation from the surface and the more effective is the olfactory stimulus. The intense smell of warm foods, excreta, etc., is a well-known fact. On the other hand, particles of substance can without difficulty condense on previously indifferent surfaces by decreasing the vapor tension in the situation. Every hunter knows that a dog does the best job of following its prey if the wind is still and the weather is slightly humid. Under these conditions, the odors of the game animal stick best to the shrubbery, the moss, and the ground. A dry, warm, and windy climate hastens evaporation, dissipates odors rapidly, and thus interferes with a prolonged chase. On the

[4] F. Geldard, *The Human Senses* (New York: John Wiley & Sons, Inc., 1953), pp. 291–94.

other hand, in very wet conditions the vapor tension remains so low that the watery ground binds the olfactory particles completely, and virtually no evaporation takes place.

Thresholds and Classification of Odors

Many odorous substances have a remarkably low *absolute threshold*. Even the human nose can sense incredibly small amounts of certain strongly odorous materials. We know that chemists often resort to their sense of smell when discriminating among different substances. Artificial musk is perceivable even if the inspired amount is only about 0.000000000003 g. It has been calculated that there need be only 1 molecule per 50 trillion molecules of air for

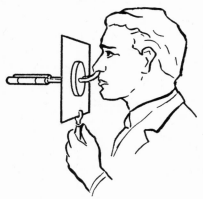

mercaptan to be detected. Diethyl ether (the anesthetic) has a threshold concentration of about 0.5 mg. per cubic meter of air.

Most determinations of smell thresholds were made with *Zwaardemaker's olfactometer* (Figure 7–1). It consists of a glass tube, open at both ends, over which is loosely slipped a hard rubber or plastic tube, the inner surface of which has been impregnated with an odorous material. A scale etched on the inner tube indicates

FIG. 7–1. The Zwaardemaker olfactometer.

the position of the outer one, and thus the amount of odor-bearing surface exposed to the stream of air created by the subject's inhalation. The instrument's scale may be calibrated in smell units, "*olfacties*," one olfactie being the number of centimeters exposed when the threshold is reached.

Many attempts have been made to classify odors on the basis of their phenomenal and physical characteristics. Most of these classifications have been theoretically dubious listings of impressions without clear reference to the physical correlates of smell experiences. The most serious effort was made by Henning in 1915. He created an analytic three-dimensional scheme known as the smell prism (Figure 7–2). Just like the color solid, this diagram, too, maps only "reduced," "pure" odors and neglects the immediate natural appearances of smells. It is a reduced system of "floating smells," just as the Ostwald system of sight concerned only "film colors." "We must be satisfied with such a description," Henning claimed, "if we are to achieve something like the level of color classification in the almost futile task of introducing some order into the vast multitude of smell experiences."[5] Henning's primaries have already been mentioned. These primary qualities are found at the corners: flowery, fruity, foul, spicy, resinous, and burnt. *Spicy* is, for example, a smell which gradually changes to resinous if one varies it along one dimension, and into flowery if it is varied along

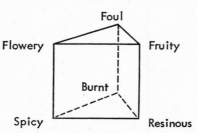

FIG. 7–2.   Henning's smell prism.

another dimension. Between *flowery* and *spicy* odors there are no qualitative, only gradual quantitative, differences. Henning's prism contains a number of undesirable implications. A Turkish oil of roses, for example, belongs not to the flowery but to the fruity class. Most important is the fact—as pointed out by Henning—that the system is phenomenal. The actual odor itself is important, not its verbal connotation. As raw material for the "oil of roses" just mentioned, orange peel has been used, not roses or other flowers as the *name* would make us believe. Between fruity and resinous we find the acetones and the turpentines. Odors lying along the *diagonal* lines should have four reference points, and they should form a sequence of gradually increasing similarity as either of the opposite corners is approached. Thus between foul and spicy there should be found the mediating qualities of onion, dill, celery, goats, and cheese, starting from the lower left corner and approaching the upper center one. Glue made from fish products ("syndeticon" glue) smells simultaneously resinous and foul. In the perceptual complex of a *burnt* smell, a prickling component is often included, because of the additional stimulation of the trigeminal nerve.

Let us briefly consider some of the research upon which Henning's system was based. Geldard rightly points out that it was developed partly from some experimental findings and partly from purely rational considerations.

Odorimetric measurements were performed on a sample of 20 subjects. The method of paired comparisons was employed. Among

[5] Henning, *op cit.*, p. 363.

the stimuli were 415 standard odorous chemicals and 51 additional commercial perfumes, mixed chemical substances, mixed drinks, and odorous household materials. The odorous liquids were poured into small bottles, from which outlet tubes led to the nostrils. Such an olfactometric apparatus can be constructed in two forms, single and double, for stimulation of one nostril (*monorhinic*) or of two simultaneously (*dirhinic*); same odor in both nostrils, or (*dichorhinic*), different odors in the two.

We probably can consider it analogous to the results from experiments on binocular vision and binaural hearing that the absolute and the recognition thresholds are lower for dirhine than for monorhine smell sensations. The difference is larger than that obtained in vision or audition. The vivid impression of reality disappears from the odors perceived in monorhinic experiments.

When tested monorhinically, most subjects can discriminate better with their left nostril than with their right one. This fact might reflect the *dominant role of the left hemisphere* in most human beings. As we know, the *olfactory tracts do not cross* at a subcortical level as do the optical tracts, at least in part. In this connection also, the asymmetric position of the septum and the differences in size between the two nostrils deserve some consideration.

Like other geometrical constructions, Henning's smell prism is subject to criticism from a physiological as well as from a psychological point of view. More significant than most superficial objections against it, however, is the fact that it represents a first productive attempt to depict the system of odors by means of a three-dimensional model like that used for phenomenal colors. Former criticism concentrated *either* on the point that the smell prism fails to represent the stimulus conditions *or* on the other point, that it is insufficient as a model of phenomenal odors. Geldard raises an essential objection in pointing to the intermodal complexity of most of our natural smell experiences. The question is not settled by simply referring to the failure of physiological experiments to establish the validity of the model. The smell prism cannot correspond to the system of stimulus relationships for the simple reason that it, like the color solid, was not intended to provide a model of stimulus constellations. What is worse is its failure to represent even the phenomenal system of perceived smells very well.

CHAPTER 8

Principles of Sensory Functioning and Interaction

The chapter on sensory evolution gave us an opportunity to consider some common principles of perceptual events which transcend the conventional borders separating various sense modalities. Now that we have reviewed the main functions of the different senses, it is feasible to pause and inspect systematically the instances of similar processes in, and cooperation among, these perceptual fields. Such an examination can provide the basis for a coherent model of our total phenomenal world.

STIMULUS BASIS OF SENSATIONS

Adequate stimuli for a sense organ are those which activate the receptors of the organ in the most effective and differentiated way. They are the proper, immediate, natural stimuli, such as light radiation for our eyes, sound waves for our ears, pressure and temperature variations for our skin receptors, and some soluble substances for the organs in the nose and mouth. It is well to remember, however, that all receptors tend to respond in their own particular way to almost all kinds of stimuli if they are at a sufficiently high intensity.

Inadequate stimuli are the other nonspecific ones. Electricity is an inadequate stimulus for most receptors. Johannes Müller's *law of specific nerve energies* provides an interesting formulation of this reciprocity between specialized sense organs and stimulus specifity. A little later we shall examine it more closely.

The relationship between stimulus and sensation has been described in the following way by Ekman:

1. The sense organs communicate to us only a very small portion of the physical reality of our environment.
2. This portion is communicated by the sense organs in a way which depends intimately upon the structure of these organs.[1]

Neural Transmission

The neural potentials initiated by receptor stimulation and the transmission phenomena connected with them have been thoroughly investigated during the last few decades. What goes on in the nerve fibers had remained rather obscure until recent years. Our knowledge has profited from the modern electrical methods employed by *neurophysiology*. One simply cannot ignore these findings in a chapter on the characteristics common to all of sensory activity. They shed clear light on the nature of the nerve impulses and of the process of neural stimulation. But they presuppose some orientation in the functions of any *living cell* in the organism. Let us consider especially the neural cells, which conduct impulses.

For neurophysiology the *membrane* is the most significant part of the cell. It segregates the *cytoplasm* and the *nucleus* of the cell from the environment. The membrane has regulative functions, maintaining a state of equilibrium between the inside and the outside of the cell. Physically speaking, it is *semipermeable* in that it permits some substances to pass through it while it prevents others from doing so. As a prototype of an entire living organism, the individual cell is astonishingly capable of self-regulation by means of something like *homeostatic* equilibration mechanisms. This regulative activity maintains an equilibrium between the inside and outside of the membrane with respect to temperature, fluid pressures (by means of osmotic interchange), and the concentration of positively and negatively charged ions on both sides of the membrane's surface.

Experiments have yielded evidence to support the view that the cell fluids act as electrolytes, within which ionized atoms move about and which are selectively admitted by the membrane. The state of *polarization* which is typical of a resting nerve fiber consists of antagonistically loaded ion concentrations (+ and − ions) facing each other on opposite sides of the membrane. If the membrane is slightly damaged somewhere, the potential is decreased and a so-called *depolarization* occurs, which implies a

---

[1] Gösta Ekman, *Psykologi* (Stockholm: Almqvist & Wiksell, 1953), pp. 38–39.

mutual neutralization of antagonistically loaded ions. These changes in outer and inner potentials can be measured with specially constructed refined instruments (Figure 8–1). Clearly, the polarization is an essential part of the vital function of a cell, and what we know as tonus phenomena in the body probably form its counterparts on a macroscopic level. The conditions of these bioelectric loadings and potentials are still not fully understood.

More important for the conductive property of neural cells than the above-mentioned *resting or injury potentials* are *action potentials*, which proceed along the membrane, following the "all-or-none" law. The energy consumed by the action potential comes from the neural tissue itself, the sensory stimulus serving only as a kind of trigger which disturbs the polarization. Thus the intensity of sensory stimulation affects only the number of simultaneously activated fibers and the density of successive action potentials. The action potential begins as a neutralization of the positive charge outside the membrane by negative ions streaming out to the surface. This disturbance of the equilibrium spreads to neighboring parts of the membrane by means of a local bioelectric current, producing a corresponding depolarization of adjacent parts of the membrane. Thus the "state of depolarization" travels along the entire fiber and even crosses over to subsequent neurons, initiating a continuous transmission through the network of connections. But it is important to note that through a chain of successive neurons the depolarization proceeds only in one direction from the originally stimulated spot. The propagated zone of depolarization is called the "absolute refractory period." It has a local duration of about 0.001 second, and corresponds to the strong, brief impulse, the so-called *spike potential*. During this state the fiber is completely insensitive. After this comes the "relative refractory period," several milliseconds in duration (Figure 8–2), in which the fiber can be discharged only by a stimulus that is stronger than usual. Neural transmission consists of a rapid series of successive action potentials.

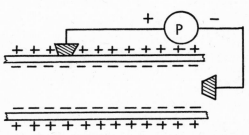

FIG. 8–1. Application of the electrodes when recording rest potentials.

Most of the methods used to measure these impulses and their density, i.e., the *impulse frequency*, were developed by the English neurophysiologist Adrian. He presented his techniques and their significance in his books *The Basis of Sensation* and *The Physical Background of Perception*. Records were taken from the optic nerve of the eel, from some frog motor neurons, and from touch fibers in the cat leg. The anaesthetized cat was decapitated, but respiration and circulation were artifically maintained so that the research worker could perform his measurements in living stimulated fibers. The neural impulses were amplified and led to a basin containing sulphuric acid in which a capillary tube with mercury stood vertically. The oscillations produced by the potentials caused the

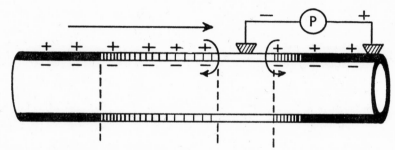

FIG. 8–2. Propagation of depolarization zones along a nerve fiber.

upper level of the mercury to rise and fall, yielding a vertical variation which could be recorded with a movie camera. The resulting graphs proved very similar irrespective of which nerves and which stimuli were employed. Whether or not adequate stimuli produced the impulse, if a fiber fired at all, the physiological record was the same as in all other conducting fibers—with variations only in frequency. The impulse is like an electric current in nature.

Undoubtedly the nerves conduct impulses in this way from the receptors to the brain and also through it and out to muscles and glands and, as a feedback process, down to the receptors again. The impulse frequency varies greatly with the intensity of stimulation, but the amplitude stays rather constant. The higher the stimulus intensity, the higher the impulse frequency—in other words, the denser the sequences of action potentials. If the stimulus intensity remains constant, the impulse frequency gradually decreases. If the stimulus intensity is increased very slowly, the nerve can "keep up" with this gradual change in the stimulus. No traveling spike potentials occur if the polarization equilibrium is promptly achieved without neighboring sections of the fiber being involved. To produce a spike, a sudden stimulus of sufficient intensity is required—a fact which is psychologically significant.

The clearest results were achieved by stimulating the isolated fiber electrically, but stimulation via the receptors by adequate stimuli produced essentially equivalent results. An unbroken continuous activation of the pathway is impossible; the impulses always appear as a series of successive instantaneous excitations, each impulse forming an isolated action potential of its own with clear cut absolute and relative refractory periods. Adrian illustrates the influence of stimulus intensity on impulse frequency by comparing

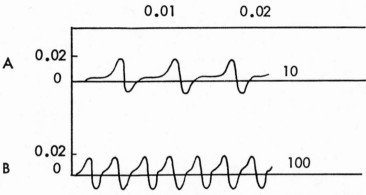

FIG. 8–3. Double-phase record showing the effect of the stimulus intensity on the impulses of a kinesthetic nerve of the frog.

two graphs recorded from the kinesthetic nerves of a frog. The muscle was stretched in the first instance (A in Figure 8–3) by a weight of 10 g., while in the second (B in the figure) a 100-g. weight was applied. Figure 8–3 shows the two records when the electrodes were placed outside, that is, on the surface of the fiber. The double-phase record becomes a single-phase one, as shown in Figure 8–4, if the fiber is damaged and one of the electrodes is inserted into the fiber.

From the point of view of visual perception, Adrian's experiments with the eel optic nerve are the most important. The eye and its neural pathways were dissected, and in a dark room, visual stimuli were projected on the living retina through a system of lenses. The results essentially confirmed earlier findings on neural conduction, but the visual fibers had a longer latency period as compared with, for example, the pressure sense, in which the first impulses fired much faster than in visual fibers.

After Adrian's pioneer studies, several research workers, especially Granit and Hartline, have continued with the electrophysiological investigation of the visual organs. They developed amazingly accurate methods by means of which they explored a range of animals at different phyletic levels. *Electroretinograms*, which are impulse sequences recorded directly from the eyeball and photographed on photosensitive bands, show some variations from one species to another. They nevertheless are essentially consistent with the results obtained by Adrian: they consist of series of electrical impulses varying in density. The frequency is maximal at the

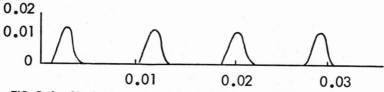

FIG. 8–4.   Single-phase record from the kinesthetic nerve of the frog.

initiation of stimulation. If the stimulation continues with unchanged intensity, the impulse frequency gradually becomes slower and smoother after only a few seconds (see Figure 8–5). However, the stimulus intensity does not affect the amplitude of the potentials, which remains fairly constant. The impulse frequency and latency are the only variables affected by variation of the stimulus.

When considering the basic functions of a living cell, we noted its capacity to *regulate itself*. The state of equilibrium inside the cell and between its inside and outside tends to remain as constant as possible, due to the physicochemical and electrolytic regulatory mechanisms. If the concentration of a substance in the cell's environment should increase greatly, the immediate result would be increased absorption of it through the cell membrane, followed by some kind of metabolic process such as its oxidation. Another consequence is an increase in the concentration of metabolic by-products inside the cell, followed by their excretion out into the cell's invironment. Thus the concentration of glucose, of oxygen, and of hydrogen ions in the cell's protoplasm remains constant within rather narrow limits.

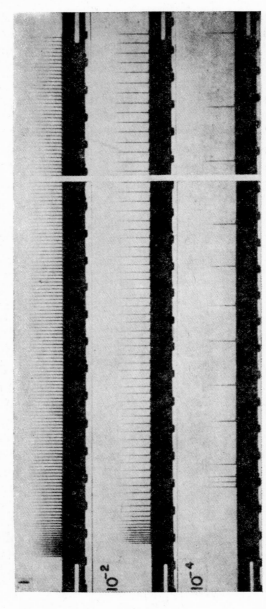

FIG. 8–5. Oscillograms showing the bursts of impulses in a single optic nerve fiber in response to short pulses of light of various intensities and durations. Relative intensity for each horizontal row is given on the left (1.0 = 3 × 10⁶ meter-candles). Signal of light pulse blackens the white line above the time marker (arrows mark position of signal for very short pulses). Time marked in ⅕ second (Hartline, 1934).

General Considerations about Threshold Phenomena

During the last few decades, investigators have inclined toward the view that regulation processes of this kind in receptor cells can serve to explain *threshold phenomena*. Hecht, the American physiologist, expresses this idea in the following way: biologically speaking, sensation is nothing but a loss of equilibrium within receptor cells. This statement, originally formulated in connection with the *photochemical theory of vision*, has, among others, the following implications. Stimuli produce external conditions which affect the inner state of equilibrium of the receptors. Because of its capacity of *self-regulation*, the cell responds with an antagonistic process, aimed at restoring the disturbed equilibrium. If this counterreaction is rapid enough to keep up with the consumption of energy caused by the initial input, the depolarization phenomenon stops without affecting enough of the cell to cause it to fire. No spikes and consequently no phenomenal percepts occur in such a case.

It has long been known by sensory physiologists that all receptor tissues require a stimulus intensity beyond a certain minimum if spikes are to be produced. Intensities below the minimum, even if applied for prolonged periods, are insufficient to result in sensory activity. The lowest intensity which can produce a sensation is called the *absolute sensory threshold* (minimum perceptible). Whenever this threshold intensity is reached, the antagonistic process in the receptor cells cannot keep up in restoring the equilibrium, and the result is a rapidly increasing density of spikes at higher stimulus intensities. At these intensities the spread of depolarization is not inhibited. The lower its absolute sensory threshold, the higher the *sensitivity* of a particular sense organ.

This threshold is not constant, but shows considerable individual variation. There are even differences among different parts of the same receptor tissue at any given time. The following representative threshold values have been obtained in several modalities. (The measurement unit is the *erg-second*, which is the energy required to move a mass of one milligram straight up one centimeter in one second.)

Most sensitive touch receptors, about . . . . 1/10,000 erg/sec.
Auditory receptors at middle frequencies, about . . . . . . 1/10,000,000 erg/sec.
Visual receptors stimulated by green light, about . . . . . 1/100,000,000 erg/sec.

Sensory thresholds can be determined and experimentally measured by the changes that stimulation produces in the organism's behavior. The changes need not be accompanied by conscious experiences. Conscious awareness generally requires a longer lasting or more intense stimulation. This is the reason for the introduction of the concept of the *threshold of recognition* (*Erkennungsschwelle*) or *threshold of perception* (*Wahrnehmungsschwelle*), or *threshold of awareness* (*Bewusstwerdungsschwelle*). Such terms have proved useful especially for dealing with stimulation of the sense of smell. Whenever these thresholds cannot be distinguished, there presumably are no noticeable differences as intensity is increased beyond a minimum, and then one can speak simply of the sensory threshold. Sometimes it appears reasonable to discriminate among *degrees of specificity* in thresholds. A person might sense a light without being clear about its color. Or one might sense some kind of strange color, whose clear identification is impossible below a certain threshold of intensity.

There is also an *upper threshold* or a *maximum perceptible*, that is, an intensity above which specific perceptions no longer occur. Although the stimulus continues to evoke a sensation, it loses its familiar character at these extremely high intensities, which are so strong that they may result in direct damage to the receptors. The sensory quality in this case is accompanied by new additional impressions, such as experiences of *pain* and *agony*.

The *differential threshold* or the just noticeable difference (jnd) is a concept which must not be confused with the absolute sensory threshold or the upper threshold. The differential threshold is the smallest *change in intensity* which can be noticed. If changes in stimulus intensity cannot be perceived, they are said to fall below the differential threshold: although the experimental subject continues to have sensations, because the stimulus is above the absolute sensory threshold, the sensation appears constant to him since the changes in intensity are too small for him to notice.

Differential thresholds can, however, be explained as special cases of the absolute sensory threshold. If a stimulus intensity reaches the level defined by the absolute threshold, the antagonistic process in the receptor cells, which has been overcome temporarily by the stimulus, gradually gains in effectiveness and *eventually compensates for the disturbance of the equilibrium*. At this stage *minimal variations in the intensity are not enough* to produce a loss of equilibrium and new phenomenal changes. Before resulting in a new sensation, different from that achieved at the absolute threshold intensity, a new minimum intensity limit must again be exceeded. It is this new minimum limit which is the differential threshold. *The stimulus intensity must be changed suddenly to overcome the compensation afforded by the antagonistic process, if the intensity variations are to be perceived.*

Weber's and Fechner's Laws

At an early stage of experimental psychology, in 1834, Weber showed that differential thresholds are roughly proportional to stimulus intensities. This fact can be expressed by the equation

$$\Delta R = kR$$

in which ΔR is the differential threshold, R is the original stimulus intensity, and k is a constant, the value of which varies from one modality to another and also from subject to subject. This formulation of Weber's observations was provided by Fechner, who called the functional relationship *Weber's law*. Sometimes it is called the Weber-Fechner law, which is misleading because there is another relationship between stimulus intensity and sensation which owes its name to Fechner.

Fechner's law states a systematic, measurable relation between the perceived and the physical intensity of the stimulus. Fechner's attempt rests on the assumptions that separate successive differential thresholds (ΔR) could be considered equal to the corresponding phenomenal units (ΔS), and that the sensation scale (S-scale) is metric and equidistant, that is, that all ΔS steps are subjectively equal. If S stands for any magnitude of sensation, C stands for the absolute threshold and k again is a constant, Fechner's law could be given the formulation

$$S = k \log R + C .$$

If one starts with the equation $\Delta S = k\Delta R/R$, which defines Fechner's concept of the "just noticeable difference," the above-mentioned logarithmic formula can be arrived at by means of integration.

Fechner's law is difficult to test empirically for the simple reason that there are no methods for determining whether two phenomenal

ΔS values are equal or how they are metrically related. The law has, accordingly, been widely criticized; Weber's law, however, has been rather generally accepted.

Although some perceptual investigators have looked askance at intermodal analogies, we are reasonably safe in assuming that, within certain limits, Weber's law generally holds true as a basic description of sensory function in all, or at least most, modalities. Most modern research methods, regardless of which modalities were investigated, have provided further empirical support for the law. We know that the law is valid in vision and hearing, with certain qualifications which will be discussed later. The same is true of the senses of pressure, touch, and kinesthesis. It is symptomatic that those modalities within which investigators cannot agree about the applicability of Weber's law happen to be precisely those which are least well explored and least well understood from a scientific point of view. Characteristically enough, Fröbes considers the law "dubious as far as smell and taste are concerned," while Skramlik in his huge handbook argues for the validity of the law for smell sensations, but doubts its general validity for the taste modality. Further, Skramlik cites Pütter's measurements of temperature sensation thresholds, which failed to follow Weber's law.

This brief orientation in the criticism which has been leveled at Weber's law again brings to mind the narrow and amazingly restricted interpretation of smell and taste experiences which characterizes Skramlik's works. If we recall the painstaking efforts of physiological psychologists to isolate all olfactory components from gustatory sensations and to accept as "taste" only something functionally restricted to the activity of the mouth, many of the alleged exceptions to Weber's law would hardly be surprising. How could one possibly try to derive the phenomenal complexity of an unarticulated perception from isolated "pure sensations"? We might safely presume that verification of Weber's law is apt to be more difficult the less differentiated the modality investigated, because it is in just these areas that the correspondence between perceptual experiences and their stimulus patterns has not as yet been successfully delineated.

The situation is somewhat different in the "higher senses." Not until Rubin's contributions appeared was it generally admitted that taste, psychologically defined, is the result of an interaction between the functions of smell rods and taste buds, a complex of olfactory and gustatory components. How, then, could the sense of smell be expected to conform to Weber's law at the same time that the sense of taste does not, which is what Skramlik assumed? If the stimulus correlates for neither of these modalities are clearly circumscribed, how could their stimulus conditions prove so different? One explanation might be that threshold measurements have been performed on isolated receptor units in accord with traditional physiological definitions. When exploring taste, investigators have generally confined themselves to stimulating only the inside of the mouth, and because of temperature factors they may have run across precisely the same rules as those formulated in research on the "isolated" temperature sense.

It is worth observing that, according to Skramlik, some investigators regard Pütter's law (based on threshold relationships in the temperature sense) as also valid for taste sensations. After showing that differential thresholds for temperature do not follow Weber's law, Pütter proposed replacing it with another, which has come to be known at Pütter's law: *The differential threshold is an exponential function of the stimulus intensity.* Repetition of Pütter's experiments with modern methods is urgently needed. As long as that remains undone, we had better face the possibility that thermal thresholds diverge from Weber's law.[2]

As already pointed out, Fechner's law is based on rather suspi-

---

[2] The whole discussion of Weber's and Fechner's laws has come into a new phase after Stevens published the equation of his *power law* (1962). He too proposes a single general psychophysical law for the relation between increments in the intensity of the stimulus and the sensory differential threshold. This relation, according to his experiments, proves to have something other than the logarithmic shape postulated in Fechner's law (cf. above p. 169), rather it is a power function. This psychophysical power law can be written:

$$\psi = k(\phi - \phi_0)^n$$

It relates the psychological magnitude ψ to the physical stimulus ϕ; k in the equation is a constant determined by the choice of units, and the exponent n varies with such parameters as adaptation and contrast. Defined in this way, the relation appears surprisingly simple: if data are plotted on log coordinates, the power function results in all points falling on a straight line. Throughout a wide variety of sensory judgments in many different modalities (electric shock, warmth and cold, weights held in the hand, vibration, pressure, pitch, and brightness discrimination), Stevens was able to demonstrate the linearity of his data, employing a method of magnitude estimation: the subjects reported verbally on the subjective magnitude of the stimuli by assigning numbers of them. Furthermore, in an interesting series of cross-modal validations, Stevens had his subjects match the force of their handgrip alternately to warmth, to pressure, to noise, and to light intensities, always ending up with the same law, with variations only in the value of n for different modalities.

cious assumptions. It is nothing but artificial to substitute phenomenal entities like ΔS for increased levels of intensity (ΔR). The likelihood that a scale like ΔS, $2\Delta S$, $3\Delta S$, etc., has equal intervals is very low indeed. While Fechner's law is speculative, Weber's law is purely empirical.

Hecht's Work

More than 30 years ago Hecht, on the basis of neurophysiological discoveries about the photosensitive processes in visual receptors, formulated a far-reaching theory of the fundamental events that

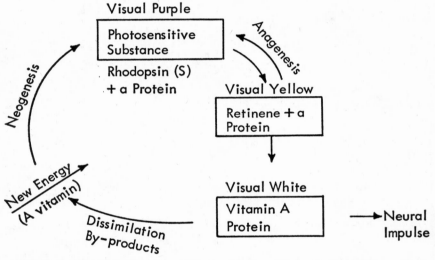

FIG. 8–6. Wald's explanation of the metabolic cycle in photosensitive cells.

occur in receptive tissues. According to him, the facts of thresholds, Weber's law, adaptation phenomena, Talbot's law, etc., could all be regarded as reflections of a broadly uniform chain of events. There is every reason to inspect his theory more closely, especially in regard to the up-to-date interpretation of Weber's observations.

Hecht chose as his starting point Wald's description of the absorption functions of *rhodopsin*, the photosensitive substance in the rods. The metabolic cycle from visual purple or rhodopsin to by-products, enzymes, and regenerative substances, as proposed schematically by Wald, is shown in Figure 8–6.

Under the influence of light the visual purple (S) is first decomposed into *visual yellow* and *visual white*. *Retinene*, one of the components of visual yellow, is produced only in the dark-adapted retina. Light adaptation produces a comparable amount of vitamin A. Wald has therefore concluded that the retinene is always capable of being transformed into vitamin A. The regeneration of rhodopsin *S* requires a process working in the opposite direction (anagenesis):

Vitamin A—retinene (visual yellow)—rhodopsin (visual purple)

As soon as the vitamin A has played its role in contributing to neural activation, it breaks down and dissipates. The organism must constantly replace the vitamin from outside sources. It is clear that visual purple does not function as the immediate initiator of the nerve impulses. The actual firing is probably triggered by visual yellow. If a dark-adapted eye is momentarily dazzled by a flash of light, the dark adaptation is restored in a relatively brief time by a process of anagenesis. Prolonged exposure to light would require an elaborate *neogenesis* to compensate for the absorbed substances. This slower building-up process results in a longer adaptation time for the receptors. After a momentary flash of light, some surplus retinene usually remains available, immediately ready to be absorbed as soon as the light is off.

Hecht generalized Wald's observations to *all* receptor activity, suggesting that the same prototypic equilibrium governs all living receptor cells

$$S \rightleftharpoons P + A.$$

During equilibrium the antagonistic process compensates fully for the breakdown of the substance *S* into its components. Psychologically speaking, this means that under these conditions no perceptual process is initiated. A stimulus sufficiently intense to speed up the breakdown process is required to produce a percept. When the breakdown process achieves a sufficiently high rate, the antagonistic process is incapable of compensating for it because of accumulating intermediate and waste products which gradually disappear from the picture.

Hecht's interesting suggestions need not by any means be limited to photochemical receptors. He explicitly states,

Any outside agency will have a threshold when its primary effect is accompanied by another process which removes or inactivates the effects of the primary process. Obviously this can happen in the mechanical stimulation of the ear and in the electrical stimulation of nerve. . . .[3]

Moreover, Hecht stresses the significance of thresholds as a general physiological fact. There are even thresholds in functions other than those of the sensory apparatus.

Hecht's method is rather convincing. Starting with some axioms based on our present knowledge about the structure of the visual cells, about processes involving visual purple, and about various other functions of retinal tissue, Hecht constructed some mathematical formulas which predict, for example, the expected threshold values for the new states of equilibrium achieved when previous intensity thresholds are exceeded. Hecht tested his formulas with painstaking experiments—at first investigating the photosensitive organ of the clam (*Mya arenaria*), later measuring thresholds and adaptation levels on the human eye. His experimentally obtained values generally confirmed his hypothetically calculated values surprisingly well. The main significance of Hecht's research lies in the fact that from the *same* relatively simple *basic hypothesis* he managed to derive a wide variety of regularities in sensory functioning. The core of his explanation consists of the assumption that thresholds depend on two antagonistic processes which maintain a mutual equilibrium. The same fundamental rules are encountered everywhere; the theory of thresholds can be considered a *universal* explanation.

Figure 8–7 summarizes the data of four separate investigations of light intensity discrimination over the total illumination range visible to the eye. The abscissae show logarithms of adapting intensity (in millilamberts); the ordinates, the ratio $\Delta I/I$. Theoretically, the relation between $\Delta I/I$ (ordinates) and Log I (abscissae) yields the curves in Figure 8–8 as computed from Hecht's equation

$$\Delta I/I = \left(\frac{X_2}{X_1}\right)^n \left(\frac{a - X_1}{a - X_2}\right)^m - 1$$

in which X_1 is the original concentration of photoproducts and X_2 the concentration after the increase in stimulus intensity. Given for the curves are different values of $X_2 - X_1$. In the equation a stands for the initial concentration of the photosensitive material, and m

[3] S. Hecht, "The Nature of the Photoreceptor Process" in C. Murchison (ed.), *Handbook of General Experimental Psychology* (Worcester, Mass.: Clark University Press, 1934), p. 712.

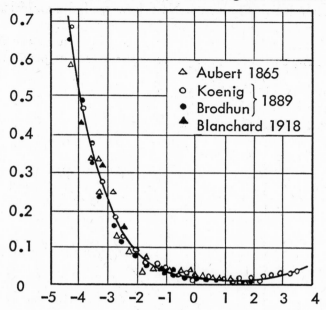

FIG. 8–7. Intensity discrimination over the total illumination range.

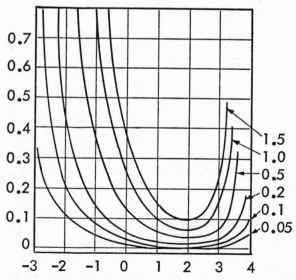

FIG. 8–8. Theoretical curves conforming to the empirical ones in Fig. 8–7.

and n are velocity exponents. Note how well the empirical curve conforms to the theoretical curve of parameter 0.05.

The Finnish chemist Erämetsä has developed a new formula for Weber's law, based essentially on measurements he performed with

Threshold unit = percent of
the maximum intensity of
the Pulfrich photometer

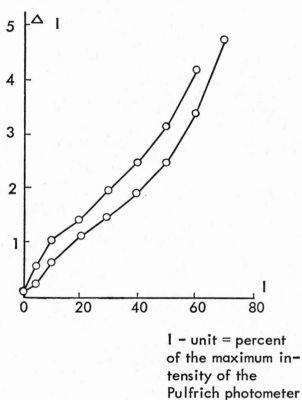

I - unit = percent
of the maximum in-
tensity of the
Pulfrich photometer

FIG. 8–9. Two examples of the differential threshold function (Erämetsä).

a Pulfrich photometer. His calculation of the events in the visual cells uses an analogy with the function of a Geiger-Müller computer. Like Fechner, he defines a secondary set of differential thresholds, which are thought of as "phenomenal units," S, and which correspond with the impulse units of the computer. His theoretical model, as well as the derivation of his formula, is therefore subject to the same criticism as that leveled above at Fechner's law. Erämetsä's empirical finding diverges from the usual differential threshold function mainly in the initial form of its ascending slope. His curves are initially concave, then show a quite short convex slope until they turn concave again. Figure 8–9 shows two individual examples from his material. He reports considerable individual differences due in part at least to personality characteristics of the subjects. A more detailed survey is given in his paper, published in *Acta Polytechnica Scandinavica*.[4]

ADAPTATION

In discussing the recorded neural spike potentials published by Adrian and his successors, we observed that the highest impulse frequencies occur at the start of the recorded reaction, immediately after the initiation of the stimulation. The frequency of spikes per unit time thereafter gradually reduces to a slower, yet relatively constant, rhythm if the intensity continues unchanged. After a while there is still a further gradual loss of frequency. The higher the stimulus intensity, the longer is the initial period of very high frequency firing. After a momentary intense stimulation, the densest part of the firing sequence lasts longer than it does after a relatively weak stimulation of the same duration. Furthermore, the time between the initial application of the stimulus and the appearance of the first spike potentials, i.e., the *latency*, varies with the stimulus intensity. This period is shorter the more intense the stimulus. In these processes, in the necessity of a period of latency as well as in the gradual transformation of the originally high impulse frequency, the highly developed organism reveals itself as fairly delayed in its mode of reaction. The sensory processes often need to warm up, as it were, but are apt to continue their activity beyond the termination of the stimulation. On the other hand, as has been shown experimentally, it is possible to increase the stimulus intensity without arousing any spike potentials if the increase is sufficiently slow and gradual. In such a case the organism is said to *adapt* to the gradual changes in the environment. The differences in the resting potentials are insufficient to fire the impulse sequences and the antagonistic process manages to compensate for the slight depolarization.

---

[4] O. Erämetsä, "The Principles of Visual Measurements," *Acta Polytechnica Scandinavica* (*Ph. 18, 317/1962*) (Helsinki, 1962).

Both rapid immediate adaptation and the delayed longer lasting adjustment have their biological significance, which varies with the phylogenetic and ontogenetic level of the individual organism. The more primitive the organ or the organism, the faster is the reaction to the stimulus. Reaction times of insects are of the order of magnitude of 0.003 second, a fact not surprising to anyone who has ever tried to catch a fly. The more differentiated the organism, the larger the number of way stations along the neural pathways and the slower the reaction. Different parts of the human organism exhibit corresponding differences, such as those among sense modalities. Relatively poorly differentiated modalities, such as smell and taste, have a high transmission rate but also show weaker and shorter lasting aftereffects. Phenomena corresponding to physiological afterimages are at best poor; it is also more difficult to rate the intensity of the stimulus after it has terminated. The highly differentiated structure of the human eye is related to a prolonged reaction time of visual tissue, and it is precisely this slower adaptation which makes it possible to judge the intensities of visual stimuli more accurately and to compare the different aspects of stimulus variations better than can be done in other modalities. An increase of about 30 percent in stimulus intensity is required to produce a phenomenal change in the strength of an odor, but only a 1 percent change suffices for a visual stimulus. A slow adaptation is also characteristic of muscle proprioceptors; thus we continue to perceive even slight changes in our position for a relatively long time. The adaptation of touch receptors to clothing, as is familiar to everyone, is such that we normally notice the pressure of our clothes only if we test it with intentional movements.

The speed of adaptation is vitally important for many species which must react promptly to *sudden changes* in their environment. More differentiated organisms, on the other hand, interrelate experiences from different modalities so that there is not necessarily a reaction to every haphazard stimulus. The organism may wait and collect information through several modalities until the time comes to react in an adaptive way to the changes in the situation facing it.

Adaptation might therefore be considered a tendency to withhold reaction to continuous stimuli which do not change enough to exceed the differential threshold. In primitive animals this failure to react may characterize the total organism, in higher animals generally only the receptor tissue. The organism behaves, in a sense, as if a part of the receptor tissue were satiated by the continuously invariant stimulus (which would be consistent with Hecht's ideas about how the chemical processes enter upon a new state of equilibrium that involves a higher differential threshold than before). This locally reduced sensitivity can, however, be restored by a movement of the stimulus pattern relative to the receptors or a movement of the receptor field in relation to the stimuli. When a tidbit is savored with the gustatory receptors, it is moved along the mucous membranes of the mouth; when we look at colors, the satiation effect of staring is avoided by moving the eyes; and being aware of the touch of our clothes requires appropriate movements because an invariant, unmoving stimulation of the skin surface rapidly leads to adaptation. According to recent investigations, satiation phenomena in receptor cells and nerves are similar to the metabolic processes of muscular fatigue.

After considering these general biological aspects, we should be more specific and look at a few examples of research on adaptation. Visual dark and light adaptation provide good illustrations.

When a room is suddenly darkened, we first see nothing at all. We are surrounded by a diffuse unarticulated darkness. After a while weak illumination differences appear. As dark adaptation proceeds, the threshold of stimulation drops, and light sensitivity improves. The adaptation is slow at first, but then speeds up again after about 10 minutes, followed once more by a retardation, which after another 20 minutes or so reaches a fairly constant asymptote. In the dark-adapted human eye the threshold drop is so enormous that, according to Piper, sensitivity improves by a factor of 8,000. Already in the first three minutes, sensitivity reaches 1,000 times its original value. After half an hour the absolute threshold is down to 0.0001 of the threshold intensity for the light-adapted eye.

When we enter the outdoor bright environment from a dark room at noon, we at first see no objects, because all stimuli initially exceed the upper threshold. We are just dazzled. Only after the eyes have adapted to daylight do we start perceiving objects distinctly.

Earlier investigators thought that light and dark adaptation could be explained as due to a delay in the function of rods and cones, caused by the division of labor assumed to exist between them. At the moment when a different set of receptors "takes over," some "inertia" could be expected to occur. It is well known that cones are mainly responsible for daylight vision and rods for vision in darkness. In sensory physiology, as we pointed out in Chapter 3 this explanation is known as the "duplicity theory."

More recently, numerous experiments have demonstrated that the light-sensitive substance is not immediately available in the rods as soon as stimulation at high daylight intensities ceases. This state of affairs could have been predicted from Weber's law. For a long time the necessary warm-up period of the rods could not be satisfactorily explained. It was thought of as a "property of the rods," much as "ease" and "heaviness" were considered "attributes" of objects in the Aristotelian mode of thought. During the last decades, and most convincingly as a consequence of Hecht's research, it has become quite clear that the most essential role in the adaptation to darkness or to light is not played by the division of labor between rods and cones but rather by the fact that, *whether it is in the rods or in the cones, the threshold phenomenon produces a comparable process of adaptation.* The only difference seems to be that the adaptation of the cones occurs much faster than that of the rods. This difference cannot be observed at low intensities. The decline of the threshold has the same general form in all visual receptors, and the threshold curves are all comparable in shape.

At the outset, only the performance of the rods was examined because the fact of adaptation was ascribed to them. The first experiments were quite crude and were able to detect only changes in the rods even when the measurements aimed at "mapping" the retina as a whole. The first investigator to make systematic observations concerning the increased sensitivity of the eyes in darkness was Aubert (1865), who greatly influenced Schultze. After him measurements were carried out especially by Piper (1903) and Nagel (1911). Already in this early phase is seemed possible to interpret the obtained curves of thresholds as a function of amount of time in the dark as composed of two temporally separable reductions in the threshold intensity. If we compare Piper's results (Figure 8–10) with those of Hecht and Wald (Figure 8–11), the characteristic difference in the shapes of the curves is immediately observable. The abscissae show time (in minutes) after entering total darkness, the ordinates the absolute threshold (in log values of the measured intensity). Piper's results suggest a continuous decline of the threshold values. The fall is steeper at first and more gradual after a few minutes. Hecht and his collaborators suggested that thresholds for the entire receptor tissue should be measured as soon as possible after the end of the preadaptation exposure to light.

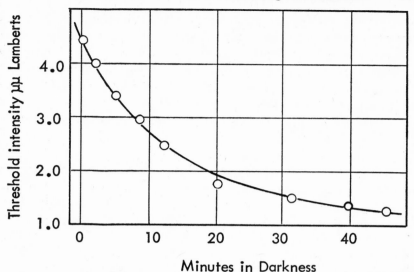

FIG. 8–10. Dark adaptation of the human eye as measured on the rods (Piper).

If this strategy is followed, curves with two distinct legs can be obtained. The slope of the adaptation function for times exceeding 30 minutes has been investigated by Achmatov (1930), Kohl-

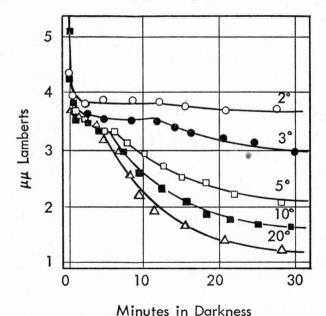

FIG. 8–11. Results of Hecht and Wald with the method of Kohlrausch.

rausch (1922, 1931), Dieter (1929), Sheard (1944), and others, who found that the absolute threshold continues to fall up to 25 percent further than the level it reaches during the first 30 minutes if the experiment is carried out for 24 hours. The curves in the figure represent the declines of thresholds, using test circles of light subtending 2°, 3°, 5°, 10°, and 20° of visual angle.

If the steeper initial part of a two-phase adaptation curve is considered a function of the adjustment of the cones and the second flatter part a function of rod adaptation, we may ask why changing the size of the fixated area produces differences in the

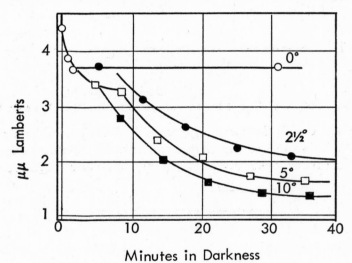

Minutes in Darkness

FIG. 8–12.   Dark adaptation of a 2° stimulation area at different distances from the fovea.

shape of the curve (Figure 8–11). As the test patch area increases, the cone leg drops further, indicating a greater sensitivity. Furthermore, the rod portion of the curve sets in earlier, the larger the fixated area.

As pointed out by Saugstad and Saugstad, the *size of the area* as such is not significant; what counts is *how far it extends beyond the fovea*. If the experiment is repeated with only a single stimulus area size, the 2° one, but the position of this stimulus is varied so that it is presented at different distances from the fovea, one obtains a family of curves highly similar to those from the previous experiment (Hecht, Haig, and Wald, Figure 8–12). The increase in the sensitivity of cones farther out in the periphery cannot possibly be explained by an increase in their number, since there are actually fewer of them. Probably both types of receptors support each other, at least in part.[5]

Early research concentrated primarily on peripheral reactions. It was only later that the *dark adaptation of the fovea* itself became an object of systematic investigation. Among the first investigators, however, were Nagel and Schaefer, who had already shown in 1904, 1911, and 1912 that adaptation also occurs in the fovea proper. Yet their results were incomplete and scientifically unsatisfactory. It was not until 20 years after Piper's contributions that Hecht carried out the first reliable measurements (1921–22) of the dark adaptation of the fovea. The method involved stimuli of very pure, long-wave red light which presumably cannot affect the rods. His results indicated that the dark adaptation of the fovea is extremely rapid, the process being complete in only a few minutes, a rapidity comparable to the speed of light adaptation when the subject is moved suddenly from a dark room into sunlight. That light adaptation should occur very rapidly indeed sounds quite reasonable when we consider that it is primarily a matter of foveal adaptation.

Starting with observations like these, Kohlrausch (1922, 1931) demonstrated experimentally that two phases must be distinguished in the dark adaptation of the human retina. His measurements were done on the peripheral cells of the fovea, thus involving both cones and rods. He obtained adaptation curves which showed an initial cone adaptation leg, followed after a clear-cut break by a phase of rod adaptation. In Kohlrausch's experiments the light stimulus subtended 1° of visual angle, and it was shown at most at a distance of 5° outside the fovea. With red stimuli the break occurred later than with blue ones, and the location of the break clearly affected the remainder of the curve, which lasted correspondingly longer or shorter (Figure 8–13). Hecht and Yun Hsia experimentally demonstrated in 1945 that the rods are not really insensitive to red light but that they may even be slightly more sensitive to it than cones. These findings would make us expect that a curve of red thresholds for rods, if it could be obtained, should follow approximately the cone curve. Recently adaptation curves have been recorded electroretinographically directly from the receptor tissue. Some of these,

---

[5] P. Saugstad and A. Saugstad, "The Duplicity Theory: An Evaluation," *Fortschritte der Augenheilkunde-Advances in Ophthalmology-Progrés en Ophthalmologie*, 9 (Basel–New York, 1959), pp. 44–45.

obtained on the frog retina, were reproduced by Morgan, and clearly confirm Kohlrausch's earlier results. Even the levels of sugar and oxygen in the blood have been shown to affect the shape of the curve. Adaptation is more rapid at higher concentrations of these chemicals in the blood, as it generally is during phases of increased metabolism. Differences in the rate of adaptation may depend, e.g.,

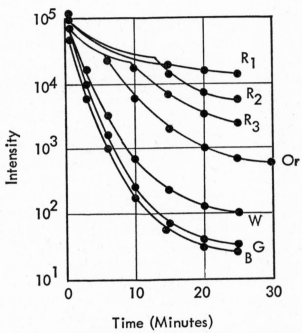

FIG. 8–13. Kohlrausch's experiments on foveal adaptation. R = red; Or = orange; W = white; G = green; and B = blue.

on whether the subject did or did not have his breakfast before the experiment was begun.[6]

These facts again support Hecht's photochemical theory of adaptation. According to him the following explanation may be offered for visual light adaptation. A sudden increase in the light intensity brings about a breakdown of rhodopsin at a higher speed than the antagonistic reaction can keep up with, the amount of rhodopsin in receptor tissue which is in equilibrium being proportional to the threshold intensity. The level of the absolute threshold,

---

[6] Saugstad and Saugstad, *op. cit.*, pp. 17–21.

according to Hecht, directly indicates the amount of rhodopsin available. The greater the sudden increase in light intensity, the longer is the temporary lag suffered by the compensatory antagonistic process. Gradually the regenerative process gains ground, and at an accelerating rate it finally restores the equilibrium. One observable effect is the rise of the threshold. At high metabolic rates all these organic processes are speeded up.

Recent Studies in Sensitivity and Adaptation

The rate of adaptation is also influenced by the emotional state of the subject. In some investigations reported by Eysenck, it was shown that neurotics take longer to achieve dark adaptation. It is tempting to regard these results, too, as outcomes of differences in metabolic rate, for neurotic disorder may well involve a reduction in metabolic efficiency.

The influence of *motivational states* on visual *thresholds* was studied by L. A. Shvarts in 1953 at the Teplov Laboratory in Moscow. After the subjects had been placed in darkness they were allowed a 50-minute period for dark adaptation. A Kravkov adaptometer was used in order to determine the thresholds for recognizing shapes of a series of figures from so-called Snellen charts. All the figures were equal in size and they could be presented in four different positions. The figure to be recognized was mounted on a rotating disc. The description given by the author goes as follows:[7]

The illumination of the stimuli could be varied by means of a diaphragm from a point at which the letter stood out clearly to a point when not even a white patch was visible to the untrained eye. A value, inversely proportional to the amount of light admitted by the diaphragm, was taken as a comparative measure of the sensitivity of peripheral vision. Thresholds for recognition of the shapes were defined by the minimal illumination at which the subject could distinguish the letter presented at a given distance.

In each experiment there were 40 stimuli. The order in which they were presented was changed from one experiment to another. The investigator noted the correctness or otherwise of the subject's answers, and the time elapsing between stimulus presentation and response.

From the point of view of psychometrics one could strongly criticize the author's method of computing his threshold values. We

[7] L. A. Shvarts, "Raising the Sensitivity of the Visual Analyser," in B. Simon (ed.), *Psychology in the Soviet Union* (Stanford, Calif.: Stanford University Press, 1957), p. 101.

know that with increasing sensitivity the original threshold goes down. As the relationship between *jnd*'s and the stimulus intensity, however, is never linear, the author probably has not been quite justified in his taking 100 percent as the index of "the level of sensitivity at the beginning of series *I*" as he reports having done. He could have computed an equation for scaling *jnd*'s. Instead, he has been operating with changes in the original basic level of illumination, which changes in terms of a logarithmic scale if the *jnd*'s are following a constant scale. Because the intensity of the illumination can be reduced from the original level as a consequence of his experiment, and because he keeps recording *values inversely proportional to the amount of light admitted by the diaphragm*, he ends up with tremendously increasing percent-values. One could object to his taking 100 percent as the index of the original value of sensitivity.

Probably all percentages given by Shvarts should be transformed into a scale of *jnd*'s or into a logarithmic scale of *I*'s in order to work out properly. In the following, however, we are going to quote his descriptions.

During the first session the subject was given no feedback about whether his answers had been right or wrong. He simply was asked to try his best in continuously lower illumination. The recognition threshold dropped an average of 40 percent. In the second session the subjects were informed about whether their answers were right or wrong. Sensitivity improved by 170 percent up to a level of 310 percent better than the standard intensity. During the third session the subjects were punished by weak electric shocks for wrong answers. Sensitivity increased again, this time by 160 percent, and remained at the level of 470 percent without rising further with a long series of trials.

In the fourth session the subjects were informed about the progress they had made in sensitivity and were given new goals to try to achieve after reaching earlier ones. Sensitivity improved again at an average of 375 percent, or a rise from 470 to 845 percent. The improvement took longer than before, the highest values requiring 300 presentations, while the corresponding numbers of presentations were 25–30 for the first session, 230–250 for the second, and 55–65 for the third.

In the fourth session "all subjects were active and interested in their results, and tried to reach their goals as fast as they could." A retest after a period of five months still yielded a sensitivity of 830 percent better than the initial intensity.

With a second group of subjects the first session was performed in the same way as before. Sensitivity improved by 50 percent. Thereafter the procedure of the fourth session of the first group was used with this new group. Now the subjects were immediately given goals to try to achieve, the next goal always higher than the preceding one. Sensitivity finally went up to 1,200 percent! This ascending trend continued for 570 presentations. Despite the accumulated experience with the stimuli in the first group, the second one did even better. A third group, whose sensitivity again improved by 50 percent during its first session, was thereafter presented with an "easy goal session," that is, with clearly defined, more easily achieved intermediate goals. This session brought sensitivity up by 150 percent, ending at 330 percent. Next, the last session given the two earlier groups (the original fourth session) was used with this third group. It improved its sensitivity further by 920 percent, up to a level of 1,250. Thus, even the challenge of the task seemed to influence the improvement in sensitivity. In addition to generally favorable motivation, the level of effort is decisive for progressively better performance.

Shvarts sums up:

1. New cues for recognition apparently are available at lower levels of illumination, which shows the increased influence of the cortex in the process of recognition.
2. In very weak illumination the cortex displays an increasing alertness.
3. Changes in the motivating procedure produced results exceeding the previous extreme threshold.
4. Most effective was the setting of new goals in addition to providing information about the correctness of the answers.
5. The improved sensitivity seems to be relatively permanent and to transfer to analogous stimulus situations.

Before coming to final conclusions from the highly striking data given by Shvarts, there remains the task of checking the effect of a quite natural training process as a consequence of repeating the same test figures several hundred times. Although they varied in order, there were consistently only four alternatives to be looked for. This training effect could easily have been proved in a more affirmative way than that shown by Shvarts, by simply repeating a series of Snellen's figures in ordinary daylight without introducing dark adaptation at all.

In 1953 Blackwell published a sensational experimental investigation of methodological factors which can greatly improve the differential thresholds for brightness.[8] He employed two parallel methods, *phenomenal report* and *forced choice*. A relatively large field of brightness *Bo* was presented continuously and served as a background brightness. From time to time a small increment of brightness, Δ*B*, was added to *Bo* over a small portion of the field for a brief period of time.

In the phenomenal report situation the brightness increment, a circular light spot subtending 18.5 minutes of visual angle at the subject's eye, and varying in luminosity, was always projected 7° to the right (east) of the center of the background. The subject had simply to report whether or not he had noticed the Δ*B*. In the forced choice situation the spot rotated on the background, flashing four times during each turn (at compass points, N, E, S, and W). The subject had to report at which location the increment was most likely to have occurred. It turned out that when this "indirect method" was applied, not only was the threshold far lower, but the variability of the threshold estimations decreased, and there was also a greater reliability than in the "yes-no" data. Blackwell suggests that his procedure should be generally applied as a new method for threshold measurement.

INTERACTION OF MODALITIES

Is there an interaction paradox? Müller's law of specific nerve energies (1826) has been mentioned before. It implies that all sensory organs are tuned to react in their own specific way even to inadequate stimuli. There are some ancient observations concerning this phenomenon. Even Aristotle mentioned that a sensation of light can be aroused by mechanical stimulation of the eye. Sulzer (1752) reported that electricity gives a "taste," and Volta specifically referred to the qualities it can evoke when applied as an inadequate stimulus. The Czech Purkinje (1823) thoroughly described the visual phenomena produced by mechanical, electrical, and organic stimuli. A theoretical controversy later developed around these questions because of the rather strict and literal interpretation which before long was given to Müller's law. This view has been called the *modality axiom*. According to it the various modalities work independently of each other, obeying their specific laws of

---

[8] H. R. Blackwell, *Psychophysical Thresholds. Experimental Studies of Methods of Measurement* (Engineering Research Institute Bulletin No 36) (Ann Arbor: University of Michigan, 1953).

stimulation. As though pigeonholed, the senses are seen as completely isolated and incapable of mediating anything other than their specific types of messages, each its own. It was especially the authority of Helmholtz which helped to consolidate this viewpoint. Let us remember the assumption underlying Helmholtz' color theory: different hues are developed on the basis of stimulations mediated by specific different fibers. His theory of hearing, too, is based on the assumption of separate and specifically tuned fibers in the cochlea. Henning's theory of olfaction, in assuming groups of separately stimulated receptors, comes rather close to Helmholtz' explanation. This general view, gradually developed by several investigators, could briefly be labeled the *theory of specific nerve fibers*. It is worthwhile to give some consideration to the controversies it has engendered.

Psychologists who tend to base their approach on an analysis of the phenomenal facets of our perceptions, such as Rubin and to some extent Katz too, have belittled the significance of the theory of specific nerve fibers from the point of view of *psychological* explanation. They stress common sense observations from our everyday life, which tend instead to yield instances of astonishing interaction and immediate cooperation across the conventional boundaries of sense modalities. From a traditional point of view, it is a case of what one could call an *interaction paradox* in the operation of the sense modalities.

As an example, Rubin (1934) considered the views concerning the sense of *taste* commonly held by scientists. The experience of flavors is a psychological fact, although investigators have been inclined toward descriptions in terms of clear-cut separate specific modalities, treating smell and taste as isolated senses. Rubin begins his paper with a severe criticism of this prevailing view. He remarks that research workers always tend to limit the number of specific tastes, implying only four: *sweet, sour, salty,* and *bitter*. Earlier investigators such as Linnaeus are mostly criticized for having listed as many as 7 to 10 categories of taste, but according to Rubin, their chief mistake was that they still had too *few* instead of too many of them.

The fact that scientists resort to four taste primaries must, Rubin claims, be due to the finding that our taste sensations are specific to various local areas inside the mouth cavity. We *sense* sweet, sour, salty, and bitter with different parts of the mouth. This physiological fact has led to two misunderstandings concerning taste perception:

1. The specific receptors for taste are located exclusively in the mouth cavity.
2. What we usually consider "tastes" are perceptual contents not mediated by the sense of taste as such, but which (except for the above-mentioned four taste primaries) depend on simultaneous activity of the senses of smell and of touch.

If this scientific view were to be taken literally, Rubin goes on, one would come to a number of strange conclusions. Vanilla, strawberry, and chocolate ice cream should all be said to *taste* the same, because all of them stimulate only the *sweet* receptors. But since we notice different flavors when enjoying these desserts, we would be forced to ascribe the differences to other senses. Maybe to different odors? Furthermore, a cup of tea with sugar, a candy cane, and all three kinds of ice cream should be regarded as equal in *taste:* they are all sweet. We would have to say that bouillon and cheese *taste* alike: they are both salty. And it would be impossible to say that a rotten egg *tastes* bad. What is bad is only the smell component.

Rubin fights vigorously against a theory which in this way diverges from our natural verbal expressions. If we want to know, he remarks, how things look phenomenally, which is psychology's primary task, we get the best hints from how our everyday language is used. Actually, the flavor of a bit of food, its *taste*, is built up of a complex of receptor stimulation. Gustatory receptors play a role in it, but what we experience as taste is based on the activity of olfactory, thermal, and tactual receptors too. During a cold, when the nasal membranes are insensitive to odors, we cannot really taste our food, although we might be able to discriminate between what is sour and what is salty. Figure 8–14 schematizes these receptor relationships. Out of these sensory stimulations develops a coherent, unified experience, which is called the taste of the food. It is not like the sum of all the impulses from the specific nerve fibers, but it is an

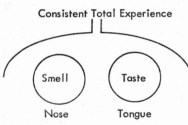

FIG. 8–14. Functional connections behind a flavor.

autonomous, diffuse, immediate totality, something that we could call a *complex quality.*[9]

Katz ends with similar statements, although he follows a path somewhat different from Rubin's. He applied evolutionary thought to the study of sensory processes and of the interdependence of the senses. When he was exploring the phenomenal world of colors, he asked whether any *specific receptors* could be identified for the perception of illumination. According to the law of specific nerve energies such receptors would be necessary. As we remember, the eyes receive their light either directly from the light sources or as reflected radiations from surrounding surfaces. There is nothing separate in the physical stimuli specifically responsible for perceiving "the illumination" or for perceiving "colored surfaces through a prevailing illumination." Suppose an object is illuminated by red light. In terms of the law of specific nerve fibers it would be difficult to explain why the red light reflected from the surface of the object as an object color does not fuse with the radiation coming to the eye directly from the light source. Why do we on the one hand see *illumination* as something separate in its own right and on the other hand *hues,* as well as degrees of *brightness* and *saturation* as something immediately specific and different? In our perceptual world, colored surfaces always appear in some illumination and to a certain extent retain their proper color even despite changes in the illumination.

Thus the law of specific nerve energies, narrowly understood, does not fit with actual impartial observations. There are many exceptional cases, constituting a kind of "interaction paradox."

Katz assumes that the immediate autonomous color experiences were omitted because laboratory experiments originally were performed on artifical spectral colors without sufficient attention to actual everyday perceptual reality.

The objections raised by phenomenally oriented psychologists against the theory of specific nerve fibers sound quite convincing, if we consider its limited psychological explanatory value. Yet research in physiological psychology has in the meantime made further progress, which makes it reasonable to hope for a solution to the problem. Morgan, after summarizing the physiological facts discovered so far, ends with the comment that they fully confirm the

---

[9] E. Rubin, "Taste," *British Journal of Psychology*, 24 (1934).

assumption of specific nerve energies.[10] In any case there is undoubtedly separate, isolated stimulation of different receptors. The theory
of specific fibers has been confirmed throughout various different
modalities. At the same time, theories denying specificity have been
proved untenable or remain unverified. As examples of explanatory
models which conform with the law of specificity Morgan lists the
modern theory of hearing, the Young-Helmholtz color theory, and
the models of specific skin receptors. The fact that he did not
mention "flavor sensations" seems to speak for Rubin's point of
view. Physiologically speaking, Morgan might be right in pointing
out that we know too little about the sense of smell. When we
discussed Weber's law, we pointed to the undeveloped level of smell
and taste, arguing that they can be considered rather diffuse,
unarticulated sense modalities.

From the standpoint of *phenomenalistic perceptual psychology*
these physiological statements need some modification; although
sensory qualities generally depend on the firing of specific receptors,
there might be *some* sensed qualities which can appear only as an
outcome of *specific receptor combinations*. That would enable
natural complex perceptual qualities to arise out of various different
possible combinations of specific fibers.

Moreover, the physiological arguments we have considered concern *peripheral characteristics* of perceptual qualities, i.e., the
specificity of the receptor fibers. Specificity of the peripheral nerves
does not necessarily require complete specificity of the *central
pathways* and *brain loci*. The cortico-spinal situation should therefore be explored. Unfortunately we find ourselves on a field which so
far is empirically almost totally uncultivated. It has been claimed in
favor of the specificity hypothesis that the optic nerve consists of
three types of fibers in accordance with the three-color theory of
vision. Granit (1955) ventures to say that structural correlates to
this specificity could be found at the cortical level. As the Finnish
neurophysiologist Tunturi has shown for the modality of hearing,
isomorphic correlates of the organ of Corti could be found in the
cortex, in spite of the fact that auditory pathways are more intricate
than the visual ones.[11] Tunturi's experiment involved electronic

---

[10] C. T. Morgan, *Physiological Psychology* (New York: McGraw-Hill Book Co.,
1943), p. 297.

[11] A. R. Tunturi, "Physiological Determination of the Arrangement of the
Afferent Connections to the Middle Ectosylvian Auditory Area in the Dog,"
American Journal of Physiology, 162 (1950).

mapping of the cortical auditory area in dogs. He found contiguous areas, each covering about 2 mm. and corresponding to one octave's interval on the stimulus scale. This result Granit considers one of the most convincing demonstrations of the reciprocity of peripheral and central perceptual loci.

As far as other modalities are concerned, prevailing opinion is primarily based upon assumptions. Specific connections in the central nervous system can be inferred from some general scattered observations. If sense organs of the skin are stimulated, experiences of *pressure* are more usual than experiences of *temperature* or *pain*. This could simply be explained, however, by assuming the central correlates of these sense organs to be located in different layers of the brain cortex. Even if we accept the theory of specific fibers, there is no need to assume specific cortical loci for different experienced qualities. A synaptic junction between fibers representing the same sensory function could be sufficient to produce the same perceived quality. Morgan believes that chemical differences in synaptic activity could explain the well-preserved specificity of the modalities in the central nervous system, while Granit and with him the electrophysiologists support a *frequency-code interpretation*. According to the latter, impulses representing separate modalities maintain their identity, by firing at different rates of frequency, even if they travel along a common fiber and occur simultaneously. This specific frequency of impulse view could be considered analogous to the transmission of various simultaneous radio waves. Correspondingly, it assumes that different cortical areas are specifically tuned to pick up code messages of a particular frequency. These electrophysiological assumptions have been submitted to intensive investigation. Their verification would render the theory of specific nerve fibers superfluous.

Hartshorne's Dimensional Explanation

As an alternative to the modality axiom, the American psychologist Hartshorne, in his *The Philosophy and Psychology of Sensation*, proposed what he called a *dimensional approach*. As a starting point he referred to the fundamental connection between different modal contents, which is immediately apparent in many verbal expressions. Thus, for example, the pitch of a tone and the brightness of a color may be fairly analogous, as can be concluded from expressions like "loud colors," "the gaiety of yellow," "light" or "bright" and "dark" sounds, etc. Hartshorne assumed that common dimensions exist across modalities, intermodal dimensions which make us able to restore the connections broken by the modality axiom. These connections reflect *affective continua* which arise during early developmental stages in the evolution of qualities out of some primary, relatively vague primordial dimensions.

Hartshorne began his presentation with a critical survey of the prevailing situation in the perceptual psychology of the early 1930's, pointing out a wide variety of errors directly ascribable to the modality axiom. After only some 30 or 40 pages he arrived at the question which proved to be central in his examination. Everyone willing to entertain Hartshorne's theoretical construction must try to face squarely the problem he raised. Hartshorne blamed orthodox perceptual psychologists for having proceeded too rationalistically. Perceptual qualities have, according to him, been treated as too isolated, too dispassionate, deprived of the attitudes, evaluations, and emotional connotations generally involved in all sensory activity. Dimensions of feeling have been excluded from studies of the dimensions of sensory experience. Even "striving" and "willing" should, according to Hartshorne, be treated as much more closely related to pure "sensation" than had hitherto been generally admitted. Perceptual spatio-temporal configurations gain their significance from the fact that the "emotional tone" of biologically primitive sensations is directed toward objects, toward goals in external phenomenal space. The coding of changes in this environment, giving direction to primitive conative striving, is interpreted by higher organisms as modal contents, that is, as perceptual experiences. "Sensation" is always connected with "striving" and "willing."

Hartshorne also stressed the importance of the social continuum in trying to understand the directedness of our perceptions. A social dimension implies a relation of at least two individuals, and individuality in the social sense means a certain freedom, or independence of action. "What does not undergo and react cannot belong to the great community of socially continuous individuals." Finally, sensory experience as a whole can vary along the dimension of intensity, independently of how vividly and intensely the "self" is experienced, as contrasted with others, activity as contrasted with passivity, positive values as contrasted with negative ones.

The direction and the content of perception are determined by the actual situation. "Neither vocal cords nor ear were physiological necessities, apart from the need to communicate, the need for language and social awareness . . . ," Hartshorne points out. He goes on to say that the prevalent theory of sensory experience is dualistic in its treatment of sensory evolution: New sense organs are conceived of as gradually evolving from some simple fundamental forms. On the other hand, new sensations "emerge" full-blown as if they were hermetically isolated from each other. Hartshorne wishes to bridge these gaps in the description by using his concept of the *affective continuum*. That contents from different modalities are experienced as similar or even as equivalent is due to the affective tuning associated with our perceptual activity. This tuning affects our whole organism, acting like a guideline for more specified, differentiated sensory activities. Because of this close relationship there is no sharp, essential break between feeling on the one hand and sensation on the other. "Feeling and sensation are the two main forms of sheer intuition or having of qualities."

The facts discussed in Chapter 2, page 24, can help us understand Hartshorne. Recall that at a primitive level perception consists of general *irritability*. The attitudes, the adaptation and the adjustment of an organism to the demands of its environment, require some degree of irritability. Perceptual contents which are valuable to human beings are irrelevant to primitive organisms. On that level, integrated reflex arcs might suffice. Against this background Hartshorne's definition of feeling makes sense: "The form in which active tendencies become conscious is feeling." The primitive function of the senses is action and not information, and this fact gives even more meaning to the role of irritability. While traditional perceptual psychology has been deeply engaged in exploring the *ability to initiate sensations*, the more primitive and the more widely distributed *capacity to excite action* has been deplorably slighted. The feeling tone is the only intrinsic reference to action which an experience, as a conscious event, involves. Hartshorne considers feeling a *primordial matrix* out of which sensory qualities evolve, "the very stuff out of which they are made." Characteristic is the next conclusion: "The first layer of sensory awareness must be the sense of activity, and the subsequent associative addition can only be the objectification of this activity feeling upon the environment, together with the intellectualization of the direct feeling content." Direct appearance of other socially emotional elements is all-pervasive in experience, and shows itself as an Ehrenfels quality, as an expression.

Hartshorne's idea that no perceptual act can occur without a feeling tone being connected with it, and that even an "intellectually advanced" organism keeps recording affective nuances, properties of its own motives mixed with sensory qualities, is not new. From an evolutionary point of view it also makes good sense. It is a reminder of the place *feeling* deserves in modern textbooks of psychology. A phenomenally oriented psychology of perception cannot be handled without considering the role of experienced emotional qualities. They decisively embellish our percepts. This undercurrent of feeling is the most central common factor in the correspondences among different sense modalities.

Pfaffmann's Studies

This point of view has been clearly emphasized by Pfaffmann in some of his most interesting articles. When discussing the recent advances in neurophysiology, he calls attention to the fact that the reticular activating or arousal system is, apparently, also able to modulate and influence activity within the classical sensory pathways themselves. "Most sense organs," he keeps repeating, "have at least two neural pathways. One, the well-known primary projection pathway—to the cerebral cortex; and the second, a nonspecific pathway by way of the reticular activating system with diffuse projections to the cortex and other neural structures."[12]

The reticular system is multimodal and intramodal in contrast to what is known about the classical discriminative projection systems. The former mediates, generally speaking, physiological and behavioral arousal.

Pfaffman furthermore pointed to the evidence given by the famous intracranial stimulation experiments (Olds, *et al.*) that stimuli as such can act as positive primary reinforcers. There exist, according to him, certain correlations between gustatory nerve discharges and food preferences in animals.

Carefully conducted studies on the sense of taste have shown that this same sense modality possesses easily demonstrable discriminative and reinforcing functions. Detailed investigations were carried out by recording discharges in the gustatory nerve fibers originating

---

[12] Carl Pfaffmann, "The Pleasures of Sensations," *Psychological Review* (Vol. 67, No. 4), pp. 253–68.

in the specific receptors on the tongue surface. From the point of view of behavior, the basic response to taste solutions is either acceptance or rejection, so that the classical manifold of four tastes, salt, sour, bitter, and sweet, may be reduced to two behavioral classes, acceptance and rejection.

His preferential ingestion method rendered it possible to register the preferences by a choice of two solutions and to record the intake of the preferred one. Pfaffmann's results demonstrate that there do exist certain hedonistic aspects of sensory stimulation. It turned out that sugar solutions are basically hedonically positive for the rat irrespective of the nutritional value of the solution and the actual "nutritive state" of the animal. It is rather conspicuous that even prolonged stomach loading of saccharine solutions did not bring about "extinction symptoms" in the experimental animals. On the other hand, it turned out that even a bitter taste is apt to gain in acceptability if the tasted "bitterness" conditionally is combined with thirst reduction.

Pfaffmann remarks that affective or hedonic rating-scale methods have been generally applied in the field of flavor technology. He has been impressed by the apparent similarity of his rat preference curves with those obtained by scientists who investigated actual food preferences in human subjects, asking them to rate different intensities of taste stimuli as either pleasant, unpleasant, or indifferent. If graphs are computed for the rating scores of four different taste modalities, expressed as percentage of pleasant ratings minus percentage of unpleasant ratings, we have a picture similar to the trends of the graphs—which is what is found in the preferential reactions of the rat.

Thus, there most likely exists a hedonically founded, striking interaction in the perception procedure of some fundamental sensory qualities.

Evaluation of Hartshorne

Hartshorne's argument is largely based on expressions from everyday language, which certainly reflects analogies between different modalities and feelings. A passion, for example, is often called "warm" or "burning." He also refers to experiments on "dynamic movement" from one color to another, performed by von Allesch. "It is possible, for example, to see yellow either as a cold or as a warm color, for red is warmer and green is colder." Those who misunderstand Hartshorne must have overlooked his statement: "Thus the rule is sustained that the occupancy of a certain portion of experience by a given sensory quality, say a color, constitutes the complete qualitative determination of that portion of experience." "If tertiary qualities, 'characteristics,' appear in phenomenal space, these *characters* are the *sensory qualities themselves, their constitutive natures.*"

Hartshorne faces the question of whether feelings could be considered attributes of sensation. He concludes that such a claim does make sense, if we replace the term "attribute" by the term *affective continuum*, so that dimensions of sensory quality are translated into dimensions of affective quality. Hartshorne's theoretical presentation traces the evolution of the idea of dimensional continua and of the concept of variable back to Plato. He completes his system with the social continuum, within which polarities such as "self-others," "dominance-submission" and "individuality-sociality" occur.

Hartshorne's view of the sense continua and of the analogies among modalities should be examined against the background of his general theory. He looks everywhere for continuities and for general dimensions. He objects to the color solid as a description of the dimensions in color perception and to the color square as a diagram of the spectrum. He argues that perceptual psychologists should not consider hue, brightness, and saturation as separate unitary dimensions, and points out that colors phenomenally show a gradual transition from red to green, from yellow to blue. They do not follow straight diameters across the circle. He suggests his own system of phenomenal colors, but we need not go into it here.

Hartshorne's ideas generally are consistent with findings from comparative psychology. At least he is familiar with the intermodally important phenomenon of *synesthesia*. It is, according to him, an indication of a feeling of intermodal reciprocity, which is very salient in some individuals. He objects to an associationist explanation of the phenomenon, and considers talk about presumed pathological traits of synesthetics as reminiscent of a tendency among conventional psychologists to deny the reality of events which not everyone can perceive. "When certain persons, often those distinguished for their fine, accurate, and trained powers of sensory discrimination, have declared that to them sensations from different modes appeared very distinctly and indubitably comparable, the psychologist has formed the suspicion that these persons were characterized by odd personal idiosyncrasies," Hartshorne remarks ironically.

In his quest for intermodal dimensions Hartshorne uses some of Hornbostel's observations. The dimension of *brightness* is the first one both of them mention, established as it is by well-founded empirical evidence. Hartshorne reminds us in this connection of the striking fact that *high tones* are immediately experienced as *light* or *bright*. The dimensions of smell are not especially considered. After examining brightness, he surveys the opposites of *high* and *low* throughout several sense modalities. When tones of different pitch are listened to, a *visual* vertical line might serve as a basis of reference. Even the fact that we speak of the *volume* of sounds testifies, according to Hartshorne, that intermodal spatial experiences exist. Impressions of three-dimensional space are not obtained exclusively through vision and touch. They occur abundantly in auditory perception.

The next intersensory analogue mentioned is *weight*, which Hornbostel had also already observed. Colors appear light or heavy, as do odors and flavors, and even tones. Seeking observational material to support his dimensions, Hartshorne, unlike Hornbostel, makes excursions into the vast material of poetry and epic literature: "There are hot perfumes and cold . . . Lucy's gardenias seemed to fill his throat and lungs with tropical and sultry sweetness." Hartshorne asks, "Is warmth, like brightness, a genuine intersense notion?" And he goes on, "Is there any reason to suppose that the orthodox view of mere association is a truer answer to this question than it proved to be to that of the elevation and brightness of sounds?"

Polymodal Impressions

Most people have capricious, barely analyzable global and multivariate perceptual experiences, which cannot quite be captured verbally by referring them to a specific sense modality. We all know the expression of feeling "bitterly cold." In some Finnish dialects the verb *maistaa* (taste) can be used for strong sensations even if they have nothing to do with the smell-taste modalities. If a hiker breaks through the ice into a creek he might speak of having "tasted cold with one of his feet." And Hartshorne's example of "the silver needle notes of a fife" sounds quite understandable to the present author when examined against the background of some personal experiences of his.

On a lovely February morning one could remark to his friend that a foretaste of spring is in the air. What does the expression "foretaste" actually imply? It refers to a complex quality unmistakably composed of a host of sensations associated with spring. Components of this perceptual totality might be (1) the illumination conditions, (2) the mildness of the air recognizable on the skin surface and in the respiratory organs, (3) the transparency and light colors of the landscape and probably, (4) some scents mixed in with all the rest. This holistic music of the sensory contents is picked up and responded to by the human organism as adequately as by the plant which prepares for the approaching summer by swelling its roots and extending the first timid and fragile leaves out toward the warming sun. We do not by any means exhaustively analyze these signs of the season when we speak so strikingly of a "foretaste of spring."

A similarly global, polymodal impression has been described by Hornbostel:

I find myself in a very definite state of consciousness—"mood" would be too vague—there simply is no term. I cannot say whether it comes from a day in the Black Forest, a picture by Schwind, the work of Möricke, or from the seventy-third bar of Wolf's *Fussreise*. Perhaps from none of these, though each embodies it identically, captures its essence. I cannot give an exact account of it or communicate it to others, for I am neither painter, poet, nor singer, and was born a hundred years too late simply to express it in my way of life.[13]

Let us turn back to Hartshorne: The transition from heat to practically pure pain is as continuous and gradual as that from orange to red. Cold bites and pinches until pure pain is felt. Dynamically central continua like these dramatically show us the consistency and interaction of perceptions and feelings.

Criticism

One rather telling problem with Hartshorne's approach is his tendency to generalize without reservation from certain phenomenal events in the field of comparative psychology to the life of adult

---

[13] E. M. v. Hornbostel, "Die Einheit der Sinne" (quoted from English trans.) in W. D. Ellis (ed.), *Source Book of Gestalt Psychology* (London: Routledge & Kegan Paul, 1938), p. 215.

educated people. In criticizing Hartshorne's chain of thought, Nyman points out that the lion's share of our perceptual world is a world of differentiated modalities.[14] Hartshorne's theory must be considered a *working hypothesis*, he thinks, taking him to task for not mentioning it explicitly, although Hartshorne probably intended it to be precisely that. The affective continuum proposed by Hartshorne thus remains a programmatic ideal, not thoroughly confirmed by empirical research. Nevertheless, the search for inter-modal dimensions and their analysis has brought certain important facts and realities to light, and we must thank Hartshorne for this. But as Nyman points out, his analysis and argument leaned too heavily on *qualitative* analogies and *similarities*. An orientation along scientifically better founded *relational similarities* could have prevented his going adrift, which does occur occasionally in his presentation.

Following Hornbostel we might presume that the qualities Hart-shorne calls intermodal dimensions became differentiated only in part and ontogenetically rather late. Probably they form the basic ontogenetic events in our perceptions. It is striking that in the most differentiated modalities we can, at early stages, e.g., during infancy, observe events which seem to confirm an interaction paradox. The same holds true of the impressions and reactions of primitive tribes. Hornbostel reports that a certain African language has a special word for "*see*," but only a common general expression for "hear," "touch," "smell," and "taste." "It matters little through which sense I realize that in the dark I have blundered into a pig sty," he ironically remarks. In French too, *sentir* simultaneously means to smell, to touch, and to feel, and when a German boy asks for a "bright" trumpet (*eine helle Trompete*) he returns to the original meaning of the German word for *bright*, which referred only to sound in Middle High German.[15]

Werner has shown in his work on comparative psychology that *synesthesias* are normal events throughout the perceptual life of children, primitive tribes, and the mentally retarded. One of the best-known syndromes of synesthesia is *chromatism* (*audition colorée*) or colored sound. When he is listening to sounds, colored images appear to the observer. Modern investigation tends to regard

[14] A. Nyman, *Nya vägar inom psykologin* (Stockholm: Norstedt & Söner, 1951), p. 105.
[15] Hornbostel, *op. cit.*, p. 210.

these as extreme cases along a continuum which also contains the complex qualities of modal interaction occurring in most ordinary people.

Children may be afraid of a stranger because of his voice: "The man has such a black voice." Or when one can't quite recognize a voice on a phone: "That isn't Henry. Henry has a light voice, and this voice was dark."—Once I gave my four-year-old daughter some cough drops, explaining to her that they are useful because they relieve hoarseness by making the throat feel clear. After sucking on the drops, she opened her mouth wide and asked: "Well, is my throat all shiny now?" An expression denoting "clear" in vision was effortlessly applied in a new connection. Shiny things also feel smooth and clear when they are rubbed, so perhaps touch too played a role in this spontaneous analogy.

CHAPTER 9

Perceptual Constancy and the Frame of Reference

Shapes at Different Angles of Inclination

LET US IMAGINE, in a farmer's cottage, an old rocking chair facing a small, square window so that the sun's rays hit the solid backrest at a right angle. The light spot on the chair, projected through the square window under these conditions, is clearly square too. If the chair is gently tilted back and straightened again, the shape of the rectangular light spot changes. It will, for example, look more elongated the more the backrest is tilted. It is not perceived as possessing "shape constancy"; it is regarded as something unessential, as something quite incidental, "not belonging to the chair" and devoid of any "object character."

On the other hand, let us assume that the cloth covering the chair back has a square-shaped pattern on it. Each of the squares in the pattern is seen not as "a projected spot" but as "belonging to the surface." When the rigid surface of the chair back, bearing the squares, is turned away from the frontal plane, the perspective and the *retinal image of each square is compressed*. It becomes *shorter* in the vertical dimension, the more we tilt the rocking chair away from the spectator, looking at it from straight in front. *In this case the squares on the chair surface are perceived as maintaining the form first ascribed to them.* The figures on the cloth are seen as tilted backward from their original frontal plane, as belonging to the chair, and as participating in its movements, thereby *maintaining their constant square shape* as do other "real objects" in our environment.

How should we explain the difference between these two instances? In both cases the projected retinal image is a square which, from the point of view of optics and of the physiological stimulus, becomes deformed according to the angle of tilt given to the stimulus surface. Why do we perceive this deforming projection as variable and accidental in one instance and as a stable and invariant "thing-gestalt" in the other?

Here we encounter a central problem in perceptual psychology, the problem of *perceptual constancies* or *invariances* in our world of perceived objects. Apparently the difference in the experience of the two situations is partly due to the fact that simultaneously with the stimuli from the deforming squares of the cloth we receive a rich flux of stimuli from surrounding areas, from the rest of the cloth, and from the whole chair back, all of which participate in the projective transformation. The spot of sunlight, contrariwise, grows and shrinks alone, without being accompanied by consistent concomitant changes in the other visual forms of the chair surface. Their retinal projections change in a way altogether different from the changes in the projection of the window. The psychologist calls the backrest of the rocking chair and all the other figures changing in an orderly, consistent way, a *frame of reference*. How we perceive the figural characteristics of a single part of the cloth depends on this frame of reference. The fact that we see perceptual objects as having a constant form, determined by their frame of reference, is known as the *formation of object constancies* or *object invariances*. We must recognize, however, that the viewing conditions allowed for reception of reliable, direct stimuli indicating the *degree of tilt:* a sufficient amount of the cloth's surface was visible all the time, so that the spectator's eyes could obtain the information that various parts of the figures were adopting new positions at different distances from their initial location.

The Problem of Shape Constancy

Our example corresponds to the much-quoted case of viewing circular objects in their natural environment from different angles of sight and yet experiencing them as circular (e.g., plates in their natural surroundings on a rigid table surface). Were we not equipped with these tendencies to perceive constancy, we obviously would be forced to get along in a most curious perceptual environment. Because of the continuously changing shape of retinal images, our visual world would appear to be constructed of continuously expanding and contracting rubbery objects. The plates on the dinner table would assume a variety of elliptical shapes, changing as the angle of regard changes.

Experimenters have worked with a more and more *impoverished* (*reduced*) frame of reference in perceptual laboratories. In the case of the rocking chair, a reduction procedure would mean that the visual field of the spectator would be restricted, screening most parts of the backrest and the cloth except, say, for one of the square decorations. The spectator would be prevented from observing that the decoration belongs to the chair. If, in a carefully conducted experiment, a bright white circular disc is slowly tilted around its horizontal axis *in an environment which is sufficiently dark, devoid of surrounding objects and at a sufficient distance from the observer* so that accommodation of the lens to the various parts of the disc's surface is impossible, shape constancy no longer occurs. Subjects soon report seeing an ellipse. Employed as a measure of the degree of shape constancy in such an experiment has been the size of the angle between the plane of the tilted object when it can still just be seen as circular and the original orientation in the frontal plane. Numerous investigations of shape constancy have used this technique.

A series of careful later experiments has shown, however, that the phenomenon of shape constancy actually consists of seeing *the form of the object as permanent and invariant* while it *at the same time* is *perceived as tilted away from the frontal plane* facing the observer. Subjects who continued to report seeing a circular shape as a rule perceived it as *a tilted circular disc.* A variation of the experiment in which all cues for the angle of tilt are excluded produces a zero constancy except for the initial frontal-parallel position: the subjects report varying elliptical figures.

This kind of finding has resulted in an extension of the original problem of perceptual constancies. Apparently the issue should be stated in the following way: what is most significant is the *constancy of the relationship* between one set of stimulus factors (e.g., form of the retinal image) and another set of stimulus factors (e.g., cues indicating the slant of the figure surface). One single stimulus variable, e.g., the shape of the retinal image, can therefore not be considered *the* stimulus factor responsible for object constancy. On the contrary, *the relation between this retinal pattern and the stimuli for the degree of slant must be considered the decisive stimulus*. This insight has recently resulted in a reevaluation of the concept of invariances. What is constant or invariant is typically certain relational aspects of the stimulation.

Relational Invariances in Size Perception

We have thus been brought to regard as central an idea rather incidentally mentioned by Koffka in his discussion of *size constancy*. As we know, within certain limits perceived size is invariant. A person moving away from us does not seem phenomenally to shrink in proportion to the optical change in the size of the retinal image, that is, in proportion to the square of the distance. The fact of size constancy is well established.[1]

As Koffka pointed out, what is really important for bringing about this phenomenon is the maintenance of a *consistent relation* among the *real*, measurable *size* of a physical object, the size of its retinal image, and its *distance from the eye*. Research carried out by Gibson, Patricia Smith, and Olin W. Smith has confirmed that *size constancy* is greatly diminished if stimuli for perceiving distance are artificially reduced.[2] In most of their experiments, the frame of reference or the distance cues consisted of texture gradients of inclined surfaces. When the term *perceptual invariance* is used in the following discussion, it will sometimes still refer to the old meaning, to *object constancies*, but will usually indicate what are now considered the real stimuli for these constancies, that is: *invariances of relational variables*.

One of the cornerstones of Gibson's perceptual theory is his hypothesis that two or more variables together can form relational stimuli, stimuli of a higher order than, say, simply the locus of a two-dimensional pattern. Out of his idea that our perceptual system actually is not stimulated by the isolated, elementaristic reflected points of a stimulus pattern, but rather by a system of relationships among these elements, grows a new need in modern psychophysics. It should concern itself with looking for and finding those systems of relationships among single stimuli which prove to be crucial in determining what we perceive. E. Kaila once mused about this line of thought. He observed how accurately our eye can follow the

---

[1] K. Koffka, *Principles of Gestalt Psychology* (London: Kegan Paul, 1935), pp. 222–23 and 229.

[2] O. W. Smith, P. C. Smith and D. Hubbart, "Perceived Distance as a Function of the Method of Representing Perspective," *American Journal of Psychology*, 71 (1958), pp. 662–74.

increasing curvature of a logarithmic spiral, so that for most people a freehand drawing of its continuation would come out amazingly well. "We have," Kaila said, "actually been reacting to a relational stimulus." Each spiral has its own particular gradient of curvature, and this gradient is capable of directly affecting our visual apparatus: we can sense it. Metzger points in the same direction with his statement that every stimulus, in addition to having its specific function, serves as a stimulus for a system. Gibson can use his gradients to explain two of the object constancies: size and shape invariance. The following presentation will make it clear that the *relative constancy of surface colors* can also be accounted for by recourse to the gradients which have been discovered to exist under certain conditions of light radiation.

Dimensions of Perceptual Space

The frame of reference of perceptual space is composed of several sets of "higher-order stimuli" (relational stimuli) from many modalities. We are informed about the influence of gravity, which acts in a direction parallel to our vertically oriented body, via receptors in the inner ear, and via the senses of equilibrium, muscle tension, and posture, as has been shown in experiments especially by Mach, Kleint, Werner, and Wapner. The gravity dimension, together with the one crossing it at right angles, form the *cardinal dimensions*, the vertical and the horizontal of our perceptual space. Takala (1951) demonstrated their unique position and role in our perceptions in some beautiful experiments on asymmetries in visual space. His results also showed that our visual world diverges from Euclidian space in the asymmetric distribution of areas of equal acuity; it resembles the visual field of the right eye.[3]

With numerous experiments Jaensch in 1911 demonstrated *the tendency towards orthogonal localization* (*die orthogone Lokalisations-tendenz*).[4] There seems to exist a perceptual tendency to localize objects in a way which keeps their main dimension in a plane at right angles to the line of sight. Thus Jaensch showed that visually perceived static objects are experienced in an "optimal position" on the coordinate axes, either parallel or orthogonal to

---

[3] M. Takala, "Asymmetries of the Visual Space," *Annales Academiae Scientiarum Fennicae*, B 72, No. 2 (Helsinki, 1951).

[4] E. R. Jaensch, "Über die Wahrnehmung des Raumes," *Zeitschrift für Psychologie*, Ergänzungsband 6 (1911).

either of the two basic planes (frontal and horizontal). Later Rausch gave the concept a more generalized meaning. He described a tendency of observers to flatten out zigzag lines. Quite a few of the so-called geometric illusions can be reduced to this phenomenon of an increase in the apparent size of angles. Experimental subjects are inclined to overestimate the angles between adjacent straight parts of a zigzag line. The phenomenal line is closer to a straight line than is the zigzag line. This tendency is supported in visual perception by another tendency demonstrated by Rausch, which can also be interpreted to support the validity of Jaensch's observation: subjects tend to reproduce a parallelogram (Figure 9–1) so that the angles

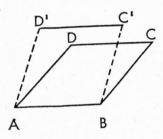

FIG. 9–1.   The phenomenal image (e.g., the memory image) *ABC'D'* is more upright than the original parallelogram *ABCD*.

are closer to 90° than those of the physical stimulus. The "pheno-gram" *ABC'D'* as drawn by the subject on the basis of his memory image, or as constructed on the basis of psychophysical experiments (by production method), is more erect, more square-shaped than the "ontogram" *ABCD*, which was originally exposed.[5] When asked to provide metric descriptions of the dimensions of objects and figures we generally rely on our *touch experiences* if we wish to reproduce the ontogram as closely as possible. This procedure of seeking information through touch is considered as more dependent upon the physical stimulus pattern, as more reliable, than vision. Similarly, we regard our *physical picture of the world*, which is metric and thus based on tactual experiences, as more real and trustworthy than our visual world. Visual objects whose perceived dimensions differ from their tactual ones are called "illusions."

Orthogonality and Anisotropy of Space

It is quite possible that the immediately experienced visual world of a child does not conform at all to our Newtonian space, the latter

---

[5] E. Rausch, *Struktur und Metrik figural-optischer Wahrnehmung* (Frankfurt am Main: Kramer, 1952), pp. 2–3, 89–96.

being an inferred construction, based on what we know from our past kinesthetic and tactual experience. As soon as the child starts handling objects, however, he learns to match his visual environment with tactual, postural and kinesthetic *cues*. Touched edges and surfaces provide a kind of frame of reference for what is perceived visually. It is not accidental that our visual world, even at more mature ages when it is fully developed, adjusts itself rather smoothly to a transformed tactual-postural system of reference. After having worn spectacles which turn the visual world upside down long enough, we do not react to streets and vehicles which look inverted by trying to stand on our heads. Rather, we try to correct our visual impressions by reference to what we *feel* is correct about the world around us. We rely more on reports from the tactual, postural, and kinesthetic senses and, as the experiment is continued, we gradually become able to adjust sufficiently to the topically distorted world. This developmental trend has been observed in experiments by, for example, Stratton, Erismann, and J. Kohler.[6]

The frame of reference is a necessary condition for the appearance of object constancies. The more richly and finely articulated the frame of reference, the more is perception able to record objects in conformity with their metric, distal (i.e., physical) dimensions. Constancy in the traditional sense of the word is considered greater the better the perceived object corresponds to its distal stimuli, and poorer the more it corresponds to its proximal stimuli. Most of our percepts appear to owe their constancy to the frame of reference offered by simultaneous, parallel stimulation affecting all available modalities. The more impoverished the differentiation of the entire stimulus pattern, the poorer is constancy.

A procedure similar to Stratton's was used in one of Wertheimer's experiments. The subject sees the room through a convex mirror, which reflects verticals and horizontals as curved lines. The subject looks at the mirror through a tube which masks those parts of the visual space which otherwise could be seen surrounding the mirror. At first everything looks odd. People walk on a curved floor, falling objects follow a curved path, etc. However, it does not take longer than a few hours before the "mirror space" is corrected: the

---

[6] See, e.g., Ivo Kohler, "Über Aufbau und Wandlungen der Wahrnehmungswelt insbesondere über bedingte Empfindungen, *Österreichische Akademie der Wissenschaften, Phil.-historische Klasse*, p. 227, Vol. I.

floor looks horizontal and objects fall vertically, once again obeying the law of gravity. Koffka applied the frame-of-reference concept to this case too. In our immediate natural environment there are no isolated straight or curved lines. What we could call lines are mostly contours, borders, or edges of substantial, unitary three-dimensional objects. These perceptual totalities have their rules of appearance, and how we experience their lines depends on the roles of the larger, more complete surfaces and objects to which they belong. Visual space is entirely determined by the frame of reference of the total field. What Koffka presumably was pointing out with this statement is that the *mutual relations* among the local elements were maintained even in the distorted "mirror space," because they were all lawfully displaced together according to a consistent rule. When the mirror space becomes "corrected," this is achieved simply by changing a common factor, a *coefficient* as it were, in the prevailing relationships. Perception records the *invariances of the situation*, the *constant ratios* or *relationships* embedded in it. Once this invariant is realized and the appropriate single substitution is made, all the elements change or are displaced simultaneously. As long as the distortion remains, a general invariance nevertheless governs the outcome of the perception.[7]

Inadequacy of the Learning Assumption

Explanations that refer to the contribution of past experience are unsatisfactory in this connection. Whatever we know about the "correct" position of telegraph poles, trees, and houses cannot prevent us from seeing them as tilted again and again when looking at them from the window of a cog railway car. The same is the case when we look at houses built on steep slopes. In any actual perceptual world there always develop cardinal dimensions corresponding to the primary dimensions of the stimulus situation. In a tilted cog railway car the frame of the rectangular window determines the apparent vertical and horizontal. The objects in the "window space" are referred to the dominant cardinal dimensions of the window itself, which provides the frame of reference. Therefore, physically vertical objects when seen through the tilted window are phenomenally tilted. The *invariant relation* in the stimulus situation to which we referred above (page 206), as stressed by Koffka,

---

[7] Koffka, *op cit.*, pp. 215–18.

shows up again: it is the angle of inclination between the tilted frame and the vertical object which is significant.

The same principle can account for the famous case of the "tilted house" on the west bank of Lake Cayuga (Figure 9–2). The long slanting slope forms a frame of reference which tends to turn into one of our cardinal dimensions, that is, to get identified as a

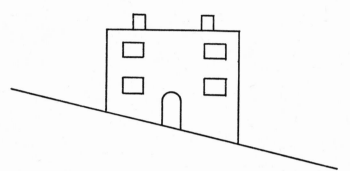

FIG. 9–2. Koffka's example of the "tilted house" (on the bank of Lake Cayuga).

horizontal line. A building which is not perpendicular to it, therefore, looks tilted. The same rule holds too of most instances of phenomenal colors and phenomenal movements because of their numerous relational invariances, as will be shown later.

Size and Distance

If two squares are presented as in Figure 9–3, the visual experience of them depends on which of several alternative stimulus possibilities is accepted. The squares *A* and *B* may be physically at

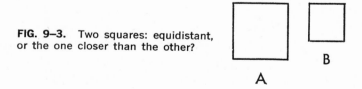

FIG. 9–3. Two squares: equidistant, or the one closer than the other?

the same distance from the subject's eyes, with *B* actually smaller than *A* (condition I). *Or*, he may have before him two squares of the same size but at different distances from him. Then the retinal image of *B* is smaller because it is farther away (condition II).

Suppose we have an experimental subject who is completely unaware of the physical conditions of the setup. With enough patience, we could easily construct these two alternative situations. We can make two *B* squares of different sizes, such that the retinal image of the smaller square, when it is as close to the subject as *A*, corresponds exactly to the retinal image of the larger, when it is a certain specified distance farther away than *A*. We may ask whether the subject is able to discriminate between conditions I and II. It can be shown that he does so amazingly well, provided that the perceptual situation supplies him with cues not only of the *two-dimensional size* but also of the *distance* of the test objects. Whenever we naturally perceive objects in our visual environment, we always have more or less clear-cut cues for distance at our disposal. The most effective system of stimuli for articulating the experience of depth, according to Gibson, is the texture-gradient of a receding horizontal surface. In natural life, objects at various distances always appear along extended surfaces. If in an experiment this ordinarily visible *gradient of depth* is artifically eliminated, and other distance cues are also reduced by, e.g., asking the subject to close one eye, it becomes much harder to distinguish between situation I and situation II. In the natural environment, people tend to preserve the perceived visual size of an object with moderate variations in its distance. *Relational invariance* comes up again: *sensed size in relation to sensed distance.*

Careful experiments have confirmed that absolute size constancy does not occur. Perceived size is preserved to a considerable degree when the viewed object is moved farther away, but the perceived size does not correspond entirely to the dimensions of the distal stimulus object itself. Rather, constancy almost always involves a compromise between distal and proximal stimuli. Faced with the alternatives of incessantly varying proximal stimuli and an absolute constancy of a seen object, size perception ends with a modified constancy, a biologically adaptive solution. It would be most difficult indeed to get along in a world in which a moving car or truck decreases to $\frac{1}{10}$ its former size when it is 10 times further away from us.

MEASUREMENT OF THE DEGREE OF CONSTANCY

The degree of shape constancy can, as mentioned on p. 205, also be quantitatively determined. The circular standard disc, which can be turned at an angle to the subject's line of vision, is paired alternately with various different frontally oriented elliptical discs until one is found whose shape looks identical to that of the tilted standard. These paired comparisons yield equations not unlike the mixture equations for matching colors of different hues.

Koffka gives an example of the traditional formulation of the problem of constancy (see figure 9–4). The subject is at point O and looks at an ellipse the length of whose larger diameter is $AB = r$ ("real diameter"). If this ellipse is turned around its other axis, the diameter assumes the new orientation $A'B'$. The retinal angle of the axis in position $A'B'$ is a projection of the line CD, which is located at right angles to the line of vision. $CD = p$ ("projected diameter"). The task of the subject is to compare the tilted ellipse yielding this retinal projection with other orthogonally located elliptical figures. Suppose an ellipse with a diameter s ("seen diameter")

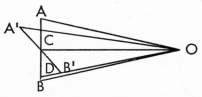

FIG. 9–4. Koffka's experimental situation (seen from above).

fulfills the conditions. Generally speaking, $p < s < r$. If $s = r$, that would mean perfect constancy; if $s = p$, there is no shape constancy at all.

Starting with these concepts, Brunswik developed his technique of measuring the degree of object constancy. We must relate the perceived s to both r and p. The difference $r - p$ indicates the total distance between the distal and proximal poles in terms of the measuring units used in the experiment. If the seen diameter s differs from p by the distance $s - p$, we could relate s to both r and p by expressing the distance $s - p$ as a percentage of the distance $r - p$. This yields the *Brunswik ratio*, in which the number R directly expresses the degree of constancy:

$$R = 100 \frac{s - p}{r - p}.$$

Brunswik considers this method of measurement and calculation generally applicable, irrespective of what kind of constancy is studied. It is a characteristic trait of our perception to yield *intermediate compromises*. The process of perception always starts with what is available as the proximal physiological representation of the object; in vision, it starts with the retinal projections (p) and "strives" or "intends towards" the distal stimuli, toward the real size, shape, color, etc. (r) of the physical object. Borrowing Brentano's descriptive approach for these purposes, Brunswik frequently speaks of the perceptual constancies as occurring within what he calls an *intentional system between two opposite poles*. The poles consist of the proximal, retinal projective conditions p, and of the distal stimulus object r. The process of perception begins, as it were, with p as raw material and the constancy coefficient R measures the degree to which r is achieved. The percept undergoes a kind of active *transformation process* (to borrow a term from Katz). Nevertheless, the constancies are at best only compromise solutions. Thus the perceptual constancies are, according to Brunswik, symptoms of a general, pervasive compromising tendency in our perception.

Koffka sharply criticizes this method for determining the degree of constancy. Especially in shape constancy R-values exceeding 100 have been obtained, which looks like a kind of "hyperconstancy."[8] Suppose $A'B'$ (Figure 9–4) has a length of 15 cm. and that the length p, corresponding to the retinal image of $A'B'$ at a visual angle of 45°, is 10.7 cm. Clearly, there are problems in using Brunswik's equation for any ellipses whose phenomenal diameter exceeds 15 cm. or is below 10.7 cm. Yet values like these do occur every now and then in laboratory experiments.

Koffka presents several examples of investigations which confirm that the relation between the *plane form* and *the plane of orientation* of a figure can act as "higher-order" relational stimuli. A constant relation seems to persist between the figural shape of an object and its phenomenal tilt. Eissler, Thouless, Langdon, and others have found that shape constancy decreases when the angle of inclination exceeds a certain maximum.[9] With only slight tilt, however, as in our example of the rocking chair, the perceived inclination in combination with an appropriate deformation of the remainder of the retinal image may even contribute to the perceptual constancy of the seen figures. A study performed by Eissler is specially valuable

---

[8] Koffka, *op. cit.*, p. 227.

[9] K. Eissler, "Die Gestaltkonstanz der Sehdinge," *Archiv für die gesamte Psychologie*, 88 (1934); R. H. Thouless, "Individual Differences in Phenomenal Regression," *British Journal of Psychology*, 22 (1932); J. Langdon, "The Perception of Changing Shape," *Quarterly Journal of Experimental Psychology*, 3 (1951).

for clarifying the relationship between shape constancy and certain perceptual cues for three-dimensional space. The descending order of effectiveness of the best-known depth cues, in contributing to shape constancy, came out as follows: *binocular disparity, accommodation, visual acuity, motion parallax, overlap,* and *perspective.* When they were successively eliminated one by one in a reduction experiment, the degree of constancy decreased accordingly. In accord with what we said before (page 205), a simultaneous elimination of all distance criteria led to a *reduced visual mode,* to an almost complete lack of shape constancy.[10] However, Eissler did not include the texture gradient of receding surfaces (page 212) among his criteria.

Size Constancy

We have concentrated so far almost exclusively on *shape constancy.* Size constancy too, however, deserves our full attention and interest. What we said about the decisive role of *stimulus ratios,* of relational stimuli in perceived invariance, can be applied to these constancies too. Sensation of distance as well as of the size of the retinal image is tremendously important in size perception. The degree of size constancy is directly related to the degree of articulation of visual space. Only binocular disparity seems to be less crucial than it is in shape constancy. The closer examination of the relative role of each of the depth cues in size constancy remains a task for future research. The role of the *cardinal dimensions,* however, is known to be crucial if moving objects recede along either of them. When they recede from us horizontally, familiar objects maintain a higher degree of size constancy than they do when their vertical distance from the observer is increased. A metal plate on the ground 15 meters away from the observer looks larger than a similar plate the same distance above his head. Unlike what is true for shape constancy, in which a frontally oriented pattern yields maximal constancy, Koffka points out that no optimal stimulus conditions have been found for size constancy. There is no such thing as "a normal distance" for seen objects. In other respects, however, the explanation of size constancy is fully analogous to the explanation of shape constancy. Size constancy can be derived from a scientific description of perceptual space.

---

[10] Eissler, *op. cit.;* cf. B. E. Holaday, "Die Grössenkonstanz der Sehdinge," *Archiv für die gesamte Psychologie,* 88 (1934), pp. 440 and 473.

Color Constancy

Color constancy has been systematically investigated for over a century. This invariance is directly related to the phenomenal appearance of colors (described in Chapter 4) in that only surface colors, in other words the colors of the light-reflecting surfaces of objects, are sufficiently invariant to warrant speaking of constancy. It should also be remembered that a certain degree of constancy of surface colors holds only of objects seen in natural daylight, with its relatively minor variations in brightness and in chromaticity. The traditional artificial experiments, too, used only light sources which varied only slightly in light energy and spectral distribution. When gas, carbon, and incandescent electric light were replaced by fluorescent tubes, the intensity gradients of the reflected radiation became steeper and more variable. The following examples are traditional in the sense that they do not hold true throughout all spectral radiations, especially not for illuminations which are particularly strong in the "yellowish" and "reddish" portions of the spectrum.

The traditional problems are most understandable if we recall some of the phenomenal changes which we experience in ordinary daylight conditions. Looking at the galvanized iron roof of a low neighboring house at dawn, we might see a bright, "shiny" color which in the late fall yields a compelling impression of *snow*. The brilliant reflected light is seen as something "substantially" connected with the surface, as a white color belonging to it. Capricious climate may have misled us once again, though. The iron roof is actually wet, reflecting light very efficiently from its moist, cold surface. As soon as the error is noticed, the phenomenal color of the roof instantly changes. Instead of a white surface color, we perceive a nearly black one, but now the color is *far more lustrous and glowing* in the morning light *than it was when it was perceived as snow*. Or we may notice a grey spot of dust on the arm of our jacket. The slightest movement, however, can reveal it as a spot of sunlight coming from a small hole in the curtain. As soon as our movement displaces the spot it is impossible to see it as grey dust any longer. These examples concern *brightness constancy* with variations in light intensity and illumination and surface conditions. Correspondingly, one could point to *hue constancy* with varying chromatic illumination.

Interest in these problems was awakened by Hering with his insightful remarks in his textbook on the "light sense." He introduced the concept of "memory color" (see page 86), which refers to the "specific color" we tend to ascribe to objects. We regard the color as though it were constant, that is, as though it were a *property* belonging to the object.[11] Memory color plays a central role in Hering's attempt to account for color constancy phenomena. He also resorted to various physiological mechanisms (pupillary reaction, successive adaptation and simultaneous contrast) often omitted in later explanations. The concept of memory color served Katz as a point of departure for constructing his color theory. In the second edition of his chief work, color constancy is treated in a way not fundamentally different from his handling of the other types of object constancies; he does not reduce it to factors of previous experience, which is what memory colors are undoubtedly considered to be.

Already in his first edition Katz aimed at a synthesis of the dualistic view shared by both Hering and Helmholtz. Just as Hering included both physiological and "higher-order" psychological (memory colors and learning) among his explanatory principles, so Helmholtz too referred both to traditional physiological determinants and to something reminiscent of cognition and reasoning, his famous "unconscious inferences" (*unbewusste Schlüsse*). "Pure" sensations, i.e., proximal ones, act as signals for cognition, which bases its unconscious inferences about distal stimulus objects upon them.[12] Explanations founded on two different levels and therefore dualistic in structure were an unavoidable outcome of sensory elementism. It was inconceivable that something like an interactional pattern of relations among elements could serve as immediate stimuli. Even Katz cannot be considered successful in his attempt to avoid a dualistic explanatory principle operating on two parallel levels. Katz assumed two sensory processes to account for his results. According to him, the most primordial is the perception of film colors, something which we can accomplish in the periphery of the retina. Thus all "retinal vision" is governed by the ordinary optical rules of refraction and reflection. This elementary

---

[11] E. Hering, "Grundzüge der Lehre vom Lichtsinn," in Graefe-Saemisch (ed.), *Handbuch der gesamten Augenheilkunde* (Leipzig, 1905–11; Berlin, 1920).

[12] H. v. Helmholtz, *Handbuch der physiologischen Optik III: Die Lehre von den Gesichtswahrnehmungen* (Leipzig: Voss, 1896), pp. 582, 947.

mode of perception can always be reinstituted by the "method of reduction." "Reduced vision" thus equals elementary, retinal vision. Immediate, natural visual perception is, however, also governed by a "higher," "central" component. This was the assumption which led Katz to his concept of "transformation." Color constancy is a kind of transformed color vision. When constancies occur in our visual world, they are the result of optically determined elementary sensations the content of which has been transformed to fit the conditions of the total situation better.

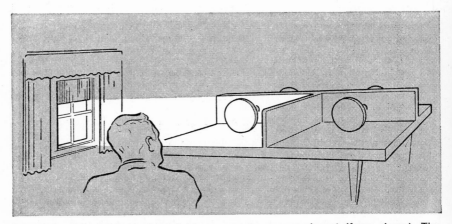

FIG. 9–5. The fundamental brightness constancy experiment (from above). The motors of the color mixers are hidden behind the background screen. The subject sees two colored discs.

These considerations can be readily illustrated by reference to one of Katz's experiments (Figure 9–5). In front of the subject on a table are two color mixers with black and white sectors. They stand parallel against a neutral grey background which also screens the motors of the mixers from the subject. All light falling on the circular discs on the mixers comes from a side window. Between the discs is a vertical screen which shadows the disc which is further away from the window. Before starting the experiment, the same proportions of black and white are mounted on both mixers. The two mixtures, as soon as they are seen, look different in two different ways. First of all, the shadowed disc looks darker. To produce a color equation, the white sector on the shadowed disc must be enlarged. The existence of a certain amount of *brightness constancy* can easily be demonstrated by reference to the optically surprising outcome of the experiment. *The white sector of the shadowed disc does not need to be enlarged to the extent which would optically compensate for the decrease in the amount of reflected light produced by the shadow.* Even a slight increase in its albedo will make the disc in shadow phenomenally similar to the other one, *because it looks rather light all along, almost invariant in color* but at the same time standing *in the darkness of the shadow.* The equation which can be produced by slightly increasing the white sector of the disc in shadow does not correspond at all to the equation produced by viewing the two discs alone, without the surround, through the openings in a reduction screen. In this reduced situation the subject compares two *film colors*—the articulation into a colored surface and a shadow cast upon it cannot occur.

Second, however, the discs look different in another way too. Even after the appropriate equation has been found in the first, "free observation" situation, so that a maximum similarity in brightness has been achieved, the grey discs are not experienced as equal. Katz has convincingly described this other category of dissimilarity. The grey surface which is seen "through the shadow" looks *clearer*, more intense, and shinier, even when both discs have an identical albedo. Katz calls this greater *salience.* Such differences constitute "additional stimuli," which contribute to the appearance of object constancies. Analogous to these illumination cues are the "concomitant stimuli" used in arriving at the divisor in the invariance ratio in shape and size constancy. Perception of the angle of inclination thus affected the appearance of the ellipse; the determination of the distance of the parallel squares rendered their size perception more accurate, etc.

Degree of Color Constancy

In his color psychology Katz devised a method for measuring brightness constancy. He defined his B quotient as the ratio of the albedo of the unshadowed disc to that of the shadowed in the "free observation" situation (measured in degrees of white of the color-mixer sectors when the two discs look equal in albedo). The other, the Q quotient, gives the ratio of the albedo of the unshadowed disc freely observed to the albedo of the same disc in the "reduced situation." For example, if the shadowed grey is at 300° white and the unshadowed equals 200° in the free observation situation, then $B = 200/300$ and Q might equal 200/20 (i.e., the shadowed disc looks 10 times darker in the reduced situation). Clearly, we could also apply Brunswik's equation to these values. This time r in the equation is the degrees of white in the freely observed shadowed disc (the "real" grey of the color behind the shadow), s is the corresponding value for the unshadowed disc (that is, the "seen color" of the shadowed grey, or how bright r looks) and p is the value for the unshadowed grey when it is viewed through the reduction screen (that is, the "projective color" of r in the reduced situation). Consequently, we could write:

$$R = 100 \frac{200 - 20}{300 - 20} = 64 \, .$$

Theoretical Explanations

After the publication of the first edition of Katz's book in 1911, several investigators attempted a synthesis by relying only on "physiological" arguments. There were, for instance, the rather odd "parallel laws" formulated by Jaensch and Müller, according to which color constancy and color contrast could be analogously explained by common principles. Quantitative measurements of brightness contrast performed by Hess and Pretori could be directly applied to the determination of brightness constancy according to the second parallel law, if the inner field in contrast experiments is considered parallel to the illuminated color surface and the contrast-inducing surrounding field is considered analogous to the prevailing illumination. These efforts of Jaensch and Müller were heavily criticized, and even Gelb has his doubts.[13] About 1940 the correlation between contrast and constancy phenomena was studied in a research project at the University of Helsinki. Measurements were performed on about 100 subjects and the results, with Pearson product-moment correlations as well as with related techniques, were entirely negative.

Bühler, too, tried his hand at getting rid of the dualism of simultaneous recourse to psychological *and* physiological explanations.[14] According to his theory, the difference Katz noticed between free and reduced visual perception can be accounted for by reference to the luminous "specific light" (*Eigenlicht*) of the air produced by the billions of microorganisms in the atmosphere, but Bühler's theory has not been supported by empirical evidence.

---

[13] A. Gelb in Bethe's *Handbuch der normalen und pathologischen Physiologie*, 11, No. 1 (Berlin: Springer, 1929), pp. 663–66.

[14] K. Bühler, "Die Erscheinungsweisen der Farben," *Handbuch der Psychologie*, I, Heft 1 (Jena: Fischer, 1922).

It was the authority of Gelb that provided the impetus for what can be called relational explanations. With this approach, the old problem of reconciling "psychological" and "physiological" aspects disappears and becomes a pseudoproblem. It turns out that Gelb's relational considerations can fully account for *brightness constancy*. Furthermore, the brightness gradients that accompany virtually all spatial chromatic hues can also, as mentioned above (page 88), form the basis for explaining *hue constancy* in terms of relational systems among stimuli. The basic principle of gradients of reflected intensity thus leads to a theoretically significant broadening of Gelb's original formulation.

Gelb does not consider the conventional descriptive distinction between "the illumination" and "the illuminated surface" very fruitful. Whenever a perceptual event involves color constancy, we can always discover a constant ratio, a relational invariance in the prevailing stimulus constellation. What generally matters are the ratios of the intensities of radiations reflected from different visible surfaces. If the stimulus pattern did not contain a system of relations among reflected light intensities, or, more specifically, if the amount of light reflected from one area A could not be seen *in relation to* the amount of light reflected from another area B, we could not experience brightness constancy. According to Gelb, our reaction to ratios of light intensities is primordial, and hue discrimination is acquired much later.

A related issue concerns the effect on color perception of the structure of the total visual field. Gelb not only pointed to intensity gradients as bases for color constancy, but also stressed how these gradients depend upon spatial conditions. With his brilliant "paradoxical experiment," Gelb laid to rest Katz's concept of "normal illumination." Using Katz's paradigm (Figure 9–5), Gelb placed the experimental subject in the same screened illumination which darkened the shadowed disc; under this condition, the phenomenal change occurred within the color of the *other* disc, the unshadowed one Katz considered the "standard" disc in "normal illumination."[15]

Consider another famous experiment of Gelb's. Suppose the stimulus constellations for color perception can be described by the formula

$$P = f(S, p, q \ldots) ,$$

<hr />

[15] Gelb, *op cit.*, pp. 652–53.

that is, the percept is a function of the light intensity (S) and of various physiological conditions p, q . . . (pupillary reaction, adaptation, contrasts). We could also add some letters, X, Y, Z for "spatial conditions." The experiment uses a large, black rotating disc carefully illuminated by a beam of light which is precisely confined to the surface of the disc. The light source is screened from the observer. Thus this "really black" disc, because of the strong illumination and of the rotation which eliminates its surface structure, phenomenally appears white. Since there are no additional reflecting surfaces, no brightness constancy occurs, and it is impossible to see the disc in its "own," "real" black color. A naïve observer brought into the room unequivocally sees a white disc. If now a narrow strip of white paper is inserted into the light beam just in front of the disc, so that two surfaces, reflecting light to a different extent, can be seen, the disc which had previously looked white instantly turns black. If the strip is removed, the white color returns.[16] Only someone who has actually seen the experiment with the dramatic changes in the disc's appearance, can fully understand how convincingly it proves that *there is no such thing as a brightness specific to an object, unless some neighboring reflecting surfaces are simultaneously visible.* But if they are not, the factors in our above formula are reduced. Then the perceived color depends only on S and *some* of the factors p, q . . . On the other hand, if the white strip is present, it produces *a ratio between two reflected radiations, a gradient*, and the experienced brightness promptly conforms to the gradient.

Wallach's Contribution

Köhler's student Wallach elegantly developed Gelb's experiment further. A grey disc was surrounded by a white ring, and the disc and the ring could be illuminated independently. The apparent greyness (the phenomenal albedo) of the disc proved to depend on the brightness of the surrounding ring. Then Wallach doubled the whole arrangement. By means of four separate light sources he illuminated four areas independently, yielding two circular discs, each surrounded by a ring (see Figure 9–6). Let us call the light intensity reflected by the left-hand disc i_1 and the intensity of its surrounding ring I_1. Wallach chose intensities which stood in a

---

[16] *Ibid.*, pp. 674–75.

simple relation, such as 1:2. Then an intensity I_2 was given to the ring on the right, this intensity being some fraction of I_1. The task of the subject was to set the intensity of the right-hand disc, i_2, *so that the brightness of the two discs would be as similar as possible.* It turns out that the subject, without any conscious intent, succeeds in giving i_2 a value which fits astonishingly well the equation

$$i_2 : I_2 = i_1 : I_1 .$$

Wallach's experiment clearly demonstrates that the grey color of an object depends on a system of relations, i.e., on gradients of reflected radiations. It is important to remember, however, that all four color fields in Wallach's experiment were located on a *common plane sur-face.* The outcome could well also be the result of contrast. It remains an

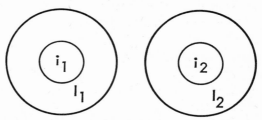

FIG. 9–6. Wallach's experiment.

unsettled question whether Wallach's finding is a "retinal" or a "central" perceptual achievement.[17]

Thus we may agree with Gelb in assuming that color constancy is generally an inherent primordial tendency to adjust to reflectance gradients on surfaces. We must not forget, however, that man can also *experience hues.*

Hue and Brightness Constancy

The hue of a color depends to some extent on the adaptation level of the receptors, on contrast effects, and on the size of the colored surface. It depends primarily on the wavelength of the radiation. Phenomenal brightness, however, rests on an immense number of factors. It is determined by psychophysical relations such as light intensity, wavelength composition of the radiation, adaptation, length of exposure, pupillary reaction, and brightness contrast conditions.

From what experiments have shown so far, we would expect the *hues* of objects to exhibit a high degree of constancy, while

[17] Charles Osgood, *Method and Theory in Experimental Psychology* (New York: Oxford University Press, 1953), pp. 281–83.

brightness should be less constant and rather variable because of its dependence upon the entire illuminated area.

Immediate experience confirms these conclusions. All visually sensitive organisms are subjected daily to enormous changes in reflected intensities. What the "absolute" or "specific" brightness of some object would be does not greatly concern the organism, which, rather, is greatly affected by how constant the brightness of object surfaces remain *relative to each other*. Brightness constancy is highly relational indeed. On the other hand, hue constancy is easily lost as soon as the light course exceeds a habitually low level of *saturation*. In the illumination at a gala masked ball all objects seem to change color. Apparently we must revise our recent conclusion. The claim that the hues of objects maintain a very high degree of constancy holds only for colors in daylight. Normal natural changes in daylight have no noteworthy effect on the hues of objects in our environment. On the other hand, hue constancy disappears at night due to the disruptive effect of dark adaptation. When man turned to the use of artificial lights, it was *only a natural consequence that this change should disturb his hue constancies*. It is worth noting, however, that not all kinds of artificial light affect our vision to the same extent. The more similar the artificial light is to natural daylight in its physical properties (spectral distribution, consistency, levels of intensity, etc.) the better can a naïve organism adjust with color discriminations learned in the original biologically natural illumination.

The emphasis here that hue perception presupposes a different frame of reference from that affecting brightness perception should not obscure the general fact that every hue at the same time has its own brightness. For that reason, when the hues of various surfaces around us appear constant, this "order of hues" as a spatially successive series also presupposes characteristic gradients of reflectance intensities. *The substance of the matter of color constancy in perceptual objects is thus given by the systems of relationships of wavelength zones and of the interrelated intensity gradients produced by these wavelengths.*

The Factors of Field Size and Complexity

If, as in Gelb's ingenious approach, color constancy is to be explained by means of stimulus gradients, then Katz's famous *laws of field size* could be considered axioms on the significance of gradients. Katz states his laws as follows:

> If within an area of the visual field which is filled with objects the intensity of the illumination is uniformly reduced, the changed impression thus induced varies with the way in which this area is filled. If only a small section of the external world is seen within it, the colors of the objects are then in essential correspondence with the intensity of retinal excitation and with the illumination perceived in the total visual field. If a large section of the external world is seen within this area (at a correspondingly greater distance), the illumination within it appears reduced, and the colors undergo such changes as they would undergo if the illumination of the whole visual field were reduced.[18]

> This consistent relationship between change in illumination impression of part of the visual field and change in its *real* size (i.e., change in its retinal size) or in *apparent* size (retinal size held constant) may be expressed in two laws. These we may term the *first and second laws of field size.*[19]

Presumably the laws refer respectively to the *retinal* and the *apparent* size of the field. The larger the field *actually is* (law I) or *appears to be* (law II), the less likely is a color to look like a film color.

Shortly after Katz's book on color appeared, Henneman systematically studied the role of field complexity in brightness constancy.[20] Interested in how accurately the "real" color of a grey mixture on a disc in the *left* part of the perceptual field could be measured by adjusting the black and white sections on an exactly similar disc on the *right*, he filled the left part with successively more and more "visual objects," as shown in Figure 9–7. The white sector values required for the right-hand disc in the different situations were entered as *s*-values in Brunswik's ratio. Thus, for example, the *R*-index in situation 1 scored 0.03, it went up to 0.32 for situation 2, to 0.44 for situation 3, to 0.50 for situation 4, and to 0.53 for situation 5. Hence, as the differentiation of the perceptual field was successively improved, the *R*-values increased accordingly.

Object constancies in modalities other than vision will be examined in Chapter 14.

[18] D. Katz, *The World of Colour* (London: Kegan Paul, 1935), p. 217.
[19] *Ibid.*, p. 219.
[20] R. H. Henneman, "A Photometric Study of the Perception of Object Color," *Archives of Psychology*, 179 (1935).

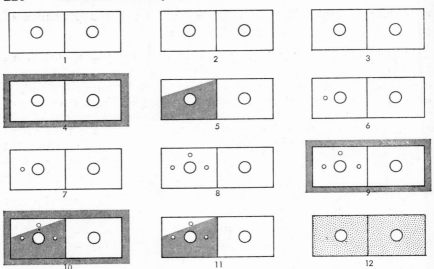

FIG. 9–7. The successive experimental conditions used by Henneman. The left circle in each numbered field is the standard color wheel. The perceived brightness of its grey is measured by mixing black and white on the right-hand color wheel (the variable). Except for the rectangles, other parts of the visual field are screened. The conditions are: (1) The two discs viewed monocularly and alternately through tubes. (2) Binocular perception through a reduction screen. (3) Same as condition 2, but with larger openings. (4) Free observation, with a border visible around the rectangles. (5) Standard wheel shadowed. (6) Small grey circle added close to the standard. (7) Black circle introduced. (8–11) Combinations of earlier situations. (12) Observation from a closer distance, 2½ feet from the discs. The "object constancy" of the standard grey increases up to condition 11 (in other words, the variable must be made more and more different from its setting in the reduced situation).

CHAPTER 10

The Differentiation of Visual-Tactual Space

Biological Origins of Perceptual Space

THERE HAS BEEN much argument about whether vision or touch is prior in the development of our clearly articulated perceptual space. If we consider again what was said in previous chapters about the interaction of modalities, we may safely state that phylogenetically such alternatives hardly exist. At the dawn of human history there was probably a "primitive space" supported in an unarticulated and diffuse way by several different sense modalities. Apparently, *all receptors* originally participated in the mediation of *biologically relevant* information concerning events in the surrounding habitat. As soon as some kind of division of labor came about, vision and touch formed a kind of framework for experiences of depth, a framework to which all spatial perceptions are constantly referred.

Admittedly, up to now phenomenal space has generally been treated as primarily *visual*, but Révész deserves our appreciation for having pointed to the original and independent existence of what could be called a *tactual space*. And, to be sure, the difficulties with this sense are much less complex than when we try to conceive of an original, independent auditory space. According to prevailing opinion, supported by much research, man has a phenomenal *world of visual-tactual objects* (*Dingwelt, Gegenstandsraum*) into which he places his other, especially auditory, spatial experiences, to coordinate them in the most natural way with perceived objects. Thus we use a *visual-tactual frame of reference* in perceiving spatial relations. For ease of exposition, visual and tactual spaces will, to some extent, be handled separately in the following discussion. It should not be forgotten, however, that they actually constitute a coordi-

227

nated, unitary basis for spatial perception. Their interaction will be examined on various occasions.

COMPONENTS OF VISUAL SPACE

According to Hofmann, *visual space* is a system of relations among points of location, among the size and shape characteristics of visual objects, whether they are organized in two or three dimensions. The individual's organism, his living body, forms a kind of origin for his spatial frame of reference. The three cardinal dimensions for our visual space, the vertical, the horizontal, and the sagittal planes, meet at right angles right between our eyes. The sagittal plane can be conceived of as standing vertically, as it were like a partition between the eyes, continuing forward and back from the head and body of the observer and dividing all of phenomenal space into a left half and a right. This plane, which is parallel to the line of vision, is also sometimes called the *median plane*. The frontal plane is vertical and parallel to the forehead of the subject, intersecting his line of vision at right angles; and the horizontal plane runs through the line connecting the pupils of the eyes.

If we stand upright, looking straight ahead, these *subjective* planes coincide with the imaginary *objective* ones. The objective planes constitute a system of reference governed by gravity, which provides the criterion position for our vertical and sagittal planes, with the objective horizontal plane tangent to the surface of the earth. This imaginary objective coordinate system appears to be in some sense constant, and people refer their spatial experiences to it when talking about perceived space; they do so independently of their own bodily orientation. The placement of perceptual objects in this objective system of coordinates is called *absolute localization*, while *relative localization* refers to the spatial relationship of two perceptual objects to each other. If the localization is not absolute but is performed according to what might be considered a subjective coordinate system, with the observer at the origin, it is called *egocentric localization*, e.g., of directions, displacements, and distances. Let us begin with an examination of the organization of two-dimensional perceptual space.[1]

Metzger, a student of W. Köhler, studied monotonous, uniform visual stimulation by producing a *homogeneous visual field* (a *Ganzfeld*) in the following way: The experimental subject sat op-

[1] F. B. Hofmann, *Die Lehre vom Raumsinn des Auges*, I–II (Berlin: Springer, 1920, 1925), pp. 215–17.

posite a wall painted a homogeneous flat white and fixated on a point in its center. All seams along the corners and the edges of the walls were optically concealed by rounding them with bent cardboard sheets fastened to the wall. The illumination was homogeneous and began at a very dim level, from which it could be gradually increased. In the dimmest illumination all subjects reported a diffuse "light fog," which phenomenally was *space filling* like the *space colors* described by Katz. It was impossible to localize this white light as being on any clear-cut surface or as at a given distance from the subject. He was simply surrounded by it. After the intensity of the illumination had been increased beyond a certain threshold, the subject experienced his visual world as a concave surface. It seemed to curve around him, always oriented at right angles to his line of sight. The white was experienced as a *film color* at a distance almost corresponding to the physical distance of the wall, but devoid of what could be called the depth articulation and the micro structure of a real colored surface. When the illumination was sufficiently increased beyond this level, the surface of the wall finally appeared normally articulated and attained the character of a surface color.[2]

Gradual Differentiation of a Homogeneous Space

The experiment indicates that it is possible to see an object surface as having a surface color *only* if the illumination is sufficiently strong to permit the eye to accommodate to the irregularities of the surface—in other words, if it exceeds the *threshold* determined by the distance and other factors which reduce the ease of focusing. If accommodation is successful, the diffuse visual field becomes differentiated into object surfaces. Any structural irregularity in the visual field promotes the formation of a *system of reference*, which in turn serves as a basis for the further articulation of the percepts. A frame can develop from the smallest observable differences in the roughness of the surface.

Koffka sums up Metzger's results with the following four statements:

1. First, there is a diffuse undifferentiated visual field which appears space-filling. Even the lowest degree of articulation requires some minimally visible irregularities in the thing surface.

---

[2] W. Metzger, "Optische Untersuchungen am Ganzfeld, II Mitteilung: Zur Phänomenologie des homogenen Ganzfelds," *Psychologische Forschung*, 13, p. 10 ff.

2. The perception of a surface is already evidence of a considerable degree of articulation: objectless space and the colored surface have been differentiated.
3. Perception of a film color is a more primitive, early stage in a sequence of gradually increasing differentiation.
4. Phenomenal space assumes the minimum degree of volume articulation that is possible given the actual situation.

Metzger's statements also imply that even when the prevailing conditions are quite simple, as in the perception of two-dimensional plane patterns, no formed figures or gestalten can arise unless the stimulation contains some *unevenness* or *irregularity*. As soon as any inhomogeneity is introduced, numerous differentiations suddenly take place. What is actually meant by a perceptual gestalt on a two-dimensional surface? As a simple demonstration, take an inkblot on a sheet of white paper. The first condition for a gestalt to occur is some kind of inhomogeneity, some discontinuity in the situation. Given some discontinuity, the parts of the whole configuration which are sufficiently internally consistent and unitary are *segregated from the rest of the stimulus field*. The emergence of gestalten presupposes the formation and shaping of figural patterns as well as sheer segregation. Generally speaking, *homogeneous* stimulation initiates cohesive unifying field tensions, while *inhomogeneous* stimulation brings about isolating segregating tensions.

Visual gestalten emerge from the interaction between inner and outer conditions. If the field's homogeneity is disturbed for some reason, different *articulation possibilities* arise. In bringing about the fundamental differentiation between plane figures and their backgrounds, these articulation possibilities follow the familiar gestalt laws of perceptual organization.

Ambiguous Patterns—Figure and Ground

Rubin examined reversible or *ambiguous patterns*, using a variety of visual plane figures (cf. pages 14–15). A pattern is ambiguous if it or some parts of it can be seen in either of several ways. In Figures 10–1 through 10–4, if one part is perceived as a figure, the rest of the pattern becomes a ground, which seems to continue behind the part seen as figure. The ambiguous parts reverse, with what was previously seen as ground becoming figure while the previous figure becomes ground. In these patterns the contours of the seen figures do not look like sharp breaks in the

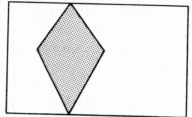

FIG. 10–1. An example of phenomenal figure-ground articulation.

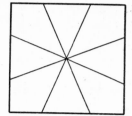

FIG. 10–2. Ambiguous figure-ground articulation.

plane on which the figure is seen, yet the figure seems somehow closer to the observer than the rest of the pattern, as though it were lying on top of the ground. Gestalt psychologists have tried experimentally to isolate the physical factors contributing to the emergence of particular phenomenal figure-ground articulations. The following principles have been proposed to account for the typical phenomenal appearance of patterns such as those illustrated in Figures 10–1 through 10–4.[3]

FIG. 10–3. Brightness differences and factor of proximity as contributing to figure-ground alternatives.

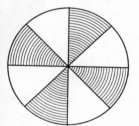 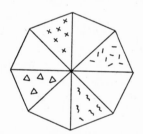 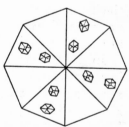

FIG. 10–4. Effect of the degree of articulation on the segregation of figures.

1. If several alternatives are otherwise equally salient, those subparts aligned with the vertical and horizontal cardinal dimensions are preferred as figures.
2. A part which is *smaller* than the entire patterned field or is *completely surrounded by it* is more likely to be seen as figure.
3. More *richly detailed* and *better articulated parts* tend to become figure.

---

[3] K. Koffka, *Principles of Gestalt Psychology* (London: Kegan Paul, 1935), p. 153.

4. *Symmetrically* organized parts of the field are more likely to be seen as figures.

Koffka considered the possibility that a part of the retina may have developed especially as an organ for the detection of figures (he was thinking particularly of the foveal cones). Some experimental evidence is consistent with such an assumption but is insufficient to provide strong, convincing support for it.[4]

Learning Effects Closely Investigated

Perceptual learning is a field which has been fraught with almost insurmountable difficulties. If previous learning does have a major influence on what is perceived, the most ubiquitous gestalten must, it seems, be formed at a very early stage of learning, probably during the first month or two of life. It is very difficult to demonstrate any effect of learning on the gestalten perceived by older persons; established perceptual functions typically look as though they must have been congenital. Systematic research aiming at a reconstruction of previously traversed stages has been difficult to perform. What have been carried out are comparative experiments on animals. Some hints have also been obtained by observing perceptual development in persons born blind who later recover sight. Improving medical knowledge and social care have reduced the incidence of such cases of children born blind who do not regain normal vision until long after birth. The previously reported cases are mostly rather poorly documented.

In 1932 Von Senden published a monograph summarizing a large number of cases, reported from 1695 to 1928, of congenitally blind persons whose sight was later restored by an operation. Révész (1950), in his book on psychology of the blind, carefully inspected Senden's material and concluded that the majority of the cases had been poorly examined or reported. He eliminated the cases which for various reasons seemed totally untrustworthy, and this left only 22 cases, from 1810 to 1928, which still were rather vague and unclear. The age of the patients averaged 17, with a range from 7 to 46, and including five children below 10 years of age. According to Révész, the following conclusions can, with considerable reservations, be drawn:

---

[4] See, for example, W. Köhler, *Die physischen Gestalten in Ruhe und im Stationären Zustand* (Erlangen: Philosophische Akademie, 1924), p. 207.

1. Differences in sizes of objects could, on some unexplored basis, be correctly discriminated immediately after the operation.
2. The recognition of visual forms immediately after the operation has not been clearly confirmed or disconfirmed.
3. Objects familiar to the patients as tactual forms could generally not be identified visually after the operation.
4. Recognition of familiar persons solely on the basis of their visual appearance could not be achieved by any of the patients immediately after operation.
5. Nothing general can be concluded about the patients' condition and ability visually to perceive movement.
6. In most cases two- and three-dimensional forms could not be distinguished solely on the basis of vision (a circular disc looked like a ball, not to mention difficulties with plane and perspective figures).[5]

Révész also called attention to the training period required after the operation for the patient to gain control over his eye movements, a fact later emphasized by Wertheimer.[6] If we assume that some visual learning occurs after the operation in the congenitally blind, no unequivocal evidence can be obtained until the patients have had this training period. Most writers appealing to Senden's material omit this postoperation period and just emphasize the poor visual performance of the patient.

Hebb (1949) has pointed out that in some cases the patients evidently were not able to recognize simple visual figures (circles, triangles, squares) even several weeks after the operation, although they could easily recognize them tactually. In one case the patient was able visually to recognize only a few faces even after two years, although this subject was considered exceptionally intelligent. Disabilities like these have occasionally been interpreted as indicating something about the role of early learning in the development of form perception.

Dember (1961) speculates that perceptual learning normally occurs rapidly, much as does the *imprinting* familiar from animal experiments. At some early stages children show an improved learning capacity, according to Montessori; during these periods they pick up experiences more rapidly and efficiently than earlier or later (e.g., the age of five seems to be the best for early reading

---

[5] G. Révész, *Psychology and Art of the Blind* (London: Longmans, Green & Co., Ltd., 1950), pp. 14–17.

[6] Michael Wertheimer, "Hebb and Senden on the Role of Learning in Perception," *American Journal of Psychology*, 64 (1951).

instruction). This argument would suggest that very young pre-school children can learn to form visual gestalten as soon as they have reached the appropriate level of development.[7]

Riesen (1949) tried to solve the problem by his method of rearing chimpanzees in darkness from birth. Although their visual performance was indeed impaired, it was discovered that the lack of light had caused deterioration of their retinas, a fact which interfered with any conclusions concerning the role of learning in perception. So, in 1950, Riesen repeated his experiment, with the difference that one chimpanzee was reared in complete darkness until age seven months, while another was allowed experience with a homogeneous light fog (a *Ganzfeld*, described above, page 228) for 1½ hours a day. These conditions were achieved by means of a translucent plastic helmet which completely encased the head of the animal, so that no objects, shapes, or figures were discernible. A third animal spent the daily time of 1½ hours in a normal illuminated environment. Some deterioration was again observable in the eyes of the chimpanzee raised in complete darkness. The retinas of the two others appeared normal. The animal reared in regular daylight perceived normally. The two others were immature and undeveloped in their performance; they only gradually learned to follow moving objects with their eyes. Their behavior was also deficient in other ways which Riesen interpreted as a retardation of their form perception. Yet there remains the possibility that the main cause of their poorer vision was the lack of training in eye movements, not principally the insufficient conditions for perceptual learning.[8]

Comparable results have been obtained in other sensory deprivation experiments. Some research workers prevented chimpanzees from having normal touch experiences during their early months of development (Nissen, Chow, Semmes, 1951); others impoverished the visual environment of birds and rats (Siegel, 1953; Walk, Eleanor J. Gibson, Tighe, 1957). A few experimental results clearly argue against the significance of previous learning. Thus, for example, Wertheimer in 1961 reported that a newborn baby, less than 10 minutes old, was able to turn its head and eyes in the

[7] W. N. Dember, *Psychology of Perception* (New York: Holt, Rinehart & Winston, Inc., 1961), pp. 240–41.

[8] See A. H. Riesen, "Arrested Vision," *Scientific American*, 183 (1950), and "The Development of Visual Perception in Man and Chimpanzee," *Science*, 106 (1949).

direction of a sound; this finding indicates that learning is not essential for at least some crude forms of space perception.[9] A more extensive series of studies was done with rats by the Gibsons and their collaborators. They found that for the development of correct visual size perception the rats were unaffected by their previous experiences. On the other hand, rats kept in homes as children's pets developed faster and became more intelligent than rats reared in the

FIG. 10–5. Sensory deprivation is a method for studying the role of early experience in perceptual learning. The picture shows a 30-month-old chimpanzee who was raised from birth with hands and feet encapsulated. In the test situation the ape could not be conditioned to discriminate between touches in two places on the back of his hand as a signal for getting food, a performance which is easy for normal chimpanzees.

usual way in cages (Hebb, 1949). Hymowitch (1952) showed that the visual characteristics of the immediate postnatal environment are significant for the development of visual form perception in rats, a conclusion confirmed in a study by Forgus (1956). E. J. Gibson and her students found that rats raised in cages decorated with geometrical figures later were better at discriminating among these shapes than animals reared in ordinary bare cages (Gibson and Walk, 1956; Gibson, Walk, Pick, and Tighe, 1958).

In experimenting with the visual cliff (shown in Figures 10–6 and 10–7), which they designed and constructed, E. J. Gibson and R. D. Walk (1960) observed that all infants and young animals used in the experiment, and who were able to move around, stopped at the edge of the cliff and could not be persuaded to go straight

---

[9] Michael Wertheimer, "Psychomotor Coordination of Auditory and Visual Space at Birth," *Science*, 134 (1961).

ahead. This happened even with a completely artificial cliff, made by choosing patterns of squares so as to conform with the perspective transformation of the size of the squares in accordance with the distance gradient of texture.[10] The investigators did not insist that depth perception is innate in the children and animals, but nevertheless pointed out that it would probably have been difficult for many species to survive if they had been forced to learn depth perception through trial and error. E. H. Hess repeated this argument in a study

FIGS. 10–6 and 10–7. The striking experiment of the visual cliff (performed by E. J. Gibson and R. D. Walk at Cornell University). A four-week-old kitten, as well as a half-year-old human baby, stop spontaneously at the "edge" (which is actually covered by glass), refusing to proceed when confronted with the edge the first time. Visual depth perception thus occurs almost immediately as soon as general visual functioning develops.

(1961) in which he tried to show the extent to which learning can be considered responsible for the depth articulation of surfaces with various distributions of light and shadow (see Figure 10–20, page 248). Hess could, first confirm the priority of a phenomenal articulation which corresponds to the surface being illuminated consistently from the left and above as reported previously by Metzger and von Fieandt (1938).[11] His results are not inconsistent with Metzger's

_____

[10] E. J. Gibson and R. D. Walk, "The Visual Cliff," *Scientific American*, 202 (1960).

[11] W. Metzger, *Gesetze des Sehens* (Frankfurt am Main: Kramer, 1936); also K. v. Fieandt, *Über Sehen von Tiefengebilden bei wechselnder Beleuchtungsrichtung* (Helsinki, 1938).

and Fieandt's conclusions in that he conditioned chicks from the moment of hatching to receive their grain in a unilateral directional illumination. Different groups of chicks were always fed in differently oriented light. The two other authors, however, found that one particular prevailing perceived illumination, that from above left, is pre-

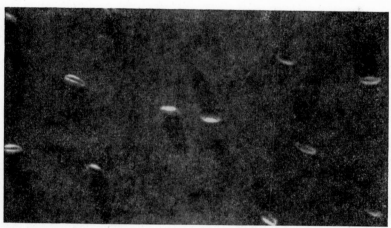

FIG. 10–8. Hess's photograph of wheat grains, which was presented to the chicken in an upright (frontal) position. In the left half of the picture the grains are illuminated from above, in the right half from below.

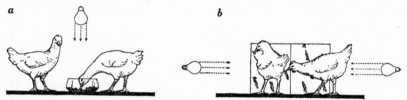

FIG. 10–9. In order to study the influence of previous experience on the role of light distribution in the perception of "bulges," Hess reared two groups of chickens in different feeding conditions. One group always had the grains illuminated from below, the other from above. Confronted with the photograph in Fig. 10–8, the birds chose either the left or the right half in accord with the distribution of shadows during training feedings.

ferred to all others without the need for any kind of motivated training in the experiment. Metzger and Fieandt are not inclined to interpret the results of their experiments as due to a "learning effect" (Figures 10–8 and 10–9).

Ames (1951) and his collaborators, the "transactionalists," claim to have shown with deceptive visual arrangements like that in

Figures 10–10 and 10–11 that visual organization in ambiguous situations follows the sensible expectations arising from extensive prior experience. There is, however, no systematic experimental evidence which unequivocally supports this interpretation of the pervasive effect of learning.

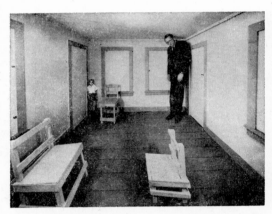

FIGS. 10–10 and 10–11. Ames's famous "distorted room" at Princeton University. If the subject looks monocularly through a small opening in the front wall, he obtains the paradoxical view shown in Fig. 10–10. The man standing in the right-hand corner appears to be a giant while the boy looks like a dwarf. Fig. 10–11 reveals the true structure of the room (here shown as a mirror image, that is, with left and right reversed). When only a part of the interior is seen without cues to the actual shape of the room and without a wider frame of reference than the walls and corners of the room itself, it appears rectangular in shape.

Organization of Three-dimensional Space

So far our discussion of visual gestalten has been restricted to relative localization of objects in two dimensions and to the determination of directions. Phenomena of *distance localization* have traditionally been explained as depending on binocular vision. The visual fields of the two eyes are ordinarily smoothly combined, the fusion being better the more the images on the two retinas hit corresponding points. This arrangement enables us to localize certain stimulus objects as closer or farther away than the fixated part of the visual field. The retinal images of such objects are disparate in the two eyes; that is, they hit noncorresponding spots in the left and right retinas. All points in space which have corresponding projections on both retinas are said to lie on the same *horopter circle*. The horopter is the locus of all points seen as single in binocular vision, i.e., the locus of all points whose images fall on corresponding points of the two retinas. In the horizontal plane the horopter is a circle which passes through the fixation point and the centers of the two eyes. The horizontal horopter can be extended into the *total horopter*, which is a spherical surface containing all loci which stimulate corresponding points, irrespective of the direction of the line of sight.[12] Although we shall not completely disregard sensory physiology in our description of the conventional cues for depth perception, we shall concentrate primarily on the psychologically interesting and relevant laws of organization of three-dimensional visual space.

The perception of direction in phenomenal space is based upon a number of interesting relationships. When on shipboard in a rough sea, we might be surprised by the predominance of *visual* directions inside our cabin. Although we are aware of the rolling of the ship, the phenomenal vertical dimension is still given by the walls and the horizontal one by the ceiling and floor of the cabin. Our clothes, hanging on clothes hangers on hooks on the wall, swing out into the space of the cabin, phenomenally approaching a horizontal position in a rather ghostly manner. *This immediate part of our visual space*, outlined by the sides of the rectangular cabin, *takes over the role of a visual system of reference*, and the *cardinal spatial dimensions are likely to be identified with the dominant directions of this subordinate system;* the rectangular frame of the window and the corners and the edges of the cabin outline this system. It is especially difficult to maintain perception of the objective, real cardinal directions in a banking aircraft, as when coming in for a landing. Phenomenally, the passengers typically perceive the surface of the earth or of water as steeply tilted with respect to the predominant, phenomenally normal orientation of the cabin.

Kleint has been especially interested in such phenomena.[13] Among other things, he studied phenomenal experience in various amusement park devices, such as a small cabin which can be turned around its horizontal axis while the subject sits in its center on a stationary chair. A string from which a small weight hangs is fastened on the ceiling. When the cabin is slowly tilted, the only

---

[12] Hofmann, *op. cit.*, pp. 231–33, 296 ff., and W. Trendelenburg, *Der Gesichts- Zeitschrift für Psychologit,* 1940.

[13] B. H. Kleint, "Versuche über die Wahrnehmung," in F. Schumann (ed.), "Beiträge zur Analyse der Gesichtswahrnehmungen," *Zeitschrift für Psychologie,* 1. Abteilung, 11 Heft, 1940.

thing the subject sees as diverging from the usual upright position of the little room is the string, which starts turning sideways. Soon the subject feels *himself* as turning with his chair, while the walls, the ceiling and the floor phenomenally maintain their normal position, their main directions being uncritically identified with the cardinal dimensions of normal three-dimensional gravitational space.

In another of Kleint's studies, slides of landscapes were projected on the white wall of a darkened room. The subject stood about 7 m. from the projected picture, which was about 2 × 2 m. large, and was asked to report the apparent position of the picture, i.e., whether it appeared tilted, and if so, how many degrees. Although the projected pictures were physically tilted, they were seen as normally oriented until a considerable inclination threshold had been exceeded. The subjects were amazingly slow to report any tilt, and oriented their own bodies according to the cardinal dimensions of the *picture*, with the danger of falling because of their hazardous posture. It is remarkable that the projected pictures after a while seemed to conform with the cardinal dimensions of the room. We have here a case parallel to the results obtained by Rausch. In Kleint's experiment the picture "normalizes," "straightens up" as did Rausch's parrallelogram. The sense of equilibrium seems not to provide sufficient control. The visual orientation, determined by the cardinal dimensions of the *picture*, seems to operate so autonomously that the subject orients himself according to the frame of the picture, rather than according to the actual structure of physical space. It is not until he is about to lose his equilibrium that a correction of the faultily seen "up" and "sideways" occurs.

Kleint concludes that what has often been claimed concerning visually produced variations in tonus really makes very good sense. Witkin and his collaborators studied some characteristic individual differences in spatial orientation. More independent and self-sufficient subjects relied primarily on gravitational and postural cues, while dependent, insecure subjects trusted more in their visual frame. The latter appeared not to count on their inner controls, but instead to conform throughout with their phenomenal environment. This strong dependency was also reflected in some of their difficulties in observing visceral changes in their own bodies. The dominant visual orientation can, however, reflect itself in the behavior of self-sufficient persons, too.

In addition to the above-mentioned everyday experiences in ships and aircraft, we could mention a number of further examples that demonstrate the priority of the visual localization of directions. Sometimes this preferred localization of directions is combined with illusory movements—as when we look at a landscape through the window of some moving vehicle. The cardinal interior dimensions of the vehicle are phenomenally identified with the gravitational, physical dimensions of space. If a railway car tilts on a curve because of the banked roadbed, we perceive tilted trees and buildings in the frame of the window, and the car phenomenally remains stable and upright in its orientation. The impression changes instantaneously as soon as one's head is put out of the window. Instead of the narrower system of reference provided by the walls of the car we suddenly can use the broader and larger outside dimensions which make us see the "outer world" corrected and our train as considerably tilted instead. The modes of appearance of colors demonstrated by Katz and reported in Chapter 4 can reasonably be compared with different modes of perception of directions. Here, too, we notice some "transformations," for example, disengagement from an impoverished frame of reference and the transition to richer and more articulated systems of relationships. The frame determined by the window or the closed cabin is a more restricted or *reduced situation*, corresponding to the "aperture colors" or film colors. An unrestricted view brings about greater object constancy, as was also the case with perceived surface colors.

If Metzger's experiment with the Ganzfeld is performed in opposite order, starting with the clearly differentiated, well-illuminated background, and a short, straight vertical line of light is projected on this ground, the so-called Aubert phenomenon may occur. As long as the level of illumination remains high enough, the line will be perceived as vertical if it is vertically exposed. During the next phase, if the weakening illumination renders the microstructure of the background and the richness of its cues invisible, the apparent orientation of the line becomes less accurate. The ambiguity is worse yet if the background is totally dark. Visual cues for the actual cardinal dimensions are then altogether unavailable and the frame of reference is confined to impressions based upon the observer's proprioceptive sensations. If he tilts his head, that affects the appearance of the line, which looks as though it is inclined in a direction opposite to that of the tilt of the head, even though the stimulating line actually remains physically vertical.

Depth Cues for Perceptual Space

The depth cues for three-dimensional vision investigated by traditional sensory physiology are listed in most textbooks of psychology. Best known are the following.

1. *Binocular disparity* (due to the binocular parallax mentioned in connection with the horopter circle, page 238) has for a long time been regarded as the primary depth cue. It is still considered important, although we must remember that its influence is greatest at short distances, within what might be called the biologically "near space." A sharply fixated spot or object will be projected on corresponding loci on the retinas. This makes it possible to localize points which do not fall on corresponding loci as either closer to us or further away than the horopter surface on which the fixated point is always located. If the edge C in the prism ABC is foveally and correspondingly projected, the other edges are noncorrespondingly projected on the retinas, resulting in the impression of three-dimensionality (Figure 10–12). That perception can be artificially misled by retinal disparity is demonstrated by the stereoscope (Figure 10–13) and the haploscope

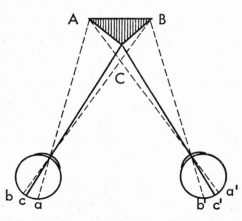

FIG. 10–12.   Demonstration of binocular disparity.

(Figure 10–14). These devices were explicitly designed to produce disparate projections of lines or pictures on the two retinas, and thus to yield illusions of three-dimensionality while using two-dimensional stimuli. Systematically slightly different plane figures, drawn so that they stimulate disparate parts of the retinas, can be made to fuse even without a stereoscope or other technical aids. A small amount of training is generally enough to make us able to look at these stereograms with appropriately converging eyes so that the pictures are retinally superimposed and phenomenally fused.

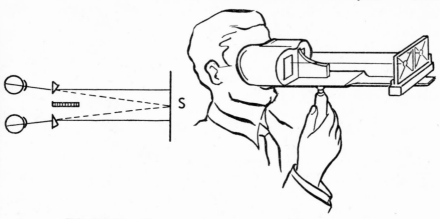

FIG. 10–13. Structure and function of the stereoscope.

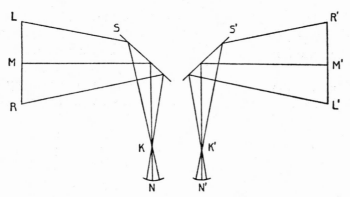

FIG. 10–14. Optical system of the mirror-haploscope.

2. *Motion parallax* sometimes complements or takes over the role played by binocular disparity, especially if we are compelled to look monocularly. The perceiver uses this cue if he moves his eyes or his head back and forth horizontally. As a result of these movements the projections of close objects are displaced to a greater extent than the corresponding projections of more remote objects, thus providing a cue for their distances.

3. *Accommodation of the lens* is a depth cue of minor psychological significance. The principle of its function can be seen in Figure 10–15. When focusing at remote objects the lens is flattened out as compared with its increased convexity when focusing at closer distances.

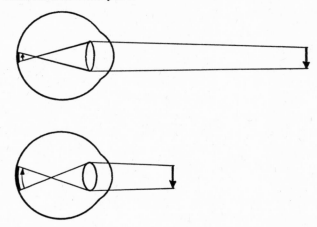

FIG. 10–15.   Principle of the accommodation.

4. *Visual acuity* is defined as the differential threshold for discriminating between two points located close together on the same horizontal line in a frontal plane. It is a significant depth cue.

5. *Convergence of the eyes* aims at producing sharply corresponding projections of objects at various distances (Figure

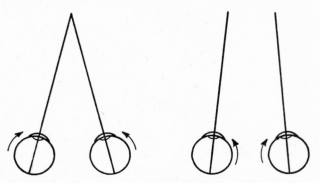

FIG. 10–16.   Two different degrees of convergence.

10–16). These eye rotations are accompanied by changes in the innervation and tension in the eye muscles and may function subconsciously as depth cues.

6. *Perspective transformations* have always been considered among the strongest cues for perceiving depth. They are equally effective in monocular and binocular vision. Their operation has

often been interpreted simply as an outcome of previous learning, which is somewhat too one-sided a point of view. Actually, perceptual organization of a stimulus pattern in accord with the principles of perspective constitutes choice of that alternative, among all other articulation possibilities, which achieves the *most uniform and most invariant total percept* or, in other words, *the minimum variability*.

The following are less important cues than those mentioned previously because they are quite often ambiguous, irrelevant or erroneous and may be due to accidental or incidental characteristics of the stimulus situation.

7. *Number of interposed space-filling objects.*
8. *Partly overlapping contours.*
9. *Distribution of light and shadow.*
10. *Color perspective.*
11. *Aerial perspective.*

Their role is to some extent shown in Figure 10–17 and Figure 10–18.

Gibson has emphatically pointed out that there are numerous depth cues which have been completely omitted by traditional perceptual psychologists. The cues considered so far have mostly resulted from an artificial concept of some kind of "empty," "abstract," three-dimensional space. Investigators have seemed to conceive of perceived or experienced depth as a vague kind of *distance*, as the shortest line between the retina and the seen object. This concept of distance is

FIG. 10–17. Effect of overlapping contours.

clearly an abstraction. In any case it has led research workers to look for physiological bases for our ability to locate various objects in this abstracted third dimension. Actually, *vision of differentiated distances* consists of *seeing objects standing on or located on substantial surfaces, mostly receding surfaces slanting away from the viewer.* The distances are not psychologically represented by straight lines running horizontally at eye level. Phenomenally, when we see

FIG. 10–18. The effect of aerial perspective. The interposed layers of air and dust, etc., clearly contribute to the impression of distance among objects.

objects at a distance, we conceive of them as located on a plane which begins below eye level and stretches out from us toward the seen objects. This entire articulated surface—not an empty space between us and the object—is what we have projected on our retinas. The distances are quite concretely represented on the retina. Among the more significant cues for perceiving depth are, therefore, the *retinal gradients* included in these projections of surfaces. Especially important are *gradients of increasing or decreasing density of elements in the surface structure*, or gradients of texture density. If a pattern of dots or objects of systematically increasing or decreasing size is projected on the retina, what is perceived is a surface which

FIG. 10–19. The gradient of texture density in a surface. Even if the upper half of the picture is covered, the simultaneously seen pieces of gravel tend to appear approximately equal in size, and hence a receding surface is clearly perceived even though other distance cues are absent.

recedes from the viewer, with the texture density greater at greater distances (Figure 10–19).[14]

Gibson's contribution is particularly valuable in that it points to some factors in space perception which were admittedly overlooked by earlier investigators. Furthermore, his observations confirm the importance of the role of organization, of articulation, in the effective perception of wholes. On the other hand, it might be wise to remain cautious about endorsing Gibson's view that such gra-

---

[14] See J. J. Gibson, *The Perception of the Visual World* (New York: Houghton Mifflin Co., 1950), pp. 59–76.

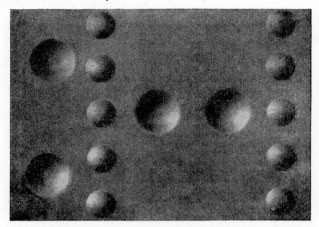

FIG. 10–20. The role of light and shadow in the depth articulation of a surface.

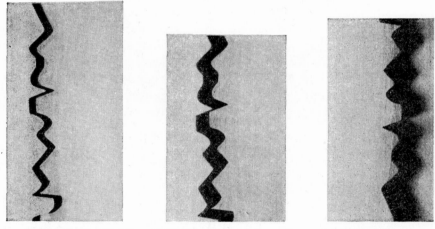

FIGS. 10–21, 10–22, and 10–23. Figures from Lauenstein's experiment.

In order to demonstrate the role of light and shadow in depth articulation, Lauenstein carried out a series of experiments on a board, the indented edge of which was illuminated by a hidden light source on the right of the spectator. The board was always experienced as closer compared with the background. When the illumination came almost directly from the front of the setup (Fig. 10–21), no shadow was actually perceived. The subject reported a plane, the edge of which was seen as equal in height, like a kind of step. This invariance was achieved instead of seeing a black stripe varying in width and direction. It was not until an extremely lateral illumination was adopted (Fig. 10–23) that the spectator experienced a shadow on the background.

dients, which are completely retinal, constitute the ultimate primary stimulus basis for all visual perception.

That the distribution of light and shadow can influence the perception of spatial forms decisively is clearly shown by the examples in Figures 10–20 through 10–23. Some principles of the operation of these depth articulations can be observed by looking at the figures from different angles of sight or by turning them upside down.[15]

THE INDEPENDENCY OF TACTUAL SPACE

Perceptual psychologists have sometimes been castigated for restricting themselves too exclusively to visual factors when exploring space perception. This one-sidedness need not surprise us, however, if we consider how dominant the sense of sight has been in the adaptation of the human species. We orient ourselves primarily with our visual impressions in three-dimensional space. Vision is so predominant that if a normal person is asked to imagine his location, his posture, and the limits of his body relative to the nearby environment, he immediately uses his visual memory images in his answer. When a normal-sighted person receives perceptual impressions which are diffuse and unarticulated (e.g., smells or sounds) he starts *looking for* the source of the smell or sound. His otherwise rather vague experiences can be visualized and objectified, can achieve a "real," "substantial" character, if he can *see* what is going on. People who lose their sense of sight maintain a visual attitude toward their spatial experiences for a long time, some of them even for life. As mentioned above in terms of its effects, visual space is interwoven functionally with tactual space, and the latter is more reliable if the surrounding world is to be described metrically. Furthermore, we stated that human beings tend to correct their ambiguous or distorted visual world by means of simultaneous touch experiences. Spatial touch perception is autonomous in several respects. Although the principles of the perceptual organization of our environment remain basically the same across all modalities, it must not be forgotten that haptic-tactual space exhibits particular regularities of its own. They can best be observed in *persons born blind*, and so tactual perception in its purest form must be studied in them. In the behavior of persons born blind, it is the sense of touch that takes over most of the *space-determining functions*. It has often been noticed that blind people show a tendency to *objectify smells* by means of their sense of touch. They try to touch the source of smell in order to perceive it accurately. That the sense of touch is

---

[15] As for references, cf. K. v. Fieandt, "Das phänomenologische Problem von Licht und Schatten," *Acta Psychologica*, 6 (1949), and Lotte Lauenstein, "Über räumliche Wirkungen von Licht und Schatten," *Psychologische Forschung*, 22 (1938), pp. 367–419.

capable of taking over this role of corroborating and checking attributes sensed in other modalities shows its high degree of adaptability. In addition to sight and hearing we have here a sense which can be developed to mediate symbolization, as shown by the invention and widespread use of the Braille alphabet.

The successive constitution of a differentiated world of tactual objects is reminiscent of corresponding visual phenomena. Analogous phases of structuring and articulation have been experimentally demonstrated. Recall what happens to visual space if the intensity of the illumination is gradually reduced. Such reduction produces a most diffuse visual space. The organizing effect of the illumination has its counterpart in tactual space in the form of *kinematics*, or the space-enriching influence of movements by the perceiver. If a sightless person stands or lies completely motionless, an egocentric organism space is developed, a *body space* which phenomenally is extremely narrow and restricted in all its dimensions. Only subjects born blind can reliably report on this phenomenal space, because even a person who was blinded later in life could hardly forget his earlier, richer visual world, nor could he avoid projecting visual memory images onto his impoverished environment.

This organism space is functionally a "near" space. All spatiality is restricted to proprioceptive experiences from one's own body. The only tactual component is the experience of weight against a supporting surface. In all other respects it is phenomenally nothing but an *empty space* without dimensions. The primary position of the vertical or the horizontal is greatly diminished.[16]

An immobile person living in his body space is certainly an extreme case. If he is allowed to perform the slightest movement, the body space changes into a *movement space*. It is more extended than body space, with some primitive distances and dimensions, but the individual himself still feels rather dimly and uncertainly located.

Both *body* and *movement space* are early, more primitive stages of *object space*. In order to understand how tactual object space gradually builds up, we must again consider some facts about our sense of touch as a sense for short distances. Contrary to what holds true in vision, touch really presupposes the establishment of some form of contact between the individual and the objects serving as

---

[16] G. Révész, *Psychology and Art of the Blind* (London: Longmans, Green & Co., Ltd., 1950), pp. 38–46.

stimuli. Our sense of touch is characterized, as already mentioned in an earlier connection, by a kind of bipolarity, in that it has its subjective pole, or sensation of what is going on at the receptor surface, and its objective pole, or sensation of the object making contact with this surface. Let us imagine that a person born blind, moving about in his movement space, makes contact with a chair, hitting its backrest with his arm. Immediately, the somatic experience of the subject's own body weakens or disappears, and what he actually experiences is something in the "outside world."[17]

The fundamental conditions for space perception are the same in the tactual as they are in the visual articulation of space. In both cases a sufficiently differentiated total situation is a prerequisite to the perception of objects. Kinematics, i.e., a moving receptor surface and moving limbs, plays a decisive role both in vision and in touch, although it is considerably more essential for faultless performance in touch than in vision. In tactual perception, movements are a counterpart to illumination in visual articulation.

Following Révész, we can refer the facts with which we have dealt so far to what we could call either *thing* or *space haptics*. Far more important however is the *form haptic*, which thus deserves attention.

A basic distinction among various kinds of perceptual performance the hand can engage in was made by Heller. He distinguished among tactile perceptions by (1) the stationary hand, (2) the moving hand, and (3) the grasping hand. If we call our immediate general impressions of the visually observed part of the world *synthetic*, it is clear that the most important portion of our haptic impressions, the two kinds which include *hand movements*, cannot be regarded as synthetic at all. Only what we obtain when touching with the immovable surface of the skin might be called a *synthetic perception*. Both movement of the hand surface and grasping movements provide us with what we could call an *analytic perception*. Révész in his account distinguished between *simultaneous* and *successive* tactile perception. We can, according to him, gain simultaneous general impressions not only with our immobile limbs but also by means of kinematics. All detailed, well-structured, tactile perception is successive in nature. If expressions like "tactual forms" and "tactual gestalten" are to be used, we must think of them

---

[17] *Ibid.*, pp. 49–51.

as temporal configurations in the same sense of the word as a melody is a temporal unit. Visual gestalten are mostly simultaneous; the time dimension is not essential for their structure, although successive, gradual development of them may occur in some cases. When Révész makes a distinction between *static* and *dynamic* touch experience, he considers the role of the continuously moving hands in their attempt to achieve a reliable judgment of the structure of a tactual object. Dynamic touching is far more important, because it implies intentional motion in an effort to obtain a clear impression of the object.[18]

Structuration Principles of Tactual Forms

In experimental investigations of blinded persons and those born blind, it was found that they use the following principles, which are generally not applicable in visual perception:

1. *The stereoplastic principle*, i.e., a strong tendency to *grasp* the object or successive parts of it gives the patient conditions for simultaneous *three-dimensional* articulation, conditions which are different from those used in the perception of instantly comprehended visual stimuli.

2. *The principle of successive perception.* No real haptic gestalten are possible without constructions based on successive sensations. In this respect touch is in a sense "atomistic" or "elementistic," to borrow an old expression.

3. *The kinematic principle* can be seen in a compulsion to move the hands and fingertips during the whole process of touching. It takes place even when the whole explorable surface is already in a state of motion, e.g., as a procedure of rubbing the fingertips opposite each other when the perceiver has to estimate the thickness of moving paper sheets.

4. *The metric principle.* Through touching we obtain contact between the receptor tissue and the surface of things. All measurement, familiar to us from everyday life, presupposes contact between corresponding points on a thing surface and a scaling or measuring device.

5. *The principle of an alternately receptive and purposive attitude.* If the patient stops in a passively receptive position similar to what is often said to be typical of visual perceivers, he may gain only raw material for *haptomorphic gestalten*. Persons who have

---

[18] *Ibid.*, pp. 60–69.

become blind, as well as normal subjects, not only receive impressions, but they also strive to complete their percepts through active intent. These intentions may, in any groups which engage in visual imagination, even result in visualized tactual forms, which are called *optomorphic gestalten*.

6. *The schematic principle.* "Preferred forms" are typical of blind and blindfolded subjects. Thus, for example, modeling in clay, or sculpture, follow a scheme from which it is difficult to free oneself.

7. *The principle of transposition.* People with normal sight and persons who have become blind tend to visualize their impressions.

8. *The principle of structural analysis* refers to the method used in forming analytic perceptions and temporal gestalten.

9. *The principle of constructive synthesis.* In contrast to immediately perceived visual forms, a successive construction takes place in the tactile modality. In so doing, the parts gradually added to a total form do not preserve their mutual harmony.

10. *The principle of autonomous formative activity.* If we want to use the word "gestalten" for tactual configurations, we should remember that these gestalten follow laws of their own.[19]

These principles are most salient if we compare object perception in people born blind with the perceptual processes of normal-sighted persons. It has already been pointed out that detailed articulation, no matter what modality is concerned, always involves successive *structural analysis.* Although our visual gestalten are usually simultaneous, we sometimes even go through a visual structural analysis. To borrow a striking example from Révész: if we are confronted for the first time with a complicated building, say a Gothic cathedral, maybe standing a little too close to it, we may resort to a gradual structural analysis.

Such an analysis is necessarily *successive.* A global, *simultaneous* perception could probably be obtained at a greater distance, if there were an opportunity to capture the entire building in a single glance. The form perception of the blind never contains such simultaneous gestalten. They always must proceed as if they were analyzing a Gothic cathedral. Therefore, the elaborated, well-articulated apprehension of forms is possible for the blind only with

---

[19] See G. Révész, *op cit.*, pp. 92–131.

successive perception. Whenever simultaneous tactual gestalten seem to occur, it actually is a matter of persons with visual memory traces (blindfolded persons or those blinded in childhood) learning to represent spatial forms by means of their simultaneous visualization. The congenitally blind would not be capable of generating such representations.

The specific nature of sculptures and of other modeled reproductions of perceived objects, when performed by sightless patients, especially the congenitally blind, must therefore be explained via their particular touching methods. Through a successive kinematic structural form analysis, they develop a topographical "map" of isolated details of the sculpture. These details are often accurate, but they cannot be fitted together, because a total overall impression is lacking. The nose of a human head points in an impossible direction, the folds of the face are exaggerated, etc. The process of construction is slow, stereotyped, and piecemeal and lacks the idea of a harmonious totality. In his thesis E. Ketonen, a Finnish psychologist, compares the working procedure of the congenitally blind with that of a child: the latter also forgets about the whole to be constructed when he is painstakingly preoccupied with elaborating a detail.

Later (in Chapter 13) we shall return to some of Révész' conclusions in relation to the expressive value of artistic products of the blind.

As pointed out at the beginning of this chapter, it is only the purpose of *clarifying the presentation* which justifies our isolation of visual and tactual functions to the extent that has characterized our discussion so far. An emphasis on the autonomous and self-determined nature of tactual gestalten is essential when we try to understand the picture the blind person has of the world or when we wish to examine the potentials and limits of visual components in sighted people's construction of three-dimensional space. Let us not forget, however, that in all normally sensing people the perceptual functions are *global* and *synthetically intermodal*. We have already seen that the localization of perceptual objects is intermodally determined. Each animal species has its dominant sensory modality. The diffuse impressions from various senses which lack clear-cut object or substantial character (in man the primitive "short-distance" modalities) are referred to the frame of reference offered by the better-developed telereceptors.

Analogies between Tactual and Other Modal Space Determinants

In dogs and related animals probably the *sense of smell* produces a framework which corresponds as it were to the human visual-tactual reference system. Kaila (1960) pointed to this priority of smell impressions in his dog when he described how the animal preferred to rely on the olfactory stimulation from a moving ball rather than follow its visible track. The role of olfaction in human object perception is much weaker indeed than that of other human telemodalities. The role of olfactory stimuli is already weakened by the fact of much longer *reaction times* in olfactory tissues. Our sense of touch, on the contrary, is superior to both vision and hearing if we want to determine precisely where and when a sweep of stimuli contacts our body surface. Yet as an actual telerecorder our tactual system is admittedly poor save for its vibratory components.

Relatively accurate *after-images* occur on the skin following fairly prolonged simultaneous patterns of pressure. Completion phenomena in the sense in which this word is used when investigating visual effects have rarely been observed in connection with simultaneous touch figures or immediately after them. If the skin surface is stimulated with a ring out of which a small section has been cut, the opening is still felt in the after-image produced by the pressure. No completing closure of the kind generally observed in visual after-images occurs. On the other hand, a tendency toward "good gestalt," or the so-called prägnanz tendency, has been demonstrated in successive tactual patterns. Thus Benussi, for example, was able to produce an apparent circular motion on the skin surface by having three thin, sharp identical pointers, arranged as the corners of an equilateral triangle, touch the skin alternatively in a tight regular rhythm (*ABCABC* . . . . . .).

Findings concerning tactual *eidetic phenomena* are controversial. What Révész has reported about the inadequacy of tactual form perception does not seem to support the likelihood that such phenomena occur.

There is an articulation into *figure* and *ground* in tactual perception. Touch experiences, too, are referred to a *framework*, which consists of a *haptic peristasis*. All tactual objects are localized by the observer in some way or another in relation to this system of reference. This framework has not been demonstrated to exist in the world of normally sighted persons, because it is completely dominated and covered over by the visual coordinates which usurp its function.

Tactual components always contribute to the phenomenal orientation of one's own body. Research workers have constructed special rotation apparatus which eliminates normal touch sensations of constant body pressure and other cues such as visceral and postural sensations occurring in longer lasting stable positions. The experimental subject reclines on a bed or is fastened at two or three points to a rotating frame. His task is simply to report on his phenomenal position. One thing showing the role of the cardinal dimensions is worth mentioning. Révész repeatedly pointed out that a reduction of the visual frame of reference would abolish even the priority of the vertical and the horizontal in phenomenal space. A person relying only on his tactual, kinesthetic, visceral, and vestibular sensations would not experience certain cardinal dimensions. Yet the experiments show us that a subject does succeed best in judging his objective position if his body is actually oriented along the horizontal or the vertical dimension. Any other position generally results in a discrepancy of some 10, 20, or more degrees between the estimated and the physical orientation.

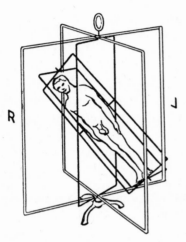

FIG. 10–24. Rotation apparatus used in the experiment on the recognition of body orientation.

It would really be surprising if this were not the case. The cerebellum has its centers of equilibrium. They are connected with the thalamic way stations of most sensory pathways. Kinesthetic sensations, tactual and visual orientation, thus all cooperate with the *sense of equilibrium.*

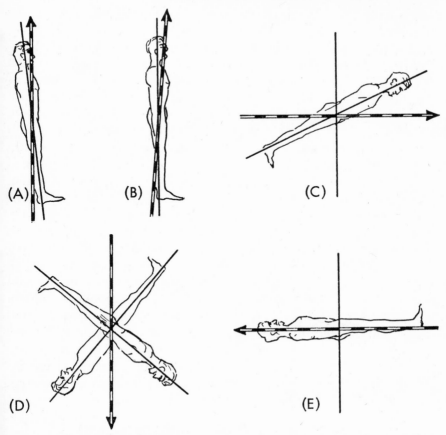

FIG. 10–25. Some illusions in the experience of body orientation. The wide arrow indicates the experienced orientation when the body is given the physical position shown. Apparent lying down on one's back corresponds the closest with the actual physical position. Leaning slightly backward is felt as about vertical, etc.

CHAPTER 11

Movement and Time Perception

IN RECENT YEARS psychologists have tended to emphasize the study of movement perception as a special field of its own. Among others, Vernon considered phenomenal motion autonomous in the sense that it does not simply and directly reflect displacements in the visual field; nor does the immediate perception of velocities imply awareness of the prevailing distance or time conditions. Confronted with a complicated moving pattern, the organism tends promptly to perform a perceptual motion analysis reminiscent of the Fourier analysis which occurs in the hearing of complex sounds. Also, according to Vernon, in movement perception those alternatives among the possible organizations are preferred which achieve the simplest and most elegant articulation of the pattern.

THE ANALYTIC CHARACTER OF MOVEMENT PERCEPTION

Consider a lecturer wandering back and forth in front of his audience. If he nods his head several times during his wandering, we perceive his face moving up and down vertically and at the same time see him moving horizontally. *We do not see* single points on his face moving along a sinusoidal line, which is what actually is happening physically to the local stimulus elements constituting his face.

Similarly, if we look at a waving passenger standing on the platform of a moving railway car, we see his hand going up and down simultaneously with the other movement component included in the stimulus pattern, the horizontal translatory motion of the person together with the train.

When performing such an analysis, perception follows *the law of the common motion state* as pointed out by Johansson in his doctoral thesis. Metzger had already concluded that the entire human sensory apparatus is especially sensitive to stimuli which are systemic, that is, serve to represent the total stimulus situation as well as having their specific local function. These systemic stimuli are generally *gradients which act as cues for physical invariances embedded in the pattern* (brightness invariances, invariances in surface texture, shape and size invariances, etc.). The law of the common motion state means that consistent displacements of a group of elements are perceived as a *change in the state of the whole system of stimuli.* In the above-mentioned examples the horizontal motion is seen as common, as belonging to all elements; it is the "system-determined" component of the pattern, and the vertical component is separated out because it does not participate in the common horizontal displacement.

When perceiving movement, we thus perform visual analyses which are comparable to mathematical analyses of physical motions. Certain combinations of components, among all the mathematically possible alternatives, appear *phenomenally* as the only real ones. The superiority of those alternatives which are customarily and immediately accepted as "natural" and self-evident becomes apparent in exceptional situations, for example, in darkness, when we cannot use familiar cues. The invisibility of the total stimulus system in night vision can destroy the entire system of reference, including the cues for discriminating the various components of a complex movement. The results of an otherwise clear analysis may then not be attainable. It is told that late one night Galileo came across the equation of the epicycloid while watching some Tuscan farmers amuse themselves by rolling wagon wheels, to which burning torches had been fastened, downhill. In daylight the entire rotating wheel is visible; all its elements participate phenomenally in the rotation, and the rotating wheel as a whole is experienced as performing a horizontal translatory motion. Usually the analysis results in these two components, but in darkness only the luminous track of one or two moving points is visible, so that without the possibility of analysis, all that is left as immediately visible is the epicycloid path.

The Finnish test psychologist Vahervuo chose this difficulty in visualizing the moving paths of single elements in a rotating figure as the starting point for constructing his rotation test of spatial imagination, which includes subtests like those shown in Figure

11–1. Forming a mental image of the path of movement which a single point in a rotating figure would trace, and drawing it with a pencil, proves to be surprisingly difficult. Because we conceive of a figure or an object as a whole which maintains its unity and rigidity when turning and moving, the specification of the path of movement of single elements feels like an artificial, unnatural request. It is unlikely that there have been opportunities to learn the skills required for such performances.[1]

The perception of movement and of time are closely related simply because phenomenal motion involves displacement in time

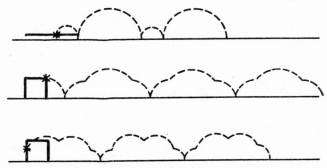

FIG. 11–1. Typical tasks in Vahervuo's rotation test.

and space. Furthermore, in physics, velocity is defined as a function of both time and distance. We have stated before, however, that phenomenally both motion and speed are autonomous experiences in themselves. When they are perceived, it is not necessary that there be simultaneous impressions of displacements in space or time. Therefore, throughout this presentation we shall consider the perception of motion and of time separately. Later we shall take up some phenomena which include parallel time and motion experiences within the same total impression.

Conditions for Apparent Motion

Phenomenal motion occurs under the following conditions:

1. The retinal image of a physically actually moving object proceeds over a stationary retina (= perception of "real movement").

---

[1] T. Vahervuo, *Tutkimuksia keskikoululaisten matemaattisesta suorituskyvystä* (On the mathematical ability of high-school students) (Helsinki: WSOY, 1948), pp. 43–45.

2. The projection of a physically stationary object is displaced across the retina as a consequence of eye or head movements. Presumably the intermodal receptor systems sensitive to changes in eye and head position (such as in the eye muscles or in the proprioceptors of the inner ear) are inhibited. It is, for example, possible to produce apparent motion of visual objects by pressing the eyeball lightly on one side. The usual sensory-motor cues of eye movement are absent in such a procedure.

3. The projection of a stationary object on a stationary retina can be seen as moving in the visual field as a consequence of certain endogenous conditions (e.g., movement after-images).

4. Stroboscopic apparent motion occurs when two different areas on the retina are successively stimulated. The appropriate time interval depends upon the intensity of the illumination, the viewing distance, the distance between the areas, and the total situation (e.g., the particular stimulus pattern). As a rule the interval should not exceed 200 msec.

Gestalt psychologists have emphasized that the operation performed by our perceptual apparatus in organizing single stationary successively ordered cell firings into a continuous perceived motion is analogous in cases 1 and 4. It is a fact that the phenomenal analysis of perceived "real movement" was begun only after stroboscopic phenomena had been studied for decades. These studies had led investigators to realize that the problems and processes in perceiving real physical motion are not peculiar, are not different from those in apparent motion. Apart from movies and television, case 4 plays only a minor role in everyday life.

What happens when we look at a movie? A series of successive stationary pictures evokes an illusion of movement as a consequence of rapidly presented minimal changes in the pattern of the pictures. The momentarily varying pictures are identical except for these small local changes which cause corresponding displacements in the retinal image of the onlooker. The successive, actually stationary pictures are projected for equal short moments on the screen, a rotating disc hides the phase of picture change from the viewer, and appropriate timing makes the successive stimulations fuse. What our visual system achieves is a *synthetic perception of movement*. The synthesis of the single local displacements is somewhat less effective when the film is run backwards, because then the synthetic fusion feels somewhat unnatural.

Superficially, one might be inclined to regard the visual perception of real physical movement as something fundamentally different. It has been claimed that when the stimulus consists of real continuous motion, our visual organs are not faced with the task of synthetic completion. Let us not forget, however, that although we may speak of a continuous displacement of the retinal image, the receptor tissue is actually composed of discrete elements. Not unlike what happens when we look at a movie or watch television, even in the case of "real physical movement" *the gaps between separately stimulated receptor units must be phenomenally filled.* The techniques of movies and television roughly reproduce the physiological situation on the receptor surface when real movement occurs and is perceived in our natural environment.

There is no need here to go into the cortical correlates of the successive retinal stimulations. In some stroboscopic experiments phenomenal movement has been obtained even with rather great distances between the stimulated parts of the retina. Despite the tight mosaic of adjacent receptor units, the stimulation can be permitted to skip intermediate zones of visual cells without reducing the apparent smooth continuity of the movement. On the other hand, DaSilva has observed—as have some other investigators—that stroboscopic motion is not as easily perceived as physical motion; the two are confused, he reports, only if the physical motion is presented in darkness or at high velocities. Precise exposure and time interval thresholds have been determined for various categories of apparent motion in careful experiments. DaSilva's results are controversial. Now, with the results of Piéron's, Humphrey's, and Springbett's experiments available, it is impossible to doubt the central, cortical contribution to these synthetic completion phenomena.

Fifty years ago, research concentrated on the question of the optimum length of *"the blank interval"* (i.e., the time elapsing between the two successive stimuli) in the production of stroboscopic motion. The limits 30 msec. and 200 msec. proved significant in many experiments. If the interval is as short as 30 msec. or less, the experience of succession is entirely lost, and one sees both stimuli *A* and *B* simultaneously without any impression of motion. If, on the other hand, the interval has a duration of 200 msec., two discrete stationary stimuli are seen as flashing and fading successively, without any apparent motion being involved in the alternation. It has turned out that the threshold for stroboscopic motion varies widely between these limits, but that it can readily be determined for every individual.

Stroboscopic and Pure Motion as Compared

Around 1910 Max Wertheimer set to work at Frankfurt with the recently invented Schumann tachistoscope, a laboratory device which permits several successive monocular exposures of extremely short durations (a few msec.). In his most crucial study (1912), Wertheimer presented successive views of two short vertical lines, A and B, 1 cm. apart and at a reading distance. He observed a peculiar phenomenal motion, never clearly described before if the blank interval was brief enough, i.e., close to the lower threshold (30 msec.) for stroboscopic motion. Because the interval was very brief (usually 60 msec.), both straight lines were seen simultaneously; nevertheless, something was perceived as moving from A to B. This was not a stroboscopic motion proper, because line A was not seen to leave its place and move over to B. Rather it was an objectless movement, or "pure motion" as Wertheimer called it. Without seeing any moving objects or figures, there is a clear impression of motion from one place to another. Instead of being a "sensation" in the traditional sense of the word, this experience could properly be called a *phenomenon*, as that word has been used by the phenomenologists. Thus Wertheimer called it *phenomenal movement* or ϕ-*phenomenon*, and it has been considered the starting point of the gestalt-psychological phenomenalistic method of describing the perceptual world.[2]

Investigating the Wertheimer Phenomenon

Another of Wertheimer's setups consisted of an old-fashioned slide projector in which movable wooden frames were used to hold the slides. Instead of slides Wertheimer placed pieces of cardboard in the frames. Two rectangular openings, a and b in Figure 11–2, were cut out of the stationary cardboard. The second frame, which slid over the stationary one, held a cardboard sheet with only a single rectangular opening, c, of the same shape and size as a and b. In the first position of the movable frame, c revealed only the opening a; in the second position it uncovered b. When exposure of

[2] Max Wertheimer, "Experimentelle Studien über das Sehen von Bewegung," *Zeitschrift für Psychologie*, 61 (1912).

openings *a* and *b* was alternated at a moderate velocity, the *vertical rectangle was seen to move from its initial position* a *to position* b. This is a case of stroboscopic movement, without the ϕ-phenomenon.

The latter would require a shorter "blank interval," so that *a* and *b* would be almost simultaneously visible, yet also giving an impression of *something moving from* a *to* b. What is interesting in the projector experiment is the similarity of the stroboscopic motion to the perceived motion of *c* when it actually is moved continuously across the visual field in a comparable amount of time. Especially interesting are the cases reproduced in Figures 11–3 and 11–4. The oblique line in Figure 11–4 is seen as turning along the shortest path, i.e., down to the right, and ending with an angle of 180°.

FIG. 11–2. A basic arrangement in an experiment on phenomenal movement.

Since Wertheimer published his pioneer article in 1912, various investigations of the same phenomena have been carried out, contributing to our knowledge of this field with studies of previously unfamiliar motion phenomena. If the arrowheads of the Müller-Lyer illusion are presented alternately or Wertheimer's rectangles in Figure 11–2 are varied in size, phenomenal shrinkages or enlargements occur in the moving figure, depending among other things upon the direction of the motion. More differentiated parts of the total pattern generally tend to be mobile in contrast to the less differentiated ones, which form the background for the ϕ-phenomena.

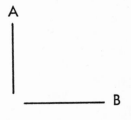

Korte later repeated Wertheimer's experiments, trying systematically to discover the principles of the occurrence of ϕ-phenomena. He investigated the role of the intensity of the illumination, of the distance between the end positions, and of the duration of the blank interval. The synthetic closure of gaps among separately stimulated parts of the retina has been shown to occur even under

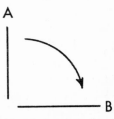

FIG. 11–3. An example of a phi-movement.

conditions less restricted than those described by Korte. The structure of the sequences in a movie shows that a biologically familiar set of displacements can successfully challenge the laboratory rules for stroboscopic motion (DaSilva).

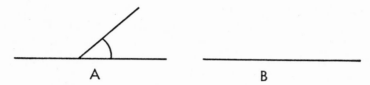

FIG. 11–4. Preconditions for another phi-movement.

Johansson's Contributions

Especially facinating is the *wandering-* or *w-phenomenon* discovered by Johansson (1950). In the most general terms, his results suggest that the gestalt law of common fate should be stressed more than it has been so far. Parts of a visual pattern which follow an identical path of movement are perceived as belonging together and as forming a "motion gestalt." Most interesting are Johansson's experiments on *motion analysis*. The main idea is shown in Figure 11–5, which illustrates one of his arrangements. The circles are

FIG. 11–5. An experiment in motion analysis.

spots of light on a common frontal plane in a dark room, and moving along the paths indicated by the broken lines. If all vertical and horizontal components in the motion pattern are in phase, i.e., if all spots are (1) at the top, (2) in the middle, and (3) at the bottom of the figure precisely at the same moment, *the subject is unable to see two circular and two vertical paths. What he sees instead is the common up and down movement of all four spots, while the two end spots, in addition to participating in this common motion, swing horizontally from side to side.*[3]

---

[3] G. Johansson, *Configurations in Event Perception: An Experimental Study* (Stockholm: Almqvist & Wiksell, 1950), pp. 78–80.

Johansson's w-phenomenon is a strange perceptual event, comparable to the original ϕ-phenomenon. If two circular translucent discs are illuminated from behind in a dark room, and the brightness of each is varied so that when the left disc decreases in brightness the brightness of the right disc is simultaneously increased by the same amount, *something is perceived as wandering from the darkened disc over to the brightened one* (and back again if we reverse the brightness change and return to the initial situation). *No moving object or figure is seen during this state of phenomenal motion.* The discs simply retain their positions. Analogous phenomena have been observed in sound perception if the intensities of two sound sources increase and decrease alternately in reciprocal proportion. A wandering phenomenon can even be demonstrated in the vibration sense, for example, if the intensity of the vibrations applied to one hand is increased proportionately to the simultaneous decrease of the intensity of vibratory stimulation to the other hand.[4]

In the wandering phenomena, too, perception seems to conform with an optimal meaningful invariant proportion among elements in the stimulus pattern. Ekman again points out that the perceptual system seems to carry out a physical analysis which could have been predicted mathematically from the characteristics of the stimulus.

Stereokinetic Motion

Another kind of apparent movement, the *stereokinetic phenomenon*, has been studied by Benussi and Musatti in Italy, by Renvall in Finland, and by Flock in the United States.[5] Large circular discs the size of dinner plates are viewed monocularly in a dim illumination and slowly rotated (five or six revolutions per minute). Drawn nonconcentrically near the edge of each disc is an asymmetrical figure (overlapping circles, ellipses, points, curves, etc.). The rotation also displaces these different elements of the inconsistent figure relative to each other. The perception of such a moving pattern undergoes successive organizational stages. At first glance the inner articulation of the presented pattern is minimal. The impression is almost chaotic: the elements appear to rotate around

---

[4] *Ibid.*, pp. 146–51.

[5] V. Benussi, *Archiv für die gesamte Psychologie*, 33 (1915); C. L. Musatti, *Archivio Italiano di Psicologia*, 3 (1924), pp. 105–20; P. Renvall, *Theorie des Stereokinetischen Phänomens* (Annales Universitatis Turkuensis), B 10, No. 1 (1929); H. R. Flock and C. Bartoli, translation of Musatti's paper with preface, notes, and comments (Cornell University, 1962).

each other with hardly any coherence or cohesiveness. In the second stage the partial or subordinate motions of the elements are gradually reduced. Different parts appear to move together, following common paths, resulting in a decrease in the endless variability and ambiguity of the seen whole. The end result of maximum invariance of the figural pattern is achieved when it is perceived as a turning plane projection of a three-dimensional object. Suddenly—and without any deliberate intent on the part of the observer—the pattern on the disc takes on a three-dimensional form and seems to stretch quite realistically out from the surface of the disc toward the observer. This solution allows maintenance of constant spatial relationships among the rotating elements of the total pattern. Investigators who appeal to the influence of habit, expectation, and previous learning on perception have a difficult time accounting for the results of such experiments.

Perceived Motion Directions

Perception of directed movement follows, at least in part, the principles of spatial organization which we formulated in considering the dimensions and directions of stationary space. Takala, in Finland, examined the predominance of the cardinal dimensions and left-right asymmetry in plane figures moving across a frontal plane. The present author performed analogous experiments with three-dimensional situations, paying particular attention to the frontal and sagittal dimensions.

In Takala's fundamental experiment, a single spot of light moved along a cardboard track in a dark room. The track could be placed in different positions, varying the direction of movement from horizontal up to vertical. The subject had to match the phenomenal direction of movement seen in darkness by turning a pointer to indicate the judged angular direction. Table 11–2 gives the results, in average degrees of error, for seven different actual inclinations at two rates of velocity (Takala's experiments 20 and 13a).

Takala interprets his findings as follows. At lower velocities the deviation of the phenomenal track from the horizontal direction is smaller than the corresponding deviation from the vertical. The phenomenal deviation is determined by two factors: (1) *the phenomenal direction recedes from each of the cardinal directions and assimilates toward the bisection of the angle between them (the "warding off influence")*; (2) *the tendency to deviate from the*

TABLE 11–1

RESULTS OF K. v. FIEANDT'S EXPERIMENT

Deviation of the Direction of Motion from the Frontal Plane (Angle, in Degrees)	Moving Silhouette of Airplane		Photograph of Airplane in Varying Flight Angle	
	Constant Error	Standard Error (Times 3)	Constant Error	Standard Error (Times 3)
0	−0.1	0.7	+3.0	1.2
10	−2.9	2.9	−4.0	1.4
20	−5.2	3.9	−6.0	1.7
30	+0.6	4.0	−3.7	3.3
40	—	—	−17.2	1.9
50	—	—	−10.9	2.4
60	−13.1	2.3	−16.8	2.1
70	−12.3	2.1	−8.4	2.3
80	−6.6	2.0	−4.5	1.2
90	−1.5	0.7	—	—

horizontal toward the vertical direction is stronger than the opposite tendency.[6]

It has often been stressed by research workers that the frontal plane in three-dimensional configurations should play a role comparable to that played by the horizontal dimension in plane figures. Correspondingly, the sagittal plane is said to act as a counterpart to the vertical dimension in plane situations. This correspondence was not supported by the results of Takala, nor of the present author. The data in Tables 11–1 and 11–2 and Figures 11–6 and 11–7 convincingly demonstrate the warding-off tendency in the situations

TABLE 11–2

RESULTS OF M. TAKALA'S EXPERIMENTS

Deviation of the Path of Motion from the Horizontal (Angle, in Degrees)	Experiment 20		Experiment 13a	
	Constant Error	Standard Error (Times 3)	Constant Error	Standard Error (Times 3)
0	+1.2	1.1	+5.1	1.6
15	+4.8	1.1	+7.2	1.6
30	+3.9	1.0	+2.9	1.6
45	−0.6	0.5	+2.8	1.1
60	−3.5	1.2	+0.9	1.4
75	−3.6	0.9	−4.9	1.6
90	−0.2	0.4	−0.1	0.8

[6] M. Takala, "Asymmetries of the Visual Space," *Annales Academiae Scientiarum Fennicae*, B 72, No. 2 (Helsinki, 1951), pp. 43–44.

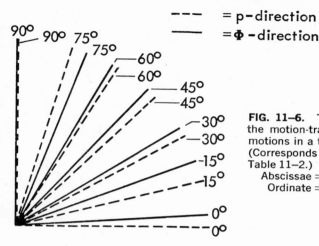

= p-direction
= Φ-direction

FIG. 11–6. The constant errors in the motion-track experiments using motions in a two-dimensional plane. (Corresponds to the right half of Table 11–2.)
Abscissae = the horizontal axis
Ordinate = the vertical axis

of both investigators. On the other hand, in von Fieandt's experiment the deviation from the true physical direction does not—as the above-mentioned analogy would presuppose—tend toward the sagittal plane, but instead seems to aim at the frontal plane. Another indication of our visual asymmetry can, however, be observed in the results: The constant error (CH) or the deviation from the true physical direction is greater for motions occurring in the right (shown in Figure 11–7) than the left half of our visual space. It must be recognized, however, that the two studies cited used quite different setups, and there was no intent to make them comparable.

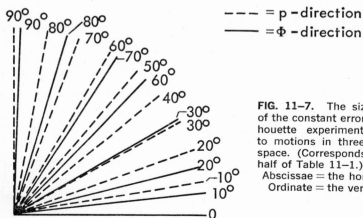

= p-direction
= Φ-direction

FIG. 11–7. The size and trend of the constant errors in the "silhouette experiments" referring to motions in three-dimensional space. (Corresponds to the left half of Table 11–1.)
Abscissae = the horizontal axis
Ordinate = the vertical axis

The impetus for the present writer's experiments came from reports during World War II by aerial observers in antiaircraft batteries. When seen from a high tower, an enemy plane passing horizontally looks as though its course were oriented at right angles to the line of sight. When following the plane with his eyes, the observer therefore got the impression that the plane curved around him when it actually maintained a straight course, as shown in Figure 11–8. This is reminiscent of Jaensch's orthogonal localization tendency, referred to in Chapter 9. Our working hypothesis is, accordingly, that this tendency should also show up in situations in which *directions of movement* instead of figures or rigid objects are

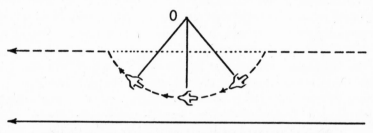

FIG. 11–8. Erroneous perception of an aircraft's path.

to be located in visual space, especially when they are viewed monocularly. (The observation distance in the airplane example was so great that binocular cues had no practical significance.) The hypothesis was consistently verified in several of the present author's studies in which moving miniature silhouettes of bombing aircraft were projected on the white ceiling of a room, or stationary photographs of horizontally flying aircraft, varying in their orientation toward the sagittal line, were presented. The expected tendency always appeared, but was sometimes overcome by the warding off influence when the physical direction came close to the frontal plane (deviating from it at angles less than 30°). A more detailed description can be found in the report of the 1950 Göteborg congress of Scandinavian psychologists.

Perception of Velocity

It took a good deal of independence for psychologists to realize that perception of the speed of motion has problems of its own. At first it was assumed that phenomenal speed was simply a function of time and distance, but before long it became clear that other factors play a role. Brown found that phenomenal velocity is determined, among other things, by the shape and position of the moving object in relation to its direction of motion and to the entire visual constellation. Everyday observations again yield a host of examples. A motorboat and an ocean liner going the same speed look as though they are moving at different rates. The smaller vessel seems to be going faster than the larger one. When tiny insects gather on a sunny rock, each of them moves at an objectively, i.e., physically, low speed, yet they are perceived as scurrying around in a great rush.

Phenomenal velocity, too, seems to follow a principle of perceptual constancy or invariance. We know that the angular speed of images projected on the retina changes considerably as a function of the distance from which the same motion is perceived. Nevertheless, seen speed displays a remarkable degree of constancy, approaching the velocity of the true physical motion.

Koffka cites an experiment by Brown in which standard and variable figures are placed in a dark room at equal distances from the observer, whose task it is to match the speed of the standard figures moving inside a frame by adjusting the speed of the variable. Suppose the standard display has black circles with a diameter of 1.6 cm. separated horizontally on a white ground by 4 cm., and the variable stimulus is half as large in all its dimensions (diameter 0.8 cm. and a separation of 2 cm.). Further, imagine the standard frame is twice the size of the variable frame, so that their dimensions are, say 5×15 cm. and 2.5×7.5 cm. respectively. Then it turns out that *the subject must set the speed of the variable at about half the velocity of the standard* to achieve a satisfactory match of phenomenal speeds. As Brown put it, the physical velocity of motion must be changed proportionately to the change in the dimensions of the circles and the frame, if phenomenal velocity is to remain constant.[7]

Most essential was Brown's finding that if both motions are presented in identical frames, but with different-sized circles, the velocity of the one with smaller figures is overestimated.

It has already been mentioned that the speed of peripherally perceived motion is generally overestimated. Brown was able to show that reduced illumination also produces overestimation of velocity. According to the duplicity theory, the peripheral parts of the retina take over at low intensities of illumination.

---

[7] J. F. Brown "Über gesehene Geschwindigkeit," *Psychologische Forschung*, 10 (1928), pp. 85–90.

Still another of Brown's observations: if the main dimension of the moving figure coincides with the direction of motion, it seems to have a higher speed than if the main dimension of the figure is oriented perpendicularly to its direction of motion.[8]

The results obtained in investigations of *the velocity of stroboscopic motion* were at first surprising. Any increase in the distance between *a* and *b* in Wertheimer's experiment (Figure 11–2) was expected to require a directly proportional decrease in the duration of the blank interval to maintain the ϕ-effect if the speed was to be sufficiently increased. The equation $C = s/t$ was expected to hold, even for stroboscopic motion.[9] Brown's factors, however, proved also to influence this kind of perceived movement, which is what should have been expected if the Wertheimer velocities had been rightly understood as phenomenal rather than physical magnitudes.

In Finland, Takala, in 1948 and 1949, continued with Brown's work, designing analogous experiments and using technically improved apparatus. His results could not be handled by a single, uniform principle, but the role of the frame of reference was once again beautifully demonstrated. The dispersion of the estimated velocity as well as the constant error increased, the more the experimenter reduced the total situation. When the experiment was carried out in a completely dark and "reference poor" environment, the dispersion and the systematic underestimation of the velocity were considerable. When more richly organized reference criteria were admitted (normal daylight, objects passing one another, structured background, etc.) the judgments were immediately made with greater accuracy and with a reduced variance. A single cue, such as a stable point of light in the dark room, was often enough to produce a clear reduction in error and in variance. Analogously, the influence of the reduced stimulus configuration can be demonstrated when the moving object is *a black figure on a black background*, a situation in which the function of the fovea is minimal and the role of the retinal periphery increases.

Perception of Time and the Phenomenal Present

Organisms seem to have an awareness of the lapse of time. Scientists have sometimes asked whether we should postulate a

---

[8] J. F. Brown, "The Visual Perception of Velocity," *Psychologische Forschung* 14 (1931), p. 232.

[9] C = velocity, s = distance, t = time.

specific time sense, and if so how we could explain its function. Careful observations have shown that animals and other organisms orient themselves according to regular periodic astronomic or climatic cycles with surprising accuracy. They also adjust remarkably to their own metabolic rhythms. It is not only humans, with their timing devices, or in other words, with their mechanically divided systems of time coordinates, who are capable of periodic reactions; yet on the other hand we do not *experience* the flow of time as though it were accurately divided up into equal duration elements, although our precise timing devices can make such a division credible.

It is important to discriminate between the sense of time and periodic changes in the behavior pattern of the organism. Mental events are extended in time, have a certain duration as do events of movement, but this does not imply that any event or movement must be perceived as a time phenomenon. It makes sense to speak of time perception only when an organism notes the flow of time and articulates it, divides it up in one way or other.

The fact that some kind of temporal awareness developed long before there existed any measurements of physical time is probably not as impressive as it first appears. All life processes have a rhythm; a subjective timing operates in our heartbeat, in our breathing, in our cycles of sleep and wakefulness, and in our motor behavior.

Because no specific receptor for a time sense has been found, we have to postulate some correlative connection between time experiences and the organic processes we just mentioned. There are striking examples of punctuality in animals despite their lack of a time sense in the just-used meaning of the word, not to speak of the nonexistence in them of a concept of physical time. The feeding periods of titmice and other birds have been carefully observed. They regularly search for food at the same hours, at least during the hatching season, the intensity and the angle of the radiating sunlight probably being the cue for initiating and terminating the periods of activity. The time perception of insects such as ants and bees has also been carefully investigated. The role of the varying sunlight has been experimentally controlled and altered, yet the animals have nevertheless arrived punctually at their customary feeding places. Dogs are frequently reported to go to meet a train at a certain hour, expecting either food or the arrival of some agreeable familiar person. In this sense of the word we humans, too, have an awareness of time which reflects itself, for example, in our ability to tell the time of day without looking at a watch for hours. How deeply rooted this habituated time articulation can be is illustrated by some people's capacity to carry out prior decisions to arise at a certain hour the next morning. This intention to wake up may be so effective that it rarely fails if the performance is sufficiently motivated.

Jørgensen[10] mentions some results obtained by François and Hoagland according to which body temperature has a noticeable influence on the perception of time. In high fever, time appears faster, which can be shown, for example, by having fever patients count numbers in a prescribed rhythm. Katz says that we can be aware either of the nature of the contents or of the temporal character of our conscious mental processes. When we pay attention to the contents, the sense of time may almost completely disappear. During a long-winded dull lecture, time seens to pass at a snail's pace; but if the presentation is fascinating, "time becomes winged." Compared with physical time, phenomenal time varies widely. Attitudes and expectations play a decisive role. Waiting times are generally long.

Katz enumerates—analogously with his phenomenal attributes of touch—certain *modifications* in the perception of time. *Duration* and *succession* are most essential; *change* and *simultaneity* are their opposite poles. Some events are immediately experienced as instantaneous, lacking in duration, as a pistol shot or lightning, while others, like an organ tone or a stable neon light, appear more enduring. It must, however, not be forgotten that perceptual configurations require at least a minimum temporal duration, since they are not only spatial patterns but also temporal units—especially tactual and auditory gestalten. On the other hand, the speed of these organizing processes varied widely among modalities and also among individuals.

The difference between phenomenal and physical time is particularly clear in the different definitions they provide for the concept of the "present moment." The present, in the mathematically defined continuous dimension of physical time, has no duration; "right now"

---

[10] For references on this page, see J. Jørgensen, *Psykologi paa biologisk grundlag* (Copenhagen: Ejnar Munksgaard, 1941), pp. 319—23, and D. Katz (ed.), *Handbuch der Psychologie* (Basel: Benno Schabe, 1951).

is a mathematical point along this dimension, and continuing from it in one direction is the future, in the opposite direction the past. Phenomenal "right now" differs from this mathematical, dimensionless dividing point. Experimentally, the duration of the "phenomenal right now" has been found to be between about 0.4 and 3.0 seconds. If the interval between two stimuli exceeds 3 seconds, they are not experienced as simultaneous; sometimes there is even an impression of succession if the interval goes down to 0.4 second. In most cases stimuli falling within these limits are experienced as occurring in the same present moment. This *succession within the present moment* can be readily distinguished from *temporally unitary configurations*. If we strike lightly on two empty drinking glasses, we can hear a difference between the case in which "*A* sounds but *B* doesn't yet," "*B* sounds but *A* isn't sounding any more," and the case in which "*AB* is audible," i.e., the *A* sound has not faded before *B* comes in. The totality *AB* implies that two successive sounds are discriminated, yet are present simultaneously.

In another respect, too, phenomenal time differs from physical and is reminiscent of the spatial differentiation of the perceptual world. Present time, too, has a *center* and a *periphery*. What a moment ago was the phenomenal "right now" is still somehow nearby; it is more vivid, clearer, and closer to the present moment than things expected in the immediate future. The differences between phenomenal time and the physicist's time concept are not as great, however, as we would expect when we compare phenomenal time with abstract mathematical time. Both in macro- and micro-events physical science (astronomy and nuclear physics) has, in looking for measuring devices and appropriate scales, encountered much the same difficulties as man has in exploring his everyday sensations. The mathematically defined concept of time is like the concept of causality in mechanics, as it were, a tool useful to the human though not equally efficient in all cases.

TIME AND MOTION RELATIONSHIPS

The rest of this chapter will be devoted to the problem of interrelationships between time and motion perception phenomena, since it is obvious that there are interactions between them in our daily experience.

We can also put the same thing in another way by stating that time and space are fused in movements. Physically, all motion is spatial displacement in time. In such terms, there is no break or discontinuity in the physical scale of velocity from extremely low speeds (e.g., tiny displacements in a period of weeks or months) to the highest measurable velocities (e.g., the speed of light). As stated before, no actual physical displacement is essential for an impression of motion. Two points in the physically continuous scale of velocity mark the limits of phenomenal speed. First, the velocity has to exceed a minimum threshold in order to be perceived at all. Second, the velocity must not exceed an upper threshold, because the eye is incapable of recording extremely high speeds. The growth of the familiar plants in our immediate environment is clearly noticeable, but *we do not experience these gradual changes as motions*, nor do we perceive the changing positions of the hour hand of our clocks as movement. On the other hand, a projectile fired from a gun is generally invisible too.

If we look more closely at these thresholds we observe a rather significant connection between man's time perception and his ability visually to discriminate motions. This relationship has been pointed out by many investigators, most convincingly perhaps by Michotte.[11] There is a correlation between the rhythm of the organic processes in an individual and his optimal limits for perceiving motion. Gerontology has shown that metabolic processes are progressively slower in a gradually aging organism and that the speeding up of phenomenal time parallels this retardation. If human beings had a metabolic rhythm approximately the rate of growth of plants, we might well perceive these growth processes as expressive dynamic movements. By running botanical films at higher rates of speed, analogous to those observable in man's usual activities, the plants rise, bend, and twist in an almost meaningful personal manner. Michotte, in his ingenious experiments, has shown that human beings perceive motion only within a limited section of the entire range of velocities. The lower and upper limits of these perceivable rates of speed appear to be related to the organic life rhythm of the experimental subject.

In addition to these thresholds, there is another time limit which has been especially interesting to psychologists. How do the variations in the time of exposure of adjacent stationary stimuli and of the blank interval affect stroboscopic motion? The upper limit for

---

[11] See M. D. Vernon, *A Further Study of Visual Perception* (Cambridge, England: University Press, 1952), pp. 183–99.

the blank interval has, as mentioned before, been considered to be about 200 msec. Other investigators, however, have reported experiences of motion at intervals up to 800 msec. Clearly, much of this phenomenon depends on the particular experimental setup.

Roelofs and Zeeman, in a series of articles (1949 to 1953),[12] explored the influence of these stimulation times, using a simple experimental design for all these investigations. Two equal sized squares, varying from 100 cm.² to 144 cm.² were alternately and regularly presented on a black background, and the exposure times and the blank interval could be varied; the subject's task generally was to estimate the length of exposure of each square. Additional experiments on phenomenal movement were also carried out.

If the two alternating stimulus squares are presented at different durations, estimates of how long they were exposed depend on whether there is an interval between the times of their appearance, and on whether this interval is blank or contains a stimulus; in this latter case the content of the interval has a decisive influence. The investigators also point to the significance of the two "framing stimuli," in other words to the whole configuration formed by the interval plus the two alternating squares. Measurement of the seen interval was achieved either simultaneously (matching standard and variable durations) or successively (by comparing two successive durations). The latter method is based upon recall of perceived events, and therefore is burdened with numerous sources of error. It was already known that the *intensity* of the stimuli framing the interval decisively affects its appearance.

Meumann, on the basis of his experiments, correctly pointed out that there are actually no completely "blank" or empty intervals. Rather, at the same time as visually empty intervals, there are always impulses which come from other sense organs. Irrespective of whether the stimuli during the interval are visual, auditory, or tactual, a number of common regularities have been found to hold. When experimenting with longer durations, one finds that an interval which contains a stimulus is overestimated; but with very brief durations, overestimation tends instead to refer to the blank intervals. The zone of irrelevant equivalent durations lies between

---

[12] O. Roelofs and W. P. C. Zeeman, "The Subjective Duration of Time Intervals," I–II, *Acta Psychologica*, 4 (1949); O. Roelofs and W. P. C. Zeeman, "Influence of Different Sequences of Optical Stimuli on the Estimation of Duration of a Given Interval of Time," *Acta Psychologica*, 8 (1951).

about 1,800 and 2,500 msec. If the stimuli are bunched at the center of the interval the duration appears longer than when they occur late in it.

The investigators began by comparing blank intervals with those filled by stimulations, using squares successively flashed on the right, then the left, or the other way around. The first square was shown for 420 msec. but the exposure was briefly interrupted either after 140 or after 350 msec. The other was shown continuously but with considerable variations in duration from exposure to exposure. The framing stimuli were important. The blank interval was mostly overestimated, and sometimes the interval presented last in the whole series was the most overestimated one.

Thus there appeared two competing reasons for the overestimation. Inserting a break into the interval regularly brought about an underestimation of it: the total interval could appear abbreviated by up to 30 or 40 percent of its original duration. If the subject is asked also to estimate the duration of either of the luminous framing squares, he will underestimate the interval between the two squares (by about 14.5 percent) if the square he estimates precedes the interval. This underestimation, however, is significantly less than that produced by inserting a break in the interval. Locating the stimulus material left of the subject's median plane causes a slight overestimation relative to locating it on the right. Generally *a blank interval appeared shorter than a regularly articulated interval.* The underestimation is as great as 12.3 percent if the total length of the interval is 1,800 msec. This phenomenon is reminiscent of Oppel's illusion (i.e., filled space looks larger than empty: ╠╫╫╫╫╫╫╫────┤) and also, for that matter, of the role of rich texture (as a gradient cue) in producing more articulated depth in distances in the third dimension.

The later papers of these investigators were not quite as interesting. Their subsequent work consisted in a painstaking replication of their earlier results, and in looking for the optimal location of temporal "zones of indifference." They pointed out that the break must be long enough, for if too short a break is used, it sometimes becomes phenomenally tied to the first part of the interval, forming a new temporal unit with it, *which makes the second part of the interval appear shortened.* If the total interval falls below 800 msec., this effect is especially likely to occur, and with intervals longer than 800 msec. an overestimation of the last part of the interval regularly results. The part intervals on both sides of the break must be at least 800 msec. long to make the break period appear as an independent temporal unit (gestalt).

These last results have some relevance to the perception of movement. Some of the experiments used only one square, flashing for two equally long periods interrupted by a break. The first period was divided into a series of shorter flashes, the number of which was varied in the different experiments, while the second period was always constant. The unarticulated continuous period produced more overestimations. On the other hand, the articulated period with a constant series of short flashes was likely to be overestimated compared with a period with slightly varying series of flashes. The investigators also arranged some stroboscopic presentations of two squares, varying the distance between them and the length of the blank interval (from 167 to 2,500 msec.). At a spatial separation of 40 to 80 cm. and a 500 msec. time interval, a "tunnel motion phenomenon" (like Johannson's w-phenomenon) occurred, such that there was motion without any visible moving object. The ϕ-phenomenon proper could be seen at the 1,250 msec. interval, and the squares produced dim, phenomenally mobile after-images.

Michotte's Experiments

We have already encountered some of Michotte's elegant experiments. His problem has a far-reaching importance and therefore offers an appropriate conclusion to a chapter on the perception of motion and time. The point of his experiment is illustrated by describing one of his surprisingly simple setups. A cardboard screen is placed in front of a horizontal kymograph drum, and the screen has a horizontal slit (15 cm. in length and 0.5 cm. in width) at that height on the screen which comes closest to the rotating drum surface. The drum is covered by white paper on which two 0.5 cm. wide lines are painted in such a way that they cross the slit and appear through it as two parallel short portions of the entire lines. (As a matter of fact, because of the proportions, they look like two parallel small colored squares in the slit.) When the drum is *slowly* rotated, these squares look stationary in the slit as long as the two lines run strictly parallel on the drum surface and both remain at a right angle to the slit, but if the lines curve and cross, the squares are seen as moving horizontally. These are real movements, which Michotte prefers to ϕ-phenomena. Interesting situations can be produced by varying the slopes of the lines and the speed of rotation.

Generally the two squares are experienced as *depending on* or *related to each other in a certain way*. Michotte distinguished among a "throwing effect," a "transporting effect," and a "tunnel phenomenon." The most essential experience in them all is the impression of causality produced if the stimulus conditions are appropriate. For example, the throwing effect occurs if originally one square, say A, moves horizontally until it stops by the other square, B, which immediately starts moving at the rate and speed A had before it stopped. An experience of causality is inevitably included in this perception: the observer *sees* A as producing B's movement. The transporting effect is obtained if, for example, B is stationary until A comes by, then A touches B and they both continue together: A carries B along. If one part of the path of movement is screened, or a part of one line is omitted, one square is seen as moving through a tunnel even if physically A is stopped behind the cover and B starts at its other edge, as long as A and B are sufficiently similar.

These results made Michotte speak of the *perception of causality*. What is especially interesting in his presentation is that movement configurations, according to him, appear to exhibit regularities equivalent to those demonstrated for plane figures. Thus Michotte points out, for example, that as a rule the background or the environment of the moving object serves as a frame of reference for the perceived motion, but when two squares are followed visually and are experienced *in relation to each other, a sudden reorganization of the system of reference* may occur. One of the moving squares can take over the role of frame of reference for the other; when something concerning one of them is reported on, it is done so in comparison to the state or position of the other. In one of his later experiments he was able to isolate the components which strikingly evoke the impression of a "crawling" movement: he used a rectangle which shrank and stretched rhythmically while simultaneously undergoing a translatory horizontal movement. He has also been interested in exploring the role of projected human characteristics in the interpretation of the interrelations among figures moving in a common arena. The time dimension seems crucial for these effects. Michotte feels that perceptions are never completely devoid of expectations, intentions, and emotions.

These research perspectives provide a tentative glimpse at the intimate connections between "space" and "time" in the context of the total personality. They are phenomenally created and experienced by the continuously changing and spontaneously moving perceiver himself.

CHAPTER 12

Differentiation of Auditory Perception

THE EXPERIENCE of time leads naturally to evaluations of the role of rhythm and of the time dimension in *auditory perception*. The time dimension is quite central in our auditory impressions although *temporal units* can be found wherever changes and movements are perceived, such as in successive visual or tactual stimulations. Auditory gestalten always involve time. Auditory totalities such as rhythmic patterns or melodies would not be possible without temporal articulation.

The old controversy concerning the independence and the genesis of auditory space is usually handled nowadays by the conjecture that three-dimensional visual-tactual space provides the frame of reference for auditory experiences as well. It can hardly be denied that we do have spatially localized auditory impressions. In such cases the time dimension often enriches the otherwise static three-dimensional visual-tactual articulation. On the other hand, although our immediate auditory experiences are in some way or another spatially determined, and especially music is typically and richly spatially differentiated, the localization of our auditory impressions is nevertheless spatially imprecise and diffuse. Aside from the two-component theory of tone perception with its spiral model, which provides a kind of spatial organization for musical experiences, it appears reasonable to assume that all discernible sounds are referred to the visual-tactual system of coordinates. Auditory impressions are perceived within the framework of visual-tactual space, and if in addition they have their own particular spatial character, this is due at least in part to the time dimension.

ANALOGIES BETWEEN VISUAL AND AUDITORY SPACE

Visual and auditory space are analogous in many respects; for example, there are temporal figure-ground phenomena: "behind" a brief sound we may hear another longer lasting, persistent one. In general, the gestalt laws seem to hold for auditory as well as for visual perception.

Such analogies have led some investigators to draw far-reaching parallels between these two modalities, sometimes giving rise to loose and speculative thinking which is not properly tied to empirical facts. The previously mentioned "octave law of vowels" might be considered one such attempt. One must take more seriously the theoretical consequences of the fact that man is able to discriminate among as many sounds as colors, if one considers all the nuances of hue, brightness, and saturation. Whether or not there is a common organic basis for this correspondence, or how else one could explain it, remain unresolved questions.

The musical world of a listener with absolute pitch can well be compared with the natural appearance of colors to a normal eye. For a person with absolute pitch the *tone qualities* of the tonal scale, depending upon successive pitch steps, clearly give impressions not unlike those a normally sighted subject experiences when looking at color hues. Persons devoid of the gift of absolute pitch react in a manner comparable to the *completely color blind*, who are able to discriminate only among brightnesses. Even regional pitch, a weaker form of absolute pitch, implies a crude discrimination only among nuances of tonality. The tonal scale, unlike the color spectrum, has no phenomenal nodal points like the primaries or fundamental hues of the spectrum. According to Stevens and Davis, this can provide an explanation for the rarity of absolute pitch discrimination; they consider the usual crudity of the pitch sense as due to the undifferentiated homogeneity of pitch gradations, an assertion which is difficult to test empirically.[1] It is true that distinctive points corresponding to the primaries in the color spectrum do not occur within the tonal scale, which weakens the analogy, but much depends on whether we consider tonality as a series of qualities in the same way as different hues constitute different qualities.

---

[1] S. S. Stevens and H. Davis, *Hearing: Its Psychology and Physiology* (New York: John Wiley & Sons, Inc., 1947), p. 108.

In any case *there are striking similarities in the way the visual and auditory receptors react to certain physical components of the stimulus situation*. Changes in *frequency* influence colors as well as sounds; if the *amplitude* of the respective adequate stimuli changes, the intensity of colors on the one hand and the loudness of sounds on the other is affected.

Physically as well as phenomenally, color and tone scales are reminiscent of one another.

Physically, a *linear dimension*, frequency, stimulates both modalities. Phenomenally, this variable produces a *cyclic dimension*, so that all hues on the one hand and the tones within one octave on the other can be represented on a circle (Figure 12–1).

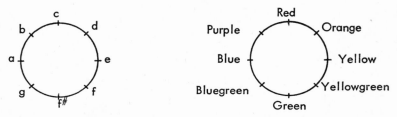

FIG. 12–1.   Presumed correspondence between tone and color scales.

Hornbostel pushes the parallel so far as to compare the middle region of color intensities with the middle of the tonal scale, that is, the fourth octave, C_4–C_5 (American standard pitch). *Tonality is strongest in this region*, as are the *saturations of the various hues*. In spite of the dominance of tonality, the transitions from one tone step to the next are as clearly perceivable within the range of the whole octave as are the differences between subsequent hues on the color circle.

Wellek objected to Hornbostel's comparison that the linear dimension of the tonal system cannot accurately be considered a counterpart to the vertical white-black axis in the color system (*"die Parallele ist nicht wörtlich durchführbar"*). The entire analogy between the tonal system and the color solid is also shaky in some other essential respects, which even Révész did not especially stress. *While frequency is the variable determining the linearity of the pitch scale, this cannot correspond to the linearity of brightness in color vision*, i.e., to the vertical axis of the color solid. As we know, the linear brightness axis in color vision depends not on frequency (or wavelength) but on *intensity*. The counterpart to the linear pitch scale is the *cyclic* dimension of the color circle. One easily encounters this kind of confusion if one exaggerates the analogies between two modalities.[2]

A genuine parallel, on the other hand, can be seen in the fact that *the world of sounds has qualitative peculiarities* corresponding to the *modes of appearance of colors*, that is, *to film color, surface color, and space color*. Tones of the same pitch may appear *sonorous, sharp, dull, or bright* and have the timbre of a *singing voice*, a *violin*, a *clarinet*, etc.

Synesthesias (e.g., colored hearing or *audition colorée*) will not be discussed in this chapter because they lead to broad questions which also involve other modalities. These problems have been touched upon in another connection, in which we also observed that certain visual and auditory contents can be thought of as representing common emotional complex qualities.

Temporal Units

The fact that auditory percepts involve temporal units reflects itself in visual parallels other than color experiences. Music is above all a series of gestalten; it is built up of units larger than separate isolated tones. The law of the immediacy and priority of the whole relative to part impressions holds throughout all auditory experience. Auditory gestalten are perceived as immediate wholes the differentiation of which is a later step. Gestalt theory is in effect second nature to a practising musician, because he knows without stopping to think about it that melodies are gestalten, are something more than just aggregates of single tones.

The sound of a trumpet stands out as a distinct figure against the background of strings, whose intensity may even be greater. Mellow, weak, and low qualities (timbres) sound remote to the listener. The depth localization of different timbres can, according to Wellek, be directly compared with the immediate phenomenal localization of hues: "warm" hues such as red are seen as approaching, "cold" hues such as blue tend to recede. Wellek assumes that red and yellow could be represented tonally by sharp, brilliant, substantial timbres like those of the trumpet, the trombone, the

---

[2] A. Wellek, "Der Raum in der Musik," *Archiv für die gesamte Psychologie*, 91 (1934). Cf. A. Wellek, "Die Ausspaltung der 'Tonhöhe' in der Hornbostelschen Gehörpsychologie und die Konstanztheorien von Hornbostel und Krueger," *Zeitschrift für Musikwissenschaft*, 16 (1934), p. 487.

piccolo, or the clarinet.[3] The comparison is rather bold if we consider the great individual differences in the phenomenal localization of colors of different hues.

The significance of the time dimension for auditory gestalten can be seen in the role of *rhythm* in certain auditory articulations. Some musicians speak of "the sense of rhythm." This term refers primarily to body movements, but applies, according to Roiha, equally well to auditory events, in which rhythm is conceived to develop in parallel with the development of motor patterns of rhythm. Preschool children nicely display the coordination of both kinds of rhythm. Roiha remarks that the auditory rhythmic pattern of our own gait is more easily recognized than is the visual one. At early stages of human development, rhythm is strongly and inextricably intermodal. Roiha declares:

Rhythm is temporal. That is, it is a whole which is differentiated and integrated in a certain way, with the differentiation arising from the listener's appreciation of the relation between the stressed and the unstressed phases of a sequence, and even only a dim awareness of the relations can suffice. Integration means that the stressed elements occupy a central position within the rhythmic whole, and that the unstressed elements are referred to these central components. In music stresses are beats, accents or cadences, but unstressed elements lack emphasis. Such words make us think about loudness, and undoubtedly loudness is of great importance for rhythmic accents, but they do not reflect loudness exclusively. Accents can be produced by other components as well. Loudness, duration, pitch, timbre and harmonic as well as tonal factors all interact, influencing each other to a different extent and in different ways in different conditions. Attempts to force rhythmic articulations solely on the basis of varying intensity have not been very successful.

The duration of tones is an important factor in rhythmic articulation. In ancient music the lines of tempi were not indicated and accents were produced by relationships of durations, with the rhythm based upon the "width" of the elements. The phenomenal connections between the "weight" and the duration of a tone seem to be rather close, as shown by many psychological investigators. The stressed tone often is prolonged—a so-called irrational prolongation, not written in the note manuscripts. On the other hand, unstressed elements are sometimes really produced by tones of long duration inserted among shorter ones.

Leibold remarks that one condition for the occurrence of a genuine experience of rhythm is the formation of successive gestalten (as articulated totalities); there is no rhythm if the phenomenon investigated is completely unarticulated, as is the case, e.g., with a roaring waterfall

---

[3] A. Wellek, "Der Raum in der Musik," *Archiv für die gesamte Psychologie*, 91 (1934), p. 414 ff.

or a thunderstorm, nor does it show up in situations in which regularly successive functions or acoustical stimuli are presented unless these are experienced as differentiated. Functions of the latter type are, e.g., our gait and respiration.[4]

All kinds of rhythm imply regularity which must, however, not be taken too literally. Instead of the "regular metric" of the old classicists, modern composers use a number of fixed intervals in the continuous tone series. These intervals are linked together in larger combinations.

Direction and Distance Localization

The localization of sounds is in many respects analogous to the localization of visual objects, whether we consider it merely a process of *fitting auditory percepts into a visual-tactual frame* or whether we consider such localization as perception of an auditory space in its own right. The physiological conditions for an auditory space are in any case harder to determine than are the conditions for visual localization. Even the factors which contribute to perceived direction in auditory space have proved complex.

The perception of auditory distance is determined by intensity and by the components of the sound spectrum in the field extending from the sound source, according to Békésy, with lower frequencies in the sound spectrum relatively stronger near the sound source. This is due to differences in ease of absorption among sounds of different frequencies. Engelmann showed in a series of experiments that cats have a very well-developed capacity for auditory distance localization. The cat is a nocturnal animal, and the proper timing and coordination of its pounce upon moving prey in twilight or darkness is highly dependent on its ability to "scan" the right distances. The human auditory apparatus is, by comparison, quite underdeveloped.

The auditory localization of directions depends upon three different primary factors, all of which are *binaural: intensity, phase,* and *time* differences at the two ears. They are all based upon physical differences in proximal stimuli, i.e., at the very moment the sound waves arrive at the ears.

1. Binaural Intensity Differences

If the sound source is located on the sagittal plane, straight ahead of the listener, directly above him, or behind his back, the sound

---

[4] E. Roiha, *Johdatus Musiikkipsykologiaan* (Jyväskylä: K. J. Gummerus, 1949), pp. 161–63.

waves stimulate both ears with equal intensity. If the source is moved to one side of the sagittal plane, the ear nearer the sound source receives a higher intensity of stimulation than the other ear. This binaural intensity difference permits the sound source to be localized; one hears the sound as coming from the side receiving the higher intensity. The difference in intensity is caused not only by the different distances of the two ears from the sound source; the farther ear is also partly screened by the head. The density of this acoustic "shadow" is a function of the stimulus frequency. Relatively low sounds penetrate the "shadow" more efficiently, while sounds above 5,000 cps. may suffer shadow effects as great as a 30 db decrease in intensity. If the stimulus is a complex impure tone, the sound shadow of the head may also produce binaural differences in *tone quality* or *timbre* in addition to the differences in intensity.

High frequency components are somewhat damped before they reach the far ear, and some investigators (e.g., Wilska) have suggested a tone quality factor in addition to the customary intensity difference. In laboratory experiments the role of intensity has been studied by presenting separate stimuli, differing in intensity, to the two ears. Subjects can readily point to the apparent location of the sound source on the basis of the intensity difference as soon as the differential threshold for intensities at the two ears is passed. This threshold is easily measured, but varies with the stimulus conditions, as thresholds generally do. Stewart claimed to have found a simple relationship: phenomenal deviation (in degrees from the sagittal plane) is directly proportional to the intensity difference (in db). It is, however, hazardous to generalize this simple equation to all audible frequencies and intensities.[5]

Binaural intensity differences unquestionably play a major role in the localization of the direction of sounds, but this role becomes somewhat complicated when complex sounds and noises are considered. The screening head, the structure of the outer ear, and the ear canal affect the intensity differences in complex ways.

2. Binaural Time Differences

If two identical sound stimuli reach the ears *at different times*, the sound is localized toward the side of the first stimulated ear. One of the early studies of the role of time differences in auditory localiza-

---

[5] Stevens and Davis, *op cit.*, p. 171.

tion was published by Hornbostel and Wertheimer in 1920.[6] They found that the optimum difference in time of arrival of a sound at the two ears has two thresholds: if the difference is too small, the auditory apparatus is unable to discriminate which ear was stimulated first, and the upper limit consists of a difference so large that *two different sounds are heard*, one in each ear. The lower limit is about 0.1 msec., the upper limit about 2.0 msec. The angle between the sagittal plane and the apparent direction of the sound is determined by where the time difference falls between these thresholds, i.e., it is approximately directly proportional to the time difference.

Hornbostel and Wertheimer found in their experiment that if the difference in the distance from which the two ears receive the sound is 1 cm., the phenomenal direction barely diverges from the sagittal plane. Such a distance difference equals a time difference of the magnitude of 30 $\sigma\sigma$ or 0.03 msec. The phenomenal angle ϕ (between sound direction and sagittal plane) of perceived sounds is determined by the values of s and of the time difference. If s (the difference in length of path from sound source to the two ears) is 21 cm., ϕ in increased to 90° and the time difference to 630 $\sigma\sigma$. In an actual hearing situation the angle ϕ can be assumed to coincide with the actual physical angle α from which the sound is coming. Then s can be computed from the equation $s = k \sin\phi$, in which k stands for the distance between the ears. We know from elementary physics that the speed of sound can be computed from the equation $t = s/34{,}000$ (34,000 cm./sec. is the speed of sound traveling through air). If we insert this value for s, we then have a method for calculating the time difference. Actually, however, this simple trigonometric technique ignores the shadowing effect of the head on the more remote ear. This can to some extent be taken care of by including a correction for D, the diameter of the head, so that we end up with the new s:

$$s = D\left(1 \pm \frac{\sin\phi}{4}\right) \sin\phi.$$

3. Binaural Phase Differences

This factor is generally considered separately, although it actually is nothing but a kind of binaural time difference. The phase of

---

[6] E. M. v. Hornbostel and Max Wertheimer, "Über die Wahrnehmung der Schallrichtung," *Sitzungsberichte der Preussischen Akademie der Wissenschaften*, 1920.

the *sound wave* at which the proximal stimulus arrives at each ear clearly depends upon the frequency of the oscillation and the angle of the sound source. If the same oscillation is transmitted to both ears from a constant sound source, the waves arrive at the closer ear at an *earlier phase* than at the farther ear. This binaural difference in the phase of the sound wave provides the basis for the third factor. Physical analysis and careful experiments have shown that the phase difference is greatest if the sound source is completely lateral to the head, on an extension of the binaural axis, the line connecting the ears. The maximum phase difference corresponds to a binaural distance of 21 cm., which is equal to s in Hornbostel and Wertheimer's equation in the special case in which the sound is received at a ϕ angle of 90°. Generally, it corresponds to their constant k.

Phase differences are relevant only for tones and within a certain range of frequencies. The limits of this region have been theoretically and experimentally determined. The frequency which has a period of 2 k or 42 cm. is 800 cps. At higher frequencies phase differences are ambiguous, because if the difference in phase between the oscillations at the ears exceeds half a wavelength it is impossible to determine which of the ears was ahead in receiving a certain phase of the wave. This circumstance restricts the significance of the phase cue to a considerable degree, because the major part of the discernible tones in the auditory area lies above this frequency—consider the components of most natural sounds, the physiological range of the voice, and the sounds of instruments and various animals. As Hornbostel and Wertheimer have stressed in other respects, this factor has explanatory value primarily for *pure* sinusoidal *tones*, and even then the factor is reducible to time differences. For more complex auditory stimuli, especially for noises, the factor probably plays a minor role, if any at all.

Wilska[7] investigated the size of the discriminative threshold for the direction of sounds presented in the horizontal and frontal planes by determining the just noticeable difference between two successively presented sound directions. This jnd for *auditory directions* was measured on either plane using a calibration of equal sized angles (30°) among successive directions of stimulation. The threshold values proved amazingly symmetrical irrespective of the

[7] A. Wilska, *Untersuchungen über das Richtungshören* (Helsinki: published by the author, 1938).

physical planes and directions employed. Furthermore, the thresholds were remarkably similar when two correspondingly located azimuths on the different planes were compared. Wilska considers this equality of threshold values in two different planes of sound direction strong support for the importance of time differences (although they are also consistent with the role of intensity and phase differences), because time differences sensitively reflect the angle between the physical sound direction and the sagittal plane irrespective of the planes on which these stimuli are presented. The ratios between successively determined threshold values also correspond rather closely to their predicted value as calculated from the time differences.

Among the binaural factors in sound localization, time differences have proved experimentally to dominate the others. Stevens and Davis assume that time and phase differences are crucial at low frequencies while intensity differences become relatively more important at higher frequencies.

Other Cues for Scanning and Localization

Some auditory localization is even monaurally possible. Several investigators have, indeed, considered auditory direction finding primarily monaural. Tullio and Kraus suggested that the impression of an auditory direction may depend upon displacements in the labyrinthine endolymph, caused by pressure variations on the eardrum. There are known to be cases in which vestibular damage has produced anomalies in auditory localization, but such cases have been insufficiently investigated.

Monaural scanning and localization are also facilitated by differences in timbre and intensity. In familiar settings we may, on the basis of previous experience, accurately locate a well-known sound by recognition of its timbre.

Recent physical and psychological research in hearing has used a new approach to these problems, an approach which is more global and more dynamically oriented than earlier work. Especially interesting are the new attacks by Gemelli on auditory scanning and localization. No single cue alone can fully account for auditory discrimination of sound direction. In some studies of binaural stimulus differences, the experimental procedure did not involve localization proper, but rather only the *lateralization* of a perceived sound. The subject estimates the approximate angle of the sound source rather than performing a genuine localization. The binaural cues can be conceived as operating on the horizontal plane running through the imaginary binaural axis connecting the ears. Wilska argues that the traditional approach, which has generally explored only the horizontal plane, reveals a kind of "astigmatism" for localization on other planes. According to Wallach, equivalent binaural differences can be produced by all the loci on the surface of a cone whose central axis coincides with the binaural axis, and whose apex is centered directly between the two ears. Wallach has shown experimentally that the *change* in binaural differences with head movement relative to the sound source, resulting in changes in the cones of possible locations, is also a major cue in auditory localization.[8]

Gemelli suspects that the problem of discrimination among auditory directions cannot be solved on the basis of physical stimulus differences alone. If that were the case, auditory scanning and localization would be primitive sensory functions. He feels that the fundamental fact of discrimination among directions must be considered due to some kind of frequency analysis by the ears. However, binaural theorists are also right in pointing out that auditory stimuli display a variety of binaural *physical* differences in accordance with the prevailing conditions.

On the other hand, it is clear that a given aspect of the auditory stimulus itself constitutes only a part of the total structure governing our impressions of directions and loci. Successful sound localization is apparently based upon complex, multidimensional processes in which separate features of the physical auditory stimulus constitute the chief factors and are complemented by one another as well as by further integrative and developmental factors. Scanning and localization of sounds cannot be considered "qualities" of auditory perception; rather, they constitute a differentiated perceptual process striving to achieve a clearer specification of the stimulus.

In actual life situations we not only localize sounds in our stationary system of coordinates, but, as pointed out among others by Wallach, move about and complement the usually considered localization processes with kinetic trials. This fact, too, conforms with our frequent emphasis upon the interaction among modalities. The perception of a sound is influenced not only by the auditory

---

[8] H. Wallach, "On Sound Localization," *Journal of the Acoustical Society of the Americas*, 10 (1939), pp. 270–74.

stimuli proper but also by proprioceptive messages from muscles controlling the head position, as well as by visual and vestibular stimuli. Furthermore, in most cases we also use our past experience of the probable location of particular sound sources to assist us in our attempts to localize familiar sounds.

Some experiments performed at the Psychological Institute of the University of Helsinki may serve to illustrate these problems. In 1944 the Institute cooperated with the Finnish Broadcasting Company in a study of the localization of simple mobile and stationary auditory stimuli in the horizontal plane. The results were intended to assist antiaircraft batteries in the nocturnal localization of enemy planes. The experimental procedure, designed and carried out by Somerkivi, consisted in confronting the subject with loudspeakers in a large, darkened anechoic chamber. Monotonous recorded aircraft engine noise was transmitted from different positions on the front wall of the room. The subject pointed at the estimated direction with a 2½ m.-long stick which was attached at one end on a support at his eye level. The far end of the stick held a reference sound source, a buzzer which could be operated electrically by the subject.

Most important in the present connection were the following results: The scanning and the location of a moving sound source actually is no more difficult than pointing to stationary sources. Best results were obtained when the subject succeeded in keeping the observed sound continuously in his median plane (which results in the lowest thresholds for directional sound localization). The improvement produced by a reference sound source in auditory localization tasks had already been pointed out by Wilska. In Somerkivi's experiment the "acoustic-optical condition," in which the tip of the pointer could be illuminated by the subject in addition to permitting the subject to sound the buzzer, was the most effective. Less accurate, but still very comparable results were obtained with the "optical condition" (illuminated pointer without the sounding buzzer) or the "acoustic condition" (tip of the pointer could be heard but not seen because of the darkness).

THE ROLE OF DIFFERENTIATION

From these results we might conclude that the additional information yielded by visual space articulation decisively supports sheer *auditory* scanning and localization of directions. The additional spatially differentiating perceptual cues seem to be equally effective whether they are visual or auditory. The best result is obtained with a combination of cues from both modalities in reciprocal interaction. *The more detailed and richer the differentiation of a stimulus situation, the greater the degree of constancy or invariance in the perceptual relationships investigated.* The experiments also revealed that subjects confronted with the task of discriminating between two identical sounds presented simultaneously from different directions did surprisingly well. If one of the stimuli kept moving, especially clearly differentiated percepts were achieved. The subjects reported an auditory figure-ground articulation: the stationary sound formed a background to which the moving sound source was referred, as something more temporary and incidental than the ground. Kock later demonstrated that our capacity to detect weak sounds in a complex of disturbing noise is directly proportional to the size of the angle between the directions of the sound and the noise sources.

Interaction of Visual and Auditory Cues

In the Psychological Institute of the University of Helsinki, Pentti in 1954 undertook an investigation of auditory localization in an effort to develop a critical evaluation of some of Gemelli's theoretical proposals.[9] The experimental subject was seated inside a vertical rotating cylinder. The inside wall of the cylinder consisted of narrow vertical stripes, about 10 cm. in width, alternating black and white. The subject was given the task of indicating the apparent direction of a sound coming from outside and presented successively from randomized points on the same horizontal plane. The nystagmic movements of the subject's eyes, and the visual stimulation from the rotating cylinder, soon produced the illusion that the subject and his chair were turning in an opposite direction, while the physically moving cylinder looked stopped. This illusion produced a systematic displacement in judged localization relative to performance inside the stationary cylinder. The subject's pointer had a strong flashlight which enabled the experimenter to record the readings precisely. The displacement averaged 17° and systematically followed the direction of rotation of the cylinder.

Roelofs, Van der Waals, and Gemelli stressed that the body

---

[9] L. Pentti, "Auditory Localization during Rotation of the Visual Environment," *Reports from the Psychological Institute, University of Helsinki*, No. 2 (1955).

image serves as a frame of reference for auditory localization. When localizing auditory stimuli, at least, the human being relates them to the position of his own body. Pentti's experiment confirms this explanation and the above-mentioned results of Wertheimer demonstrate that this phenomenon may involve a primordial, inborn human capacity.

The Problem of Auditory Space

The term *auditory space* may, according to Wellek, be appropriately used for any of the following three alternatives: (1) *auditory space* proper (*Gehörraum*), (2) *tonal space* (*Tonraum*), and (3) *musical space* (*Musikraum*). By auditory space he means the auditorily determined framework for spatial orientation, which we have already considered here at sufficient length. Apparently we could also just as well share Révész' view that auditory space consists of a transposition of points localized by hearing into a visual-tactual perceptual system, on the assumption that differentiated geometric space is built upon these two sense modalities. Tonal space, on the other hand, describes the three-dimensional system of tonal attributes and cannot be regarded as a space in the usual perceptual or psychological sense of the word. Yet the spiral diagram of the tonal system has its fruitful aspects, pointing at least to the conclusion that some *musical components can be objectively symbolized only by placing them in a spatial framework*. Indeed, as Wellek has rightly pointed out, the *representation of the temporal dimension by* horizontally continuous *staves of notes* is precisely such a symbolization.

Wellek holds that the time dimension has an essential significance for the formation of auditory gestalten.[10] Therefore, the customary three-dimensional spiral model must be expanded into a fourth dimension, the time continuum. It is especially the succession of articulated components that brings about the *dynamics*, the *directedness* and the *lack of simultaneous symmetry* so characteristic of musical configurations. Musical structures do not provide us with simultaneous patterns as visual perception does. We concretize and objectify our tonal impressions into a geometrical, physical system in space in the line of notes, written as a continuum from left to right and using the horizontal dimension to symbolize

---

[10] A. Wellek, "Der Raum in der Musik," *Archiv für die gesamte Psychologie*, 91 (1934), p. 402.

time. The lines of the staff further permit spatial representation of the brightness variation, the most important attribute of tonal pitch. Wellek does not hesitate to claim boldly: "Without musical space there would be no writing in notes" (*"Ohne musikalischen Raum keine Notenschrift"*). Yet we must object that the staves of notes do nothing more than refer temporal units to a visual-tactual spatial framework; it need not rest on any further assumptions.

When we turn to *musical space*, we run into a terminology which is totally unrelated to the concrete space of perceptual objects. Révész, reflecting upon the concept of "auditory space," admits that it is, of course, *possible* to define perceptual space in terms of the musical one described by Wellek, but this would imply the introduction of a new concept of space, entirely different from the traditional one. This statement of Révész' could, perhaps, be taken literally in evaluating Wellek's position. Révész repeatedly suggests that the way to find out whether we are actually using a space concept or not is to ask whether accurate locations and metrically measurable distances can be specified as they are in visual-tactual space. In this connection Révész' prerequisite appears rather irrelevant. The concept of a *space color* is generally accepted in perceptual psychology without any attempt to consider Révész' criteria. Apparently we could, in a similar sense of the word, denote as "space" the immensity which we often experience in listening to music.

Wellek's reference to the connection between phenomenal musical space and our feelings is reminiscent of the instances of sensory-emotional interaction which we encountered in a previous chapter.

Synesthetic primordial space is also a space which applies to some emotions: we feel joy or happiness at its *highest*, but we also sometimes are in *low spirits;* an experience may be *elevating*, another can make us *downcast* in a somewhat spatial sense of the word.

More light has recently been shed upon the *physiological background* of this intimate connection between tone sensations and human emotional life by investigations of the functions of our reticular and *thalamic* systems made possible by advances in electronics. A decade or two ago the detailed description of sensory representation in the thalamus was mostly restricted to the modalities of touch and pressure. Modern EEG recordings of brain waves have shown that *tonal stimuli* exert inhibiting or modulating effects on the regular alpha rhythm. It now appears very likely that musical tones, by affecting various thalamic centers, have a pronounced influence on emotional arousal and excitement in the behavior of experimental subjects. Even more recent electrophysiological findings (e.g., Morrell, 1961) suggest that the cognitive understanding of musical sequences rests upon some subcortical "storage process of temporal units."[11] Sound-induced activation of thalamic reaction patterns seems to facilitate the formation of temporary connections. Resting potential fields are produced which affect larger "cell assemblies" in Hebb's sense of the word, and thus influence the unification in memory of successive single temporal elements. Maybe, then, the kind of central tonal deafness Révész calls *amusia* (intact auditory perception of single tones but no ability to understand *melodies* or musical sequences) could reflect inadequate functioning on the thalamic level. Patterning of temporal units is already important for the successful formation of some visual gestalten; even more so, the trace-determined formation of temporal units must be quite indispensable for the achievement of musical understanding.

[11] F. Morrell, "Electrophysiological Contributions to the Neural Basis of Learning," *Physiological Reviews*, 41 (1961).

CHAPTER 13

Complex Articulations in Tactual Perception

NEXT WE TURN to a series of tactual or haptic phenomena and will attempt to relate them to the general schema of our perceptual world developed in the previous chapters. We shall again resort mainly to simple, natural life situations. As in other fields, in the area of tactual perception such immediate experiences seem more reliable than the artificially produced "pure stimuli" which were the main subject of study in the laboratories of the turn of the century. If we stick to real-life situations, we encounter tactual events which correspond closely to various visual phenomena.

Dimensions of Touch and Modes of Appearance

Just as, in the chapter on color perception, we could distinguish between "dimensions of color" and "modes of appearance of color," it seems reasonable to characterize *modes of appearance of touch.* On the other hand, the dimensions of color, like brightness, saturation, and hue, lack definite counterparts in the world of touch. It would not seem appropriate to construct "touch solids" to depict the various dimensions of touch. Superficially, even the illumination seems to have no parallel in the tactual world. Should we, because of these limitations, give up any attempt to enumerate appearances?

According to Katz, the poverty in the kinds of tactual dimensions which could be arranged in some sort of "solid" diagram is amply compensated for by a wonderful richness in the modes of appearance of touch. Although we must abandon a strict analogy to color dimensions, we can readily distinguish between two modes of appearance, which Katz called *modifications* and *specifications.*

Titchener, who was interested in the dimensions of touch experiences, in his time described only one continuum, which could probably best be compared with the brightness dimension in color vision. This continuum contains the various steps from the lightest, gentlest, "airiest" contact to the "heaviest" pressure. This bare, qualitatively restricted variable, which we met already among Hartshorne's continua, would represent the only dimension comparable to what is included in the three-dimensional color diagram. Richer and more varied are the following tactual modifications:

Surface touch (*Oberflächentastung*) corresponds to surface color. It can be observed when touching rigid objects (metal, wood, wool, or, for example, paper surfaces). The surface phenomenally forms a spatial boundary around the three-dimensional object, separating it from the rest of perceptual space. It is experienced as corresponding closely to the shape of the object. Even a thin sheet of cotton, smoothly spread out over the table, has a surface quality when touched during an experiment. Surface touch can be localized at any distance from the subject. "Space" is here referred to as the tactual space experienced by a normal blindfolded person.

Space-filling touch (*Raumfüllendes Tastquale*) is the touch experience of a medium. When walking against a rather strong wind, we experience a pressure which is diffuse, homogeneous, and without any reference to familiar surrounding objects. When the body surface is stimulated by a strong wind, no definite three-dimensional form can be experienced. Because this touch quality lacks articulation in form and location in space, Katz compares it to film color. It is the most reduced touch experience. This same touch quality also occurs when we move our limbs around in a liquid of a certain viscosity (e.g., splash in a pool with our feet). This phenomenon provides an opportunity to discuss the old question of the two poles, the subjective and the objective, of certain sensations. When sensing a space-filling touch, we do not feel the distal stimulus as "something out there" or as an object in the way the distal stimulus in vision usually is represented, according to Gibson, in the light flux of the proximal stimulation. The objective pole fades in an impression of space-filling touch, yet it remains as an extremely weak component connected with the dominant subjective pole in tactual perception.

Touch transparency (*Raumhafte, Durchtastete Fläche*). This phenomenon occurs when a rather small, well-bounded object is perceived *behind a layer of softer material*. We can, for example, perceive a wristwatch through a sheet of cotton which completely covers the watch. The cotton is felt as *tactually transparent*—as a medium, as it were—behind which the object is perceived. In the psychology of vision, *space color* refers to something seen in chromatic illumination. Touching through a contact surface is in some sense of the word equivalent to perceiving a space color. The same general rule holds, according to Katz, for both modalities: *The depth impression improves with increasing articulation of the object behind the medium.*[1]

In recent years Gibson has extended his interest from an exclusive concern with vision to an exploration of related phenomena in other modalities. He has looked for general applications of his principles concerning gradients of stimulation. Consistent with this point of view are cases in which the experienced quality of an object could be explained as due to certain *relational characteristics* of a sequence of *stimulus elements*, for example, of a *gradient* of scaled intensities. We have already noted that the theory of temperature stimulation based on the concept of gradients of thermal conductance offers rather a good parallel to the theory of the role of retinal gradients in visual perception.

The everyday experience of *feeling something hard behind a layer of softer material* must probably be explained as an effect of a *pressure gradient*, a gradient of successive degrees of deformation of the points of the skin contacted by the stratified layers of various materials. These applications of the gradient concept should be kept in mind when considering theories which hold that simple point-to-point stimulus-response connections represent the essential releasers of all sensory activity. In this connection it seems wiser to endorse the more general points of view maintained by organismic theories of behavior.

Intermodal Correspondence

When considering the differentiation of visual space, we introduced the concept of *frame of reference*. Correspondingly, differentiation of the tactual world involves *a tactual framework* with certain *figures* standing out from it. This can be demonstrated by stroking the stiff hairs of a short-bristled brush with the palm of one's hand. Perceived are the tips of the bristles together, forming a

---

[1] D. Katz, "Der Aufbau der Tastwelt," *Zeitschrift für Psychologie,* Ergänzungsband, 7 (1930), p. 30.

kind of coherent, consistent figure on an indeterminate background. The spaces among the hairs provide a kind of tactual frame, articulating the distinct configuration. What is amazing in a case like this is the impossibility of reversing this figure-ground configuration. There are few, if any, reversible tactual patterns. True, if we press a coarse-pronged fork against the skin we may sometimes perceive the "background" as more pronounced than the widely scattered "figure." These simple tactual figures convincingly demonstrate some features parallel to those observed in the articulation of visual stimulus configurations. For example, the *discrete patterning* of the discontinuous receptor surface does not prevent the perceiver from tactually experiencing a cohesive continuous plane. The five fingers of our hand together represent an "unbroken," consistent receptor field. Physically speaking, there are gaps in this phenomenally continuous sensorial field, for the fingertips are distinctly separated when scanning a tactual object. The spaces between the individual fingers correspond to the blind spot in the receptor field of the eye. Yet, in the same way as a moving retina can compensate for the lack of continuity and complete the discontinuities of the visual receptor area, so our five fingers can report continuous unitary surfaces without any breaks or "openings" between the tracks of the fingertips moving together across the object.

The problem has even more relevance when, say, we *move* our hand along the edge of a table. There occurs a certain *invariance phenomenon* not too different from the one we encountered when we considered visual examination of physically stationary objects by moving one's eyes along their contours. Although various groups of single receptor cells on the retina are successively stimulated, there is no phenomenal motion. On the contrary, there is a phenomenal constancy in the perceived stationary objects. According to Katz, the *moving sensory surface* is of major significance in tactual invariances. As mentioned before, he is inclined to assign to the motion of the receptors a role in maintaining tactual constancy comparable to that assigned to the prevailing illumination in accounting for color constancy.[2] Only by a stroking movement or through increasing pressure on the skin are we able to develop our surface touch experiences, which actually are the most ubiquitous

[2] *Ibid.*, p. 58.

impressions of touched objects. These conditions enable us, among other things, to experience constancy of surface touch at varying velocities of tactual movement.

To avoid misunderstanding we must emphasize with Katz that the immediate experience of surface touch is always completed by a *specification* of the tactual object. Such specification represents a tactual analogy to various color hues. Human beings are so much less differentiated in tactual perception than in vision that there are simply no specific "touch names." Terminology for touch has no expressions comparable to "red," "blue," "green," etc., the specific names for various color impressions. This fact has many implications for the psychology of language. When speaking about touch qualities we must resort to expressions like "wooden," "leatherlike," "silky," etc.[3]

Preferred Forms

Révész was especially interested in the form perception of the congenitally blind and carried out some experiments connected with these questions on them. It is generally known that there are certain *preferred forms* (*ausgezeichnete Formen*) in *our visual world*. Their importance can be shown, for example, by referring to the tendency to maintain and reproduce shapes having a simple structure (circles, squares, symmetrical forms, etc.) that are so conspicuous in visual perception. These preferred forms also emerge in the salience of certain proportions for the main dimensions in familiar plane figures. Occasionally it has even been claimed that some kind of aesthetic judgment tends to influence visual perception in a choice situation in which rectangles of varying proportions are to be compared. These influences have been referred to as the principle of the "golden section," which appears to govern our preferences for proportions. If a subject with normal sight is presented with a series of rectangles differing in the proportions of their main dimensions, and if he is asked to point to the "most agreeable," he usually chooses a rectangle the proportions of whose sides are as 21 to 34. Despite the exaggerated emphasis some investigators since Fechner's time have given this principle as an "aesthetic achievement," it has some general implications from, for example, the point of view of gestalt psychology. Révész began his experimental study

---

[3] *Ibid.*, p. 33.

of this statement by presenting rectangular pieces of cardboard to subjects with normal vision. A clear majority preferred a rectangle with proportions of 1:1.6, or even more extreme ones, going far from the other extreme, the cardboard square (the maximum discrepancy in the length of the sides was 1:2).[4]

When the same series was presented to blind subjects, a completely different result was obtained. The rectangle whose proportions were closest to the golden section was no longer most preferred, but instead the square (proportions 1:1) was. There apparently is a tendency to choose proportions explicitly avoided by the normally sighted (see Figure 13–1). When the blind were

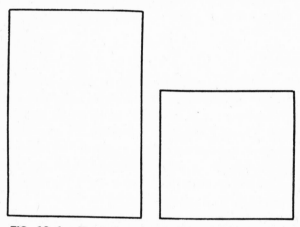

FIG. 13–1. The left rectangle is preferred by visual perceivers, the square is preferred by tactual ones.

asked to choose the "most agreeable," the task hardly made any sense to them. The majority choice of the square was regarded by them as rather arbitrary. Révész is of the opinion that no genuine aesthetic judgment can be expected to occur in pure tactual perceptions. The square is chosen on the basis of the metric principle; it is a form which is easy to handle kinesthetically and rhythmically, i.e., submits readily to a successive scanning process. Révész holds that form perception even of normally sighted individuals up to an age of 10 to 16 years follows the principles of construction and of simple symmetrical structure. This method of structural analysis in touch

---

[4] G. Révész, *Psychology and Art of the Blind* (London: Longmans, Green & Co., Ltd., 1950), pp. 197–99.

perception is a more primitive form of perception in general, and only later do the normally sighted become able to go further and appreciate relatively more complex structures.[5]

Conspicuous is the *absence* of *gestalt completion phenomena* in tactual forms in comparison with visual ones. A visually presented open, unclosed ring is phenomenally completed in tachistoscopic or after-image experiments. Nothing of this kind happens in tactual experiments. *Missing parts in the concrete physical stimulus pattern cannot, contrary to what occurs in visual perception, appear in the complete final phenomenal configuration.* An opening remains an opening, a torso of a human figure remains a torso, without being *completed* as a total impression. Further still, as we have seen, predominantly tactual structural analysis proceeds *slowly* and *gradually, bit by bit.* Since no gestalt completion is possible in, for example, the sculpture or clay modeling of certain blind people, their productions mostly remain an *incidental collection of successive partial impressions of an unintegrated totality* (see pp. 253–54).

Expressive Value of Works Made by Congenitally Blind

Révész goes so far as to deny any expressive value to works created by congenitally blind subjects.[6] According to his observations visually normal people are incapable of entering into the "spirit" of a product of these patients, to say nothing about their inability to grasp its meaning. In one of his experiments Révész showed a series of 14 clay sculptures produced by the patients of the Institute for the Blind in Vienna (Wiener Blindeninstitut) to about 80 university students. The task was simply to write down for each of the sculptures what the students thought they might represent. Some of his results are shown as percentages in Table 13–1. Révész himself pointed out that interpretations which can be considered "adequate to" or "in agreement with" (*übereinstimmend*) the original meaning were rare. In some cases there were more "opposite" or inconsistent (*widersprechend*) interpretations than ones within the "same general motif" (*dasselbe Gebiet*) as that intended by the blind sculptor.

In the Psychological Institute of the University of Helsinki a group experiment was carried out in 1950 in an attempt further to

---

[5] *Ibid.,* pp. 199–200.

[6] *Ibid.,* pp. 227–31.

TABLE 13-1

Distribution of Answers in the First Experiment Compared with Some of Révész' Results

	No. 2 "Horror"		No. 6 "Fury"		No. 7 "The Rejected"		No. 8 "Grief"	No. 1 Minné	No. 9 Picasso	No. 3 Munch	No. 7 Herzog	No. 5 Schäffner
	Révész	Exp. 1	Révész	Exp. 1	Révész	Exp. 1	Exp. 1	Exp. 1	Exp. 1	Exp. 1	Exp. 1	Exp. 1
Adequate	8.2%	37.7%	4.9%	5.3%	1.3%	2.5%	14.7%	56.5%	48.4%	26.0%	14.7%	9.5%
Same motif	34.9	36.8	34.1	17.5	28.0	24.2	30.5	17.5	—	28.4	8.4	26.0
Opposite content	10.8	3.5	—	42.8	—	14.7	1.4	1.7	6.7	—	11.2	4.9
Indeterminate	1.2	—	1.2	0.4	—	0.7	—	—	4.6	—	5.6	5.3
Other answers	42.2	23.2	56.1	30.9	69.3	55.4	52.6	20.4	30.0	41.4	47.4	51.9
No answer	2.4	1.8	3.7	3.2	1.3	3.2	1.1	3.5	10.5	4.2	12.6	2.5
	Blind sculptors							Expressionist artists				

check Révész' statements. Some of the same products of the blind were photographically reproduced and shown to 285 university students, namely "Horror," "Fury," and "The Rejected," but added to them was a series of modern artistic products all of which seemed to possess a considerable expressive value (Herzog's "Enjoyment,"

FIG. 13–2. "Horror."

FIG. 13–3. "Fury."

FIG. 13–4. Minné: "Mother and Dying Child."

FIG. 13–5. Picasso: "Face."

FIG. 13–6. Munch: "Cry."

FIG. 13–7. Schäffner: "Decency."

FIG. 13–8. Herzog: "Enjoyment."

Minné's "Mother with Dying Child," Munch's "Cry," Picasso's "Face," and Schäffner's "Decency"). The pictures were projected on a screen and the classroom was sufficiently illuminated to allow the subjects to write their responses. In the instructions the subjects were asked "to judge whether, from any one of the pictures, they could obtain an impression of a certain sentiment, a certain emotional reaction or some kind of mood and, if so, to name their

TABLE 13-2

DISTRIBUTION OF RESPONSES IN THE SECOND EXPERIMENT

Order of Preference	A	B	C	D	E	F
1	65 = 4.9%	432 = 30.7% (430)	76 = 5.4%	68 = 4.8% (66)	99 = 7.0%	669 = 47.4% (665)
2	215 = 15.3	542 = 38.4 (539)	155 = 11.0	102 = 7.2 (101)	151 = 10.7 (144)	244 = 17.3 (242)
3	370 = 26.3 (368)	180 = 12.8 (177)	211 = 14.9	166 = 11.8	303 = 21.5 (301)	179 = 12.7 (178)
4	300 = 21.3 (297)	129 = 19.1	307 = 21.8 (303)	150 = 10.6	398 = 28.1 (397)	125 = 8.2
5	306 = 21.7 (304)	80 = 5.7	435 = 30.9 (431)	280 = 19.9	252 = 17.9 (251)	56 = 3.9 (55)
6	152 = 10.8 (151)	50 = 3.5	226 = 16.0	642 = 46.9 (637)	207 = 14.7 (205)	132 = 9.3

NOTE: Elimination of psychology students (sophomores and juniors) leaves the numbers in parentheses. Percentages refer to the total number.

impression." The results, as well as Révész' comparable ones, appear in Table 13–1. The percentages vary considerably from picture to picture. Although "adequate" interpretations of the artists' products attained an average of 30.9 percent compared to 14.3 percent for the works of the blind, the difference is not overwhelming, and some of the latter products seem—according to these results—to be even more expressive than certain works of art.

Pointing in the same direction are the results of a large contest on estimating the aesthetic value of works of some well-known modern artists and of some blind artists which was arranged by the Finnish weekly magazine *Viikkosanomat* in 1958 without the contestants' knowing anything about the origin of the works to be judged. Three pictures of works by blind artists, "Loving Couple," "Old Man" and "Rejected," taken from Révész' book and called A, C, and E respectively, had to be ranked according to their estimated artistic value with three others, B (Gwen Lux's "Eve"), D (Picasso's "Face"), and F (Herzog's "Enjoyment") without the titles and artists being mentioned to the contestants. The results for the 1,409 responding readers are presented in Table 13–2. The first place votes already showed unambiguously that F (Herzog), scored highest (47.4 percent); next was B (Gwen Lux, 30.7 percent). The remaining 22 percent were shared among Picasso and the blind sculptors. E and C, works of the blind, ranged third and fourth, after them came D, Picasso, and the smallest number of first place votes was given to A ("Loving Couple"), a product of a blind person.

Thus it appears fairly safe to conclude that although the works of the blind do not seem to be particularly appreciated artistically, they cannot clearly be distinguished from certain products of modern art.

The Gestalt Completion in Tactual Experiments

Turning back to the question of completion phenomena with tactual gestalten, we should distinguish between simultaneous tactual percepts produced by a deforming object placed on the skin surface from the cases reported on p. 301. In a deformed simultaneous depression gestalt, completions may indeed occur—a ring with an opening can, on the skin surface of the trunk, be felt as a complete, continuous circle. Let us not forget, however, that touch receptors are sparsely scattered over the human chest and back. Maybe a physically missing bit of the ring did not actually stand out in the stimulus pattern because of the scarcity of receptors. We cannot quite compare these cases to visual completion of stimulus patterns which really do skip considerable portions of the receptor tissue—counterparts of visually perceived motions are "tactual apparent movements." It is possible to produce motion illusions in tactual perception by alternately stimulating two spots on the skin in a sufficiently rapid tempo. Under favorable conditions a "back-and-forth" movement appears. Some investigators report having been able to *create apparent circular movements in which the effect of a prägnanz tendency can be discerned.*

The alternation—or fusion—of after-images is rapid in visual and slow in tactual perception. If we want to draw letters in the air with a moving flashlight, we must be quick about it. If comparable symbols are drawn on the skin surface, the movements must be sufficiently slow.

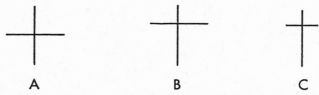

A   **B**   **C**

FIG. 13–9.   Two Latin crosses (B, C) and a Greek one (A).

It is true that in tactual perception we *notice* and *take into account certain proportions*, but the *awareness of proportions is generally not a part of the immediate synthetic apprehension of the pattern.* When limited solely to tactual stimulation, we still are often able to distinguish a Latin cross (Figure 13–9, B and C) from the Greek one (A) and sometimes even the two Latin crosses from each other, but typical forms "such as owe their existence to the impression of proportions" do not become clear.[7]

Révész' experiments show that *experienced relations of tactual percepts can even be transposed to a different scale.*

When perceiving by touch alone, we *strive for symmetry in our gestalten,* a process which is in some ways parallel to the visual prägnanz tendency. At an early stage of their *structural analysis* blind persons aim at symmetrical wholes, a tendency which is, according to Révész, an outcome of the schematic principle. The

---

[7] *Ibid.*, p. 133.

result of this procedure can be seen in experiments with blindfolded normal subjects who are presented with a piece of cardboard the shape of which they have to figure out (Figure 13–10). *Photo-*

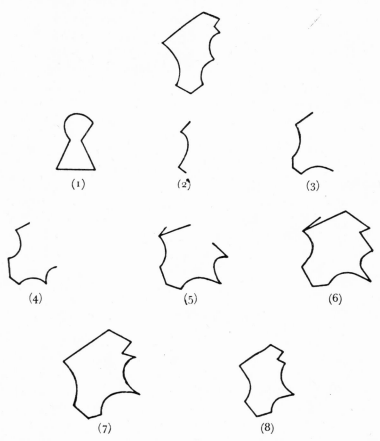

FIG. 13–10. Top center is the shape of the piece of cardboard which was handed to the blindfolded subject; the other figures are drawings made by him, showing the stages of his structural analysis, after (1) 10 sec., (2) 20 sec., (3) 40 sec., (4) 1 min. 10 sec., (5) 1 min. 20 sec., (6) 1 min. 50 sec., (7) 2 min. 15 sec., (8) 2 min. 30 sec. of handling it.

grams taken of the movements of the middle finger during this scanning procedure show how difficult such tactual form perception is (Figure 13–11).[8]

One of the most interesting peculiarities of congenitally blind

[8] *Ibid.*, pp. 110–16.

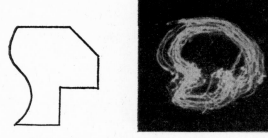

FIG. 13–11. The left-hand figure shows the piece of cardboard handed to the subject; the other figure is a photographic reproduction of a series of successive "outlining movements" during the process of his structural analysis.

artists is their inability to understand relief pictures. This may sound somewhat paradoxical, since relief actually is not a *plane figure*, and therefore we could expect that it would be easily perceived by persons without sight. But we must remember that the whole idea of representations in relief is based upon a visually determined type of articulation: the figure-ground articulation. Relief provides no opportunity for the observer to apply the stereo-plastic principle. The most natural way of perceiving forms without visual aids would be by grasping. This cannot be done with reliefs, because they are accentuated forms of plane figures on a ground. Furthermore, the ground does not present tactually plane and distinct figures. For those born blind they represent only isolated, disconnected pieces of heads, arms, etc., mixed up in a chaotic way with the rest of a larger, diffuse object surface.[9]

---

[9] *Ibid.*, pp. 183–87.

CHAPTER 14

The Perception of Objects by the Primitive Senses

PSYCHOPHYSICS OF ODORS

THE TERM "psychophysics of odors" could be used to refer to investigations of the physical correlates of smell percepts. Such research is, of course, based on the same assumptions as are other types of psychophysics; and right away we run into the difficulty that we cannot transform all immediate experience into a *system of external stimulus relationships*. Many consider it essential for scientific description that it maintain a conceptual level corresponding to that represented, for example, by mathematical physics. For perceptual psychology to be seriously considered a natural science, then, it would have to limit itself to descriptions of perceptual dimensions which are directly correlated with physical dimensions. As shown among others by E. Kaila, a psychological description on this conceptual level can be carried out, but we must be prepared to find that most of the qualities which we immediately perceive do not fit into such a restricted language of scientific description.[1]

The *psychophysics of vision* has been studied for almost a century, and important physiological functions of visual receptors have been discovered. Yet up to now appropriate starting points for psychophysical researches on odor have clearly been lacking. The reason is perhaps that the receptors for this sense are themselves relatively unexplored and hard to classify. There are, for example, only a very few studies of neural impulses in the olfactory tract.

A pioneer study in this field was performed by Ekman in

---

[1] E. Kaila, "Logik und Psychophysik," *Theoria*, 10 (1944).

Stockholm in 1954.[2] Using paired comparisons, he developed a way to *perform measurements on smell experiences which made it possible to draw certain conclusions regarding common receptor groups for structurally related chemical stimuli.*

According to the Stockholm report the 20 following odorous substances were used: (1) benzylaldehyde, (2) benzene, (3) pyridine, (4) naphthalene, (5) isopropyl alcohol, (6) ethylacetate, (7) carbon dinelphide, (8) cinnamic aldehyde, (9) methyl ethyl ketose, (10) O-xylene, (11) 3-methylpyridine, (12) methyl benzyl ketone, (13) isobutyl alcohol, (14) butyl alcohol, (15) toluene, (16) borneol, (17) nitrobenzene, (18) tetrahydronaphthalene, (19) ethyl benzoate, and (20) acetone. The experimenter and his subject were seated opposite each other at a table. The stimuli were poured into small bottles equipped with outlet tubes and were presented for paired comparison, two bottles together successively in a predetermined randomized order. The subject had to report the degree of similarity between the members of each stimulus pair, using a scale ranging from 0 (totally dissimilar) to 4 (maximally similar). A total of 23 university students served as subjects, each performing 190 comparisons twice for 380 comparisons in all.

The raw scores were transformed into a scale from 0 to 1 to achieve mean values below 1.00, which could be conveniently entered into matrices whose coordinates were the two stimuli compared. Such a matrix looks like a matrix of correlation coefficients for factor analysis and as a matter of fact could be factor analyzed in the usual way.

Ekman called his method *similarity analysis*. Each of the paired stimuli produces a physiological event, according to his theory, and the perceived similarity reflects the degree of overlap of these events. He assumes that the factor analysis could therefore reveal the proportional share of the stimulus components in the undefinable qualitative experience. An earlier investigation by the same author had applied similarity analysis to spectral colors, revealing three groups of retinal receptors. In the same way, this similarity analysis of odors was expected to show something about the specificity of certain groups of olfactory receptors.

The analysis performed by Ekman yielded three factors, two of

---

[2] G. Ekman, *Similarity Analysis of Olfaction: A Preliminary Investigation* (Reports from the Psychological Laboratory of the University of Stockholm, No. 10) (1954).

which were represented in the chemical $C = O$ structure group and in the benzene ring.

The third factor was represented by substances showing absorption spectra for red light in the region of 748 to 788 nm. Ekman's study is quite tentative in its design and its results, but it indicates some provisional possibilities for the correlation between stimuli on the one hand and perceptual experiences on the other. Unfortunately, so far our knowledge about the structural relations among the substances which are "similar" in odor are insufficient to give very useful hints for further work.

Engen, in a series of experiments conducted between 1959 and 1961, attempted to arrange olfactory stimuli into a series of gradually increasing intensity.[3] Systematically increased concentrations of the solutions did not, however, lead to transpositions of the obtained scales, nor to proportional displacements of all of the substances in the series. On the other hand, he succeeded in producing scales of phenomenal intensity for completely different substances, with the gradations of the scales perceived as directly equivalent. Such phenomenally equidistant intensity scales were constructed for amylacetate, vanillin, and diacetone alcohol, although the concentrations of the physical stimuli increased at different rates for the different solutions. Thus, proportionally increased concentrations throughout the whole physical scale of a given substance did not correspond to phenomenally equal steps between any two of the single stimuli, but the gradations of such phenomenal scales of odors did correspond to other scales based on quite different substances. It must, however, be pointed out that these experiments have so far only been performed on very small and specially trained groups of subjects (Engen, 1961).

Modes of Appearance

Odors can be analyzed phenomenally on the basis of aspects analogous to the modes of appearance of colors. Even among smells (1) the *floating smell* must be distinguished from (2) the *objectified smell experience*. The first, following Henning's descriptions, is a loose, diffuse "immaterial" smell experience without any reference to perceptual objects. If we sniff with our *eyes closed*, we obtain such experiences. The objectified smell is perceived as

---

[3] T. Engen, *Direct Scaling of Odor Intensity* (Reports from the Psychological Laboratory of the University of Stockholm, No. 106) (1961).

localized, as belonging to some object as though it were a property of it. *We feel that some object produces the odor.* Even a normally sighted subject when sensing a floating smell *intentionally* behaves in a somewhat peculiar manner. He tries to identify, to localize the source of the smell. The better he succeeds, the more the vague, indefinite floating smell gives way to a more accurate smell of an object. Henning calls this gradual change *contraction.* According to him, there are several possibilities for such objectification: (1) the source of smell may be experienced as clearly delimited in space, (2) it may be limited but without any phenomenal contours, (3) it may remain an undifferentiated "cloud of odor" associated with a definite part of space, but in which it tends to move around according to the line of vision, (4) the localization of the odor may be restricted to an unlimited yet rather specified "region," and (5) the localization may be broad yet restricted to some wider district (the "smell of the Riviera," for example).

The neighborhood surrounding a cellulose factory usually is impregnated with a constant smell, in which case it might be appropriate to speak of an odor objectified to a certain locality, for example, the particular "smell of the Valkeakoski factory" in Finland. However, if this odor is temporarily blown by the wind to far-off areas, it will be regarded there as a floating smell.

The following case illustrates the contraction phenomenon. When Henning entered a room where a richly perfumed lady was seated, he first perceived an indefinite space-filling scent. The next moment he realized that the odor must have a restricted source. Once his eyes caught sight of the lady, the space-filling, floating smell instantaneously *contracted around her.* It felt as though it became stored or piled up in the space surrounding her. Having arrived at this point the perceiver was incapable of recalling the space-filling odor again.[4]

The last sentence refers to the process of reorganization (*Umschlag*) connected with these experiences. One appearance gives way to another, to one which is more appropriate. The husband entering his home may first sense a diffuse "smell of dinner." After seeing the table he is likely to replace this floating smell by another experience: his impression probably *contracts* around the *meat platter* on the table.

---

[4] H. Henning, *Der Geruch* (Leipzig: Barth, 1924), p. 421.

We all have experienced similar cases of contraction in our everyday life. Usually a rather amusing progression occurs with them: the stimulus intensity is sufficient to bring about a sensation, but the threshold of recognition has not yet been exceeded. The source of smell cannot be successfully identified.

During a Christmas vacation the writer entered the vestibule of the University of Helsinki's main building, and immediately encountered a floating smell: a "scent of Christmas." Probably the season and the street decorations had contributed to an expectancy: something from childhood memories of Christmas was connected with that odor. What could it be? After a while it became clear: "candy store," "marzipan spiced with fruit flavors." The correct identification and localization of the source came via these flavors: the charwomen had, during this busy season, put some scented detergents into their buckets! In a moment the pleasant vague odor of Christmas disappeared phenomenally. Actually, this is the way we often sense diffuse unrecognized odors, as closely connected with strong emotional values or with objects to which we were devoted in early childhood.

Henning gives a lively description of a reorganization which occurred to him when taking a walk on the streets of his home city. There was a space-filling floating smell of "something rather dry and sweet"—"maybe pipe tobacco, from the cloud of smoke produced by a puffing gentleman in the neighborhood." At the same moment he became aware of a load of hay passing by and instantly the smell was objectified—it was perceived as a "property" of the hay.

Analogies in Perceiving Smells and Colors

When we perceive objectified odors in cases like this, they compare with constancy phenomena of illumination and colored surfaces. It is clear that even in this modality we could apply a reduction technique: we could start with smell complexes possessing object qualities and end with a diffuse homogeneous "fog of odor" analogous to what Metzger discovered in his Ganzfeld experiment. The framework of an objectified smell could easily be reduced by preventing a visual identification of its source, for example, by optically masking the source of smell from the sight of the subject. The accompanying "higher-order stimuli" for a smell percept always belong to other modalities, consisting of various relationships between sight and smell components. Accordingly, it makes sense to speak of the *constancy of an objectified smell*. In so doing we must not forget that these constancies can develop only when based on visual or tactual systems of reference. (Apparently the blind can replace visual coordinates, which are so important for the sighted, by tactual components in the act of objectification.)

In smell perception the rich and detailed relational variables prerequisite to object constancy must be provided by components from other modalities. This is mainly because of the poor differentiation of smell as a sense modality; its organizational level is insufficient to produce "self-supporting" frames of reference.

There are also smell phenomena parallel to *memory colors* in visual perception, which we shall consider here without any attempt at a theoretical criticism of such a concept. Henning observes: "When meeting a lady you inevitably sense the scent of the perfume you noticed when seeing her before." He himself made experiments with "memory smells." He had a jacket impregnated with naphthalene and also sprinkled jasmine oil on it. Wearing this coat regularly when meeting with his students, he was able to create a peculiar "Henning smell." After this, the odor was associated with his person for weeks whenever he turned up, even if he did not wear the coat and even after he had removed the smell completely with cleaning materials and deodorants.[5]

SCALING OF TASTE EXPERIENCES

If there is any modality involving interactional components from other simultaneously operating systems of receptors, it is *taste*. The complex experience of something "edible" rests on simultaneous olfactory, thermal, and tactual stimulus components. Why is it that all these parallel stimuli are needed to bring about lively and accentuated flavors? Could not isolated, "pure" gustatory sensations produce equally strong and natural taste percepts? One of the probable answers is to be found in the tight representation and the partial overlapping of adjacent sensory fields on the receptor surface.[6] Yet, more decisive than the cooperation of various receptor surfaces is probably the *role of tactual impressions for the formation of objectified taste percepts*. There are good reasons to distinguish

[5] *Ibid.*, pp. 285–86.

[6] E. v. Skramlik, *Handbuch der Physiologie der niederen Sinne*, *I* (Leipzig: George Thieme Verlag, 1926), p. 347.

even within this sense modality between two modes of appearance: an *indefinite taste* and an *objectified taste experience*.

Ekman (1961) performed preliminary experiments on the scaling of taste experiences. He presented simple salt solutions as stimuli. The concentration gradually increased from 0.06 percent to 0.72 percent in seven successive steps. Each of several of the solutions in the original series (sometimes the 0.12 percent, sometimes the 0.36 percent and the 0.60 percent solutions) were used as reference stimuli. The obtained phenomenal scales were not directly proportional to the physical scale. On the other hand, if the phenomenal scales were combined according to a certain rule formulated by the investigator, this sensory scale stood in a power relation to the stimulus scale, the equation being

$$R = 0.85 + 12.9S^{1.59} .$$

The constant (0.85) distinguishes Ekman's equation from the threshold functions in other sense modalities. Consider again, for example, the equations on page 169. Ekman provides two explanations for this difference: (1) we might suppose that the constant compensates for the error caused by the arbitrariness of the zero point on the scale; (2) even if the stimulus were given a zero value, this need not imply a zero value for the phenomenal percept, because our tasting procedure always contains some "perceptual noise" (even a solution of 0 percent concentration has a phenomenal taste). Ekman does not believe that his equation actually proves that there is a difference in the way taste perception relates to its stimuli as compared with how other perceptual modalities relate to their stimuli, but nevertheless he considers this difference very probable. Ekman wishes to stress the discrepancy between different phenomenal scales as the main result of his gustatory experiment, a proposal which merits further consideration.[7]

Various Systems of Reference for Taste

When one sucks or chews something in his mouth, all gustatory, olfactory, thermal, etc., stimulation components of the bite are objectified *in the simultaneous tactual experience*. This frame of reference is the most important. Visual and tactual coordinates of

---

[7] G. Ekman, *A Methodological Note on Scales of Gustatory Intensity* (Reports from the Psychological Laboratory of the University of Stockholm, No. 98) (1961).

our phenomenal space are decisive. The incorporation of a perceptual object into the digestive system renders it invisible and gives the tactual references special significance as a basis for constancies of objectified tastes.

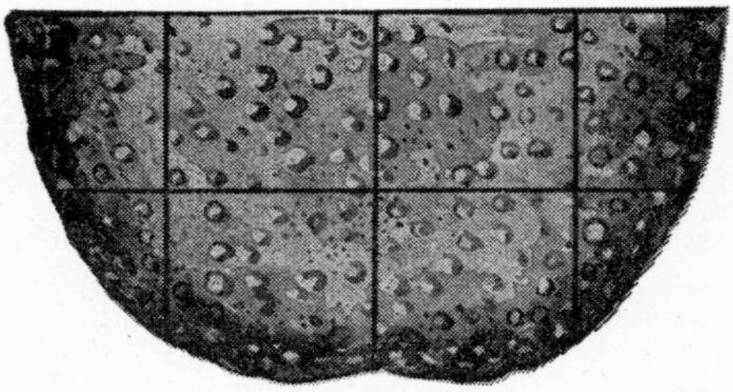

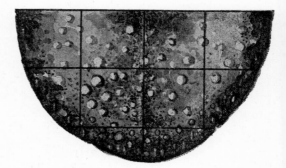

FIG. 14–1. Pattern of fungiform papillae on surface of tongue of a nine-year-old girl.

The *concentrated distribution of fungiform papillae on the surface of the tongue of a child* was mentioned in Chapter 3. Skramlik's two pictures (Figures 14–1 and 14–2) show the difference clearly. The first shows the pattern of these papillae on the tongue of a nine-year-old girl. Generally, we can notice certain asymmetries in the sensory organs of most modalities, but these asymmetries are less marked in children. When the center of the upper surface of the tongue (3 to 4 cm. back from the tip) of a person in his forties is stimulated, he does not report any taste impressions. Young persons seem to sense all of *the four qualities customarily classified as fundamental tastes with the aid of the same groups of papillae* on different occasions. At the tip of the tongue they sometimes sense sweet, sometimes sour, sometimes bitter and sometimes salty. Already in Kiesow's day it was well known that fungiform papillae in the middle of the upper tongue surface gradually turn torpid and deteriorate.[8]

Gustatory impulses, according to Katz, fire only if stimulated by adequate dissolved chemical substances. He also

FIG. 14–2. Pattern on tongue of middle-aged person.

refers to this by pointing out that the human tongue receptors are *rudimentary*. We know that at early evolutionary stages all basic

---

[8] E. v. Skramlik, "Über die Lokalisation der Empfindungen bei den niederen Sinnen," *Zeitschrift für Sinnesphysiologie*, 56 (1925).

species were exclusively *water animals* dependent on papillae spread widely over the whole body surface. "The tongue gets along in the mouth as the fish does in the water" is an often mentioned aphorism of Katz.[9] He also emphasized the significance of the *motor activity of the tongue* as contributing to the creation of taste experiences. Again, for the achievements of even this modality, a stationary receptor surface turns out to be less effective than *moving tissue*. A different approach to the perceputal exploration of our mouth organs, neglected by traditional sensory psychology, might be the possibility of testing *the projections of a person's "ego zone" by what he feels in his mouth cavity*. These considerations lead to perceptual problems associated with the "oral stage" of infants as well as to the emotional aversion against touching strange objects with the mouth if we can resort to our hand receptors. We might be able to understand the *deficiencies in size constancy* so conspicuous even with familiar objects as soon as we lose sight of them at the moment they enter the mouth. Seeds and small food particles are greatly overestimated in size—not to mention how exaggeratedly huge a tooth cavity may feel.

[9] D. Katz, "Psychophysiologische Untersuchungen an der Zunge," *Kwartalnik Psychologiczny*, 6 (Poznan, 1935), pp. 7–11.

CHAPTER 15

Perception of the Self Directly and as a Mirror Image

THE FINNISH philosopher and psychologist E. Kaila, in his uncompleted posthumous work on "Perceptual and Conceptual Contents of Everyday Experience," took up an interesting problem.

When shaving before a mirror, do we actually shave the face we feel as our own or the other face in front of us in the mirror? All the time two faces are simultaneously perceived: the mirrored face, visible in the mirror space extending behind the mirror surface, and the real face, invisible to the perceiver and located as a physical object in the "real" space in front of the mirror surface.[1]

The Shaving Paradox

A perceptual psychologist might consider a case like this rather easy to analyze: vision is for most people the dominant modality. The *visually perceived self* constitutes a preferential frame of reference, and what other senses report on as belonging to us is phenomenally projected into the mirror image. As a result of an objectification process the visual mirror image constitutes a perceptual frame into which all other body sensations may be incorporated. When we shave, some of our body sensations may be momentarily projected into the *visual object*, i.e., into the face in the mirror. The perceptual psychologist might continue by saying that we fortunately have some grasp on actual reality. We have a rich variety of sensations which accompany shaving. We feel the varying tension on the skin and hear the crisp sound of the stubble being cut. Could

---

[1] E. Kaila in *Ajatus*, 23 (1960). Quoted in K. v. Fieandt, "Erweiterung des Körperschemas im Spiegelbild," *Zeitschrift für Psychologie*, 167 (1962), p. 60.

anyone be so extremely visual as to believe seriously that he is shaving his mirror image?

The case is made more problematic if one follows Kaila's presentation: when touching the stubble before a mirror, our mirror fingers are, as it were, feeling the skin surface of the face in the mirror. This is a statement so astonishing that the reader may feel inclined to carry out a series of experiments himself before he is ready to receive more verbal information. He may want to go to a mirror and tap with his fingertips on his forehead and other parts of his face, alternately closing his eyes and looking at his fingers *in the mirror*. Without difficulty anyone can confirm that *the touch experience is referred to the mirror face, where the touch can, however, only be felt as long as one continues to look at the mirrored fingertips*. The same thing happens if we produce pain sensations in parts of the skin that can be seen in the mirror, as when, e.g., we pinch our face or prick it with a needle while looking at the mirror image of the stimulated spots.

Kaila needed these observations to support certain philosophical conclusions. According to him, the "reality" of physical objects cannot be logically distinguished from the "irreality" of phenomenal impressions. Generally speaking, his statements of the relativity of the difference between ϕ- and p-objects appears to hold true. His presentation constitutes a sound counterweight to the widespread misconception that these "two realities" can be kept distinct on the basis of some logical criteria.[2] He chose the example of the mirrored body image because he considered it a case in which "a mere image" would not be experienced as such but would, on the contrary, look even more real to the perceiver than the directly experienced parts of his own body.

Despite the illustrative value of this example it nevertheless appears to be somewhat unhappily selected from the point of view of what we know about the objectification of parallel sensory experiences.

Role of Objectified Sense Material

It turns out that the deceptive "impression of reality" or the "merely visual object which can simultaneously be perceived tactually" does not persist longer than is necessary for the touching

---

[2] Cf. our presentation above in the "Introduction," p. 6.

person to obtain a visual percept of his fingertips together with the touched body surface. Other things seen in the mirror do not achieve the same level of reality but may be regarded as "mere pictures." Probably a careful ontological examination could reveal how the localization of touch experiences, i.e., of what we feel when touching things with our fingers, has been combined with visual impressions of our fingertips. It is where we *see* our fingertips that we are likely to locate the touch objects mediated by them. And with the same certainty with which a normal person identifies his extremities, i.e., his fingertips, as the enduring permanent parts of his body, he also may well, after frequent use of a mirror, recognize his "own limbs" in the mirror image. Even the worst toothache could not be objectified to the visual frame of our mouth in the mirror as long as we refrain from touching the tooth with some object or with the finger. The visually perceived touching process is necessary for the pain to be objectified to the touched object. The proximal stimuli for the mirror experience are rays of light which are first reflected from our body surface and then once again from the surface of the mirror. Why should this turned-around or detoured array of stimuli give the perceiving organism an impression different from that produced by more direct incoming stimulation? These light rays have philosophically the *same degree of reality*, whether they are reflected twice, thrice, or still more often. It so happens that cast on the last reflecting surface, the mirror, is a complete physical as well as phenomenal representation of the perceiver's *own immediate body image*. Yet in viewing our mirror image we remain surprisingly "dualistic," and the prominent role of vision cannot abolish the peculiar experience of being a double: we remain basically aware of our own vital person—our kinesthetic, vestibular, and visceral sensations are not projected into the visual framework. And *we know it is the face of this vitally anchored person that we are shaving.*

It would not be difficult to perform further experiments of this kind. If a large cardboard box is placed upon a high chair so that it, together with the head and upper part of the experimenter's body, can be seen in the mirror, it can easily be shown that touching the surface of the box produces the impression that the fingers seen in the mirror touch the box in the mirror, provided the experimenter looks only in the mirror. Contrariwise, if the fingers touching the box surface are looked at *directly*, and not through the mirror, the experimenter feels the box tactually as located *where it actually,* *physically* is placed, and not as located in the mirror space. Anyone can produce these two alternating impressions: that of touching the box surface in the mirror space and that of touching the "real" object next to his own body. All one has to do is look alternately at the mirrored fingers contacting the image of the box in the mirror space and at the "real fingers" contacting the box in front of the mirror.

The conditions are the same as when tapping one's forehead in front of a mirror alternately with the eyes open and closed. One can feel one's forehead as located in the mirror space only if one can see the fingertips touching the forehead in the mirror. This provides a case *in which the direct objectification of touch experiences to an immediately visible part of the body is impeded,* because nobody can see his own forehead directly.[3] In this special case tactual experiences are objectified to the visible head in the mirror. The condition of seeing the fingertips seems to be crucial. If they can be seen directly without looking in the mirror, we also feel them touching our own body surface. Thus, when touching the tip of one's own nose, the fingers in this particular case reach into the visual field of the toucher, and it is therefore impossible for him to get the impression of touching his mirrored nose even while he is looking in the mirror. The problem raised by Kaila seems, when considered in terms of perceptual psychology, to be a pseudoproblem. The mirror space is simply treated as real space reflected by a mirror. When objects are perceived over this circuitous route, the same rules for objectification, etc., hold as when they are perceived immediately and directly.

Origins of the Body Image

The phenomenal body image, i.e., one's own body as a perceptual object, is a complex sensory pattern, depending to a great extent upon impressions from skin, muscle, and visceral receptors. Again the dominant role of visual experiences and the tendency to visualize sensory material transmitted by other modalities is clearly noticeable. The body image of blind persons, by contrast, reveals a corresponding hegemony of the touch modality as well as a tendency to objectify other sensory experiences tactually.

---

[3] As to the concept of "objectification," cf. K. v. Fieandt, "Toward a Unitary Theory of Perception," *Psychological Review*, 5 (1958).

Although attention was called to body image phenomena by some observations on *amputees*, the concept was typically discussed in the literature together with the somatic delusions of mentally ill and brain-injured patients. The perceptual syndromes of amputees were long handled separately without considering their interesting relationship to the body image of normal people. It was not until some research on the problem in recent decades that a coherent, systematic description of these perceptual phenomena was achieved. A. Pick in particular contributed the insight of the great significance of this concept in clinical research for understanding a number of neurotic, psychosomatic, and psychotic trends in the total personality.[4]

This kind of investigation, too, reflected prevailing conceptual tendencies characteristic of a long period of psychological research. Head referred body image phenomena to impulses from skin, muscle, and joint stimulation, the same ones which determine our awareness of body posture. These sensations, however, do not produce any percepts until they have been referred to earlier experiences within the frame of the entire organism. Jalavisto holds that tactual-kinesthetic sensations contribute only in part to the process of creating a body image.

Jalavisto seems to present a correct interpretation when she considers the body image a special case of object constancy. She appears to be the first investigator to express the psychological nature of this phenomenon so clearly. She wrote:

The fact that we perceive our mobile and sensing body as something unified and persistent despite the host of impressions overwhelming us at each moment must in my opinion be taken as an indication of some *object constancy* process in our appreciation of this sensory material—I refer to this very invariance when speaking of "body image."[5]

Jalavisto then examines the possibilities for the empirical determination of the body image in healthy people and for the stimuli upon which it could be based. The role played by skin sensations becomes quite apparent in cases of local anesthesia. A person whose straight index finger had been anesthetized later reported having felt his finger as clearly bent. This impression was so strong that

---

[4] A. Pick, "Störung der Orientierung am eigenen Körper, *Psychologische Forschung*, 13 (1929).

[5] Eeva Jalavisto, "Observations on Arm-Amputeers," *Annales Academiae Scientiarum Fennicae*, Ser. A 17 (Helsinki, 1948). Cf. *Ajatus*, 12 (1943), p. 8.

only intent visual examination of the position of the finger could abolish it. A limb devoid of its natural sensitivity feels bent, i.e., as though the muscles concerned were in a resting state. This fact has some implications for what will be considered later about phantom limb phenomena. Jalavisto presents another example of the sensory effect of anesthesia of parts of the skin. This case, too, is relevant to how we perceive clothing over phantom limbs. After a ski trip in a strong icy wind from behind, the skier's back felt somewhat odd. It had partially lost its sensitivity, so that, although it was not phenomenally missing, it was experienced as *bare*. There has been controversy about whether the clothes normally are included in the body image. On the other hand, it is clear that clothing belongs to the only crudely differentiated empirical self of a preschool child. Jalavisto wanted to introduce the concept of a sensory-motor body image when she was analyzing the role played by kinesthetic components in this phenomenal scheme. According to her, a separation of what is felt as sensations and what as motor innervations could hardly be meaningfully carried out.

The present author undertook some observations at the Psychological Institute of the University of Helsinki on the formation and the appearance of the body image. The subjects were adults, normals as well as amputees. Patients' descriptions of their body image clearly indicate that their sensations predominantly correspond to stimuli which would come from the peripheral *surface* of the body. Touch and pain are both localized on the body surface. Their sensations are rarely if ever referred to deeper, more central parts of the organism. These findings are confirmed by the observations of Jalavisto. When the experimental subject is given the task of imagining his own body while closing his eyes, the *somatic periphery*, that is, the peripheral body surface, clearly directs the formation of this mental image.

PHANTOM-LIMB PHENOMENA

As soon as the significance of the phantom limbs of amputees was properly understood, the interpretation of the body image was greatly clarified. Not to mention some remarks of Descartes, we know at any rate that Ambroise Paré (1510–90) was familiar with the phenomenon of phantom limbs, and among the pioneers in the last century, Abbatucci (1894) deserves special attention. The term refers to vivid sensory impressions of the lost limb in an amputee, persisting even for years after the amputation, and giving the illusion that the limb is intact and in its original shape and position. Since the turn of the century the phenomenon has been systematically investigated. First, it was observed that peripheral stimuli from the stump at least contributed to the development of the phenomenal limb. On the other hand, some investigators (e.g., Katz and Pitress) emphasized the influence of some central factors. It was found, for example, that phantom limbs could be influenced and transformed by means of hypnosis.

Technically outstanding were some of Katz's experiments, although nowadays his theoretical considerations sound fairly out of date. Let us consider some of his results and then give them a more recent interpretation.

The *structure* of a phantom limb does not correspond accurately with the anatomy of the amputated part of the body. Some details develop a predominant role in the perceptual pattern. In a phantom hand the surface of the palm, especially the palmar side of the thumb and the fingers, are well represented. Among the fingers, the thumb, index finger, and little finger stand out as best perceived. Tendons, wrist, and elbow are rather noticeable, but the forearm usually appears diffuse, while the upper arm is hardly felt at all. Katz presented data on 22 forearm amputees, with the following numbers of cases reporting each given part as very clearly perceived in the phantom limb:

```
Perceived forearm...................  1 case
Perceived wrist.....................  2 cases
Perceived palm......................  5 cases
Perceived fingers...................  22 cases
```

The phantom fingers appeared straight in only one case, while in the 21 others the fingers were felt as bent against the palm. There is a striking correspondence with the findings in the experiments on local anesthesia. In the long run, phantom fingers bend more and more and may in the most extreme cases even result in a permanent phenomenal fist. After a foot amputation, the patient has his strongest phantom impressions of the sole, toes, ankle, and especially the ankle bones. The legs are rarely perceived, nor are the knees. Occasionally, the clearly discerned parts can appear as separated from the rest of the limb; for example, the foot may appear to be located at a distance corresponding to the missing part of the leg.[6]

The spatial orientation of phantom limbs differs from that characteristic of ordinary extremities. Not infrequently the bent phantom forms a 90° angle, the forearm appearing phenomenally to be turned forwards or backwards, the leg being felt as lifted to a horizontal position straight back from the knee. The phantom limb behaves in either of two intriguing ways when it overlaps in space with a physical object: the phantom hand may shorten and withdraw into its stump ("inner hand") or it may just appear to penetrate visible physical objects without avoiding them ("outer hand"). Katz described these alternatives and clarified them with illustrations (Figure 15–1).

FIG. 15–1. Two kinds of phantom limbs.

If the phantom limb belongs to the type which avoids obstructing p-objects, the body image really gives way, but only to the extent necessary—the phenomenal contours of the pattern are otherwise maintained with as much constancy as possible. The fingers, for example, are phenomenally preserved, yet they might be felt as withdrawn into the stump in certain situations.

Vividness and Mobility of Phantom Limbs

Occasionally, spontaneous *involuntary movements* are felt in a phantom limb, but this only happens rather rarely. Much more common instead are various degrees of *voluntary movement*. The phantom limb may feel readily movable or, at the other extreme, almost motionless. Usually the amputee feels capable of performing voluntary φ-movements, although he experiences them as stiff and as encountering much friction; the phantom limb seems to resist them. Not infrequently a condition for feeling voluntary movements is intentional motion of the healthy, preserved opposite limb (in which case the phantom arm, e.g., is felt as swinging opposite the

[6] D. Katz, "Zur Psychologie des Amputierten und seiner Prothese," *Zeitschrift für angewandte Psychologie*, Beiheft 25 (1921), pp. 23–30.

real one), in a way which corresponds to reciprocal motor innervation. That these parallel p-movements cannot be regarded as
absolutely necessary conditions for perceived voluntary movements
is shown by the fact that even bilateral amputees occasionally feel
intentional movements in both their phantom hands. According to
Curschmann, the accompanying movements only reflect the difficulty of experiencing swinging phantom limbs. He found that the
number of these parallel p-movements increased directly with the
difficulty of experiencing ϕ-movements in the phantom limb.[7]

Least difficult is the induced phenomenal innervation of *predominant, outstanding, salient* components of the body image. Such parts
are the thumb and index finger of the hand and the big toe of the
foot. It is not unusual for the amputee clearly to perceive a
"localized effort to innervate" some of his phantom limbs; he may,
for instance, experience trying to move one of his toes, although the
effort does not result in any changes: the toe seems to have gone
numb. Katz mentioned that 22 of his forearm amputees reported
being able to move their phantom fingers. Most of them felt all their
fingers were movable, and some at least felt capable of straightening
their bent phantom fingers from their relaxed curved position. Of
the 27 upper arm amputees among Katz's subjects, 20 reported they
felt they could move their phantom fingers. Sufficient observations
of leg amputees have not yet been made.[8]

The *vividness* of phantom limbs varies considerably. Generally
they appear most vivid immediately after the operation, as soon as
the pain has somewhat subsided. It is not rare for the phantom
limb to shrink and disappear entirely after some 20 to 25 years. An
impressive exception is the case of a patient who underwent
amputation as an eight-year-old child and who vividly experienced
the phantom limb even some 60 years later. In several instances the
phantom limb maintains a *sensory vividness* for years. Patients
often tell of their efforts to catch sliding objects with their phantom
hand or to kick the door with their phantom foot when laboriously
walking through it. Usually some bitter frustrations soon lead them
to avoid reliance on such unrealistic impressions.

Especially curious was this case reported by Katz. A soldier,
shortly before he was badly wounded in the arm, got a painful local
wound just under the nail of his thumb. This painful thumb

[7] *Ibid.*, pp. 42–43.
[8] *Ibid.*, pp. 31–32.

troubled him even after his arm was amputated, the pain appearing again in the phantom thumb as soon as there was some recovery from the pain of the amputation.[9]

The phantom limb seldom shows up in patients' dreams. This fact has been considered to constitute strong evidence against Schilder's psychoanalytic explanation of the phantom-limb phenomenon. Inferiority feelings caused by the loss of a limb could be expected to show up in dreams rather than in conscious daytime imagination. According to Schilder, the phantom limb should be considered a protest against the violation of one's personal integrity.

Body Image Explained as a Thing Constancy Phenomenon

Without doubt Jalavisto's opinion represents a more modern and mature attitude toward phantom-limb phenomena. Jalavisto systematically considers each of the points we have raised as indications of how our consistent body image is developed and perceived. The constancy of this phenomenal image is the reason for perceiving the former somatic limits even in places where something is physically missing. Jalavisto stresses the central origin of this object constancy, but she also admits that in the last analysis the body image is a function of many parallel determinants.

Jalavisto's interpretation is supported by the observation that phantom limbs do not develop in infant amputees, and yet peripheral irritations in the stump are hardly likely to be different at different age levels. If peripheral factors played a decisive role, age differences in stump stimulation patterns should be readily observed. Especially impressive is the case of Meyer, as reported by Jalavisto. The patient had to undergo two successive amputations on the same leg. The first cut was just below the knee. A usual phantom limb developed, including an apparent foot. After the second amputation, which was at the thigh, the patient continued to "feel" a phantom limb which this time however did only correspond to the shape and state of his leg after the first operation. This phantom limb had already "taken into account" the missing foot and ankle.[10]

Even if the body image is regarded as a case of the much

---

[9] *Ibid.*, p. 23.

[10] Eeva Jalavisto, "Oma ruumiimme havaitomme kohteena," *Duodecim*, 1942, pp. 191–92.

discussed object constancies, according to Jalavisto this need not imply a perfect correspondence. *This* object *constancy* is apparently strongly affected by previous experience and learning. Following Jalavisto:

The way an infant reacts to visual experiences of hands and feet does not initially differ from his reactions to other visual patterns. Gradually the infant then starts to watch his limbs and tentatively performs some active movements. Even at this stage he may be unaware of the role of the skin surface in mediating touch impressions from alien bodies. After some time the infant clearly concentrates on his tactual experiences too. We can observe the child grasping his other hand or his fingers, even occasionally pinching or pressing parts of them. He looks surprised at the difference between these touch experiences and those he felt when handling surrounding objects. Characteristic of this stage of development is the reaction of the child who keeps striking the table and then suddenly, as if led by some haphazard impulse, turns the blows to his own arm or head and expresses the difference in what he experiences—sometimes even being hurt by his own activity!

Our Body as an Object of Our Perception

In her later physiologically oriented study, Jalavisto (1948) presented data on 178 arm amputees, all of them disabled veterans of World War II. The most important relationships among some of her phantom-limb syndromes are summarized in tables. Probably most valuable are her conclusions concerning the cortical representation of the various parts of the phantom limb. Her observations concerning the salience of various phantom components, as well as concerning the loci of perceived phantom movements, are compared with Penfield and Boldrey's scheme of the proportional representation of body sensations in the cortex (Figures 15–2 and 15–3). Thus, for example, the distinct experience of thumb and index finger in the phantom hand could be explained by their greater cortical representation.[11]

Another factor, however, competes with this factor of structural predominance. The *"borderline"* or *"extreme"* *parts* of a pattern stand out figurally. The index finger and the little finger constitute special, salient units in this respect. The names of these fingers are often learned first by young children. Distal extreme regions are in other ways also more strongly represented in the body image, as

---

[11] Eeva Jalavisto, "Observations on Arm-Amputeers," *Annales Academiae Scientiarum Fennicae,* Ser. A 17 (1948).

clearly shown by one of Révész' observations: if one stretches one's arms out straight ahead with eyes closed, the hands are kinesthetically perceived as the most salient and largest parts of both limbs. The parts of the arms connecting the hands with the trunk may

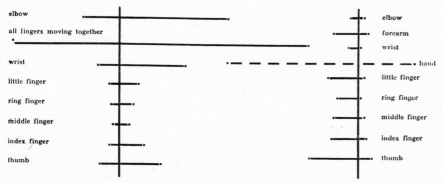

FIG. 15–2. Proportional *motor* (left) and *sensory* (right) cortical representation of the human hand.

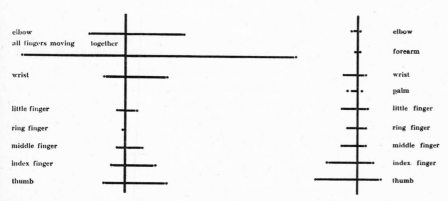

FIG. 15–3. Relative frequency of φ-movements in a phantom hand (left). Proportional accuracy of various parts of a phantom hand (right).

sometimes even phenomenally disappear. This fact probably offers an explanation for the superficially disproportionate and clumsy, yet extremely expressive, clay sculptures of the blind, who are incapable of controlling their kinesthetic experiences visually (Figure 15–5). If we compare a work like that shown in the picture with Fulton's homunculus (Figure 15–4) and Jalavisto's diagrams, the far-reaching similarity of the proportions can be readily observed.

Additional Findings

Solonen (1962) sent a detailed 91-item questionnaire to 4,000 Finnish disabled veterans, all of whom were amputees. He undertook statistical analyses on the 1,000 best described cases, supplemented by 300 individual medical case histories. The time since amputation varied from 12 to 38 years. Of all the cases investigated, 945 (94.5 percent) remembered having experienced phantom limbs, while 847 (84.7 percent) reported perceiving them "right now" at the moment of the investigation.[12]

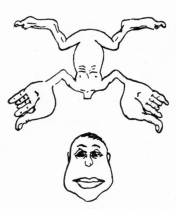

FIG. 15–4. Fulton's homunculus showing the relative proportions of various motor centers in the cortex.

The composition of Solonen's thousand cases is shown in Table 15–1. The additional individual explorations revealed that in only 5 percent of the cases was the limb perceived in its original size and shape. Generally the hand or the foot only was present, usually not more than the fingers or the toes or even the most prominent among them (thumb, index finger, big toe). Occasionally the palm or the heel could be discerned, sometimes the ankle, but rarely the elbow or knee. The closer to the trunk the amputation had been performed the more distinct was the phantom limb. It coincided with the prosthesis in 22 percent of the cases and seemed too large or too short in 9 percent. In exceptional cases the phantom limb was larger than a normal one, and as a rule it appeared shorter.

TABLE 15–1

SOLONEN'S CASES ACCORDING TO LOCUS OF AMPUTATION

Type of Amputation	N
Upper arm	163
Forearm	97
Thigh	267
Leg	433
Ankle	9
Bilateral amputees	31

---

[12] K. Solonen, "The Phantom Phenomenon in Amputated Finnish War Veterans," *Acta Orthopedica Scandinavica*, Supplementum, Vol. 54 (1962), pp. 11–14.

Ranta-Knuuttila (1962) studied 340 Finnish amputees (also disabled veterans), most of whom had phantom limbs and could feel intentional phantom movements. Continuous pain in the phantom limb was reported by 104, and occasional pain (with changes in the weather, etc.) occurred in 113. There were 123 without any distracting sensations. No significant differences could be shown to exist in this general distribution between arm and leg amputees, nor did the level of adaptation to the lesion make any substantial difference.[13]

The interpretation of the phantom limb as an indication of the permanently perceived constant body image gains additional support from cases in which the patient's limbs are all fully preserved but he is *unable to perceive one or more of them* due to some cortical damage. In patients who are able to feel phantom limbs, obviously their *intact cortex* plays a predominant role. Brain injuries can evidently in some way or another disturb the constancy of the body image. Such a patient

FIG. 15–5. "Rejected"—clay sculpture of a congenitally blind person (Révész).

may be bothered by the strange, unfamiliar, or weird appearance of one of his hands or feet. One case is known of an arm amputee who later suffered a cortical lesion. The phantom limb which had developed in the usual way disappeared immediately as a result of the brain damage.

Cases of *mescaline intoxication* give us further indications of the role played by the cortex in the articulation of the body image. The central symptom in this kind of disordered behavior is the extreme variability of all perceptual objects. Jalavisto writes: "The experimentally intoxicated subject has the feeling of his limbs being isolated from the rest of his body; he feels, e.g., as though he could pick up his foot and hand it to somebody."[14]

[13] J. J. Ranta-Knuuttila, *Amputoitu sotavammainen* (*The Amputee Veteran*) (Helsinki: WSOY, 1962), p. 111.

[14] Eeva Jalavisto, *Duodecim*, 1942, pp. 205–7.

CHAPTER 16

Perception of Pictorial Art

NOT SINCE the most remote days of antiquity has it been believed that pictorial art should strive to reproduce nature precisely. Already the great master of the Renaissance, Leonardo da Vinci, belittled mere reproduction of nature. He said, "Art is an inner, spiritual recreation of the presented objects." The transformation is so complete that an artistic representation creates another, new world superimposed on the regularly perceived world. "Painting is a matter of mind." The spirit of the artist remodels nature. And the French romanticist Delacroix develops this idea further:

Nature is only a dictionary for the artist. Most important is the need for expression. The conscientiousness of most artists only manages to make their art tedious. If it were possible, such people would even paint the backs of their pictures just as carefully.[1]

Following Katz again we can briefly summarize the role of the artist. *On the one hand*, all artists except for some atypical extremists use certain technical artistic effects to produce impressions of "reality," but *on the other hand* they make their real artistic contribution via a personal, original reworking of the perceptual material. All the well-known fads, trends, and schools in art have swung back and forth between these limits, between the framework of reality and the artist's own conception of what should be presented. The reference to "outer reality," to physical nature, is almost never completely missing; our natural experience of space provides the raw material for imaginative constructions. Yet even during pictorial art's most realistic periods, as perceptual psychologists could show, a far-reaching "poetic license" prevailed. The

---

[1] Quoted in I. Grünewald, *Henri Matisse* (Helsinki: WSOY, 1946), p. 13.

artist does not, for example, reproduce all elements, all colors, shadings, dimensions, and forms of natural perceptual space in a mechanistic, literal manner. He selects and combines: and some of his combinations often look arbitrary. Some of Rubens' and Rembrandt's paintings convincingly show that the directions of light can be represented *contrary to nature* without disturbing the total unitary effect of the canvas.

Scientific investigations of art, whether pictorial or literary, proceed from immediate descriptions of content to an analysis of structure. Structure and dynamics are closely interrelated in the production of art. At any rate, compositional factors can be analyzed separately as in an analysis of the architectonics of a piece of art. Modern perceptual psychology offers useful conceptual tools for such a structural investigation. By comparison with this interest in composition the evaluation of dynamic content factors is still scientifically in its infancy; it is reminiscent of efforts to interpret responses in a projective test of personality.

SOME PRINCIPLES OF ARTISTIC CONSTRUCTION AND COMPOSITION

Generally speaking, every closed figure has its phenomenal center of gravity. Its location is in most cases a matter of mathematical derivation and calculation—yet what we experience as the figural center of gravity cannot always be mathematically derived. Metzger has shown that the center of gravity may act simultaneously as an anchoring point (*Verankerungspunkt*) and as the focal part (*leitende Stelle*) of a figural pattern.

Within a rectangle the center of gravity is mostly determined by the crossing of the diagonals. One could also begin from the centers of the sides. If a large rectangle serves as background for a smaller circle, maximum phenomenal equilibrium requires locating the circle at the crossing of the diagonals. Next in order as locations yielding phenomenal stability are the corners, while there is an area of minimal equilibrium and stability between the center (the center of gravity) and each of the corners. If the smaller, "nearer" figure does not coincide with the center, it appears restless and unstable—and as a matter of fact this is how we phenomenally get informed of the existence of a center of gravity (Figure 16–1).

We have seen that a tendency to maintain equilibrium can be shown to exist in all organisms. Every kind of art, whether classical or modern, takes the demand for equilibrium into account in some way or another.[2] Pictorial art has several means for stabilizing interrelations among elements which would otherwise be too unbalanced as figural gestalten. If a piece of art is to have a dynamic effect, however, it cannot restrict itself to representing the level of equilibrium characteristic of systems that maintain a completely static state and remain continuously at rest. Not infrequently the impressive effect of a piece of art is due to a state of continuous tension in equilibrium, like a rope stretched by equally strong men pulling at each end. Art generally considers the tension relationships in the perceptual organization of the stimulus material; a frequently sought-after ideal is an apparently static state with strong internal tensions. This requirement becomes central, according to Josephson, whenever the static representation is intended to indicate motion. The artist tries to condense imaginary successive movement phases into the static configuration of his creation. A momentary "snapshot" posture or attitude of persons pictured in paintings or sculptures produces restless dynamics in the immediate static appearance.

FIG. 16–1.   Unstable equilibrium within a figure pattern.

A good example is the statue of Paavo Nurmi, by the sculptor Wäinö Aaltonen, in front of the Olympic Stadium in Helsinki. The bold low step of the runner simultaneously represents the backward straining movement of the foot and the powerful forward motion in the athlete's performance. A similar complex of motion has been condensed by Myron in his famous "discus thrower." Actual snapshots would probably never reveal the tremendous variety of simultaneous motor innervations and achievements which are sometimes projected into the positions of artistically represented persons.

A corresponding dynamic ambiguity probably makes the point in the frequently discussed mysterious smile of the Mona Lisa. The figural composition of the face presents two competing articulation possibilities, the tension between which provides an apparent yet strained equilibrium. In an artistic masterpiece one can experience the forces which are brought into equilibrium. Thus the configurations of the perceptual world contain more than just immediate sensory experiences. Classical painted landscapes reveal the phenomenal vanishing point of parallels converging in perspective; syncopated melodies yield the impression of induced regular beats not immediately present in the tonal pattern. Arnheim reasonably points out that every visual pattern is actually dynamic. An analysis

FIG. 16–2.   Manet: "Déjeuner sur l'herbe."

of the static relations in a stimulus field is not enough if we want to describe this play of mutual interactions. Perceptions of real life situations owe their "meaning" to the tensions produced by the various organizing factors.[3]

If two articulatory tendencies are permitted to affect each other with opposite forces approximately equal in strength, the picture may look disturbing because of its ambiguity. We know of such artistic works, but they have not generally survived very long. What is to be pictured must be placed into an appropriate frame of reference.

_____
[3] *Ibid.*, pp. 21–22.

The techniques of anchoring and accentuation can be used in paintings in various ways. If a person in perspective should look closer than the rest of the group, he can be made larger than he should be at that distance, to accentuate his role in the scene

FIG. 16–3.   Rembrandt: "Christ at Emmaus."

(Manet, "Déjeuner sur l'herbe"). A dark region must be enlarged relative to a light one if it is to counterbalance the effect of the latter.[4]

In pictorial composition, equilibrium is achieved by applying the simple principle of the physical lever. Even a small object, if placed far enough from the center, displaces the center of gravity propor-

[4] *Ibid.,* p. 12.

tionately to the distance concerned. In some of Rembrandt's paintings, for example, in "Night Watch" and in "Christ at Emmaus,"
the phenomenal center of gravity clearly differs from the center of
the picture as defined by the physical frame.[5] Comparably, Cézanne
often made his landscapes asymmetrical by displacing the center of
gravity—painting a conspicuously dominant tree or rock to one side

FIG. 16–4. Cézanne: "Mont Ste-Victoire."

of the figural center ("Mont Ste-Victoire" and especially "Rocks,
Forest of Fontainebleau"). Isolation from the rest of the group
increases the gravitational influence. If a full moon is painted in an
otherwise empty sky, it gains an accentuation out of all proportion
to its size. In pictures of social situations the position of a single
individual is emphasized by placing him to one side of the group.
Prima donnas on stage love to have plenty of empty space around
them.

In architecture the "normal weights of familiar building materi-

[5] W. Schöne, *Über das Licht in der Malerei* (Berlin: Gebr. Mann, 1954), pp.
158–60.

als" play an important role in the phenomenal appearance of a building. The Renaissance, Baroque, and neoclassical schools used coarser and rougher blocks in the foundations and lower floors, even if the same kind of stone was used all over the building, in an attempt to create apparent weight differences among successive floors. Deeper seams, producing heavier shadows, further accentuated the apparent weight effects. A granite foundation looks heavier than a brick wall, which in turn looks heavier than a wooden upper story. The modern architect must cope with a variety of problems of "weight artefacts" in his designs.

One extreme solution consists of an imaginative distribution of different colors and textures. The famous rose window above the main entrance of Notre Dame could have turned out to be a too delicate detail because of its completely symmetrical circular form. Were it located right in the center of the facade, one would scarcely avoid the uninteresting impression of a static and too well-balanced totality. But since the window is actually a little above the figural center of the lower rectangle formed by the facade below the towers of the building, it looks interesting in the way it compromises between two different centers of gravity. New building materials make it possible for modern architects to design buildings which have no outer supporting walls. Yet the phenomenal problem of "weight artefacts" forces them to maintain illusory supporting walls.[6] Most creations of pictorial art have a "fundament" or "base" which may be arrived at unconsciously and upon which higher portions of the composition are supported.

A good piece of art originates—as Pasto (1964) pointed out—in the space-frame experience of the artist.

Man feels secure in the vertical and horizontal biological fields within which he moves. Man is two right angles, i.e., the angle of sight and the vertical axis, and the horizontal on which he prefers to stand and his vertical axis. He prefers also to experience these two right angles as the terminal point of his perceptual movement into distance.[7]

Masterpieces of art are, according to Pasto, successful applications of these simple principles. Pasto's theory gains some evidence from the conclusions of Werner and Wapner which we considered in Chapter 1. The sensory-tonic postulates assume that stimulations,

---

    [6] Arnheim, *op. cit.*, p. 17.

    [7] T. Pasto, *The Space Frame Experience in Art* (New York: A. S. Barnes & Co, Inc., 1964), pp. 14–15.

irrespective of modality, always are accompanied by tonus phenomena. The various modalities are regarded, at least to some extent, as interchangeable. A visual stimulus, for example, can interfere with a posturally and kinesthetically determined experience of verticality and vice versa. So the artist creates his space frame and projects it about him as a medium within which he expresses himself. "The relation between composition and human expression hence is intensely tied up with the emotional-motor body image. . . . Aesthetic and expressive fame has been accorded those artists who have adroitly expressed their images in the perceptual motor language inherent in this concept."[8]

There are, however, artists who originally are or have become so "visually cerebral" that they are unable to extend or transfer their vertical body image to the surface of the canvas. As a consequence, in their works "no emotional message can be conveyed, only a visual assessment of data . . . , it degenerates into a map, a diagram." Too many surfaces are turned only into decorative devices. Great artists have, according to Pasto, preserved their sensitivity to the tonic tensions in their sensory motor system. The perceiver feels an effortless pleasure in contemplating such a painting. "He walks into the painting; he stands where Rembrandt stood and gazes at the portrait."[9]

Pasto considers Michelangelo, Rembrandt, and Pieter Brueghel the Elder the best interpreters of form dynamics in the early modern era. Among more recent artists he enumerates Cézanne, Seurat, and Picasso. Brueghel's "Hunters in the Snow" reveals the sensitivity of the artist to the requirements of his perceptual-motor organization. *Vertical* parallels are quite clear. A pointed rock summit is directly above a pointed house roof, the flying bird is directly over a bush below, another cliff top is over the right-hand support of the bridge, a bird is perched above the bramble bush in the foreground. If one now examines the more obvious *horizontals*, it can be seen that these parallels, too, function in accord with man's predilection for the cardinal dimensions. But there are also various *diagonals* sloping to the right, thus completing the *partly visible network of lines* and making for even more dynamics in the composition. In Seurat's famous picture "Un dimanche à la Grande-Jatte" we find a replica-

---

[8] *Ibid.*, pp. 14–15.
[9] *Ibid.*, pp. 18–22.

tion of Brueghel's sensory-motor construction simplified into a system of cylinders and balls. There is a persistent harmony between vertical and horizontal elements. For the same reason Picasso's "Still Life with Guitar" deserves consideration, although it is a rather abstract creation of art indeed. Piet Mondrian, among purely abstract painters, can be mentioned as a skillful interpreter of motor form dynamics.

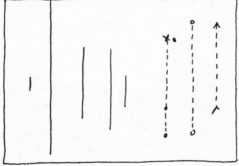

FIG. 16–5. Some vertical parallels in Brueghel's painting (according to Pasto).

What has been generally pointed out regarding *kinesthetic proprioceptive stimulation* might serve as a background for investigating visual equilibrium tendencies in relation to the vertical-horizontal coordinates. However, as has been shown in Chapters 9 and 10, if there is a conflict between the kinesthetically sensed cardinal dimensions and what is *seen* as vertical and horizontal in one's own body or in a picture, the visual organization usually, at least for some time, overrides the kinesthetic frame of reference.

Cézanne's portrait of his wife, painted in the years 1888 to 1890, can serve as an example. The viewer is impressed by the apparently restful yet rather powerful dynamics. The tensions are achieved by skillful use of various balanced accents in the composition. The person portrayed appears to be a well-supported configuration, slightly in front of and above the chair cushion. The figural proportions are about 5:4. An oval form surrounds the geometric center of gravity. The background is divided into two rectangles, the higher of which is farther away. The chair inclines to the left, as does the vertical center line of the woman and of the chair.[10]

---

[10] Arnheim, *op. cit.*, pp. 20–23.

FIG. 16–6. Brueghel: "Hunters in the Snow."

FIG. 16–7. Seurat: "Un dimanche à la Grande-Jatte."

The left-right symmetry of a picture is most interesting from the point of view of composition. Wölfflin was able to show the degree to which well-known paintings become flat and uninteresting if they are replaced by their mirror images. A good example is provided by Raphael's "Sistine Madonna," with the emphatic figure of Sixtus in the lower left of the picture. It is not unusual in plays to see the hero enter the stage from the left while the villain often enters from the right.[11]

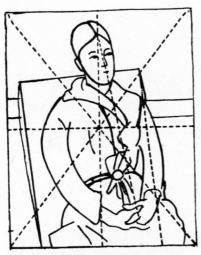

FIG. 16–3. Cézanne: portrait of his wife (outline).

Dessoir, the psychologist of art, points out that "three ways to affect visual organization are available in pictorial art, i.e., linear techniques, brightness gradients and coloration." This list is reminiscent of Katz's previously quoted remark that immediate natural perceptual space contains a rich variety of forms, dimensions, illuminations, and colors among which the artist makes his choices—and some of these effects do not fit together simultaneously. The art schools of different ages have been inclined to favor now one, now another of the organizing factors mentioned by Dessoir.

One can create hierarchical scales, centration, and balance by working exclusively either with lines, with brightness gradients, or with colors. Some modern art critics have gone so far as to maintain that the value of a piece of art is increased if the artist has used only one of these "monistically conceived" articulatory devices. To stay away from evaluative statements, one feels inclined to assume that for organizational reasons a monistically achieved line configuration or color configuration may appear better differentiated and as a more clearly structured totality than a pattern combined of line, color, and brightness articulations. It is a future task for careful experimental research to provide us with an answer to this difficult problem.

Real art, as mentioned before, does not imply a registration of all

---

[11] *Ibid.*, pp. 18–19.

FIG. 16–9. Cézanne: portrait of his wife (completed).

the available stimuli, but rather aims at indicating *essential inva-riances* in the sensory flux of variability, and fulfills this aim via sensitive, delicate choices of effects. To grasp essential components in reality we need not, thanks to our inner dynamics, have a painstakingly detailed stimulus pattern. On the contrary, if only hints or indications are presented as dominant in the pattern, a

FIG. 16–10.   Raphael: "Sistine Madonna."

richer and more effective totality can emerge. All perception probably started—from the point of view of biological development—
with the mere recognition of vitally significant combinations of
figures. Thus a "triangle" is not a late abstractive product, but a
complex quality, primordial in its generality and thus preceding

later stages of more precise differentiation. Even an infant may perceive indeterminate "dogginess" before he learns to distinguish among various breeds of dogs. A ball in phenomenal space is perceived as complete; we have the impression of a spherical object that doubtless has a "back surface" even though it is turned away from us. The back of the head of a familiar person, the "invisible part of him," has for us the same degree of reality as parts of him which are immediately perceived. When we face this person the back of his neck is an integral part of the visually perceived total object. The laws of optics taught to painters during the Renaissance rejected previous methods of illustration too sharply. Our immediate world does not generally follow a strict application of optics but appears to follow certain rules of simplicity instead.

We have already considered the favoring of a single monistic technique of creation in art. Some of the great masters, when adopting and perfecting a specific method, were actually obeying the *law of simplicity*. This principle has the following implications for the artist's work: *He should not use more artistic effects in his production than he needs for achieving his goals.* Some art historians maintain that Rubens belongs among those who resorted to the simplest methods in their creative work. This means "using the most reasonable system for assuring an ingenious understanding of what is essential in the content." At a certain stage in his development, Titian abandoned the dualism of contours and surface treatment. From that point on, his lines not only serve as contours or as a device for shading, but the entire surface is treated all over in the same uniform and well-balanced manner. The same technique is used to picture brightness differences, volume, and airiness.

A mature artistic creation is characterized by a certain stylistic invariance. It looks as if sky, water, soil, trees, and humans were made of the same substance. A viewer who has, with emotion, seen the bit of nature concerned would not call such a painting a falsification, because it captures what is essential. Thus a great artist keeps creating genuinely new products by simply following his particular system of invariances when representing quite familiar things. E. Kaila wrote in the first chapter of his *Human Knowledge:*

An interesting task would be to follow the search for and realization of invariances in the aesthetic behavior of human beings. For instance, what is an artistic style? It is a principle of uniform coherent configurations repeating itself throughout a wide variety of material.

Artistically speaking, "stylistic" means something which captures an invariance. Clarity, consistency within variability, equilibrium, harmony, beauty, all this is a fulfillment of invariances.

H. Erpf enumerates three relations in the aesthetics of music, employed as devices of organization for rhythmic, dynamic, and balanced patterning. He calls these relations *repetition, variation,* and *contrast.* Repetition can really be considered a structural device in all creative art. The act of repeating assures a unifying *invariance* among all the various elements and components which together constitute a piece of art. If we look at masterpieces of architecture, for example, at a Gothic cathedral or at the monumental center of the city of Helsinki, designed by the city planner, Engel, we find a satisfying conformity and homogeneity achieved by means of repetitive similarity in the widely varying details. On the basis of experimental findings, Eysenck tried to demonstrate that a leading principle even in pictorial art is a consistent unification of the variable elements. *Figural* style rests upon repetitive similarity of single figural elements, while the point of *compositive* style is use of a consistent device in combining elements, for example, consideration of a specific rhythm in the structure of a facade. *Qualitative* style appears as an attempt to achieve consistent similarity among all the various elements.

The process of differentiation plays a predominant role in all artistic modeling and organization. Where a multitude of forms and figures prevails without any balance or hierarchy among the details, before long we observe nothing but sheer chaos. On the other hand, maximum consistency among the elements brings about a barren totality. Throughout various fields of artistic production we have in recent years witnessed occasional lapses into one or the other of these extremes.

The principle of repetition is most profitably combined with the idea of variation.

Contrast may well be considered an extreme form of variation. The effect of this relation is a sharpening of dualistic tensions between alternative articulation possibilities.

THREE-DIMENSIONAL PICTORIAL SPACE

When we turn to techniques for representing pictorial space, we again encounter artistic expressions which are hardly comprehen-

sible without some knowledge of the cultural and historical background of the various trends in pictorial art. The purpose of the
religious art of the Middle Ages—confined as it was to illustrations
in religious books and to church decorations—was to exalt the
supernatural power of an almighty God. Therefore, the message of
the picture reached the viewer from far above, as though it came
from another world, and the human being stood facing this tran-
scendental being, constituting as it were one pole of a dualistic
relation. The consumers of these artistic productions were considered recipients of divine proclamation; the picture did not invite
them to participate in the scene on an equal footing.

The change produced by the new world picture offered during
the Renaissance was most profound. We know that it determined
new directions in Western European artistic trends for centuries.
To be sure, the Renaissance did not avoid proclamation. What it
proclaimed, however, was the eternal divinity of the human being.
The essence of this new philosophy was the love of life, the approval
of our sensory world image, the search for aesthetic values in the
human being himself. It was the mentally and physically propor-
tionate, well-balanced human figure that was emphasized and
adored. A new type of divinity was found in the beauty of living
organisms and their natural environments. Thus formalism turned
into idealistic realism, and art was given the task of revealing the
unsophisticated reality of the objects around us. A painting, it
seemed, should appear as an immediate continuation of the real
environment, as though it wished to invite the viewer to participate
in the scene occurring on the canvas. The works of Tintoretto, one
of the great masters of the Renaissance, convincingly show us that
the picture, including the painted illumination, is presented *as if it
were located in the viewer's perceptual space.*

When we turn to a discussion of three-dimensionality in paintings, we face the problem of *depth gradients* or *depth articulation*,
an extreme case of which is the differentiation of the picture surface
into figures and background. A sheer articulation into figure and
ground is, however, almost a limiting case, because most groupings
and still lifes are far more richly varied. Thus one might perceive a
figure on a background, which in turn forms a figure of its own on a
wider background, etc. In those cases one appropriately speaks of a
gradient of depth. If a homogeneous broad surface is broken up by
contours, our perceptual organization seems to prefer superposition

to mere discontinuities in a flat, even surface. In Figure 16–11 the white field (b) has two borders, an outer and an inner one, so that one could say that b has a hole through which the continuous common black background (c) is visible; another possibility would be to experience an inner black spot (a) as a figure on b, which in turn would appear as a figure on c. However, because of the homogeneity and the similar structure of the black fields this second possibility

is less popular. Superposition is always based upon the simplest possible alternative of articulation. Only rarely are there more "steps," more overlapping surfaces, than the articulating conditions make unavoidable.[12]

As we know from Chapter 10, richly differentiated, detailed, and structured parts of a field are preferentially seen as figures, and stand out from a homogeneous background. Matisse, who belonged among the artists who strove for artistic effects

FIG. 16–11. Superposition impressions in a plane figure.

which reduced spatiality on the canvas, favored ambiguity and therefore painted the background as more richly articulated and structured than his main figures. His nudes, actually the most important perceptual objects in the scene, could appear as huge light openings in a darker, detailed, and elaborated background. Several of Matisse's seashore scenes provide good examples of this kind of artistic effect ("Dance," "Lux, calme et volupté," and "Three Bathing Girls"— see Figure 16–12). The nude pinkish-tan female figures and the green meadow are painted in almost complementary colors. In such a composition the unifying factor of figural cohesion and the contrasting colors act in opposite directions, a circumstance which, as we know from the famous Wertheimer-Benussi phenomenon (see inside cover of Osgood's textbook in experimental psychology) adds to the dynamics of the picture. As a consequence of the gestalt law of closure a concave borderline gives an impression of approach, of coming closer to the viewer, while concavity tends to suggest withdrawal and passivity.

Sculptures with rounded convex surfaces (e.g., Maillol) show a

[12] Arnheim, *op. cit.*, pp. 187–89.

FIG. 16–12.   Matisse: "Luxe, calme et volupté."

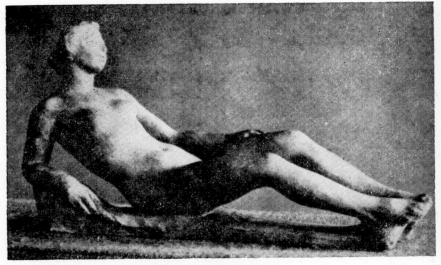

FIG. 16–13. Maillol: "Resting Woman."

FIG. 16–14. Moore: "Reclining Figure."

tendency to expand and rise, while hollow and concave ones (e.g., Moore) express a submissive, passive, reclining position and attitude (Figures 16–13, 16–14).

Jaensch's Studies in Pictorial Space

E. R. Jaensch in 1911 published his classical experimental work *Über die Wahrnehmung des Raumes* (*On the Perception of*

Space). Its point of departure was the specific function of binocular disparity as a cue for depth, but he went beyond this to broader and more significant observations. The validity of some of them has been further corroborated by later studies. It must be admitted in advance that his conception of the outstanding primary significance of binocular disparity was not sufficiently confirmed. In his basic text Gibson sharply attacked the presumed primacy and indispensability of binocular disparity by demonstrating the decisive influence of surface texture gradients on depth articulation, especially at greater distances and in monocular vision (see Figure 10–19, page 247). Jaensch had already arrived at the following conclusions in his work: *None* of the so-called *empirical depth cues*, nor binocular disparity, any more than overlapping of contours or succession, motion parallax, accommodation, convergence, or distribution of shadows, provides a *primary stimulus basis for stereovision*. They are all relatively equal in importance, and act as a kind of *releasing stimuli* for triggering a central function. According to Jaensch, a common mental process is behind the stereo tendency, a process which is dynamically based on the mobilization of *attention*.

In bookstores one will sometimes see picture postcards fastened on a frame which bends the card, making the picture surface concave toward the observer. Such a concave picture contains a new condition for depth articulation. If we look binocularly at an ordinary flat card, binocular disparity convinces us of its two-dimensionality: we do not have an impression of real depth in the picture. A concave picture surface has been shown to increase eye movements, resulting in motor cues which in turn coincide with the role of the perspective.

The fundamental device employed by Jaensch (the haploscope), as well as some of his early results, were described in another connection. It was pointed out that the perceptual product did not follow strictly from the requirements of the retinal "space values" or local signs. There appeared what were called *covariance phenomena*. If three vertical threads were shown haploscopically without disparity (so that they remained phenomenally in the same plane) and a displacement of one of the outer threads toward the center vertical line was introduced *in one* of the monocular visual fields, it brought about disparity between the projections of this outer vertical and consequently a difference in its location in phenomenal space. However, a corresponding *segregation from the frontal focal plane* (the "nuclear" plane) *was also observed in the other outer thread,* which thus phenomenally went with the newly oriented *physically* disparate other vertical, i.e., it covaried with it. Similarly, if one of the two outer threads was presented as laterally displaced to only one eye, *covariance* occurred in that the opposite *outer thread* (although no direct change in its specific stimulus context was introduced) *joined in displacement.* If, on the other hand, both outer threads were seen as belonging to the same plane the covariance phenomenon (an apparent jumping forward or back of the center vertical thread) was evidently strengthened quantitatively as well as qualitatively. Reversibility was greatest for this middle vertical. The subjects described vividly how they followed the displacement. Only two subjects were used, but each of them made 16 different matches daily.[13]

Most important from the point of view of the psychology of pictorial art was Jaensch's following observation: If the subject moves his gaze from the phenomenally nearer string to the farther one, he experiences the space defined by the verticals as *voluminous*, as filled with some kind of invisible *substance*. This impression of voluminosity is strengthened if two parallel edges are indicated and the glance is switched back and forth between them. Loeb, working with Mach's "book" (Figure 16–15) observed that the "folio" alternative, in which the book opens toward the viewer, can be reinforced if one moves a pencil along the vertical fold in the middle. Jaensch assumed that focusing on the pencil produced pursuit movements of the eyes within the "book space," movements which he considered essential for the genesis of phenomenal depth.

In his book Jaensch included a detailed chapter on the conditions of space impressions in Renaissance paintings. We know that a photograph, which faithfully reproduces perspective with correct object proportions, seems to distort immediate reality.[14] Nevertheless, in the art schools of the Renaissance, artists were instructed to depict three-dimensional objects purely in terms of a "funnel" space perspective. The use of central perspective in pictures developed among Italian artists in the early days of the Renaissance. Thus Alberti recommended suspending a fine-meshed net vertically be-

---

[13] E. Jaensch, "Über die Wahrnehmung des Raumes. Eine experimentell-psychologische Untersuchung nebst Anwendung auf Ästhetik und Erkenntnislehre," *Zeitschrift für Psychologie*, Ergänzungsband, 6 (1911), pp. 6–87.

[14] *Ibid.*, pp. 155–72.

tween the artist and the model posing for him. Dürer in his youth had already become acquainted with this method of preparing pictures on his first trip to Italy. Thereafter he designed his famous "Visualization Apparatus."[15] During his second Italian trip Dürer began to apply "secret perspective," praising the Italians as the real masters of it. Certainly not all of Dürer's works display faultless perspective, but the creations of his mature age have in this respect been almost perfectly correct. Clearly, size proportions in these pictures closely correspond to what we see in photographs. Consider the ridiculous smallness of remote buildings or trees in some of his works! The artist's eye was placed in the plane of the frontal square net, where these perspective painters of the early Renaissance projected their picture surface.

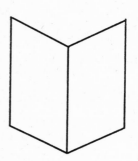

Jaensch raises the question of how it is possible that Dürer and the other Renaissance masters did not notice this distorting effect of an optically perfect perspective when they were otherwise so careful and conscientious. He finds the answer in the conjecture that they very likely noticed the effect but on the other hand did not avoid

FIG. 16–15. Mach's book.

it because it provided them with a welcome device in their efforts to stress and accentuate the voluminosity and the "life-approving roundness" of their perceptual objects. If one takes the trouble to look monocularly at early Renaissance pictures and puts one's eye close to the canvas, where the artist looked at it with his single open eye, the striking outcome is an overemphasized vividness of all the forms in an almost mysterious manner. In order to understand fully what the artists of that time wanted to show in their pictures it would thus seem appropriate to look at them as they did, that is with their observation distance and their visual angle to the canvas. The early Renaissance masters may have conceived of their products in a sensory way different from that of our contemporaries.

As a counterpart to this effect Jaensch points to the amazingly rich plasticity which can be experienced when looking monocularly at photographs with the aid of a *verant*. This device, a monocular lens, enables the viewer to place his eye at the focusing distance and optical angle from the picture at which a well-focused camera would

[15] See Arnheim, *op. cit.*, pp. 233–34.

be located. This results in a retinal image closely corresponding to the camera projection. The verant permits eye movements and side glances through the lens, thus preventing fixated staring.

Jaensch's remaining experiments were devoted to a careful phenomenal analysis of *substantially perceived space*. His manner of empirical investigation was characteristic of the turn of the century and rather different from what is nowadays considered

FIG. 16–16.   Dürer: "Visiergerät."

appropriate in experimental methodology. Mostly Jaensch worked only with three experimental subjects, he himself being one of them. The record was a kind of vague description, most of which could not be taken seriously in our time. Nevertheless, he came up with observations of "filled space" or the "superimposed medium" (*Zwischenmedium*) which seem to be of persisting scientific value.

Historically, it can be shown that Hering, the great phenomenalist in the field of physiology, was already interested in "intervening media." He wrote:

The empty space between us and visual objects is experienced differently in daylight than during the night. Gathering twilight does not appear only on object surfaces, but descends as it were into the space between viewer and objects, finally covering all visible things and replacing them in the visual world. If I look through a tiny hole into a black box it appears filled with darkness. It is impossible to perceive a dark surface color on its walls. A shadowed corner in an otherwise bright room is filled with twilight which is not conceived of as only covering the wall surfaces, but is experienced as being in that part of space which is contained by the walls of the corner.

Jaensch points out that the impression of this "medium" is a psychological event. There are no physical stimuli in the mass of air which could provide a basis for this peculiar perception.[16]

The experiments by Jaensch which we shall now describe aimed at a detailed phenomenal analysis of the space perceived in a corner. He observed that under several conditions of illumination the "space medium" impression is not so precisely determined as Hering assumed. Whether or not a "substance" is perceived can depend on the subject's attitude. First, subjects were asked to describe dark corners in an otherwise brightly illuminated room. Sometimes the corners were empty, and sometimes various different objects were scattered in them. Several of Jaensch's experiments used miniature corners made of folded sheets of cardboard (about 35 × 35 cm. in size). Projected into the corner was a light beam, the central part of which could be darkened by means of a cardboard shadowcaster mounted on a thin vertical wire. He varied the experiment by introducing different colored transparent papers into the light beam and occasionally by using an aperture screen which shaded the surrounding parts of the walls so that only the center of the corner received strong light.

The subjects reported what they saw in the following way:

If I look at a spot in the circumscribed part of space which is visible inside the corner, that is, if I keep watching the air in the corner, I actually can see the corner filled with dim light. This dim light looks material. If I concentrate instead on the walls forming the corner, I cannot see a space filling light. I can see the wall surfaces, dark but not covered by any medium.

After these preliminary experiments the setup was made more elaborate. A metal grid was placed over the upper edge of the folded, vertically erected cardboard, with thin silk strings suspended from the junctions of the grid wires. All of these thin strings were visible to the observer. When these vertical strings appeared inside the corner, the impression of a space-filling medium around

---

[16] Jaensch, *op. cit.*, pp. 250–65.

them became unavoidable. If the subject approached close to the corner, he could make the "intervening medium" disappear by concentrating his attention on the walls forming the corner. Conversely, if the light beam of the projector was emitted unscreened to the corner, it was possible to perceive the latter "as filled with a bright spatial substance" as long as one kept staring at a point in the "corner space."

In the early experiments the subjects could choose their own observation time; later experiments used *short exposure times*. The subjects unanimously confirmed that brief glancing at the corner increased the experience of a medium. Control observations revealed that these differences could not be due solely to different lengths of adaptation time.

The results are in several respects relevant for the effects that can be created in pictorial art. They show convincingly, for example, that even a completely empty corner of a room, viewed from a sufficient distance, seems to be filled with a substantial space color. If the walls of the corners are painted in saturated colors, the "medium" shows up only under conditions comparable to the silk string situation. The strength of the medium impression, therefore, is inversely proportional to the distinctness of the wall surfaces. Jaensch proposes that the perceptual set leading to the impression of a medium be labeled "*impressionistic vision*."

Additional clarification of the described regularities is yielded by Jaensch's striking experiments with *glass containers*. A prism formed by three vertical strings at different distances from the eye was shown the subject in certain chromatic solutions (various dissolved anilin dyes and tints were used). The thin strings were suspended from a plywood or cardboard sheet covering the glass basin which contained the liquid. Dim horizontal light illuminated the solution. The cube-shaped container stood at the subject's eye level, and he saw only its front wall through a rectangular opening in a masking screen.

The three subjects gave quite similar results. The liquid appears as a color which is hard to localize. The impression alternates between what Katz would call film color and space color appearances. When viewed through the aperture, the color of the solution still had something "spatial" about it. The subjects were asked to describe how the part of their visual field framed by the strings looked to them. It turns out that at the shortest viewing distances,

15 to 30 cm., the subjects reported a prismatic spatial form possessing an "object character." Although the solution was carmine red, this color did not appear to be on the planes forming the prism. The prism had a "bright red color in a red illumination" which appeared "almost achromatic in its luminosity." At greater distances, 50 to 200 cm., the carmine red color of the prism was improved. The depth articulation and the "medium" could still be seen at a distance of 50 cm., but if only the middle string was watched, the medium appeared almost invisible. A brief glance at the setup improved the depth articulation.

If the middle string was presented a little in front of the two outer ones, this difference could still be perceived at a distance of 3 m., although depth articulations and medium experiences were no longer possible. The space framed by the strings exhibited no color difference.

These experiments demonstrated that:

1. The color of the liquid did not look like a space-filling, substantial medium until the strings were suspended in the container.
2. Irrespective of the hue of the color solution, the part of space framed by the strings always looked brighter than the surrounding colored field, and it appeared brighter the closer the subject was to the container.
3. When the subject moved further away, the medium experience faded even before the depth articulation completely disappeared.
4. A short exposure weakened the depth articulation although it simultaneously improved the apparent chromaticity of the spatial medium.

Jaensch found these observations useful for a better understanding of the impressionistic art of the end of last century, with regard to the treatment of forms and colors on the canvas and the rendition of the spatial characteristics of the subject. As a consequence of the Renaissance program, European pictorial art during the first centuries of the modern age was primarily concerned with *objects*. The goal was to reproduce objects realistically, using scientific optical as well as psychological methods to obtain the desired effects. Impressionism was a pioneer movement, paving the way for later growing interest in pure illumination and in the color characteristics of the pictured subject. An art gallery in Paris in the 1870's opened an exhibition of a new style of paintings which differed radically from what was familiar in the then contemporary realism. These paintings displayed "experiences," and the new key word "impression" appeared frequently in the directory of the pictures: "My impression of a cat," "My impression of a flower vase," etc. Since then, no survey of art history could avoid reference to this word. Art historians of the turn of the century probably somewhat overemphasized the revolutionary influence of impressionism. Muther, writing in the 1890's, went so far as to speak of "these painters' new way of perceiving." "Is this talk of a new way of *perceiving* to be taken literally?" Jaensch wonders. "Or is this just jargon, a transferred meaning of words actually intended to claim something about a new way of painting."[17]

The impressionists have admitted that what they aimed at in an unconventional way was the representation of *chromatic airiness*, of the atmosphere and the regions of air surrounding objects. The main purpose of painting should be an interpretation of this spatial airiness, even at the cost of a successful "thingness" in the picture. We must not forget that the divine dispassionate and ethereal beauty of Giorgione's and Titian's nudes had already deteriorated in Rubens' and Courbet's nymphs and angels into a realism of protrusive ballooning voluminosity. According to the impressionists, when painting a landscape the artist must "grasp the sentiment of a summer day's burning illumination." No doubt Courbet could depict plasticity, but he was unable to show his human figures in a light, ethereal illumination.

The experiments we cited confirmed that in certain conditions it is as possible to experience an "intervening medium" as it is to discriminate between its color and that of the environment. A brief glance proved favorable as an economical way to obtain impressionistic experiences. This procedure allows perception of the medium and yields a maximum of chromaticity.

After the first exhibition of impressionist works an indignant critic objected: "Drawing has been completely neglected in these works. One sees a background with red spots instead of flowers. Even faces are indicated only by some hints of color; they appear as vague splotches of chromaticity." But there were others, for example, contemporaries of Manet, who admitted: "When viewed from further away, the painting comes to life, the air flickers and glows. Nature and men are bathed in a shiny ether."[18] It is

---

[17] *Ibid.*, pp. 244–45.
[18] *Ibid.*, p. 309.

noteworthy that the subjects of impressionist painters, viewed as *objects*, are rather uninteresting and commonplace: a sunny street, a man harvesting, the steel bow of a bridge. If we recall Jaensch's experiments, the objects themselves, e.g., within a corner, are not supposed to attract much attention. What the impressionists also try to stress in their pictures is the transient, temporary character of the depicted activity.

It must be admitted that classical artists who prefer to reproduce a clearly differentiated, striking depth effect fill their space with pieces of architecture, with stems of trees, and with pillared hallways in order to permit, as Pasto puts it, a promenade in depth. These objects serve the same purpose as do the strings in Jaensch's experiment, providing way stations for our wandering gaze. This solution of the problem, however, simultaneously eliminates the alternative of directly displaying a *colored spatiality*. This is what some of the impressionists, for example, Monet, working with soft, mild, scattered contours, have so skillfully contributed.

COLORS AND ILLUMINATION IN PICTORIAL SPACE

Schöne,[19] who studied the handling of pictorial space in Western European art after the Renaissance, has carefully enlarged on Katz's list of appearances of colors. Surface colors can be conceived of in two different ways in Western European painting; they can have, as it were, two different roles:

(1) They can *represent* the colors of the surfaces *shown* by the picture; (2) they can be surface colors in themselves, regardless of their symbolic function, if the picture is considered nothing but a bit of canvas covered with color. Even without the purpose of depiction, and no matter what the picture represents, a color brushed on the canvas is a surface color rather than a film color. Already the picture frame and the artistic method of painting are conditions for a *differentiation* of the picture; they prevent the appearance of film colors in the painting. Admittedly, when a surface color is indicated by the artist in a scene, the color he puts there is not the original surface color of the material on which he paints (canvas, a sheet of wood, a plastered bit of a wall, etc.). Nevertheless, it would be wrong to call them film colors; they have the characteristics of surface colors. If a red house happens to stand in the landscape of

---

[19] Schöne, *op. cit.*, pp. 222–35.

the picture, the two alternative ways of seeing that red as a surface
color presuppose changes in the set of the onlooker. When viewed
through a reduction tube (screening the edges and frame of the
picture) or when projected by means of a mirror projector or slide
projector on the screen of a dark room, even substantial classical
paintings lose their apparently concrete reality; the colors are
released from their surface character and the *illusion of the pictorial
world* feels more complete.

In addition we must not forget about the considerable dynamic
tension which occurs between experiencing a surface color just as
some chromatic material brushed on the canvas and seeing it as a
surface color which has been perceptually localized precisely where
it belongs in the three-dimensional pictorial space of the painting.
Phenomenally, and from the point of view of the artist, there is a
frontal plane somewhere in the pictorial space, either the background of a portrait, or the front of a landscape or the interior of a
room. This experienced plane is the "optical plane." In this optical
plane both the surface materially carrying the painting and the
illusory pictorial depth become integrated. The surface colors, too,
in their double function, are involved in this integrative procedure.

The distinction between "palette value" and "picture value," first
made by Bühler, is interesting in this connection.[20] The first term
has to do with the physical, technical qualities which are required
by a certain place in the picture. What he called "picture value" can
be observed and expressed only in terms of the impression given by
the complete composition. Palette value is not identical with what
Katz called "reduced color," although these expressions are conceptually related. The technical use of palette colors is supported by
what we know about the object color constancies familiar from
perceptual psychology. We must also distinguish among:

The location of the picture.
The visual field of the onlooker.
Visual space.
Pictorial space.
Pictorial depth.
The pictorial or painted illumination.
The autonomous light (e.g., luminosity) of depicted objects.
The directed pictorial radiation or light flux.

---

[20] *Ibid.*, p. 243.

The first serious restriction met by the artist is the two-dimensionality of the canvas surface and the impossibility of using binocular disparity for creating the illusion of depth. Another difficulty is the highly restricted brightness scale of palette values compared to the enormous variations in nature (the extremes of brightness obtainable on a palette are in the ratio of 1 to 60, which must be made to represent natural extreme relations as great as 1 to 800,000).

Helmholtz reported the following hypothetical experiment in 1896. Let two pictures be suspended under equal illumination. One of them shows Arabs in white clothing on an open plain in the bright light of the burning sun. The other represents a moonlit landscape in which a ribbon of moonlight can be seen on the water behind white-stemmed birches and dark human figures among the trees. Both of the paintings can give rise to the intended experience of brightness gradients and can look entirely veridical, even though we might be quite aware that precisely the same palette value of white was used for the white vestments of the Bedouins as for the ribbon of moonlight on the water. The white which the artist can use may still, even in a strongly illuminated exposition hall, reflect only one twentieth of the intensity of real white cloth surfaces under the Arabian sun. If the painting, reflecting the amount of light it does in the exhibit hall, could be moved to the sunny plains of Arabia the white color on it would still look deplorably dark. Real moonlight should have only at most one fifth the intensity of sunlight reflected from white fabric.

To surfaces in the moon landscape, if they are to be appropriately painted, the artist must give 10,000 times the brightness value they physically would have relative to what actually emanates from the moon. Helmholtz' hypothetical experiment reveals the restrictions within which the artist struggles, but also beautifully demonstrates the artistic effects and the freedom available: the best artists cannot be criticized either for slavish realism or for illusionism. They have always had their freedom. This expression refers not only to visual liberation, but also implies a technical and stylistic release from the strict requirements of nature. When Leonardo, in his famous book on art, maintained that painting is nobler than sculpture, he clearly had in mind the greater flexibility of the former despite its numerous restrictions: sculpture is more dependent on the *immediate local position* than *painting;* it is determined by the requirements of an appropriate environment. Brightness levels in a painting are dictated by the requirements of the composition; they are *system conditioned*.

SOME SPECIAL FEATURES OF THE USE OF COLORS
IN THE MIDDLE AGES

Colors in the stained-glass windows of Gothic cathedrals are not surface colors, but rather film colors with a touch of spatiality. Under such conditions a painting has a completely "thingless" appearance, looking like a colored liquid or fog, or a shapeless color substance within which events float without having any object characteristics.

The so-called Ottonic era of book illumination (in the tenth and eleventh centuries) applied surface colors in such a way as to cover the pages of the book with a layer of colored substance. Expressly in their function of covering parts of the picture intended to represent objects, these colors are reminiscent of surface colors. Nevertheless, they typically do not have the appearance of surface colors, since no microstructure is discriminable and our sight seems able to penetrate these decorated portions of the surface of the illuminated page. For that matter, a painting on a parchment page rarely indicated three-dimensional objects. The entire colored area was imprecisely and vaguely localized relative to the parchment, in a manner not unlike a film color. When used for the background of the painting, such a color was detached and independent of any spatial framework. This disconnectedness, however, also characterized the colored surface in its function of representing the figures. A frontal location perpendicular to the line of sight lifts the figures up from an indeterminate two-dimensional background. Notice that Rubin similarly was aware of the background having a film color.

It was as characteristic of modern art as of the art of the Middle Ages, that the latent possibility of finishing the colors of the picture into either film or surface colors was inherent in the production. The difference between these major historical periods shows up in the *dominant* role given to one or the other of these appearances of colors. During the Middle Ages those coloring techniques which resulted in the following appearance were dominant: (1) the film colors should have a luminescent surface, (2) the film colors had to make an immaterial impression.

Typical was the use of gold leaf. Phenomenally, it creates an

PLATE V

PLATE VI

Rembrandt: "The Night Watch"

experience of luster. Katz described luster as follows: it ". . . appears only on an object, and . . . is apprehended as a light which does not really belong to the color of the object." "Lustre light does not lie in the plane of the object to which it belongs, but appears rather either *in front of* the object or *superimposed on it.*"[21] Both of these localization alternatives make lustrous areas resemble film colors.

THE PROBLEM OF DIRECTED ILLUMINATION IN RENAISSANCE AND MODERN ART

The Renaissance, while emphasizing the voluminosity of objects and the approval of our sensory world, could not confine itself to the representation of flat surfaces which was characteristic of the religious decorations of the Middle Ages. Objects, especially human figures, should appear rounded. This could be achieved, for example, by relinquishing luminous colored surfaces and by introducing surfaces imagined as receiving *unilateral, directed illumination.* The distribution of light and shadow on the intended surfaces offered a device for the spatial representation of the three-dimensionality of objects. This technique raised the problem of the assumed location of the light source in the scene on the canvas. It also led to the requirement of visible *directed illumination* in pictorial space.[22] Either the light source or its effects should be clearly visible on the canvas, so artists were faced with the task of creating an "illumination within the picture." At first this made for considerable technical difficulties.

Before Caravaggio there had been a few fumbling attempts to let the light in the picture seem to come from outside the canvas. This was seriously attempted for the first time in the fifteenth century. Some of Caravaggio's paintings reveal this technical effort, although he must not be regarded as a Renaissance artist. His treatment of light and shadow does not always correspond appropriately to what one would expect, considering from where he let the clearly directed light beam sweep over his figures. (See Fig. 16–17.)

Since the time of the early Renaissance it has been customary to paint shiny, bent surfaces, especially armor, which allow for a complex play of light and shadow. This transitional period produced many inconsistent pictures of human figures. The torso might

---

[21] D. Katz, *The World of Colour* (London: Kegan Paul, 1935), p. 24.
[22] Schöne, *op. cit.*, pp. 107–43.

appear flat, in accord with the ideal of the religious art of the Middle
Ages, while some of the limbs already clearly show a tendency
toward "material" spatiality.

Masters of the Baroque definitely presented the correspondence
between the indicated total illumination and the light-receiving

FIG. 16–17.   Caravaggio: "Summons of Matthew."

surfaces at its best. Rembrandt sensitively combined both the
luminous luster of golden surfaces and the directedness of illumination in his canvases. Further, he was able to handle a hidden light
source in the center of the picture which produced illumination
gradients on the surrounding surfaces, on the faces and clothes of
the persons surrounding the light, as can be seen so magnificently in
his work "Conspiracy of Julius Civilis."

Besides brightness gradients, Baroque art used empirically deriv-
able *gradients of location of hues.* If a painting like "The Night

Watch" is analyzed perceptually,[23] it becomes obvious that Rembrandt was aware of the apparent difference in location of "warm" and "cold" hues. He developed the three-dimensionality of the picture by concentrating yellow and red hues in the center. Captain Cocq, with his red scarf, stands closest to the focal part of the picture. The center of gravity is moved slightly to the right by Lieutenant van Ruytenburch, dressed in light yellow. These two central figures are placed on the canvas a bit below the other people. Because of the brightness gradients amply employed by Rembrandt, these persons look ready to step out into the space of the observer. This "forward motion" component is supported by clear depth gradients. A considerable crowd of men is following the leaders, and behind the entire large group we see a house wall with a shield on the corner. Especially the transverse spear in the middle of the picture has a strong lever effect. Furthermore, the figures in the focal part of the picture are painted more accurately, while precision of detail fades as the sight wanders from the center toward the edges. The strongly illuminated girl in the left half of the painting also seems to squeeze forward into space. The movement of the boy running in front of the crowd favors the salience of the center. On the left side of the girl there is a dark musketeer, the color of whose clothing prevents her from being too obtrusive. Moreover, his weapon has the same function as the silk strings in Jaensch's experiment.

On the opposite side of the picture there are three objects serving the same purpose, i.e., the drum, the gun barrel visible behind the lieutenant, and the arm stretching from near the drum toward the gun barrel. These objects create a strong impression of space in the right third of the painting. In the center we notice the similar function of Captain Cocq's forward thrust hand. All this produces the striking feeling of space in the front center of the picture, and gives rise to the observer's impression of being able to step into the picture at the same time that the central figures appear to approach him from the canvas. In order further to accentuate depth articulation, Rembrandt spread out efficient dimensional cues at various distances in the pictorial space. Thus, well-illuminated human faces can serve as basic points for successful accommodation and convergence. Because these places catch the observer's gaze, Rembrandt

---

[23] Arnheim, *op. cit.*, pp. 256–57; Schöne, *op. cit.*, pp. 156 ff.

succeeded in making his painting convincingly three-dimensional.

Like most of Rembrandt's creations, "Night Watch" too has a mysterious unexpected distribution of light. Sometimes it looks magical or even supernatural. This picture of a shooting club which we have been analyzing contains various kinds of directed illuminations; one part of the radiation enters from outside into pictorial space, but we also suspect a hidden light source somewhere behind the musketeer on the left. In addition to this, some of the faces look luminous. Along with this skillful gradation of illumination goes a corresponding use of efficient shadow effects, varying in kind as well as in density. The gradual dimming of the shadowed areas has the characteristics of space shadows. On the surfaces of the human figure as well as on the three-dimensional objects, there are object shadows which emphasize spatial plasticity. Moreover, there are some cast shadows in the picture, especially the superb, famed shadow from the hand of the captain falling on the lieutenant's coat, which create an efficient articulation. This particular shadow keeps the protruding yellowish surface from getting too far in front of the pictorial space. Of all the many artistic effects used by Rembrandt, his use of brightness gradients may be considered the most efficient. The perceptual analysis presented above, however, indicates that this single effect alone is not responsible for the sensational fame of "Night Watch," which has persisted for centuries.

Leonardo, in his famous book on painting, listed the various forms of indirect light (*lume*). They are three: (1) diffuse daylight, (2) reflected light, and (3) transparent light.[24] In our time three kinds of interrelation between a presumed light source and the illuminated pictorial world have been enumerated:

1. The beam from a light source outside the picture extends into the scene. One can rely on lusters, object shadows, or dim illuminations filled with the shadows cast by a narrow light beam (as in Caravaggio, Figure 16–17).

2. The light source outside the picture provides a soft and mellow diffuse illumination to the entire pictured world. This luminescent space can be achieved by illuminated surfaces bearing carefully controlled chiaroscuro, object shadows, space shadows and cast shadows (as in Rembrandt).

3. The light source appears in the picture.

---

[24] Quoted in Schöne, *op. cit.*, pp. 109–10.

These varieties have been called modes of appearance of pictorial light. In addition to these one could list the following kinds of *light radiation*:

1. Natural radiation: daylight, sun, moon.
2. Artificial radiation: campfire, hearth, candle, torch.
3. Sacred radiation: gloria, visionary light, etc.
4. Indeterminate radiation: appears all over in the picture.

With the Renaissance revolution degrees of brightness gained in importance relative to mere color surfaces. The shades of chiaroscuro became more common for accentuating differences in illumination. Paint was given an opportunity to demonstrate layered surfaces.[25]

Neoimpressionism is often defined by describing its emphasis on light and motion. More important than the actual objects in such works was the *veil of light*. It is the artist's task to capture the illumination of a given moment. But this is only one side of the story. The other side is a specific technique aiming at an appropriate physiological fusion of a color mosaic in the visual organs of the viewer. It was regarded as a requirement for this school that the chromatic spots be as saturated and pure in hue as possible and that they be placed close together on the canvas. This method further required an accurate consideration of simultaneous contrast, of colored illumination, and of light reflected from surfaces.

The culmination of this trend is represented by the pointillists, above all by Seurat and by the Finnish painter A. W. Finch. If we look at Seurat's "Un dimanche à la Grande-Jatte," we can easily see that mood and the main illumination are the things of primary interest to the artist (Figure 16–7). The people on the shore do not move around, nor are they shown in any particular relation to each other or to the outside environment. They are reduced almost to geometrical solids, and their only function is to support the verticals and horizontals needed by the artist in setting up his visual coordinates. Despite this schematism, however, the many single color spots combine to give an impression of a hazy summer afternoon. The alternation of dark and light forms fits the lazy pace of a Sunday evening.

Many modern painters have been influenced by Seurat's thoughts, by the impressionistic pioneers, and by Cézanne. The

---

[25] Schöne, *op. cit.*, pp. 111–15; Arnheim, *op. cit.*, pp. 254–55, 260–65.

impressionistic era includes some of Delacroix's later works and even a few of Cézanne's. This trend in Cézanne's development dates from the time beginning with 1872 when he lived at Auvers. By that time Pissarro, influenced by Delacroix, had started mosaically covering the canvas with pure, saturated unmixed colors. Even the reciprocal neutralization of complementary colors could be achieved if the onlooker viewed the painting from a greater distance. "The House of the Hanged Man" is a good example of a work in which many pure, saturated colors were combined in different nuances.

An essential difference between Cézanne and the impressionists was that he was not primarily interested in illumination. He turned to colored surfaces and to contrast effects among adjacent parts of the picture in his treatment of surface compositions.

All artistic impressionism, according to Schildt, in addition to the above-mentioned traits, included a new ethical orientation toward life. The artists belonging to this group were rootless and superficial, yet they were also soundly affirmative toward life. In their art they prized existence, intentionally stripped of its former ideology, but containing rich sensual and aesthetic values.[26]

Paintings of the same landscape by Pissarro and Cézanne show this difference strikingly. Pissarro's picture is vivacious and realistic, while Cézanne's represents the world of an introvert. For him, the subject was only an excuse for a particular pictorial composition. The most distinctive mark of his art was a superb rising above the humdrum search for the expression of life, i.e., an elevation from the level of the beauty of nature to the level of pure *artistic loveliness*.

For the neoimpressionists color was above all a means for picturesque expression. Admittedly this scenic representative mode was already encountered even in Cézanne's paintings.

The Swede J. Grünewald describes this new school, and the experiences of one of them in Paris, as follows:

He admired Titian, Rembrandt, Raphael, Tintoretto and the other masters. He also went to the Luxembourg galleries and admired the impressionists. He dropped into a studio where he painted living models. He painted apples and towels and in the evening he drew models. Then he again went to the Louvre.

But the pulsating life of a capital, the night clubs, the Metro, the

---

[26] G. Schildt, *Riktlinjer för en enhetlig psykologisk tolkning av Paul Cezannes personlighet och konst mot bakgrunden av den allmänna romantiska livskonflikten* (*Directions for a Consistent Psychological Interpretation of Paul Cezanne's personality and Art*) (Helsinki: Holger Schildts, 1947), pp. 87–104.

FIG. 16–18. Witz: "Knight and Servant."

The gradient of the continuing perspective lines of the floor increases the effect of spatial depth.

cars and the electric lighting sang a new song with a new melody. The solemn air of the Louvre's vast galleries became heavier and more exhausting. He was able to see and experience things completely unfamiliar to the reverent old people on the walls around him. His language was different from theirs. When using their expressions he was unable to describe what was new and important. The clothes of our time did not fit their antique figures, and their dark eyes could not stand the blinding beams of our spotlights. The expressionist felt that he had to create a new language, to clear his palette and to change his brushes.[27]

There has been much argument about Cézanne's color techniques and about his interest in color depth effects. Actually, his greatest achievement was a depth-inducing application of degrees of brightness in his paintings. Cézanne was a real master in his use of brightness gradients and contrasts.

The Dutch physiologist Einthoven is the man usually mentioned in connection with color stereoscopy. He has shown that the optical axis of the eye and the line of sight form an angle subtending 5 degrees. One consequence of this asymmetry is that short-wave bluish radiation and long-wave reddish radiation have different diffusion areas on the retina. In some persons the stronger refraction of bluish light causes the illusion of "warmer" colors being closer than bluish ones. Because of the opposite asymmetry in the eyes of other people, they have a contradictory experience, bluish colors phenomenally appearing closer. Schildt found that the second physiological alternative occurred in 30 percent of his subjects. We must also not forget that at the distances from which we usually look at paintings, color stereoscopy hardly has any effect at all. The size of the pupil also affects the degree of the illusion.

Therefore, we might assume that color stereoscopy plays its greatest role, if any, when we look at generally dark paintings, such as Rembrandt's "Night Watch," which used many other techniques for achieving an illusion of space. Cézanne's pictures are mostly brighter, which would make for a smaller pupillary opening and thus act against color stereoscopy. Only few surfaces in his works can be discriminated on the basis of brightness differences—as he himself used to point out.

Actually, Cézanne generally strove for two-dimensionality on his canvases. He avoided illusory effects. Therefore, Schildt proposes that one should drop the argument of differential depth effects of various hues when speaking of Cézanne's art.[28]

Cézanne's art is mainly based on figural organization. His paintings are almost as appealing when reproduced in black and

---

[27] Grünewald, *op. cit.*, pp. 43–44.
[28] Schildt, *op. cit.*, pp. 186–90.

white. It is the brightness gradients in his pictures which contribute to their spatial frame of reference.

ART AND PERSONALITY DYNAMICS

So far in this chapter the perception of pictorial art has been analyzed primarily on the basis of the figural organization of visual stimulation. Such an approach may be useful in providing a systematic survey of the structural conditions of pictorial organization, but we must not forget that any isolation of sensory experience from the dynamic totality of personal life inevitably is an abstraction. When we are perceiving masterpieces of art, it is especially true that "attitudes, evaluations and emotional connotations are generally involved in all sensory activity," to recall the quotation from Hartshorne which was cited earlier on page 194. We certainly would be applying the principles presented in Chapter 8 poorly if we were to ignore the emotional tones of the total personality which give perceptual configurations their deeper significance.

Affective continua clearly operate in all perceptual enjoyment of pictorial art. The representation of a motif or a subject is not the only thing expected by the observer; the allegorical or symbolic meaning involved in the artistic product may unconsciously affect him even more strongly than the mere representation of a bit of outside reality. Therefore, it is not even necessary for the motif itself to appeal to us, if a picture is to be appealing.

This fact can be demonstrated convincingly if we look at the works of two artists representing exactly the same landscape. One of them might leave us completely cold despite skillful and structurally well-performed composition, coloration, and depth articulation. The other may contain those hidden artistic qualities which appeal directly to a cross-modal emotional evaluation.

Often it seems that the artist has been able to project something of his own motivation, his wishes, his needs, or his mood into the structure and coloration of the composition and that he has mastered the appropriate means for evoking the corresponding mood in us. It is not even necessary to have a topically clearly organized pictorial world in order to grasp the allegorical meaning intended by the artist. In a way similar to how a poem with an uninteresting motif can appeal to our emotions by affecting what Kretschmer called the "spheric" regions of our consciousness, i.e., physiologically speaking, by causing some "resonance" in the motivation centers of the brainstem, so a good painting can directly approach our personality without our being aware of how it does so.[29]

The Finnish artist H. O. Mäkilä has a landscape called "Spring." The rather crowded picture, with two faces and a few strokes indicating trees and bushes has nothing strongly reminiscent of springtime; yet everyone I have asked about it became aware at first glance of the spirit of spring which speaks to us unmistakably from the canvas. The symbolic meaning detectable in Cézanne's "Blue Landscape," into which he projects something of himself in an unanalyzable manner, probably is much more important than the question of how he succeeded in representing the forest.

This matter of being able to convey the artist's motivation and sentiment to the person looking at the creation is, however, an extremely delicate one. As soon as the artist discovers that he can express himself and his own problems on the canvas, he might feel tempted to neglect the perceptual treatment of space, form, and color in his pictures entirely. Exclusive concentration on one's own emotions and mood generally means avoiding the difficulties of the formal spatial elaboration of the illusory pictorial world.

Pictorial art, however, usually appeals to ordinary "normal" people, whose personality organization might not be as original, unique, or extreme as that of the artist. Man himself is a part of nature, and the immediate beauty inherent in certain creations of nature can appeal to him in the same way as do pieces of art. If the artist harshly distorts recognizable parts of nature without successfully mediating what is central in his mood and motivation, such a product usually remains unintelligible to the majority of the public.

Works of many modern painters, such as surrealists and abstractionists, might be very interesting to the clinical psychologist insofar as he can "read" the personality dynamics of the creator in the production. If the artist is not too radical, most of us can even enjoy slight compulsive repetitions like in Mondrian's skillfully composed and balanced patterns or a spontaneous gay interplay of colors and forms in a slightly manic pictorial production. Yet the majority of art lovers are no psychopathologists; what is highly satisfactory to the artist as a release of his tensions may sometimes be annoying to his public.

---

[29] Ernst Kretschmer, *A Textbook of Medical Psychology*, 2d English edition, translated from the 10th German edition, with an introduction by E. B. Strauss (London: Hogarth Press, 1952).

Pasto rightly points out that spontaneous expressions, devoid of all intended motifs or interpretations, like water colors by children or chimpanzees, impress us more than analogous apparently haphazard creations by adult artists. This level and this technique is typical and natural for children at a certain age. In chaotic water color patterns by adults we can usually discern a sophisticated or conscious striving for primitivism, which makes these creations less spontaneous and in a sense less artistic than the genuine spontaneous expressions of children. Except for art critics, most people feel as though they were faced with personality regressions, because many of the extreme modernist works display a disorganization often encountered—as Pasto strikingly shows—in schizophrenic art.[30]

One of the psychoanalytic explanations of artistic enjoyment maintains that the product should allow for the possibility of *identification*. People feel happy with a movie if they have been able to identify with the hero. This may be why some kind of space frame, including three-dimensional objects, could be an important condition for a successful painting. Human beings are typically more interested in what they see depicted and in what gives them the opportunity to identify than in the personality of the artist.

A good piece of pictorial art combines hidden emotional and mood factors with spatially balanced and agreeable pictorial space which is familiar and allows for identification. It fails in its purpose if it acts as a merely correct figural representation or as a releasing stimulus for some drive impulses or appeals to the libido of the enjoyer. Generally speaking, at least with respect to certain sensory channels, there is—as mentioned at the end of Chapter 12—physiological evidence for the participation of brainstem "arousal centers" in artistic enjoyment. Because of this emotional tuning associated with perceptual activity, our total personality resonates as it were along the affective continuum crossing and connecting the separate modalities. This is aptly described in a quotation from Hornbostel: "A dancer had a dance, 'The Lily.' Her humanity vanished in the high, waving chalice of her veil, a deep violet faded away in spirals, a dazzling white rose up, expanding indefinitely. The noises of the surburban music hall could not spoil this pure music."[31]

---

[30] Pasto, *op. cit.*, pp. 64–67.

[31] E. M. v. Hornbostel, "Die Einheit der Sinne," *Zeitschrift für Musik*, V, No. 6, Berlin, 1925, p. 290.

CHAPTER 17

The Relational Invariances of Perception

RELATIONAL INVARIANCES[1] have been considered the research object of science since the days of Galileo. The natural laws so boldly discovered and formulated by Kepler, Newton, and Galileo himself as the Middle Ages gave way to the modern age were made possible by recognizing the existence of certain constant relationships, regularities, or invariances in the endless chain of events that constitute natural phenomena. Even during continuous changes in existing reality, we sense something enduring, persistent, and unchangeable. This "regularity within variability" consists, according to Galileo, of mathematically describable *relations among*

---

[1] In Scandinavian countries there has been and still is predominant a kind of philosophy of invariance among behavioral and natural scientists which dates back to about 1930 and the influence of E. Kaila, the founder of experimental psychology in Finland. The task of all natural science is said to be the research for the highest invariances within the endless variability of single events and occurrences.

In his main work *Inhimillinen tieto* (= human knowledge) Kaila formulated the problem as follows: "Human beings have always thought that they can gain empirical knowledge only from what really exists. Since the time of the ancient philosophers *reality* has been ascribed only to what is *invariant* in a world of continuous variability. For the famous Greek philosophers only *static events* or *things* could have reality,—or even better as in Plato—only the *ideas* of single things or elements could be real, and therefore object of scientific research, because the single things and elements or their ideas were considered invariant; all of what happened and *changed* dynamically around us could not be real, because it displayed variability."

It was Galileo who, according to Kaila, came up with the statement that elements need not be invariant; instead, relations between elements can be shown—as in Galileo's laws—to be invariant. These *invariances* in relationships are the objects of modern natural sciences.

Kaila held that especially the *gestalt* view seemed appropriate and worth pursuing because it reveals the invariances behind the gestalt-regularities. In Chapter 9 we followed Koffka's way of thinking when we pointed out (see page 206) that shape constancy rests upon an *invariance* included in the stimulus situation.

phenomena. Modern science does not consist of knowledge about objects but is awareness of the *regular relationships* among objects.

Can we describe human perception by analyzing the relational invariances hidden in it? It is clear that many of the concepts used by perceptual psychology, which so far are *exclusively descriptive* and which *lack scientific definition,* could be more precisely circumscribed if we knew more about the relational regularities embedded in the stimulus situation. Phenomenally, it may well be possible to understand what is meant by a "good gestalt," by a "prägnant or outstanding form," by "good continuation," and by "gestalt complexity," but these concepts appear almost impossible to quantify. This difficulty in finding appropriate quantitative definitions indicates the crude, abstract level of such constructs and the multiplicity of relational connections in the field of psychology.

Under these circumstances we could reasonably raise the question: Is there any point in trying to find some correspondence or reciprocity between the two descriptive modes? Has not E. Kaila, among others, convincingly shown that a complete translation of the terms used in the description of immediate experience into the matter-of-fact language of the natural sciences cannot be achieved?

One answer is that we know of experimentally analyzed cases in which our perceptual system *undoubtedly responds to a combination of invariant stimulus relationships.* Even if we admit the impossibility of a complete translation from phenomenal to physical language, there remains the possibility of defining the task of perceptual psychology as a matter of describing those very cases in which a phenomenal percept can be explained by some regularities obtaining in the stimulus relationships. Such a task has been undertaken by the field of psychophysics. The fact that when we adhere to such a program we have to ignore many research questions traditionally held to be appropriate to perceptual phenomena should not obscure the possibility that such an experimental procedure may some time in the future succeed in identifying the entire system of physical relationships which underlies the direct, immediate phenomenal impression of an object.

In his 1944 paper on logic and psychophysics E. Kaila was one among the first to show how conspicuously easy it is for an experimental subject to complete freehand a drawing of the curve of a logarithmic spiral without recourse to any technical aids. Even if only a dotted line is used to indicate the trajectory of the true continuation, the subject is surprisingly sensitive to the slightest displacement of any of the dots away from the perceived smoothly continuous curvature. Kaila suggests that these observations show that the *eye can react immediately to a gradient of decreasing curvature*, such as that of a spiral. A mathematical analysis reveals that the "gestalt quality" of a logarithmic spiral is based on three regularities or invariances in the stimulus pattern: (1) the initial rate of curvature, (2) the general rate of growth (i.e., logarithmic rather than arithmetic), and (3) its general orientation in space. These regularities are once again based on specific systems of relationships.

The familiar pattern in Figure 17–1 is usually unequivocally

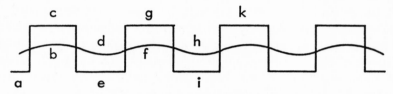

FIG. 17–1. Pattern of overlapping lines.

separated into two components, a wavy line superimposed on a line that looks like the upper edge of a turret of an ancient castle. Kaila pointed out that this predominant alternative among the many other ways in which the pattern could be divided should not and could not be explained merely on the basis of "gestalt simplicity." According to him, the immediate visual analysis of the pattern yields those two lines which, among all possibilities, best represent *two mathematical equations which characterize the most important invariances in the situation*. If maximal simplicity were the only basis, it would be hard to understand—to follow Kaila—"why a b e f i . . . and c d g h k . . . could not form the immediately perceived subtotalities." They are mirror images of each other, if one of them is displaced horizontally by half a cycle—simple enough![2]

In an earlier connection we had an opportunity to mention the Fourier analysis which is so strikingly performed by our auditory and visual systems. An analogous tendency, a striving toward regular relationships, was encountered in many of Johansson's experiments, e.g., in the wandering phenomenon (page 266).

Shape constancy was said to rest on an invariance in stimulus

---

[2] E. Kaila, "Logik und Psychophysik," *Theoria*, 10, pp. 97–193.

relationships: the ability to sense the shape of the retinal image *in relation to* the slant of the stimulus object. Whatever the object constancy, *there always are in the stimulus situation at least two components whose interrelation can offer a basis for accurate perceptual representation.* In color constancy, consideration of the *gradient* of the energies in radiations reflected from surfaces bordering upon each other proved necessary in addition to analysis of the contribution of the spectral composition and the intensity of the radiation.

Vernon called attention to the gradients of decreasing sensitivity across the retina and the central visual loci. The fovea is the region of greatest sensitivity. As a consequence of adjustments in retinal cell functions in response to certain brain injuries, this stimulation gradient may give way to some new, different ones which function to reduce the distortions caused by the injury to a minimum.[3]

It is especially the concept of gradients which has made possible the demonstration of the regularities included in the stimulus pattern. Mathematically, the term *"gradient" refers to a function which changes its value along a certain dimension according to a specific proportional ratio of transformation.* Because this is a matter of a relational variable, the rate of transformation can remain constant even when all single elements are transformed.

In 1935 Turhan, a student of Metzger's, had used the term *Gefälle* (stairway formation) to refer to the proportions of light energy reflected from objects illuminated from the side.[4] He observed that when stepwise increasing degrees of brightness were artificially introduced on plane surfaces so that the albedo increased toward one edge of the surface, imitating a natural gradient of illumination, *the subject perceived the surface as bent, i.e., as either convex or concave depending on the distribution of the illusion-producing illumination gradient.* In many of Turhan's ingenious constructions the subject was led to impressions of three-dimensional bodies by means of brightness gradients introduced on plane surfaces. It seems safe to conclude that he worked with gradients without explicitly using this expression.

Gibson deserves the credit of having shown the power of the

---

[3] M. D. Vernon, *A Further Study on Visual Perception* (Cambridge, England: The University Press, 1954), p. 83.

[4] M. Turhan, "Über räumliche Wirkungen von Helligkeitsgefällen," *Psychologische Forschung*, 21 (1935).

gradient concept in the theory of space perception. One could claim that his contribution to depth perception strikingly parallels Katz's contribution to color research. Katz broke down the old traditional views of color psychology by leaving the color laboratory to go out into the natural surroundings of human beings. He discovered that the spectral colors demonstrated by Newton were extreme, artificial cases, and he also complemented the three-dimensional color solid with the new concept of *modes of appearance*, carefully describing especially surface and space colors. Gibson, however, made a quite analogous contribution in his criticism of the three-dimensional coordinate system of perceptual space. We never see the third dimension as such, as something reduced to a straight visual line extending forward from the eye. What we see are *surfaces* receding from the observer. Gibson claims to offer a "ground theory" to substitute for the traditional "air theory." He points out that perceived objects are seen on a ground which extends from us to the objects and beyond them. Things are seen around us at different distances only on slanted surfaces. Of all slanted surfaces the *ground*, i.e., the surface of the earth or the floor, is the most important. We cannot perceive depth at a definite distance unless we simultaneously see the ground or at least a part of it. The retinal image, according to Gibson, has gradients which correspond to similar gradients in the visual field. The texture of the receding surface of the ground exhibits density variations. There are, if we put it in Gibson's terms, longitudinal and latitudinal gradients of density, and both can be called *texture gradients*. These gradients, according to Gibson, constitute a stimulus system for the perception of depth and three-dimensionality. Gibson holds that the traditional "depth cues" were treated too separately and specifically by older psychologists, and are all examples of the influence of various hidden gradients. Gradients or invariant systems of relationships are evident in binocular parallax, in brightness perspective (gradients of brightness), in motion parallax (e.g., the kinetic depth effect), in linear perspective, etc.

These gradients, according to Gibson, constitute *ordinal stimuli* in the physical structure of depth and occur over and above the punctate stimuli persistently referred to by the older classical psychologists. Many of the so-called "higher-order stimuli" actually are ordinal stimuli. In this respect Gibson's *correspondence theory* differs from traditional elementism and from the so-called constancy hypothesis. Yet his mode of thought remains entirely behavioristic. According to Gibson, there are gradients in the retinal image, and these gradients correspond to similar gradients in the visual field. The former must not be thought of as exactly duplicating the latter, but their similarity is like a kind of correlation between these variables. Once the notion of gradient had achieved general acceptance as an explanatory concept, later investigators have, not surprisingly, been looking for relational invariances of the same kind throughout modalities other than vision. Strong interest is currently centered on the possibility of the universal explanatory power of gradients. We have already mentioned that *temperature gradients* in the skin play a key explanatory role in the understanding of sensations of warmth and cold (page 62). And let us not forget "touch transparency" (page 300), which also required an explanation in terms of gradients.

A central recent extension of Gibson's theory is involved in his conception of *gradients of transformation of objects perceived as moving*. These gradients can be directly registered by our visual organs whenever we are presented with continuously moving patterns; we can perceive a movement pattern directly. Thus, in addition to all its other functions, the eye serves, according to Gibson, as an organ for the direct reception of transformations. Even if we look monocularly at objects moving on a screen, eliminating most of the standard depth cues, and producing essentially two-dimensional projections, the *gradient of perspective transformation* included in this moving pattern provides sufficient cues for depth articulation. This is one of the reasons why the "monocularly" photographed moving picture looks flat and unrealistic as soon as the camera is stopped. In experiments carried out at Cornell by Gibson and Gibson, by Gibson, Smith and Flock, by Gibson and Fieandt, and later by Johansson, with moving objects projected on opalescent screens or with specially designed perspective figures produced on the face of an oscilloscope, it became evident that our visual system reacts immediately to gradients of transformation of patterns projected on a surface.[5] Fieandt and Gibson found that subjects can distinguish the projected motion of a rigid surface from

---

[5] See, e.g., K. von Fieandt and J. J. Gibson, "The Sensitivity of the Eye to Two Kinds of Continuous Transformation of a Shadow-Pattern," *Journal of Experimental Psychology*, 57, pp. 344–47; and G. Johansson, "Perception of Motion and Changing Form," *Scandinavian Journal of Psychology*, 5, pp. 181–208.

the "elastic motion" of forms in a two-dimensional plane. Continuous perspective transformations of the projected shadow of a "fish net" pattern made of elastic thread could be distinguished amazingly well from its nonperspective transformation, i.e., from displacements of all its elements in a "rubbery" manner.

It is tempting to refer some of the famous experimental findings of Erismann and I. Kohler to the influence of certain gradients. After wearing distorting lenses for weeks, their experimental subjects gradually reestablished their previous behavioral world, developing a systematic correction for the distortion. Such an effect might be explained by the assumption of an "ordinal stimulus" which serves to establish a certain invariance in the variability caused by the distortion. All prismatic lenses, even if they are extremely distorting, have their fixed, regular gradient of refraction. An optical distortation is never completely ambiguous or haphazard. The gradient of refraction, as a common factor, governs all displacements which may superficially look irregular and chaotic. As soon as our visual system "catches on" to this common denominator, it becomes possible to compensate for it in sensory-motor behavior.

Even if we might feel disinclined to go along with Gibson's particular way of trying to quantify all visual, auditory, tactual, and other modal experiences, his approach does provide a way of identifying the gradients which determine at least some of our perceptions. Only when a specific quantification of such gradients has been achieved could we permit ourselves to speak of "gestalten" in a genuinely scientific sense of the word.

Bibliography

AALTO, OTSO. *Zur Psychologie der euklidischen Raumanschauung.* Annales Academiae Scientiarum Fennicae, B LV, No. 2. Helsinki, 1946.

ABRAHAM, O., and v. HORNBOSTEL, E. M. "Zur Psychologie der Tondistanz," *Zeitschrift für Psychologie,* IIC (1926).

ADRIAN, E. D. *The Basis of Sensation.* London: Christophers, 1934.

———. *The Mechanism of the Nervous Action.* Oxford: Press of the University of Pa., 1935.

———. *The Physical Background of Perception.* Oxford: Clarendon Press, 1947.

ALLERS, R., and SCHMIEDEK, O. "Über die Wahrnehmung der Schallrichtung," *Psychologische Forschung,* VI (1924).

ALLPORT, F. *Theories of Perception and the Concept of Structure.* New York: John Wiley & Sons, Inc., 1955.

AMENT, M. "Über das Verhältnis der ebenmerklichen zu den übermerklichen Unterschieden bei Licht und Schallintensität," *Philosophische Studien,* XVI (1900).

AMES, A., JR. "Reconsideration of the Origin and Nature of Perception," *Vision and Action* (ed. S. RATNER). Rutgers University, 1953.

———. 1951, see ITTELSON *et al.,* 1951.

ANGELL, J. R. *Psychology.* 4th ed. New York: H. Holt, 1908.

ANSBACHER, H. "Perception of Number as Effect by the Monetary Value of the Objects," *Archives of Psychology,* No. 215 (1937).

——— and MATHER, K. "Group Differences in Size Estimation," *Psychometrica,* X, No. 1 (March, 1945).

ARNHEIM, R. *Art and Visual Perception.* Berkeley and Los Angeles: University of California Press, 1954.

ATTNEAVE, F. *Applications of Information Theory to Psychology.* New York: Henry Holt & Co., 1959.

AUBERT, H. *Physiologie der Netzhaut.* Breslau: Morgenstern, 1865.

AVENARIUS, FERDINAND. *Eine neue Sprache? Zweiundvierzig Zeichnungen von Katherine Schäffner. Mit einer Besprechung.* Munich: Georg D. W. Callwey im Kunstwart Verlag, 1929.

BAHNSEN, POUL. "Symmetrie und Asymmetrie bei visuellen Wahrneh-mungen," *Zeitschrift für Psychologie*, CVIII (1928).

BARTLEY, S. H. *Principles of Perception*. New York: Harper & Bros., 1958.

BAZETT, H. C. "Temperature Sense in Men," *Temperature, Its Measurement and Control in Science and Industry*. New York, 1941.

BEARDSLEE, D. C., and WERTHEIMER, M. (ed.). *Readings in Perception*. New York: D. van Nostrand Co., Inc., 1958.

v. BÉKÉSY, G. *Experiments in Hearing*. New York: McGraw-Hill Book Co., 1960.

BENUSSI, V. *Psychologie der Zeitauffassung*. Heidelberg, Winter, 1913.

———. "Versuche zur Analyse taktil erweckter Scheinbewegungen," *Archiv für die gesamte Psychologie*, XXXVI.

BLACKWELL, H. RICHARD. Psychophysical Thresholds. Experimental Stud-ies of Methods of Measurement. Engineering Research Institute Bulletin, No. 36. Ann Arbor: University of Michigan, 1953.

BLAKE, R. R., and RAMSEY, G. V. *Perception, an Approach to Personality*. New York: Ronald Press Co., 1951.

BLIX, M. "Experimentella bidrag till lösning af frågan om hudnervernas specifika energi," *Upsala läkareförenings förhandlingar*, XVIII (1882–83), pp. 87–102, 427–40.

———. "Experimentelle Beiträge zur Lösung der Frage über die spesifische Energie der Hautnerven," *Zeitschrift für Biologie*, XX (1884).

BLUMENFELD, WALTER. "The Relationship between the Optical and Haptic Construction of Space," *Acta Psychologica*, II (1936).

BOOKSCH, H. "Farbenkonstanz und Duplizitätstheorie," *Zeitschrift für Psychologie*, CII (1927).

BORING, E. *Sensation and Perception in the History of Experimental Psychology*. New York: Appleton-Century-Crofts, 1942.

———. *A History of Experimental Psychology*. 2nd ed. New York: Appleton-Century-Crofts, 1950.

———; LANGFELD, H. S.; and WELD, H. P. (eds.). *Foundations of Psychology*. New York: John Wiley & Sons, Inc., 1948.

BÖRNSTEIN, WALTER. "Über den Geruchsinn," *Deutsche Zeitschrift für Nervenheilkunde*, CIV. Leipzig, 1928.

BROWN, J. F. "Über gesehene Geschwindigkeit," *Psychologische Forschung*, X (1928).

———. "On Time Perception in Visual Movement Fields," *Psychologische Forschung*, XIV (1931).

———. "The Thresholds for Visual Movement," *Psychologische Forschung*, XIV (1931).

———. "The Visual Perception of Velocity," *Psychologische Forschung*, XIV (1931).

BRUNER, J. S., and POSTMAN, L. "Emotional Selectivity in Perception and Reaction," *Journal of Personality*, XVI (1947).

————. "Symbolic Value as an Organizing Factor in Perception," *Journal of Social Psychology*, XXVII (1948).

————. "An Approach to Social Perception," *Current Trends in Social Psychology* (ed. W. DENNIS). Pittsburgh, 1948.

BRUNSWIK, EGON. "Untersuchungen über Wahrnehmungsgegenstände," Part I, *Archiv für die gesamte Psychologie*, XXCVIII (1938).

————. *Wahrnehmung und Gegenstandswelt. Grundlegung einer Psychologie vom Gegenstand her.* Leipzig and Vienna: Franz Deuticke, 1934.

————. "Zur Entwicklung der Albedowahrnehmung," *Zeitschrift für Psychologie*, CIX (1928).

————. "Thing Constancy as Measured by Correlation Coefficients," *Psychological Review*, XLVII (1940).

————. "Systematic and Representative Design of Psychological Experiments with Results in Physical and Social Perception," *Proceedings of Berkeley Symposium on Mathematical Statistics and Probability*, 1949.

————. *Perception and the Representative Design of Psychological Experiments.* Berkeley: University of California Press, 1956.

BUCH, ANNEMARIE. "Zur Pathologie der Gestaltwahrnehmungen an der Haut," *Deutsche Zeitschrift für Nervenheilkunde*, XCV (1926).

BÜHLER, KARL. *Handbuch der Psychologie.* I. Teil. "Die Struktur der Wahrnehmungen," I Heft, "Die Erscheinungsweisen der Farben." Jena: Fischer, 1922.

————. "Gegenbemerkungen zu Katz Referat," *Psychologische Forschung*, V (1924).

BURKAMP, WILH. "Versuche über das Farbenwiedererkennen der Fische," *Zeitschrift für Sinnesphysiologie*, LV (1923).

BURZLAFF, W. "Methodologische Beiträge zum Problem der Farbenkonstanz," *Zeitschrift für Psychologie*, CXIX. Leipzig, 1931.

BUYTENDIJK, F. J. *Über den Schmerz.* Bern: Verlag Hans Huber, 1948.

COHEN, GOTTHARD. "Zur Bedeutung des Zeitfaktors für die Pathologie des Temperatursinnes," *Deutsche Zeitschrift für Nervenheilkunde*, XCVI (1927).

COHEN, NATHAN, E. "Equivalence of Brightness across Modalities," *American Journal of Psychology*, January, 1934.

CRONBACH, LEE J. "A Consideration of Information Theory and Utility Theory as Tools for Psychometric Problems," *Bulletin of Educational Research.* Urbana: University of Illinois, 1953.

————. "On the Non-Rational Application of Information Measures in Psychology," *Information Theory* (ed. H. QUASTLER). Urbana: University of Illinois, 1955.

DALLENBACH, K. M. "The Temperature Spots and End Organs," *American Journal of Psychology*, XXXIX (1927).

————. "A Method of Marking the Skin," *American Journal of Psychology*, XLIII (1931).

DaSilva, H. R. "Kinematographic Movement of Parallel Lines," *Journal of General Psychology*, I (1927).

Delacroix, H. *Psychologie de l'art*. Paris: Presses Universitaires de France, 1927.

Delay, J.–P. L. *Les Astéréognosies*. Paris: Masson, 1935.

Dember, W. N. *The Psychology of Perception*. New York: Holt, Rinehart and Winston, 1961.

Dessoir, M. *Ästhetik und allgemeine Kunstwissenschaft*. Leipzig, 1923.

Doevenspeck, H. C. H. "Über Schallokalisation," *Zeitschrift für Sinnesphysiologie*, LVIII (1927).

Drever, J. "Preceptual Learning," *Annual Review of Psychology*, XI (1960).

v. Ehrenfels, Chr. "Über Gestaltqualitäten," *Vierteljahrsschrift für wissenschafliche Philosophie*, XIV (1890).

Einthoven, W. "Stereoscopie durch Farbendifferenz," *Archiv für Ophthalmologie*. Berlin, 1885.

Eissler, K. "Die Gestaltkonstanz der Sehdinge," *Archiv für die gesamte Psychologie*, XXCVIII (1934).

Ekman, Gösta. *Psykologi*. Uppsala: Almquist & Wicksell, 1953.

———. "Nya metoder för psykologisk dimensionsanalys," *Tredje Nordiska Psykologmötet*, 1953.

———. "Dimensions of Color Vision," *Journal of Psychology*, XXXVIII (1954).

———. *Similarity Analysis of Olfaction, A Preliminary Investigation*. Reports of Psychological Laboratory, No. 10. University of Stockholm, 1954.

———. *A Methodological Note on Scales of Gustatory Intensity*. Reports of Psychological Laboratory, No. 98. University of Stockholm, 1961.

Ellis, W. D. *Source Book of Gestalt Psychology*. New York: Harcourt, 1938. 3rd ed. London: Humanities Press, 1950.

Engelmann, W. "Untersuchungen über die Schallokalisation bei Tieren," *Zeitschrift für Psychologie*, CV (1928).

Engen, T. *Direct Scaling of Odor Intensity*. Reports of Psychological Laboratory, No. 106. University of Stockholm, 1961.

———. "Psychophysical Scaling of Odor Intensity and Quality," *Annals of the New York Academy of Sciences*, 1964, 116 (2).

Erämetsä, O. "The Principles of Visual Measurements," *Acta Polytechnica Scandinavica*, XVIII, No. 317. Helsinki, 1962.

Eysenck, H. J.; Granger, G. W., and Brengelmann, J. C. *Perceptual Processes and Mental Illness*. London: Oxford University Press, 1957.

Fechner, G. T. *Elemente der Psychophysik*. Leipzig: Breitkopf und Härtel, 1862.

FELLENIUS, V. "Rörelsevarseblivning som lokalisationsrubbning," *Tidskrift för psykologi och pedagogi*, Nos. 1–2 (1946).

FESSARD, A. "Organes des Sens, Physiologie," *Revue Annuelle de Psychologie*, XX. Paris, 1939.

v. FIEANDT, K. "Dressurversuche an der Farbenwahrnehmung," *Untersuchungen über Wahrnehmungsgegenstände* (ed. E. BRUNSWIK), Beitrag VII, *Archiv für die gesamte Psychologie*, IVC (1936).

———. *Ein neues Invarianzphänomen der Farbenwahrnehmung.* Annales Academiae Scientiarum Fennicae, B XLI, No. 2. Helsinki, 1938.

———. *Über Sehen von Tiefengebilden bei wechselnder Beleuchtungsrichtung.* Reports from the Psychological Institute. University of Helsinki, 1938.

———. "Psykologiset" ja "fysiologiset" olettamukset havainto-opissa, *Valvoja-Aika*, No. 4 (1939).

———. "Versuche über Raumform und Helligkeitsverteilung," *Zeitschrift für Psychologie*, CLIII. Leipzig, 1942.

———. "Das phänomenologische Problem von Licht und Schatten," *Acta Psychologica*, VI (1949).

———. "Loudness Invariance in Sound Perception," *Acta Psychologica Fennica*, I. Helsinki, 1951.

———. "Les possibilités et les limites de la psychométrie dans le diagnostic de la personnalité," *La Psychotechnique dans le Monde Moderne*. Paris, 1952.

———. "Über den Anteil von Vestibularreizen an der optischen Wahrnehmung," *Sitzungsberichte der Finnischen Akademie der Wissenschaften, 1954.* Helsinki, 1955.

———. "Ein Beitrag zur einheitlichen Wahrnehmungstheorie," *Studium Generale*, No. 10 (1957).

———. "Toward a Unitary Theory of Perception," *Psychological Review*, V (1958).

———. "Form Perception and Modelling of Patients Without Sight," *Confinia Psychiatrica*, Separatum, II (1959), pp. 205–13.

———. "Raumwahrnehmung und räumliche Vorstellungen bei Blinden und Blindgeborenen," *Zeitschrift für Psychologie*, CLXV (1961).

———. "Erweiterung des Körperschemas im Spiegelbild," *Zeitschrift für Psychologie*, CLXVII (1962).

———. "Current Trends in Perceptual Psychology," *Psychologische Beiträge*, VI (1962).

———; AHONEN, LEA; JÄRVINEN, J.; and LIAN, ARILD. *Colour Experiments with Modern Sources of Illumination.* Annales Academiae Scientiarum Fennicae, B CXXXIV, No. 2. Helsinki, 1964.

———; AHONEN, LEA; and JÄRVINEN, J. "A Scaling Method for Measuring Color Constancy," *Scandinavian Journal of Psychology*, V, No. 1 (1964).

FORGUS, R. H. "Advantage of Early over Late Perceptual Experience in

Improving Form Discrimination," *Canadian Journal of Psychology*, X (1956).

FREUD, A. *Das Ich und die Abwehrmechanismen.* Vienna: Internationales Psychoanal. Verlag, 1936.

FREUD, S. *Die Traumdeutung.* Vienna: Franz Deuticke, 1900.

FROM, FRANZ. *Om oplevelsen af andres adfaerd.* Copenhagen: Busck, 1953.

FRÖBES, J. *Lehrbuch der experimentellen Psychologie.* Freiburg, 1932.

FUCHS, W. "Eine Pseudofovea bei Hemianopikern," *Psychologische Forschung*, I (1922).

———. "Untersuchungen über das simultane Hintereinandersehen auf derselben Sehrichtung," *Zeitschrift für Psychologie*, XCI (1923).

———. "Experimentelle Untersuchungen über die Änderung von Farben unter den Einfluss von Gestalten," *Zeitschrift für Psychologie*, XCII (1923).

GELB, A. "Die Farbenkonstanz der Sehdinge," *Bethes Handbuch*, XII, No. 1 (1929).

———, and GRANIT, R. "Die Bedeutung von 'Figur' und 'Grund' für die Farbenschwelle," *Zeitschrift für Psychologie*, XCIII (1923).

GELDARD, F. A. *The Human Senses.* New York: John Wiley & Sons, Inc., 1953.

GEMELLI, O. F. M. A. "Neue Beobachtungen über das Wesen der Wahrnehmung," *Acta Psychologica*, I. Haag, 1935.

GESELL, A.; ILG, F. L.; and BULLIS, G. *Vision, Its Development in Infant and Child.* New York: Harper & Row, 1950.

GIBSON, E. J., and WALK, R. D. "The Effect of Prolonged Exposure to Visually Presented Patterns on Learning to Discriminate Them," *Journal of Comparative and Physiological Psychology*, XLIX (1956).

———; PICK, H. L., JR.; and TIGHE, T. J. "The Effect of Prolonged Exposure to Visual Patterns on Learning to Discriminate Similar and Different Patterns," *Journal of Comparative and Physiological Psychology*, LI (1958).

———, and WALK, R. D. "The Visual Cliff," *Scientific American*, CCII (April, 1960).

GIBSON, J. J. *The Perception of the Visual World.* Cambridge, Mass.: Houghton Mifflin Co., 1950.

———. "Perception as a Function of Stimulation," *Psychology: a Study of a Science*, I (ed. S. KOCH) New York, 1959.

v. GOETHE, J. W. *Farbenlehre.* Cotta, 1810.

GOLDSCHEIDER, A. *Gesammelte Abhandlungen.* Leipzig: Thieme, 1909.

GOLDSTEIN, K., and ROSENTHAL-VEIT, OLLY. "Über akustische Lokalisation und deren Beeinflussbarkeit durch andere Sinnesreize," *Psychologische Forschung*, VIII (1926).

———, and GELB, A. "Über den Einfluss des vollständigen Verlustes des optischen Vorstellungsvermögens auf das taktile Erkennen," *Zeitschrift für Psychologie*, XXCIII (1920).

GOTTSCHALDT, K. "Über den Einfluss der Erfahrung auf die Wahrnehmung von Figuren," *Psychologische Forschung*, VIII (1926), XII (1929).

GRANIT, R. *Receptors and Sensory Perception*. New Haven: Yale University Press, 1955.

GRENIEWSKI, H. *Cybernetics without Mathematics*. Warsaw: Panstwowe Wydawnictwo Naukowe, 1960.

GROTENFELT, A. *Das Webersche Gesetz und die psychische Relativität*. Helsinki: J. C. Frenckell & Son, 1888.

GRÜNEWALD, I. *Henri Matisse*. Porvoo: Werner Söderström Oy, 1946.

GUILLAUME, PAUL. *La psychologie de la Forme*. Paris, 1937.

GURWITSCH, A. "Une théorie du champ biologique cellulaire," *Bibliotheca Biotheoretica*, II. Leiden, 1947.

HARTLINE, H. K. "A Quantitative and Descriptive Study of the Electrical Response to Illumination of the Arthropode Eye," *American Journal of Psychology*, XXCIII (1928).

———. "Impulses in Single Optic Nerve Fibers of the Vertebrate Retina," *American Journal of Psychology*, CXIII (1935).

———; WAGNER, H. G.; and MACNICHOL, E. F. "The Peripheral Origin of Nervous Activity in the Visual System," Colorado Springs: Harb. Symposium for Quantitative Biology, XVII, 1952.

HARTMAN, L. "Neue Verschmelzungsprobleme," *Psychologische Forschung*, III (1923).

HARTSHORNE, C. *The Philosophy and Psychology of Sensation*. Chicago: University of Chicago Press, 1934.

HEBB, D. O. *The Organization of Behavior*. New York: John Wiley & Sons, Inc., 1949.

———. *A Textbook of Psychology*. Philadelphia: W. B. Saunders Co., 1958.

HECHT, S. "The Nature of the Photoreceptor Process," *Handbook of General Experimental Psychology* (ed. C. MURCHISON). Worcester, Mass., 1934.

v. HELMHOLTZ, H. *Die Lehre von den Tonempfindungen*. 2nd ed. Braunschweig: Vieweg, 1865.

———. *Handbuch der physiologischen Optik*. Hamburg: Voss, 1896.

HELSON, HARRY. *Adaptation—Level Theory. An Experimental and Systematic Approach to Behavior*. London: Harper & Row, 1964.

HENNEMAN, R. H. "A Photometric Study of the Perception of Object Color," *Archives of Psychology*, No. 179. New York, 1935.

HENNING, HANS. "Der Geruch," *Zeitschrift für Psychologie*, LXXIII–LXXVI. Leipzig, 1916.

———. "Künstliche Geruchsfährte und Reaktionsstruktur der Ameise," *Zeitschrift für Psychologie*, LXXVI (1916).

———. "Die Qualitätenreihe des Geschmacks," *Ibid.*

———. *Der Geruch.* Leipzig: Joh. Ambrosius Barth, 1924.

HERING, E. "Grundzüge der Lehre vom Lichtsinn," *Handbuch der gesamten Augenheilkunde* (ed. GRAEFE-SAEMISCH). Leipzig, 1905–11. Berlin, 1920.

HESS, E. H. "Shadows and Depth Perception," *Scientific American,* CCIV (March 1961).

HOCHBERG, JULIAN. *Perception.* Englewood Cliffs, N.J.: Prentice-Hall, Inc., 1964.

HOEFER, P. F. A., and PUTNAM, T. J. "Action Potentials of Muscles in 'Spastic' Conditions," *Archives of Neurology and Psychiatry.* Chicago, 1940.

HOFFMANN, FRANZ BRUNO. *Die Lehre vom Raumsinn des Auges I–II.* Berlin: Verlag von Julius Springer, 1925.

———. "Der Geruchsinn beim Menschen," *Bethes Handbuch,* XI (1926).

HOLADAY, B. E. "Die Grössenkonstanz der Sehdinge," *Untersuchungen über Wahrnehmungsgegenstände,* Part II (ed. E. BRUNSWIK), *Archiv für die gesamte Psychologie,* XXCVIII (1934).

HOLT-HANSEN, KRISTIAN "Studien über Schallokalisation," Part I, *Zeitschrift für Psychologie,* CXX (1931).

———. "Studien über Schallokalisation," Part II, *Zeitschrift für Psychologie,* CXLV (1939).

HOLTZ, W. "Über den unmittelbaren Grösseneindruck in seiner Beziehung zur Entfernung und zum Kontrast," *Nachrichten von der Königlichen Gesellshcaft der Wissenschaften zu Göttingen,* 1893.

HONKAVAARA, S. *On the Psychology of Artistic Enjoyment,* Annales Academiae Scientiarum Fennicae, B LXVI, No. 1. Helsinki, 1949.

———. "The Psychology of Expression, Dimensions in Human Perception," *British Journal of Psychology.* Monograph Suppl., Vol. XXXII. Cambridge, England, 1961.

v. HORNBOSTEL, ERICH M. "Die Einheit der Sinne," *Zeitschrift für Musik,* V, No. 6. Berlin, 1925, pp. 290–97.

———. "Beobachtungen über ein und zweiohriges Hören," *Psychologische Forschung,* IV (1923).

———. "Das räumliche Hören," *Bethes Handbuch,* XI (1926).

———. "Eine neue Methode in der Sinnesphysiologie," *Forschungen und Fortschritte,* VII (1931).

———. "Geruch und chemische Konstitution," *Forschungen und Fortschritte,* VII (1931).

———. *Melodie und Skala. Sonderabdruck aus dem Jahrbuch der Musikbibliothek Peters,* XIX. Leipzig: C. F. Peters, 1913.

———. *Über Geruchshelligkeit. Sonderabdruck aus Pflügers Archiv für die gesamte Physiologie des Menschen und der Tiere,* CCVII, No. 4. Berlin: Julius Springer, 1931.

———, and WERTHEIMER, M. "Über die Wahrnehmung der Schallrichtung," *Sitzungsberichte der preussischen Akademie der Wissenschaften*, 1920.

HSIA, YUN, and GRAHAM, C. H. "Spectral Sensitivity of the Cones in the Dark Adapted Human Eye," *Proceedings of the National Academy of Sciences*, XXXVIII. New York (1952).

HUSSERL, E. *Logische Untersuchungen*. 1900.

HYMOVITCH, B. "The Effects of Experimental Variations on Problem Solving in the Rat," *Journal of Comparative and Physiological Psychology*, XLV (1952).

ITTELSON, W. H., and KILPATRICK, F. P. "Experiments in Perception," *Scientific American*, CLXXXV (1951).

———. *Visual Space Perception*. New York: Springer Publishing Co., Inc., 1960.

JAENSCH, E. R. "Über die Wahrnehmung des Raumes," *Zeitschrift für Psychologie*, VI (1911).

———. "Über Grundfragen der Farbenpsychologie," *Kongressbericht: VII Kongress für experimentelle Psychologie in Göttingen*. Leipzig, 1914.

———. "Parallelgesetze über das Verhalten der Reizschwellen bei Kontrast und Transformation," *Zeitschrift für Psychologie*, LXXXIII (1920).

———. "Über den Farbenkontrast und die sogenannte Berücksichtigung der Beleuchtung," *Zeitschrift für Sinnesphysiologie*, LII (1921).

———, and MÜLLER, E. A. "Über die Wahrnehmung farbloser Helligkeiten und den Helligkeitskontrast," *Zeitschrift für Psychologie*, LXXXIII (1920).

JALAVISTO, EEVA. "Perception of Weight and the Phenomenal Regression to the 'Real' Weight" (Thing Constancy Phenomenon), *Acta Physiologica Scandinavica*, XI (1946).

———. *Observations on Arm-Amputeers*. Annales Academiae Scientiarum Fennicae, A XVII. Helsinki, 1948.

———. "Oma ruumiimme havaintomme kohteena," *Duodecim*, 1942.

———, and SOURANDER, P. *Über das Stereo-Kinetische Phänomen*. Annales Academiae Scientiarum Fennicae, A V, No. 11. Helsinki, 1946.

JAMES, W. *The Principles of Psychology*. London, 1890.

JOHANSEN, MARTIN. *An Introductory Study of Voluminal Form Perception*. Nordisk Psykologi's Monograph Series, No. 5. 1955.

———. *Voluminalfigurale faenomener*. Copenhagen: Ejnar Munksgaards Forlag, 1959.

JOHANSSON, GUNNAR. *Configurations in Event Perception, An Experimental Study*, Uppsala: Almqvist & Wicksell, 1950.

———. "Configurations in the Perception of Velocity," *Acta Psychologica*, VII (1950).

———. "The Effect of Uniform and Continuous Chromatic Changes," *Essays in Psychology ded. to David Katz*. Uppsala, 1951.

————, Dureman, I.; and Sälde, H. "Motion Perception and Personality I," *Acta Psychologica*, XI (1955).

Jørgensen, Jørgen. *Psykologi paa biologisk grundlag.* Copenhagen: Munksgaard, 1941.

Kaila, Eino. "Versuch einer empiristischen Erklärung der Tiefenlokalisation von Doppelbildern," *Zeitschrift für Psychologie*, LXXXII (1919).

————. "Die Lokalisation der Objekte bei Blickbewegungen," *Psychologische Forschung*, III (1923).

————. "Über das System der Wirklichkeitsbegriffe, Ein Beitrag zum logischen Empirismus," *Acta Philosophica Fennica*, II (1936).

————. "Logik und Psychophysik, Ein Beitrag zur theoretischen Psychologie," *Theoria*, X (1944).

————. "Über den physikalischen Realitätsbegriff, Zweiter Beitrag zum logischen Empirismus," *Acta Philosophica Fennica*, IV (1941).

————. "Arkikokemuksen perseptuaalinen ja konseptuaalinen aines," *Ajatus*, XXIII. Helsinki, 1960.

Kardos, L. "Ding und Schatten, Eine experimentelle Untersuchung über die Grundlagen des Farbensehens," *Zeitschrift für Psychologie*, Ergänzungsband, No. 23 (1934).

Katz, David, "Blindheit," *Handwörterbuch der medizinischen Psychologie.* Berlin.

————. "Geruchsinn," *Handwörterbuch der medizinischen Psychologie.* Berlin.

————. "Geschmacksinn," *Handwörterbuch der medizinischen Psychologie.* Berlin.

————. "Gehörsinn," *Handwörterbuch der medizinischen Psychologie.* Berlin.

————. "Der Aufbau der Farbwelt," *Zeitschrift für Psychologie*, Ergänzungsband, No. 7. Leipzig, 1930.

————. "Der Aufbau der Tastwelt," *Zeitschrift für Psychologie*, Ergänzungsband, No. 11. Leipzig, 1925.

————. "Gestaltlagar för kroppsupplevelsen," *Svenska Läkartidningen*, XV. Stockholm, 1944.

————. *Gestaltpsychologie.* Basel: Benno Schwabe Co., 1944.

————. *Mensch und Tier.* Zürich: Morgarten Verlag, 1948.

————. *Nya psykologiska strövtåg.* Stockholm: Kooperativa förbundets bokförlag, 1945.

————. "Några fakta ur modern färgpsykologi," *Tidning för Sveriges teckningslärare.* Stockholm, 1938.

————. "Psychophysiologische Untersuchungen an der Zunge," *Kwartalnik Psychologiczny*, VI. Poznan, 1935.

————. "2. Sammelreferat über Arbeiten aus dem Gebiet der Farbenwahrnehmung," *Psychologische Forschung.* Berlin, 1929.

————. "Zur Psychologie des Amputierten und seiner Prothese," *Zeitschrift für angewandte Psychologie*, XXV (1921)

————. *The World of Colour*. London: Kegan Paul, Trench, Trubner & Co., Ltd., 1935.

————. (ed.). *Handbuch der Psychologie*. Basel: Benno Schwabe Co. 1951.

————, and KÜNNAPAS, T. "Propriozeptiver Reflex und Willenshandlung," *Acta paediatrica*, XXXIII, No. 2. Uppsala, 1946.

KELLER, HANS and BRÜCKNER, GUSTAVE HEINRICH. "Neue Versuche über das Richtungshören des Hundes," *Zeitschrift für Psychologie*, CXXVI (1932).

KIEFER, MARIA. "Experimentelle Untersuchung über die quantitativen Beziehungen der monauralen und binauralen Schalleindrücke, sowie deren Verwertung zur Deutung des Weber-Fechnerschen Gesetzes," *Archiv für die gesamte Psychologie*, XVII (1922).

KLEIN, G. S. "The Personal World through Perception," *Perception* (R. R. BLAKE and G. V. RAMSEY, eds.). New York, 1951.

KLEINT, B. HERBERT. "Versuche über die Wahrnehmung" (Beiträge zur Analyse der Gsichtswahrnehmungen herausgeg. von F. Schumann), *Zeitschrift für Psychologie*, I, No. 11 (1940).

KLEMM, OTTO. "Untersuchungen über die Lokalisation von Schallreizen," *Archiv für die gesamte Psychologie*, XXXVIII, p. 71 and XL, p. 177.

KOCH, S. (ed.). *Psychology, A Study of a Science*. Vol. I, New York: McGraw-Hill Book Co., 1959; Vol. IV, New York: McGraw-Hill Book Co., 1962.

KOFFKA, K. "On Problems of Colour-Perception," *Acta Psychologica*, I. Haag, 1935.

————. *Principles of Gestalt Psychology*. London: Kegan Paul, Trench, Trubner & Co., Ltd., 1935.

KOHLER, IVO. *Über Aufbau und Wandlungen der Wahrnehmungswelt*. Sitzungsberichte, CCVII, No. 1. Abhandlung Österreichische Akademie der Wissenschaften, Vienna, 1951.

————. "Psychophysik heute," *Studium Generale*, X, No. 1.

KÖHLER, W. "Die Farbe der Sehdinge beim Schimpansen und beim Haushuhn," *Zeitschrift für Psychologie*, LXXXVII (1917).

————. *Die physischen Gestalten in Ruhe und im stationären Zustand*. Erlangen, 1924.

————. "Optische Untersuchungen am Schimpansen und am Haushuhn," *Abhandlungen der preussischen Academie der Wissenschaften, Mathematisch-Physische Klasse*, 1915.

KOHLRAUSCH, A. "Tagessehen, Dämmersehen, Adaptation," *Handbuch der normalen und pathologischen physiologie*, XII, 1931.

KORNMÜLLER, A. E. *Die Elemente der nervösen Tätigkeit*. Stuttgart: Verlag Georg Thieme, 1947.

KORTE, A. "Kinematoskopische Untersuchungen," *Zeitschrift für Psychologie*, LXXXII.

KOSELEFF, PAUL. "Et eksperiment vedrorende Charpentiereffekten (tyngdperception)," *Tidskrift för psykologi och pedagogik*, I–II. Göteborg.

KRAGH, ULF. "The Actual Genetic Model of Perception-Personality," *Studia psychologica et paedagogica*, Series 2, VII. Lund, 1955.

KRAUSE, W. *Die terminalen Körperchen der einfach sensiblen Nerven.* Hannover, 1860.

KRETSCHMER, ERNST. *A Textbook of Medical Psychology*, 2d English ed., trans. from the 10th German ed., with an introduction by E. B. Strauss (London: Hogarth Press, 1952).

KROH O. "Über Farbenkonstanz und Farbentransformation," *Zeitschrift für Sinnesphysiologie*, LII (1921).

KRUEGER, F. "Der Sturkturbegriff in der Psychologie," *Kongressbericht: VII Kongress für Experimentelle Psychologie*, Leipzig, 1923.

KRUKENBERG, H. *Der Gesichtsausdruck des Menschen.* Stuttgart, 1923.

LAND, E. H. "Experiments in Color Vision," *Scientific American*, CC (May, 1959).

LAUENSTEIN, L. "Über räumliche Wirkungen von Licht und Schatten," *Psychologische Forschung*, XXII (1938), pp. 267–319.

LENNING, EINAR. *Färgernas system och harmoni. Handledning för envar enligt Ostwalds färglära*, Nordiska Boktryckarekonsts Fackbibliotek, XV. Stockholm, 1943.

LEWIS, THOMAS. *Pain.* New York: Macmillan Co., 1946.

LINSCHOTEN, J. *Strukturanalyse der binokularen Tiefenwahrnehmung.* Groningen, 1956.

LORENZ, KONRAD. "Die angeborenen Formen möglicher Erfahrung," *Zeitschrift für Tierpsychologie*, V. Berlin: Verlag von Paul Parey, 1943, p. 235.

MACH, E. *Die Analyse der Empfindungen und die Verhältnis des Physischen zum Psychischen.* Jena: Fisher, 1900.

MACNICHOL, EDWARD F., JR. "Three Pigment Color Vision," *Scientific American*, CCXI (1964), pp. 48–56.

MAYER-HILLEBRAND, FRANZISKA. "Zur Frage, ob nur den willkürlichen oder auch den unwillkürlichen Augenbewegungen eine raumumstimmende Wirkung zukommt," I–II, *Zeitschrift für Psychologie*, CXXXIII (1934).

V. MEINONG, A. *Gesammelte Abhandlungen.* Leipzig: Joh. Ambrosius Barth, 1913.

METZGER, WOLFGANG. *Gesetze des Sehens.* Frankfurt a. M.: W. Kramer, 1936.

———. "Optische Untersuchungen am Ganzfeld," II Mitteilung, *Psychologische Forschung*, XIII, No. 1. Berlin, 1929.

———. "Optische Untersuchungen am Ganzfeld," III Mitteilung: Die

Schwelle für plötzliche Helligkeitsänderungen, *Psychologische Forschung*, XIII, No. 1. Berlin, 1929.

———. *Psychologie, Die Entwicklung ihrer Grundannahmen seit der Einführung des Experiments.* Naturwissenschaftliche Reihe, LII. Frankfurt a. M.: Theodor Steinkopff, 1941.

MEUMANN, E. *Vorlesungen zur Einführung in der experimentellen Pädagogik.* Leipzig, 1911–14.

MICHOTTE, A. "La Perception de la causalité," *Études de Psychologie*, VI (1946).

MILLER, G. A. "What Is Information Measurement?" *American Psychologist*, VIII (1953).

———, and FRICK, F. C. "Statistical Behavioristics and Sequences of Responses," *Psychological Review.* 1949.

MOHRMANN, K. "Lautheitskonstanz im Entfernungswechsel," *Zeitschrift für Psychologie*, CXLV (1939).

MONCRIEFF, R. W. *The Chemical Senses.* London: Leonard Hill, Ltd., 1944.

MONTESSORI, MARIA. *Lapsen salaisuus.* Porvoo: Werner Söderström Osakeyhtiö, 1950.

MORGAN, C. T., and STELLAR, E. *Physiological Psychology.* 2nd ed. New York, London: McGraw-Hill Book Co., 1950.

MÖRNER, MARIANNE. *Voice Register Terminology and Standard Pitch.* Speech Transmission Laboratory. Royal Institute of Technology Report No. 4 (1963).

MORRELL, FRANK. "Electrophysiological Contributions to the Neural Basis of Learning," *Physiological Reviews*, XLI (1961).

MÜLLER, G. E. "Über die Farbenempfindungen, Psychophysische Untersuchungen," *Zeitschrift für Psychologie*, Ergänzungsbände 17, 18. Leipzig, 1930.

MUNN, NORMAN L. *Psychology, The Fundamentals of Human Adjustment.* London: George Y. Harrap & Co., Ltd., 1947.

NADOLECZNY, M. *Kurzes Lehrbuch der Sprach- und Stimmheilkunde.* Leipzig: Vogel, 1926.

NEIGLICK, H. J. "Zur Psychophysik des Lichtsinns," *Philosophische Studien*, IV (1887).

NISSEN, H. W.; CHOW, K. L.; and SEMMES, J. "Effects of Restricted Opportunity for Tactual, Kinesthetic, and Manipulative Experience on the Behavior of a Chimpanzee," *American Journal of Psychology*, LXIV (1951).

NYMAN, ALF. *Nya vägar inom psykologien.* Stockholm: Norstedt och Söners, 1946.

OGLE, K. N. *Researches in Binocular Vision.* Philadelphia-London: W. B. Saunders Co., 1950.

OSGOOD, C. E. *Method and Theory in Experimental Psychology*. New York: Oxford University Press, 1953.

OSTWALD, W. *Die Grundlage der messenden Farblehre*. Grossbother, 1921.

PASTO, TARMO. "Plastic Art: An Attempted Explanation," *Arts Magazin*, 1953.

———. *The Space-Frame Experience in Art*. New York: A. S. Barnes & Co., Inc., 1964.

PAULI, R. *Über psychische Gesetzmässigkeit, Insbesondere über das Weber-sche Gesetz*. Jena: Gustav Fischer, 1920.

PENFIELD, W., and BOLDREY, E. "Somatic, Motor and Sensory Representation in the Cerebral Cortex as Studied by Electrical Stimulation," *Brain*, LX (1937).

PFAFFMANN, CARL. "Somesthesis and the Chemical Senses," *Annual Review of Psychology*, II (1950), pp. 79–94.

———. "Taste and Smell," *Handbook of Experimental Psychology* (ed. S. S. STEVENS). 1951, pp. 1143–71.

———. "The Afferent Core for Sensory Quality," *American Psychologist*, XIV (1959), pp. 226–32.

———. "The Pleasures of Sensation," *Psychological Review*, LXVII (1960), pp. 253–68.

———. "Sensory Processes and Their Relation to Behavior: Studies on the Sense of Taste as a Model of S-R System," *Psychology, A Study of a Science* (ed. SIGMUND KOCH), Vol. IV. New York, 1962, pp. 380–416.

PIAGET, J., and INHELDER, B. *The Child's Conception of Space*. Trans. F. J. LANGDON and J. L. LUNZER. London: Routledge and Kegan Paul, 1956.

PIAGET, J.; INHELDER, B.; and SZEMINSKA, A. *La Géométrie spontanée de l'enfant*. Paris, 1948.

PICK, A. "Störung der Orientierung am eigenen Körper," *Psychologische Forschung*, XIII, No. 1 (1929).

PICKFORD, R. W. *Individual Differences in Colour Vision*. London: Macmillan & Co., Ltd., 1951.

———. "Influence of Colour Vision Defects on Paintings," *British Journal of Aesthetics*, V (1965), pp. 211–26.

PIPER, H. "Die Aktionsströme der Vogel- und Säugernetzhaut bei Reizung durch kurzdauernde Beleuchtung und Verdunkelung," *Archiv für Anatomie und Physiologie*, Suppl. Leipzig, 1910.

PIRENNE, M. H. *Vision and the Eye*. London: Pilot, 1948.

POLYAK, S. L. *The Retina*. Chicago: University of Chicago Press, 1941.

PURKINJE, J. *Beobachtungen und Versuche zur Physiologie der Sinne*. I–II. Berlin: Reimer, 1819–23.

PÜTTER, A. "Die Unterschiedsschwellen des Temperatursinnes," *Zeitschrift für Biologie*, LXXXIV (1922).

RANTA-KNUUTTILA, JAAKKO. *Amputoitu sotavammainen.* Helsinki: Werner Söderström Oy, 1962.

RAUSCH, EDWIN. *Struktur und Metrik figural-optischer Wahrnehmung.* Frankfurt a. M.: Kramer, 1952.

REENPÄÄ, Y. "Über Wahrnehmen, Denken und messendes Versuchen," *Bibliotheca Biotheoretica,* III. Leiden, 1947.

———. *Yleinen aistinfysiologia.* Helsinki: Otava, 1935.

———. *Aufbau der allgemeinen Sinnesphysiologie.* Frankfurt a. M.: Klostermann, 1961.

———. *Theorie des Sinneswahrnehmens.* Annales Academiae Scientiarum Fennicae, Ser. A V, No. 78. Helsinki, 1961.

RENQVIST-REENPÄÄ, Y. *Allgemeine Sinnesphysiologie.* Vienna: Springer, 1936.

RENVALL, P. *Theorie des stereo-kinetischen Phänomens,* Annales Universitatis Aboensis, B X, No. 1 (1929).

RÉVÉSZ, G. "System der optischen und haptischen Raumtäuschungen," *Zeitschrift für Psychologie,* CXXXI (1934).

———. "Die soziobiologische Funktion der menschlichen und tierischen Hand," *XI congrês international de psychologie, Paris* (1937).

———. "Gibt es einen Hörraum?" *Acta Psychologica,* III (1937).

———. *Psychology and Art of the Blind.* London, New York, Toronto: Longmans, Green & Co., 1950.

———. *Einführung in die Musikpsychologie.* Bern: A. Francke Ag. Verlag, 1946.

———. *Introduction to the Psychology of Music.* Norman, Okla., 1954. London, 1953.

RIESEN, A. H. "Arrested Vision," *Scientific American,* CLXXXIII (1950).

———. "The Development of Visual Perception in Man and Chimpanzee," *Science,* CVI (1949).

ROELOFS, O., and ZEEMAN, W. P. C. "The Subjective Duration of Time-intervals I–II," *Acta Psychologica,* IV (1949).

———. "Influence of Different Sequences of Optical Stimuli on the Estimation of Duration of a Given Interval of Time," *Acta Psychologica,* VIII (1951).

ROIHA, EINO. *Johdatus musiikkipsykologiaan.* Jyväskylä: K. J. Gummerus Oy., 1949; 2nd ed., 1966.

RUBIN, EDGAR. "Om det psykiske og det fysiske," *Tidskrift för psykologi och pedagogik,* I–II. Göteborg.

———. Quelques Expériences sur les rapports entre les domaines auditif et pathologique, January–March, 1938. Paris.

———. "Some Elementary Time Experiences," *Acta Psychologica,* I. Haag, 1935.

———. *Synsoplevede Figurer.* Copenhagen, 1915.

———. "Taste," *British Journal of Psychology*, XXIV (1934).

———. "Visuell Wahrgenommene wirkliche Bewegung," *Zeitschrift für Psychologie*, CIII (1927).

———. *Experimenta Psychologica*. Copenhagen: Munksgaard, 1949.

RYLE, G. *The Concept of Mind*. London: Barnes & Noble, 1949.

SALOMAA, SIRKKA. *Experiments on Visual Space*. Annales Universitatis Aboensis, B XLIX. Turku, 1954.

SANDSTRÖM, C. I. *Orientation in the Present Space*. Uppsala, 1951.

SAUGSTAD, P. "Värin konstanssista," *Yearbook of the Philosophical Society in Finland, Ajatus*, XXIV. Helsinki, 1962, pp. 105–134.

———., and SAUGSTAD, A. "The Duplicity Theory, An Evaluation," *Advances in ophthalmology*, IX (1959).

SAXÉN, ARNO. "Pathologische Anatomie und Klinik der degenerativen Erkrankungen des Gehörorgans nach den von H. von Fieandt und Arno Saxén an Greisen ausgeführten Untersuchungen," *Ergebnisse der Allgemeinen Pathologie und Pathologischen Anatomie des Menschen und der Tiere*, XXXIV.

———. "Pathologie und Klinik der Altersschwerhörigkeit nach Untersuchungen von H. von Fieandt und Arno Saxén, Vorläufige Mitteilung," *Acta Oto-Laryngologica*, Suppl. XXIII (1937).

SCHILDER, PAUL. *Image and Appearance of the Human Body*. New York: International University Press, 1950.

SCHILDT, G. *Riktlinjer för en enhetlig psykologisk tolkning av Paul Cézannes personlighet och konst*. Helsinki: Holger Schildts, 1947.

SCHMIDT, INGEBORG. *Zum binocularen Farbensehen*. Diss. Tübingen, 1927.

SCHÖNE, W. *Über das Licht in der Malerei*. Berlin: Verlag Gebr. Mann., 1954.

v. SENDEN, M. *Raum- und Gestaltauffassung bei operierten Blindgeborenen vor und nach der Operation*. Leipzig: Johan Ambrosius Barth, 1932.

SHANNON, C. E., and WEAVER, W. *The Mathematical Theory of Communication*. Urbana: University of Illinois Press, 1949.

SHVARTS, L. A. "Raising the Sensitivity of the Visual Analyser," speeches at the conference on psychological questions, July 1953, Moscow. Trans. N. PARSONS, *Psychology in the Soviet Union* (ed. SIMON, BRIAN). London, 1957.

SIEGEL, A. J. "Deprivation of Visual Form Definition in the Ring Dove: I Discriminatory Learning," *Journal of Comparative and Physiological Psychology*, XLVI (1953).

SIMON, A. A. *Models of Man*. New York, 1957.

v. SKRAMLIK, E. *Handbuch der Physiologie der niederen Sinne I. Die Physiologie des Geruchs- und Geschmacksinnes*. Leipzig: George Thieme Verlag, 1926.

———. "Über die Lokalisation der Empfindungen bei den niederen Sinnen," *Zeitschrift für Sinnesphysiologie*, LVI (1925).

———. "Psychophysiologie der Tastsinne," *Archiv für die gesamte Psychologie*, Ergänzungsband IV. Leipzig.

SMITH, G. "The Place of Physiological Constructs in a Genetic Explanatory System," *Psychological Review*, LXI (1954).

———. "Visual Perception: An Event Over Time," *Psychological Review*, LXIV (1957).

———, and HENRIKSSON, M. "The Effect on an Established Percept of a Perceptual Process beyond Awareness," *Nordisk Psykologi*, VII (1955).

———; SPENCE, D. P.; and KLEIN, G. S. "Subliminal Effects of Verbal Stimuli," *Journal of Abnormal and Social Psychology*, LIX (1959).

SOLONEN, KAUKO A. "The Phantom Phenomenon in Amputated Finnish War Veterans," *Acta orthopaedica Scandinavica*, Suppl. LIV (1962).

SOMERKIVI, URHO. "Kokeita äänen paikantamisesta horisontaalitasossa." Unpublished thesis. University of Helsinki, 1947.

SOVIJÄRVI, ANTTI. *Die gehaltenen, geflüsterten und gesungenen Vokale und Nasale der Finnischen Sprache, Physiologischphysikalische Lautanalysen*, Annales Academiae Scientiarum Fennicae, B XLIV, No. 2. Helsinki, 1938.

———. "Artikulointimme hoitoharjoituksia" in *Teatteritaide* (ed. E. Krohn), Jyväskylä: K. J. Gummerus, 1949, pp. 137–38.

STEVENS, S. S. *Handbook of Experimental Psychology*. New York: John Wiley & Sons, Inc., 1951.

———, and DAVIS, H. *Hearing. Its Psychology and Physiology*. New York: John Wiley & Sons, Inc., 1947.

———. "The Surprising Simplicity of Sensory Metrics," *American Psychologist*, XVII (1962).

STEWART, G. W. "The Functions of Intensity and Phase in the Binaural Location of Pure Tones," *Proceedings of the National Academy of Sciences of USA*, VI (1920).

STRATTON, G. M. "Some Preliminary Experiments on Vision without Inversion of the Retinal Image," *Psychological Review*, III (1896).

———. "Upright Vision and the Retinal Image," *Psychological Review*, IV (1897).

———. "Vision without Inversion of the Retinal Image," *Psychological Review*, IV (1897).

STUMPF, CARL. *Tonpsychologie I–II*. Leipzig: Verlag von S. Hirzel, 1883–90.

STÜRUP, GEORG K. *Visceral Pain*. Plethysmographic 'Pain-Reactions' Dilatation of the Oesophagus. Copenhagen: Nytt Nordisk Förlag Arnold Busck, 1940.

TAKALA, MARTTI. "On Constant Errors in the Judgment of the Degree of Inclination," *Acta Psychologica Fennica*, I (1951).

————. *Asymmetries of the Visual Space.* Annales Academiae Scientiarum Fennicae, B LXXII, No. 2. Helsinki, 1951.

THOULESS, R. H. "Phenomenal Regression to the Real Object I," *British Journal of Psychology,* XXI (1931).

————. "Phenomenal Regression to the Real Object II," *British Journal of Psychology,* XXII (1931).

————. "Individual Differences in Phenomenal Regression," *British Journal of Psychology,* XXII (1932).

THURSTONE, L. L. "Psychophysics," *Ensyklopedia of Psychology* (ed. P. L. HARRIMAN). New York, 1946.

TITCHENER, E. B. *An Outline of Psychology.* New York: Macmillan & Co., 1896.

————. *Experimental Psychology.* New York: Macmillan & Co., 1901–1905.

TRENDELENBURG, W. *Der Gesichtssinn.* Berlin: Springer Verlag, 1943.

TUNTURI, A. R. "Physiological Determination of the Arrangement of the Afferent Connections to the Middle Ectosylvian Auditory Area in the Dog," *American Journal of Psychology,* CLXII (1950).

————. "Further Afferent Connections to the Acoustic Cortex of the Dog," *American Journal of Psychology,* CXLIV (1945).

TURHAN, M. "Über räumliche Wirkungen von Helligkeitsgefällen," *Psychologische Forschung,* XXI (1935).

URBAN, F. M. "Das Weber-Fechnersche Gesetz," *Archiv für die gesamte Psychologie,* XC (1934).

————. "Über die Methode der gleichen Abstufungen," *Archiv für die gesamte Psychologie,* XXC (1931).

USTVEDT, H. J. "Über die Untersuchung der musikalischen Funktionen bei Patienten mit Gehirnleiden, besonders bei Patienten mit Aphasie," *Acta Medica Scandinavica.* Helsinki, 1937.

VAHERVUO, T. *Tutkimuksia keskikoululaisten matemaattisesta suoritusky-vystä.* Helsinki: Werner Söderström Oy, 1948.

VERNON, P. *A Further Study of Visual Perception.* Cambridge, England: University Press, 1952.

van der WAALS, H. G., and ROELOFS, C. O. "Optische Scheinbewegung," *Zeitschrift für Psychologie,* CXIV, CXV (1930).

————. "Über das Sehen von Bewegung," *Zeitschrift für Psychologie,* CXXVIII.

WALD, G. "The Biochemistry of Vision," *Annual Review of Biochemistry,* XXII (1953).

WALK, R. D.; GIBSON, E. J., and TIGHE, T. J. "Behavior of Light- and Dark-Reared Rats on a Visual Cliff," *Science,* CXXVI (1957).

————; ————; PICK, H. L., JR.; and TIGHE, T. J. "Further Experiments on Prolonged Exposure to Visual Forms: The Effect of Single Stimuli and Prior Reinforcement," *Journal of Comparative and Phsyiological Psychology,* LI (1958).

WALKER, W. "Über die Adaptationsvorgänge der Jugendlichen und ihre Beziehung zu den Transformationserscheinungen," *Zeitschrift für Psychologie*, CIII (1927).

WALLACH, HANS. "On Sound Localization," *Journal of Acoustical Society of Americas*, X (1939), pp. 270–74.

———. "The Role of Head Movements and Vestibular and Visual Cues in Sound Localization," *Journal of experimental Psychology*, XXVII (1940), pp. 339–68.

WALLS, G. J. "Land! Land!" *Psychological Bulletin*, LVII (1960).

WAPNER, S., and CHANDLER, K. A. "Experiments on Sensory-Tonic Field Theory of Perception: I. Effect of Extraneous Stimulation on the Visual Perception of Verticality," *Journal of Experimental Psychology*, 1951.

———. "Experiment on Sensory-Tonic Field Theory of Perception: II. Effect of Supported and Unsupported Tilt of the Body on Visual Perception of Verticality," *Journal of Experimental Psychology*, 1951.

———, and WERNER, H. "Experiments on Sensory-Tonic Field Theory of Perception: III. Effect of Body Rotation on the Visual Perception of Verticality," *Journal of Experimental Psychology*, 1952.

———. "Experiments on Sensory-Tonic Field Theory on Perception: IV. Effect of Initial Position of a Rod on Apparent Verticality," *Journal of Experimental Psychology*, 1952.

WATSON, J. B. *Psychology from the Standpoint of a Behaviorist.* London, 1929.

WEBER, D. O. "Versuche über Farbenkonstanz bei wechselnder Beleuchtung," *Zeitschrift für Psychologie*, LXI (1912).

WEBER, E. H. "Der Tastsinn und das Gemeingefühl," *Handwörterbuch der Physiologie* (ed. WAGNER). 1846.

WELLEK, A. "Die Aufspaltung der 'Tonhöhe' in der Hornbostelschen Gehörpsychologie und die Konstanztheorien von Hornbostel und Krueger," *Zeitschrift für Musikwissenschaft*, XVI (1934).

———. "Der Raum in der Musik," *Archiv für die gesamte Psychologie*, XCI (1934).

WENUSCH, A. *Warum raucht der Mensch.* Vienna, 1942.

WERNER, H. *Einführung in die Entwicklungspsychologie.* Leipzig: Barth, 1933.

———, and WAPNER, S. "Sensory-Tonic Field Theory of Perception," *Journal of Personality*, 1949.

WERTHEIMER, MAX, "Experimentelle Studien über das Sehen von Bewegung," *Zeitschrift für Psychologie*, LXI (1912).

———. *Productive Thinking.* New York, 1945.

WERTHEIMER, MICHAEL. "Hebb and Senden on the Role of Learning in Perception," *American Journal of Psychology*, LXIV (1951).

———. "Psychomotor Coordination of Auditory and Visual Space at Birth," *Science*, CXXXIV (1961).

WEVER, E. G., and BRAY, C. W. "Action Currents in the Auditory Nerve in Response to Acoustical Stimulation," *Proceedings of Mathematical Academy of Sciences.* Washington, 1930.

WIENER, N. *Cybernetics.* New York: John Wiley & Sons, Inc., 1948.

WILLMER, E. N. *Retinal Structure and Colour Vision.* Cambridge, England: University Press, 1946.

WILSKA, A. *Untersuchungen über das Richtungshören.* Helsinki: Acta Societatis Medicorum Fennicae "DUODECIM," 1938.

———, and HARTLINE, H. K. "The Origin of 'Off-Responses' in the Optic Pathway," *American Journal of Physiology*, 1941.

WITKIN, H. A.; LEWIS, H. B.; and HARZMAN, M., et al. *Personality through Perception.* New York: Harper & Bros., 1954.

WITTMANN, J. *Über das Sehen von Scheinbewegungen und Scheinkörpern.* Leipzig: Johann Ambrosius Barth, 1921.

v. WRIGHT, G. H. *Hjalmar Neiglicks filosofiska insats.*

v. WRIGHT, J. M. "Fechners lag och simultankontrastfenomenet." Unpublished thesis. University of Helsinki, 1948.

———, *An Experimental Study of a Regularity in the Perception of Visual Brightness.* Societas Scientiarum Fennica. Communicationes Humaniorum Litterarum, 17:1, Helsinki, 1951.

WRIGHT, W. D. *Researches on Normal and Defective Colour Vision.* London: Henry Kimpton, 1946.

WUNDT, W. *Grundriss der Psychologie.* Leipzig: Vilhelm Engelman, 1907.

YOUNG, T. "On the Theory of Light and Colours, A Bakerian Lecture (read Nov. 12, 1801)," *Miscellaneous Works of the Late Thomas Young* (ed. C. PEACOCK). London, 1855.

ZANGWILL, O. L. *An Introduction to Modern Psychology.* London: Methuen and Co., Ltd., 1950.

ZEEMAN, W. P. C., and ROELOFS, C. O. "Some Aspects of Apparent Motion," *Acta Psychologica*, IX (1953).

ZWAARDEMAKER, P. *Physiologie des Geruchs.* Leipzig: Engelmann, 1895.

Acknowledgments

The author and publisher express their appreciation to the following for permission to reproduce the figures listed.

1–4   "Subliminal effects of verbal stimuli," G. J. W. Smith, D. P. Spence, and G. S. Klein, *Journal of Abnormal and Social Psychology*, Vol. 59 (1959), Fig. 1, p. 168.

3–1   C. I. Sandström, *Psykologi*. Stockholm: Almqvist & Wiksell, 1954.

3–4   *Advances in Ophthalmology*, Vol. IX (1959).

3–7   W. D. Wright, *Researches on Normal and Defective Colour Vision*. London: Henry Kimpton, 1964.

3–8   E. G. Boring, H. S. Langfeld, and H. P. Weld, *Foundations of Psychology*. New York: John Wiley & Sons, Inc., 1948.

3–9   S. S. Stevens and H. Davis, *Hearing: Its Psychology and Physiology*. New York: John Wiley & Sons, Inc., 1947.

3–10   *Ibid.*

3–11   E. G. Boring, H. S. Langfeld, and H. P. Weld, *Foundations of Psychology*. New York: John Wiley & Sons, Inc., 1948.

3–12   S. S. Stevens and H. Davis, *Hearing: Its Psychology and Physiology*. New York: John Wiley & Sons, Inc., 1947.

3–13   *Ibid.*

3–14   *Ibid.*

3–15   *Ibid.*

3–16   *Ibid.*

3–17   R. W. Moncrieff, *The Chemical Senses*. London: Leonard Hill Ltd., 1944.

3–18   *Ibid.*

3–19   *Ibid.*

3–20 *Ibid.*

3–21 E. von Skramlik, *Die Physiologie des Geruchs-und Geschmack-sinnes, Handbuch der Physiologie der Niederen Sinne I*. Leipzig: Georg Thieme Verlag, 1926.

3–22 R. W. Moncrieff, *The Chemical Senses*. London: Leonard Hill Ltd., 1944.

3–23 *Ibid.*

3–24 *Ibid.*

3–25 *Ibid.*

3–27 F. A. Geldard, *The Human Senses*. New York: John Wiley & Sons, Inc., 1953.

3–28 C. T. Morgan and E. Stellar, *Physiological Psychology*. New York: McGraw-Hill Book Co. Copyright 1950. Used by permission of McGraw-Hill Book Co.

3–29 *Ibid.*

3–30 *Ibid.*

4–6 N. L. Munn, *Psychology: The Fundamentals of Human Adjustment*. Boston: Houghton Mifflin Co., 1947.

4–7 E. Boring, *Sensation and Perception in the History of Experimental Psychology*. New York: Appleton-Century-Crofts, 1942.

5–1 G. Révész, *Einführung in die Musikpsychologie*. Berne: A. Francke Ltd., 1946.

5–2 S. S. Stevens and H. Davis, *Hearing: Its Psychology and Physiology*. New York: John Wiley & Sons, Inc., 1947.

5–3 *Ibid.*

5–4 *Ibid.*

5–6 "Voice register terminology and standard pitch," *Quarterly Progress and Status Report*, No. 4/1963, Speech Transmission Laboratory. Stockholm: Royal Institute of Technology. Fig. 50.

5–7 S. S. Stevens and H. Davis, *Hearing: Its Psychology and Physiology*. New York: John Wiley & Sons, Inc., 1947.

5–8 *Ibid.*

5–9 *Ibid.*

5–10 G. Révész, *Einführung in die Musikpsychologie*. Berne: A. Francke Ltd., 1946.

5–11 S. S. Stevens and H. David, *Hearing: Its Psychology and Physiology*. New York: John Wiley & Sons, Inc., 1947.

5–14 G. Révész, Einführung in die Musikpsychologie. Berne: A. Francke Ltd., 1946.

8–1 S. S. Stevens and H. Davis, *Hearing: Its Psychology and Physiology*. New York: John Wiley & Sons, Inc., 1947.

8–2 *Ibid.*

8–3   R. W. Moncrieff, *The Chemical Senses*. London: Leonard Hill Ltd., 1944.

8–4   *Ibid.*

8–5   E. N. Willmer, *Retinal Structure and Colour Vision*. New York: Cambridge University Press, 1944.

8–7   C. Murchison, *Handbook of General Experimental Psychology*. Worcester, Mass.: Clark University Press, 1934.

8–8   *Ibid.*

8–10   *Ibid.*

8–11   *Advances in Ophthalmology*, Vol. IX, 1959.

8–12   *Ibid.*

8–13   *Ibid.*

9–2   K. Koffka, *Principles of Gestalt Psychology*. London: Routledge and Kegan Paul Ltd., 1935.

9–4   *Ibid.*

9–7   *Archives of Psychology*, No. 179, 1935, Fig. 5, p. 44, paper by Henneman.

10–1   K. Koffka, *Principles of Gestalt Psychology*. London: Routledge and Kegan Paul Ltd., 1935.

10–2   *Ibid.*

10–3   *Ibid.*

10–4   *Ibid.*

10–5   "Effects of restricted opportunity for tactual, kinesthetic and manipulative experience on the behavior of a chimpanzee," Nissen, Chow, and Semmes, *American Journal of Psychology*, 1951, 64.

10–6   "The visual cliff," E. J. Gibson and Donald Walk, *Scientific American*, 202 (April 1960), 4. Photos © William Vandivert.

10–7   *Ibid.*

10–8   "Shadows and depth perception," Eckhard H. Hess, *Scientific American*, 204 (March 1961), 3.

10–9   *Ibid.*

10–10   Eric Schaal, LIFE Magazine. © Time, Inc., 1950.

10–11   *Ibid.*

10–13   N. L. Munn, *Psychology: The Fundamentals of Human Adjustment*. Boston: Houghton Mifflin Co., 1947.

10–14   F. B. Hofmann, *Theory of Space Perception of the Eye*. Berlin: Springer, 1920. 1925.

10–15   N. L. Munn, *Psychology: The Fundamentals of Human Adjustment*. Boston: Houghton Mifflin Co., 1947.

10–16   *Ibid.*

10–17   *Ibid.*

10–18   Monkmeyer Press Photo Service.

10–21   *Psychologische Forschung*, Bd 22, Berlin: Springer, 1938.

10–22   *Ibid.*

10–23   *Ibid.*

11–5   G. Johansson, *Configurations in Event Perception: An Experimental Study.* Uppsala: Almqvist & Wiksell, 1950.

12–1   G. Révész, *Einführung in die Musikpsychologie.* Berne: A. Francke Ltd., 1946.

13–1   G. Révész, *Die Formenwelt des Tastsinnes. Grundlegung der Haptik und der* Blindenpsychologie. Haag: Martinus Nijhoff, 1938.

13–3   *Ibid.*

13–9   *Ibid.*

13–10   *Ibid.*

15–4   C. T. Morgan and E. Stellar, *Physiological Psychology.* New York: McGraw-Hill Book Co. Copyright 1950. Used by permission of McGraw-Hill Book Co.

15–5   G. Révész, *Die Formenwelt des Tastsinnes. Grundlegung der Haptik und der Blindenpsychologie.* Haag: Martinus Nijhoff, 1938.

16–1   R. Arnheim, *Art and Visual Perception.* Berkeley: University of California Press, 1954.

16–2   Agraci—Art Reference Bureau.

16–3   Alinari—Art Reference Bureau.

16–4   The Metropolitan Museum of Art, request of Mrs. H. O. Havemeyer, 1929. The H. O. Havemeyer Collection.

16–5   T. Pasto, *The Space-Frame Experience in Art.* New York: A. S. Barnes & Co., 1964.

16–6   Bruckmann—Art Reference Bureau.

16–7   Courtesy of The Art Institute of Chicago.

16–8   R. Arnheim, *Art and Visual Perception.* Berkeley: University of California Press, 1954.

16–9   Courtesy of The Art Institute of Chicago, Wilson L. Mead Fund.

16–10   Alinari—Art Reference Bureau.

16–11   R. Arnheim, *Art and Visual Perception.* Berkeley: University of California Press, 1954.

16–12   Art Reference Bureau.

16–17   Alinari—Art Reference Bureau.

16–18   Art Reference Bureau.

Index

A

Absolute sensory threshold, 167
Accommodation, 215
Aches, 65
Adaptation, 177 ff.
  biological significance, 178
  dark, 180–85
  defined, 178, 179
  foveal, 182, 183
  metabolic rate, 185
  photochemical theory of, 180, 183,
    184
  rate of, 185
  reaction time to stimulus, 178
  recent studies in, 185–88
  rods, performance of, 180
Ambiguity and ambiguous patterns,
  13–15, 230–32
Ames' famous "distorted room" at
  Princeton University, 238
Amputees
  body image of, 326
  phantom-limb phenomena; *see* Phan-
    tom-limb phenomena
Anesthesia, effect of, 327
Anisotropy of space, 208–10
Art, pictorial, perception of; *see* Pictorial art, perception of
Attribute, of sounds, 118–20
Audiograms, 46
Audiometer, 46
Audiometric surveys, 47
Auditory impressions, 25, 282
Auditory perception; *see also* Hearing;
  Sound perception
  absolute pitch discrimination, 283
  acoustic-optical condition, 293
  auditory space, problem of, 295–97
  binaural intensity differences, 287,
    288
  binaural phase differences, 289–91
  binaural time differences, 288, 289
  cyclic dimension, 284
  direction localization, 287, 291–93
  distance localization, 287
  frequency changes, 284

Auditory perception—*Cont.*
  gestalten, 285
  interaction of visual and auditory
    cues, 294, 295
  lateralization of sound, 291
  localization of sounds, 287, 291–93
  monaural scanning, 291
  music, 285–87
  musical space, 295–97
  rhythm, 286, 287
  scanning, cues for, 291–93
  temporal units, 282, 285–87
  time dimension in, 282
  tonal scale, 283
    correspondence between tone and
      color scales, 284
  tonal space, 295
  visual space
    analogies with, 283–93
    differentiation from, 293–97
Auditory receptors; *see* Hearing
Auditory space; *see* Auditory perception

B

Basilar membrane, 41–44
Bel, 116, 117
Binaural intensity differences, 287, 288
Binaural phase differences, 289–91
Binaural test situations, 46
Binaural time differences, 288, 289
Binocular disparity, 2, 215, 242, 355
Blank intervals, 262, 277, 278
Blind persons
  body image of, 325
  expressive value of works made by,
    304–9
  perceptual learning, 232, 233
  preferred tactual forms, 302, 303
  tactual perception, 249, 250, 252,
    253
Blind spot, 35, 36
Blindfolded subject, structural analysis
  by, 311–12
Body image, 325–27
  phantom-limb phenomena, 331, 332

409

Body orientation, 256–57
Bony labyrinth, 40–41
Brightness constancy, 216, 218, 219, 221, 223, 224, 365
Brueghel: "Hunters in the Snow," 343–45

C

Camera, analogy with human eye, 1, 2
Camera obscura analogy, 2
Caravaggio: "Summons of Matthew," 368
Cardinal dimensions, 207, 215
    direction, 239–42
Cezanne:
    "Mont Ste-Victoire," 341
    portrait of his wife (completed), 347
    portrait of his wife (outline), 346
Chemical receptors, 25, 26
Chemical senses, 48
Chemistry, 2
Chromatism, 201
Cochlea, 40, 41
    cross section of, of guinea pig, 42
Cognition, 22
Color blindness, 108–11, 283
Color constancy, 216–26, 381
    field size and complexity, factors of, 224, 225
    Gelb phenomena, 221, 222
    measurement of degree of, 216–23
    theoretical explanations, 220–22
    Wallach's contribution, 222, 223
Color perception
    achromatic colors, 79
    additive mixture, 89, 90
    appearances of color, 82–84
    basis of visual stimulation, 77
    blindness, 108–11
    brightness, dimension of, 79
    brightness constancy, 87
    chromatic colors, 79, 81
    color constancy, 88, 89
    color mixture, laws of, 89–91
    color wheel, 89
    complementary after-image, 91–93
    constancy, 86–89
    contrast phenomena, 92
    deficiencies in, 108–11
    Emmert's law, 91
    film colors, 82, 83, 92
    fluorescent lamps, effect of, 84, 85
    gradients of hue, 88
    illuminations, effect of differences in, 84–86
    incandescent lamps, effect of, 84
    integrative ability, 77

Color perception—*Cont.*
    invariance, 86–89
    memory color, 86
    mixtures of color, 77
    movement stimuli, 94
    odor perception, analogies with, 317, 318
    Ostwald's color system, 79–82
    Ostwald's double cone, 82
    phenomenal colors classified, 79
    phenomenalistic theory, 76
    physicalistic theory, 76
    point-to-point arrangement in visual cortex, 78
    Purkinje shift, 93
    radiant energy, 77
    Rayleigh's equations, 91, 108
    retina, function of, 8
    saturation, 81
    space color, 83, 84
    spectrum energy distribution, 77
    subtractive mixture, 89, 90
    surface color, 82
    Talbot's law, 89
    theories of color; *see* Color theories
    unsaturation, 80
    visual size constancy, 88
Color theories
    assimilation or dissimilation, 99
    brightness gradients, 95, 105
    Edridge-Green, 103, 104
    Hering, 99, 100
    Ladd-Franklin, 100, 101
    Müller, G. E., 101–3
    Newtonian optics, 94, 95, 104
    recent contributions, 104–7
    three-color, 91, 96–99, 105–7, 192
    Young-Helmholtz, 91, 96–99, 105–7, 192
Common motion state, law of, 258, 259
Comparative physiology, 23
Computers, programming of, 20
Consciousness, concept of, abandonment of, 11
Consonances, 131
Constancies; *see specific type, such as* Size constancy
Constancy hypothesis, 7, 18
Contrast of color, 92
Correspondence theory, 382
Corti, organ of, 42
Cps (cycles per second), 114, 116
Crista, structure of, 74

D

Dark adaptation, 18–85
    as measured on rods (Piper), 181
    of a 2° stimulation area, 182

Decay, of sounds, 115
Decibel (db), 116, 117
Definitions
    adaptation, 178, 179
    perception, 3, 4
    pitch, 120, 137, 138
    relational invariances, 378
    visual space, 228
Dichorhinic, 159
Differential threshold, 168, 169
    brightness, 188
Differentiated vision, 2
Diffuse chemical sense, 48, 52
Dimensions
    cardinal, of space, 207, 215
    of sounds, 118–20
Directed illumination, 367–75
Directed movement perception, 267–70
Dirhinic, 159
Disparity, binocular; *see* Binocular disparity
Dissonances, 131
Distal dimensions, 209
Distal stimuli, 4, 209, 212
Distance receptors, 4
"Distorted room," 238
Duck or rabbit?, 14
Duplicity theory, 32, 34, 93, 180
Dürer: "Visiergerät," 358

E

Ear, structure of, 37 ff.
Economy, principle of, 7, 8
Edridge-Green theory, 103, 104
Ehrenfels-quality, 196
Ehrenstein illusion, 16, 17
Eidetic phenomena, 255
Emmert's law, 91
Equilibrium
    in art, 337 ff.
    sense of, 256
Erämetsä's empirical findings, 176, 177
Erg-second, 167
Exteroceptive sense, 29
Exteroceptors, 4, 26, 71
Eye, structure of, 30 ff.; *see also* Retina; Vision

F

Fechner's law, 169–72
Field size, laws of, 224, 225
Figure-ground articulation, 230–32
Film colors, 82, 83, 92
Formants, 136–37
Fourier analysis, 113, 116, 380

Fovea, 31, 35, 182, 183, 381
Frame of reference, 204
    impoverished, 205
    object constancies, necessity for, 209
    perceptual space, 207, 208
    reduced, 205
    tactual perception, 300, 301
    taste experiences, 319–21
    visual-tactual, 227
Frequency-code interpretation, 193
Fulton's homunculus, 334
Functionalism, 11
"Fury," 306

G

Gelb phenomena, 87, 88, 221, 222
Gestalt psychology, 3
    auditory, 282, 285
    constancy hypothesis consistent with findings of, 18
    formation of, 2
    genesis of, 3
    patterns transmitted by eyes, 8
    tactual perception
        completion phenomena, 309–12
        preferred forms, 302, 304
Gradients, 88, 95, 105, 146, 148, 156, 212, 246, 259, 300, 351, 368, 369, 381–84
Gustatory receptors, 25, 48, 52 ff., 319, 320

H

Haploscope, 242–43, 355
Haptic peristasis, 255
Haptics, 251
Haptomorphic gestalten, 252
Hartshorne's dimensional explanation, 193–96
    criticism of, 200–202
    evaluation of, 197–99
Hauptfarbe, 99
Hearing; *see also* Auditory perception
    action potentials in auditory nerve, 44–46
    auditory area, 46–47
    ear structure, 37 ff.
    loudness perception, 44
    pitch discrimination, 44
    place theory, 44
    psychophysics of, 46
    vibration distinguished, 145, 146
Hecht's work, 172–85
Henneman's studies, 225–26
Henning's smell prism, 158
Hering theory, 99, 100
Hertz's unit (hz), 114
Herzog: "Enjoyment," 307

Hess's study of grain and chickens, 236–37
Homogeneous visual field, 228–30
Horopter, 238, 239
"Horror," 306
Hue constancy, 221, 223, 224

I

Illumination perception, 191
Illusions, 208
Impulse frequency, 163
Information theory, 19, 20
Intensity discrimination, 174–75
Interaction of modalities
    affective continua, 194, 195, 198
    chromatism, 201
    dimensional approach, 193
    Hartshorne's dimensional explanation, 193–96
        criticism of, 200–202
        evaluation of, 197–99
    interaction paradox, 188
    Pfaffmann's studies, 196, 197
    polymodal impressions, 199, 200
    sight, 191, 192
    synesthesia, 198, 201
    taste, 189, 190
Interaction paradox, 19, 188, 189, 191
Interoceptors, 4, 58, 71
Invariances, 86–89, 204, 206, 210, 212, 216, 259, 301, 347, 349; see also Relational invariances
Irritability, 24, 195

J

Jaensch's studies in pictorial space, 354–63
Johansson's contribution, 265, 266

K

Kinematics, 250–52
Kinesthetic receptor organs, 71, 72
    stimulus of, in frog, 164–65
Koffka's example of the "tilted house," 211
Koffka's experiment situation (seen from above), 213
Kohlrausch's experiments, 181–84

L

Labyrinthine sensitivity, 72–75
Ladd-Franklin theory, 100, 101
Latency period, 177
Latin and Greek crosses distinguished, 310
Lauenstein's experiment, 248
Learning assumption, inadequacy of, 210, 211

Learning processes, 11, 12
Least effort, law of, 7, 8
Loudness of sound, 123–25; see also Sound perception

M

Mach's book, 357
Maillol: "Resting woman," 354
Manet: "Déjeuner sur l'herbe," 339
Matisse: "Luxe, calme et volupté," 353
Measurable behavior, 11
Mechanistic, 11, 13, 17
    organismic differentiated, 14, 15
Memory color, 217
Mental phenomena, experimental investigation of, 1
Mescaline intoxication, 335
Metabolic rate, 185
Metric dimensions, 209
Michotte's experiments, 279–81
Minné: "Mother and dying child," 306
Mirror image
    objectified sense material, 323–25
    shaving paradox, 322, 323
Modality, 23; see also Sense modalities
    classification of, 26
    hearing; see Sound perception
    interaction of, 188–202
    receptors for, 25
Modality axiom, 188
Modern psychophysics, 12
Modulation, 129, 130
Monaural situations, 46
Monorhinic, 159
Moore: "Reclining figure," 354
Motion analysis, 265 ff.
Motion parallax, 215, 243
Motion-track errors, 267–70
Motivation, evidence of influence upon perceptual events, 21
Motivational factors, 22
Movement perception
    analytic character of, 258 ff.
    apparent motion, conditions of, 260, 261
    common motion state, law of, 258, 259
    directed movement, 267–70
    Johansson's contribution, 265, 266
    Michotte's experiments, 279–81
    movies, 261
    phenomenal motion, 260, 261, 263
    stereokinetic phenomenon, 266, 267
    stroboscopic motion, 261, 262
        pure motion compared with, 263
        variations in time, effect of, 276, 277
    velocity of, 272

Movement perception—*Cont.*
  synthetic, 261
  time perception relationship with,
    275–79
  velocity, 270–72
  w-phenomenon, 265, 266
  wandering-phenomenon, 265, 266
  Wertheimer phenomenon, 263–65
Müller, G. E., theory, 101–3
Munch: "Cry," 307
Music, 285–87
Musical scales, 131–33
Musical space, 295–97

N

Neural spike potentials, 177
Neural transmission, 161–66
Neurophysiology, 161
New-look theory, 20–22
Newtonian optics, 94, 95, 104
Nose, construction of, 48–52
  cross section of nasal passages, 51

O

Object constancies, 204, 206, 207
  body image, 326
  frame of reference, necessity of, 209
Objectified sense material, 323–25
Octaves, 131
Odors; *see also* Smell
  classification of, 157–59
  color perception, analogies with,
    317, 318
  constancies of, 317, 318
  contraction phenomenon, 316, 317
  floating smell as, 315, 316
  milk variations, 150
  modes of appearance of, 315–17
  objectified smell experience, 315,
    316
  personal aroma, 151
  psychophysics of, 313–18
  significance in everyday life, 150–52
  similarity analysis, experiment with,
    313–15
  stimuli, 150, 151
  thresholds of, 157–59
  verbal expressions for, 152, 153
  wines distinguished, 150
Olfactory receptors, 25, 48, 52, 53
Oppel's illusion, 278
Optomorphic gestalten, 253
Organ of Jacobson, 26, 50
Organismic, 11–13, 17
  cognition involved, 22
  mechanistic differentiated, 14, 15
  perceptual processes based upon, 18,
    19

Orthogonal localization, 207
Orthogonality, 208–10
Oscillation, 112–16
Ostwald's color system, 79–83; *see also*
  Color perception
Overlap, 215

P

Pain sensitivity, 65 ff.; *see also* Skin
  senses
Pasto's space-frame theory, 342–44
Perception, 22
  defined, 3, 4
Perception of color; *see* Color perception
Perception of pictorial art; *see* Pictorial
  art, perception of
Perception of self; *see* Self, perception
  of
Perception of sound; *see* Sound perception
Perceptual constancy
  distance, 211, 212
  measurement of degree of, 212–15
  relationship between sets of stimulus
    factors, 205
  shapes at different angles of inclina-
    tion, 203, 204
  size, 211, 212
Perceptual learning, 232
  blind persons, 232, 233
  chimpanzees, experiments with, 234
  learning effect, 237
  rats, experiments with, 235
  transactionalists, 237, 238
  visual cliff, 235, 236
Perceptual psychology
  current trends in, 11 ff.
  descriptive modes employed in, 5, 6
  European traditions, 11
  functional approach, 4–7
  historical background, 11–13
  new-look theory, 20–22
  phenomenal approach, 4–7
  pictorial art, 337
  pioneers in, 1
  psychophysical relations, 6
  relational invariances of concepts of,
    379
  task of, 3
Perceptual space, 207, 208
  biological origins of, 227, 228
Perceptual theory, 18
Peripheral receptors, 2, 3
Perspective, 215
Pfaffmann's studies, 196, 197

Phantom-limb phenomena, 327 ff.
  body as object of perception, 332,
    333
  body image, 331, 332
  mescaline intoxication, 335
  mobility of phantom limbs, 329, 330
  spatial orientation of phantom limb,
    329
  statistical analyses of amputees, 334,
    335
  structure of phantom limb, 328
  vividness of phantom limbs, 330,
    331
Phenomenal brightness, 223
Phenomenal image, 208
Phenomenal loudness, 118
Phenomenal movement, 260, 261, 263,
  264
Phenomenal pitch, 120
Phenomenal time, 274, 275
Phenomenal velocity, 271
Phenomenalistic perceptual psychology,
  192
Phenomenological school, 12
phi-movement, 264–65
Phon, 118
Phonetics, 113
Photochemical theory of vision, 167
Photoreceptors, 93, 95
Photosensitivity, 172–77
Physical time, 274, 275
Physics, 2
Physiological after-images, 2
Physiology, 3
  vs. psychology, 1
Picasso: "Face," 306
Pictorial art, perception of
  accentuation, technique of, 340, 341
  affective continua, 375
  anchoring, technique of, 340, 342
  artist, role of, 336, 337
  base of, 342
  book illumination, 366
  color stereoscopy, 374
  compositional factors, 337–50
  compositive style, 350
  continuous tension in equilibrium,
    338
  equilibrium, tendency to maintain,
    337, 338, 340
  figural style, 350
  gold leaf, use of, 366, 367
  hues, gradients of, 368, 369
  impressionism, 361–63
  indirect light, forms of, 370
  interchangeability of modalities, 343
  invariances, 347, 349
  landscapes, 339

Pictorial art—*Cont.*
  left-right symmetry, 346
  light radiation, 371
  Middle Ages, colors, use of, 366
  perceptual psychology of, 337
  personality dynamics involved, 375–
    77
  phenomenal center of gravity, 337
  pictorial space; *see* Pictorial space
  poetic license, 336
  pointillists, 371
  psychoanalytic explanations, 377
  qualitative style, 350
  Renaissance, directed illumination,
    problems of, 367–71
  repetition as structural device, 350
  simplicity, law of, 349
  stained-glass windows, 366
  stimulations, 342–44
  structural investigation, 337–50
  vanishing point of parallels converg-
    ing in perspective, 339
  weight artefacts, 342
Pictorial space
  attention, mobilization of, 355
  binocular disparity, 355
  brightness gradients, 365
  colored spatiality, 363
  colors in, 363–66
  covariance phenomena, 355
  depth articulation, 351
  depth gradients, 351
  differentiation of picture, 363
  directed illumination, 367–75
  dynamic tension, 364
  haploscope, 355
  illumination in, 363–66
  impressionistic vision, 360–62
  intervening media, 358–60
  Jaensch's studies in, 354–63
  material spatiality, 368
  Middle Ages, religious art in, 351
  palette value, 364
  perspective, 356, 357
  picture value, 364
  reduced color, 364
  Renaissance, change produced dur-
    ing, 351
  sculptures, 353, 354
  stereovision, 355
  superposition, 352
  techniques for representing, 350 ff.
  three-dimensional, 350–63
  verant device, 357, 358
  voluminosity, impression of, 356,
    357
Pitch, 120–25; *see also* Sound perception

Pitch—*Cont.*
absolute, 283
defined, 120, 137, 138
Point-to-point correspondence, 7, 118, 139
Polaroid Land camera, 104
Polymodal impressions, 199, 200
Postural receptor organs, 71
P-processes, 102–3
Pragmatic principle, 133
Prägnanz tendency, 255
Present moment, 274, 275
Proprioceptors, 4, 58, 71
Proximal stimuli, 4, 209, 212
Psychology, 3
Psychophysics, 6
hearing, 46
odors, 313–18
sound, 118 ff.
Purkinje phenomena, 188
Purkinje shift, 93
Pütter's law, 171
Pythagorean scale, 132

R

Radiant energy, 77
Raphael: "Sistine Madonna," 348
Rayleigh's equations, 91, 108
Receptor cell
basic function of, 23
parts of, 23
Receptors, 4
animals, 25
Recognition, 22
Reduction of stimuli, 218
Reference, frame of; *see* Frame of reference
"Rejected," 335
Relational invariances; *see also* Invariances
constancies, 380, 381
defined, 378
gradients, 381–84
pattern of overlapping lines, 380
perceptual psychology concepts, 379
Relational stimuli, 207
Relearning, 18
Resonance, of sounds, 115
Rembrandt:
"Christ at Emmaus," 340
"The Night Watch," perceptual analysis of, 368–70
Respiratory fields, 155
Rest potentials, application of electrodes when recording, 162
Retina, 30 ff.
abilities of, 8
cross section of foveal part of, 32

Retina—*Cont.*
distribution of rods and cones throughout, 34
Retinal vision, 217
Rubin's phenomenal approach to perception, 5, 189–92
Rhythm, 286, 287

S

Satiation phenomena, 179
Schaffner: "Decency," 307
Self, perception of
body image, 325–27
mirror image, 322, 323
objectified sense material, 323–25
Sensation-elements, 7
Sensations, stimulus basis of; *see* Stimulus basis of sensations
Sense classification, 26–28
Sense modalities, 19, 23, 26
evolutionary products, 28
Sensitivity
recent studies in, 185–88
threshold relationship to, 185–88
Sensory evolution
aspects of, 23 ff.
differentiation, 28, 29
dualistic treatment of, 195
Sensory functions, differentiation among, 28
Sensory physiology, 1, 2
Sensory quality, 19
Sensory thresholds, 168
Sensory tissues, 9
Sensory-tonic theory, 17
postulates of, 19
Seurat: "Un dimanche à la Grande-Jatte," 345
Shape constancy, 204–6, 380
lack of, 215
measurement of degree of, 212, 213
Shaving paradox, 322, 323
Sight, 26, 27; *see also* Vision
Simplicity, law of, 349
Simultaneous contrast, 92
Size constancy, 206, 211–15
measurement of degree of, 215
relational invariances, 206, 207
Skin, structure of, 60, 61
cross section of, 60
Skin senses
aches, 65
after-images, 255
burning pain, 67, 68
impressions available through, 9
needle pricking, 68
opinions concerning touch and pressure, 61, 62

Skin senses—*Cont.*
  organs of sense, 59–61
  pain sensitivity, 65 ff.
  structure of skin, 60, 61
  temperature sensitivity, 62–65
  three sensory systems of, 58
  visceral pain, 69
Smell, 26, 28, 29; *see also* Odors
  chemical sense, 48
  dogs and related animals, 255
  nose construction, 48–52
  theories of, 155–57
  unconscious experiences, 152
  verbal objectification of experiences,
    152, 153
Smell fields, 154, 155
Smith's subliminal experiments, 15–17
Social phenomena, analysis of, 1
Solonen's phantom limb investigation,
    334
Sone, 118, 124; *see also* Sound percep-
    tion
Sound perception; *see also* Auditory
    perception
  absolute tuning, 133
  acoustical units of measurement,
    116, 117
  amplitude, 118
  attributes of, 118–20
  beats, 127–29
  brightness, 137–40
  combination tones, 129
  density, 120, 126, 127
  dimensions of, 118–20
  formants, nature of, 136, 137
  Fourier analysis, 113, 116
  frequency, 118
  Hertz's unit (hz), 114
  human voice, 122, 133–37
  loudness, 118, 123–25
  masking, 130, 131
  modulation, 129, 130
  musical scales, 131–33
  oscillation, 112–15
  phonetics, 113
  physical acoustics, 115
  pitch, 118, 120–23, 137, 138
    human voice, 122, 136
  psychophysics of sound, 118 ff.
  pure tones, 112, 113
  resonance, 115, 135
  singing registers, 133–37
  stimuli for sound, 112–18
  summation, 115
  timbre, 119, 125, 126, 151
  tonal spectra, analysis of, 129
  tonality, 137–40
  vibrato, 128–30

Sound perception—*Cont.*
  volume, 120, 126, 127
Sound waves, 112, 290
Space; *see* Pictorial space; Tactual
    space; Visual space
Spatial specialization, 29
Spatial touch perception; *see* Tactual
    space
Specific nerve energies, law of, 57,
    188, 191
Specific nerve fibers, theory of, 189,
    192
Spectrum; *see* Color perception
Spike potentials, 177
Stabilization process, 18, 19
Sterokinetic phenomenon, 266, 267
Stereoscope, 243
Stimulation, 19
Stimulus basis of sensations
  adequate stimuli, 160
  Fechner's law, 169–72
  Hecht's work, 172–77
  inadequate stimuli, 160
  neural transmission, 161–66
  Pütter's law, 171
  relationship between stimulus and
    sensation, 160, 161
  threshold phenomena, 167–69
  Weber's law, 169–72
Stimulus-elements, 7
Stimulus-response interrelationships,
    12, 13
Stroboscopic motion, 261, 262
  pure motion compared with, 263
  variations in time, effect of, 276, 277
  velocity of, 272
Structural psychology, 13
Subliminal stimulations, 16
Successive contrast, 92
Supraliminal stimulations, 16, 17
Synesthesia, 198, 201

T

Tachistoscopic method, 15
Tactual impressions, 25
Tactual perception; *see also* Tactual
    space; Touch
  after-images, 310
  blind persons
    expressive value of works made
      by, 304–9
    forms preferred by, 302, 303
  dimensions of touch, 298–300
  gestalt psychology, 302, 304
    completion phenomena, 309–12
  intermodal correspondence, 300–302
  modes of appearance of touch, 298–
    300

Tactual perception—*Cont.*
preferred forms, 302–4
space-filling touch, 299
specification of tactual object, 302
surface touch, 299
touch transparency, 299, 300
Tactual receptors, 8, 9
Tactual space; *see also* Tactual perception
alternately receptive and purposive attitude, principle of, 252, 253
analogy with other space model determinants, 255, 256
analytic perception, 251
autonomous formative activity, principle of, 253
blind persons, 249, 250, 253, 254
body space, 250
constructive synthesis, principle of, 253
haptics, 251
independency of, 249
kinematics, 250–52
metric principle, 252
movement space, 250, 251
schematic principle, 253
simultaneous vs. successive tactile perception, 251
stereoplastic principle, 252
structural analysis, principle of, 253
structuration principles of forms of, 252–54
successive perception, principle of, 252
transposition, principle of, 253
Takala, M., experiments, 267–68
Talbot's law, 89
Taste, 26–29, 189–90; *see also* Tongue
chemical sense, 48
chemical stimuli, 56
flavors, experience of, 189–90
four primaries of, 56, 189, 190
frame of reference, 319–21
misunderstandings of perception of, 190
modes of appearance, 319
regions responsible for, 52–55
scaling of experiences in, 318, 319
tactual experience, 319
tongue structure, 53–55
traditional four primaries, 55
Tele-exteroceptors, 58
Telereceptors, 25, 58
Temperature sensitivity, 62–65, 146–49
stimuli, 147
Temporal units, 282, 285–87
Thermal gradient theory, 63–65

Three-color theory, 91, 96–99, 105–7, 192
Three-dimensional pictorial space; *see* Pictorial space
Three-dimensional space; *see* Visual space
Threshold of awareness, 168
Threshold of perception, 151, 168
Threshold of recognition, 151, 168
Threshold phenomena, 167–69
Threshold values, computation of, 185–88
"Tilted house" case, 211
Timbre, 119, 125, 126; *see also* Sound perception
Time dimension, 282
Time perception, 272–75
Michotte's experiments, 279–81
movement perception relationship with, 275–79
Tonal space, 295
Tonality, 137–40
Tongue; *see also* Taste
motor activity of, 321
papillae, 54–55
cross section of, 54
different types of, 55
on tongues of nine-year-old girl and of middle-aged person, 320
receptors of, 320, 321
structure of, 53–55
Tonic muscle tensions, 17
Touch, 26, 27; *see also* Skin senses; Tactual perception
deep, 142, 143
pressure, 141
stimuli, 141
superficial, 142
three achievements of sense of, 142
thresholds of feeling, 144
tickle, 142, 143
vibratory stimuli, 143–46
interpretation of, 146
Transactionalists, 237, 238
Transformation process, 214
Tunnel motion phenomenon, 279

U

Unconscious inferences, 217

V

Vahervuo's rotation test, 260
Velocity, perception of, 270–72
Verant, 357, 358
Vibration, 143–46
hearing distinguished, 145, 146
Vibrato, 128–30

Vibratory stimuli, 9
Vision
    adaptation to stimuli, 178, 179
    blind spot, 35, 36
    color deficiencies in, 108–11
    duplicity theory, 32, 34
    eye structure, 30, 31
    nerve structure, 31, 32
    qualities perceptible by, 7
    receptor organ for, 30
    rods and cones, 32–34
    visual field, cortical representation
        of, 38
    visual pathways, crossing arrange-
        ment of, 37
Visual acuity, 215
Visual cliff, 235, 236
Visual impressions, 2, 25
Visual perception; see Visual space
Visual space
    absolute localization, 228
    accommodation of lens, 243–44
    after-images, 310
    ambiguous patterns, 230–32
    auditory experiences, 282
    auditory perception, differentiation
        from, 293–97
    auditory space, analogies with,
        283–93
    binocular disparity, 242
    color blindness, 283
    color spectrum, 283
    components of, 228 ff.
    convergence of eyes, 244
    cyclic dimensions of color scale, 284,
        285
    defined, 228
    depth perception, 242–49
    direction, perception of, 239–42
    distance localization, 238
    egocentric localization, 228
    figure-ground patterns, 230–32
    frequency changes, 284

Visual space—*Cont.*
    gradual differentiation of a homoge-
        neous space, 229, 239
    homogeneous stimulation, 230
    homogeneous visual field, 228
    horopter, 238, 239
    inhomogeneous stimulation, 239
    interaction of visual and auditory
        cues, 294, 295
    median plane, 228
    motion parallax, 243
    perceptual learning, 232–38
    perspective transformations, 244–46
    relative localization, 228
    three-dimensional
        depth cues for, 242–49
        organization of, 238–42
    visual acuity, 244
Visual stimulation; see Color perception
Visual-tactual objects, 227
Voice register, 121, 134, 135
Vomer, 26

W

W-phenomenon, 265, 266, 380
Wald's work, 172, 173, 180–81
Wallach's experiment, 222, 223
Wandering-phenomenon, 265, 266,
    380
Weber's law, 169–72
Wertheimer's experiments, 208, 263–
    65
Wife or mother-in-law? (after Hill),
    15
Witz: "Knight and Servant," 373

Y

Young-Helmholtz three-color theory,
    91, 96–99, 105–7, 192

Z

Zwaardemaker's olfactometer, 157

*This book has been set in 11 point Monticello,
leaded 2 points, and 10 point Monticello,
leaded 1 point. The chapter numbers and
titles are in 18 point News Gothic. The size
of the type page is 27 by 45 picas.*